WHAT'S LEFT?

WHAT'S LEFT?

Liberal American Catholics

EDITED BY

Mary Jo Weaver

Indiana
University
Press

BLOOMINGTON & INDIANAPOLIS

This book is a publication of
Indiana University Press
601 North Morton Street
Bloomington, IN 47404-3797 USA

http://www.indiana.edu/~iupress

Telephone orders   800-842-6796
Fax orders   812-855-7931
Orders by e-mail   iuporder@indiana.edu

The paper used in this publication
meets the minimum requirements of American
National Standard for Information Sciences—Permanence
of Paper for Printed Library Materials, ANSI Z39.48-1984.

MANUFACTURED IN THE UNITED STATES OF AMERICA

Library of Congress Cataloging-in-Publication Data

What's left? : liberal American Catholics / edited by Mary Jo Weaver.
p.   cm.
Includes bibliographical references and index.
ISBN 0-253-33579-5 (cloth : alk. paper). — ISBN 0-253-21332-0 (pbk. : alk. paper)
1. Catholic Church—United States—History—20th century. 2. United States—
Church history—20th century.   I. Weaver, Mary Jo.
BX1406.2.W53   1999
282'.73'09045—dc21   99-28823

1 2 3 4 5 04 03 02 01 00 99

To Jeanne Knoerle,
with admiration and affection

CONTENTS

Preface: Punctuating What's Left ix
Acknowledgments xv

Introduction   1
MARY JO WEAVER

I. FEMINIST THEOLOGY AND PRACTICE

1 Catholic Women Theologians of the Left
SUSAN A. ROSS   19

2 Women-Church: An American Catholic Feminist
Movement
ROSEMARY RADFORD RUETHER   46

II. PERSONAL SEXUAL MORALITY

3 Abandoning Suspicion: The Catholic Left and Sexuality
GENE BURNS   67

4 Resisting Traditional Catholic Sexual Teaching:
Pro-Choice Advocacy and Homosexual Support Groups
MARY JO WEAVER   88

III. ACADEMIC THEOLOGY

5 Academic Theology: Why We Are Not What We Were
MARY ANN HINSDALE AND JOHN BOYLE   111

IV. LITURGY, MINISTRY, AND SPIRITUALITY

6 Progressive Approaches to Ministry
   BERNARD J. COOKE   135

7 Call to Action: Engine of Lay Ministry
   BERNARD J. COOKE   147

8 Worship in the Spirit: A Renewed Vision of Liturgy and
   Spirituality
   ANNE E. PATRICK, BERNARD J. COOKE, AND DIANA L. HAYES   155

9 A Ministry of Justice: The 25-Year Pilgrimage of the National
   Assembly of Religious Women
   ANNE E. PATRICK   176

V. RACE AND ETHNICITY

10 Catholicism in the United States and the Problem of
    Diversity: The View from History
    JOHN T. McGREEVY   191

11 Strategies on the Left: Catholics and Race
    GARY RIEBE-ESTRELLA   205

12 Representation and the Reconstruction of Power: The Rise
    of PADRES and Las Hermanas
    TIMOTHY M. MATOVINA   220

13 The Black Catholic Congress Movement: A Progressive
    Aspect of African-American Catholicism
    DIANA L. HAYES   238

VI. PUBLIC CATHOLICISM

14 What Happened to the Catholic Left?
    DAVID J. O'BRIEN   255

                      Contributors   283
                         Index   285

PREFACE

Punctuating What's Left

Although I cannot always remember my dreams, I can usually remember the titles I dream up in those shadowy hours before the dawn. "Who Is the Goddess and Where Does She Get Us?" made me laugh in my sleep in 1988 and led to an article of the same name.[1] When I began to think about right-wing Catholics in the early 90s, I had many ideas about the kinds of groups I wanted to study, but no titular description of the project. But, when I woke up with the words "being right" running through my mind, I knew I had the title for the book that eventually became the first segment of a mapping project Scott Appleby and I conceptualized in the early part of this decade.[2]

As sometimes happens with mapping expeditions, this one has taken some unexpected turns resulting in a division of labor: whereas this book about Catholics on the left has been my territory to chart, the great center or "common ground" of American Catholicism has become Scott's project. One outcome of our decision will be, I think, that the title I dreamed up for the middle-of-the-road book will not see the light of day. I wanted to call it *Who Cares*, to evoke the faithful support of those American Catholics whose dedication sustains the life of the Church and whose "caring" generally manages to transcend the territories of "right" and "left" in order to respond to the liturgical, ministerial, or educational needs of the parish. I think of "Who cares!" as an exclamation or declaration, not a question; but when I dreamed up the title of this present book—"What's left"—the words had no punctuation. Should there be a question mark at the end of that phrase? I have discovered the answer to that question in the process of working on this book.

Like *Being Right*, *What's Left?* was funded by the Lilly Endowment and also engaged a group of scholars and activists in a two-year process of conversation and learning. Although the formats of the two projects were similar, there have been some significant differences in the way the present volume was organized. The group that produced *Being Right* comprised scholars as well as activists, insiders as well as outsiders, all working together with minimal help from consultants. *What's Left?*, however, was written entirely by scholars who, in some way, identified themselves as "insiders" within the left wing of the American Catholic Church, and insiders within academia, participants who had constant stimulation from outside consultants. When the core group met for the first time, we identified six areas that we thought most clearly represented progressive American Catholicism, areas that also fit with our own interests: feminism, sexual morality, academic theology, liturgical or spiritual issues, race and ethnicity, and public Catholicism. Once we agreed that the book would address these six major topics, we divided into working groups responsible for planning the meetings and producing the essays in each area. When we met for a particular topic, we invited three or four expert consultants to join us. They were asked to help us sharpen our focus by criticizing our essays and raising questions about the project.

I think the process used for each book was appropriate to the task at hand and that each had strengths and weaknesses. *Being Right* had the steadiness that comes from a stable group of interested people able to shape and refine a project together over a two-year period. What it lost in the excitement of outside stimulation, it gained in the clarity that emerged from sustained conversation. The general organization of the book into contextual essays, insider perspectives, and outsider essays was born in the process and had its own coherence. Because we represented diverse viewpoints about Catholic issues, our arguments were usually over substantive issues and ideology, not over the general outlines of the book itself. Part of the triumph of the book was our ability to appreciate one another's differences, and it is fair to say that those differences were major. *What's Left?* also had a common core group, but since each meeting welcomed outside consultants, its process was more dynamic and confusing. When we argued, it was sometimes over ideological issues, but more often over the general shape of the project itself: we constantly queried the meaning of "liberalism," and wondered if we should substitute "progressive" or "left-wing" for it. Many of our consultants thought that making "what's left" a *question* somehow minimized the strength of liberal Catholicism or relegated it to the status of a relic. At the same time, many of the groups represented by consultants, especially in liturgy and ministry, agreed that they had a left or liberal orientation that neither they nor the programs in which they were trained wanted to reveal. Liberalism was, for them, a troubled term that could undermine their work in the Church. Others did not see how certain segments of the book fit a liberal agenda. As we gathered finished essays and thought about how to organize the chapters of the book, we were confronted with questions about the appropriateness of describing the sections on race/ethnicity and public Catholicism (or social justice) as manifestations of "liberal American Catholicism." My decision to punctuate "what's left" as a question, therefore, is meant to highlight some of these queries, and to show that half the fun of liberal Catholicism is in raising questions.

To be fair, I need to recall that when we published *Being Right*, we wondered whether a political term like "conservative" was the best description of the mental universe we hoped to elaborate. As noted in the preface to that book, the people with whom we worked and about whom we wrote often saw no need for any adjective to describe themselves. Still, since we live in a world where we regularly meet those who call themselves "recovering," "communal," "cradle," "practicing," "Tridentine," "conciliar," "feminist," "orthodox," "Roman," "American," "disgruntled," "liberal," or "conservative" Catholics, we chose "conservative" as the term that generally embraced those who share a posture of resistance to modernity that allows them to assume a common cultural context. I have chosen "liberal" as the most embracing term for those who welcome modernity and adopt many of its cultural markers. At the same time, I recognize that there is a problem with the word "liberalism."

On the one hand, liberalism seems to mean something permissive, tolerant, pluralistic, and relative. Since religion is often *not* permissive or widely tolerant of diversity, and since official Catholicism eschews moral relativism and some aspects of pluralism, liberalism might appear to be a negative way to describe a lively segment of American Catholicism. On the other hand, *political* liberalism is rooted in the belief that there are certain political arrangements that we can agree upon even while we disagree about the meaning of ultimate truth. Liberalism of this sort, born in the wake of the civil rights movement and affirmative action, is very much concerned with access: society (or the Church), it argues, should grant all its members equal access to opportunities. One problem with this kind of liberalism is that it is highly individualistic: political liberals tend to raise a wall of separation between the public and private realms that makes one's private beliefs or life choices irrelevant to the pursuit of political justice. At this juncture, Catholics have often opposed liberalism with a communitarian ethic. Bruce Douglas, for example, argues that liberals have a lot to learn from Catholics about the common good.[3]

Liberalism has never been easy to define, even in the nineteenth century when people thought they knew what it meant. Owen Chadwick, writing about secularization in the nineteenth century, called liberalism a "confused, vague, and contradictory idea . . . more a motto than a word . . . which some claimed to rest upon coherent philosophical and economic theory and others saw as the destruction of the stable structure of a reasonable society."[4] Nineteenth-century liberalism in its classic definition was an economic issue. By the middle of the twentieth century, in the context of the Vietnam war, the emergence of Third World countries, civil rights, urban riots, political assassinations, national scandals, youthful rebellion, the sexual revolution, and the women's movement, it was clear that liberalism needed to be redefined in more encompassing terms. Whatever liberalism was, it was no longer simply an economic issue: economic factors might affect sexual behaviors and beliefs, but disagreements about things like same-sex relationships were hardly economic. At the same time, some of those who were liberal on economic issues, like Blacks, were often quite conservative on personal sexual issues, whereas those who were liberal on sexual behaviors might well be economic conservatives.

Is this book—which includes material on feminists, pro-choice advocates, Blacks and Hispanics, those committed to a social justice agenda, left-wing theologians, and those whose views on ministry, liturgy, and spirituality encompass the Call to Action agenda—really about *liberal* Catholics? Perhaps, as my colleague Richard Miller suggests, this book is in part about "post-liberal" Catholics, those who define themselves in relation to identity politics where consciousness of shared racial, or sexual, or ethnic backgrounds unites those who struggle against prejudice and injustice. If the personal is political, then the desire of political liberalism to bracket personal issues does not help to identify many of the groups described in this book. The authors and groups represented here argue that experience-based perceptions of religion and religious truth should be included in Catholicism. In contrast to conservative Catholics, who accept the external source of hierarchical authority as the measure of authentic belief and practice, the groups described in this book look to the internal measure of experience to validate their beliefs.

The liberal Catholics found in this book challenge a narrow understanding of church by calling it to extend the embrace of the Gospel beyond its current confines. These Catholics ask the Church to include and welcome feminists, those who press for women's ordination, married priests, homosexuals, pro-choice Catholics, those involved in liberation or creation-centered theologies, those who often find more nourishment in personal spiritual direction than in the rules of the institution, those who understand liturgy in terms of participating in an assembly-centered moment (as opposed to focusing on the consecrating powers of a priest), and those whose definitions of ministry include groups like CORPUS, NETWORK, and the Quixote Center. *What's Left?* includes a section on race and ethnicity not because Blacks and Hispanics necessarily share this set of assumptions, but because their experience—their identity politics—is something we want to include in the ways we think about Catholicism. In the Church as in the general society, we recognize the need to embrace race, ethnicity, and other markers of personal identity as sources of cultural pride and empowerment. The real distinction, therefore, might not be so much between liberal and conservative as between those who accept or deny the importance of identity politics in defining Catholicism.

In this light, the section that may be problematic here is the one on public Catholicism or social justice. It is interesting that the social justice liberals of the 1960s (the Berrigans or Michael Harrington, for example) were clearly left-wing in their politics (pacifists or socialists), whereas those who have grabbed the public spotlight for "justice" these days are those conservative Catholics who find in anti-abortion witness a location of the sacred. They are the ones who advocate civil disobedience and are eager to be arrested.[5] Today, the broad-based social justice agenda of earlier years has been embraced by the pope, the bishops, the Campaign for Human Development, and other organizations within the institutional Church. Social justice, including support for Black and Hispanic initiatives, addresses issues within the public domain that liberals and conservatives within the American Catholic Church both embrace. Put another way, whereas race and social justice do not, inherently, challenge hierarchical authority, feminism, personal sexual issues, liberal theologies, and certain understandings of ministry, liturgy, and spirituality *do* challenge traditional religious authority. Perhaps, finally, the authority question is the hinge on which the difference swings. The challenge to the meaning and limits of authority may be the aspect of this book most consistent with liberalism. Insofar as liberalism challenges the conventional way of doing things, the essays in this book represent left-wing or liberal American Catholicism because they describe a critical, experience-based, reforming perspective in the Church. Within this general perspective, there is a wide range of possibilities about what it means to be "liberal" in the Church. It is possible that no one group in this book accepts the entire agenda described in the range of essays within this book, but we generally share a perspective that is left of certain established positions in the Church.

Liberal American Catholics share a common cultural context of pluralism and an eager embrace of both the documents and the elusive "spirit" of Vatican II. If conservative was an appropriate term to describe those who thought that the council had gone far enough (perhaps too far) in its attempts to reform the Church, then liberal is an appropriate term to describe those who think that the council did not go far enough. If conservative describes Catholics who are often oriented to the past and who accept traditional religious authority, then liberal can describe those Catholics who are oriented to the future and whose energies are attached to an array of ideas that challenge conventional definitions of religious authority even as they embrace Vatican II's definition of the Church as the "people of God." Unlike those who believe that Catholicism has been defined and must be guarded against the temptations of the world, liberal Catholics believe that we must continually define and re-define Catholicism in the modern world, embracing many of its values, responding positively to its challenges. At the same time, liberal Catholics are a new group within the Church: they look back at pre-conciliar Catholicism and recognize its power to shape their religious imaginations even as they attempt to broaden its definitions of accepted beliefs and behaviors.

This book is an attempt to provide, in some detail, the substance of this liberal sensibility and to show some of the directions it has taken in American Catholicism in the thirty or so years since the Second Vatican Council. It looks at a highly diverse group of American Catholics who describe themselves in progressive terms and asks what they do to warrant that description. *What's Left?* explores the mental universe of liberal American Catholics in order to illuminate their dreams for the future. I hope that this book also helps its contributors and readers to understand themselves as they try on various adjectives qualifying or expanding what it means to be Catholic in the modern world.

NOTES

1. This article originally appeared in the *Journal of Feminist Studies* 5 (Spring 1989), pp. 49–65.

2. Mary Jo Weaver and R. Scott Appleby, eds., *Being Right: Conservative American Catholics* (Bloomington: Indiana University Press, 1995), pp. vii–xii, 13f.

3. R. Bruce Douglas and David Hollenbach, eds., *Catholicism and Liberalism: Contributions to American Public Philosophy* (Cambridge: Cambridge University Press, 1994), p. 12. This book argues that liberalism and Catholicism are two of the most important forces shaping contemporary political culture in the United States and urges a constructive conversation between them.

4. *The Secularization of the European Mind in the Nineteenth Century* (Cambridge: Cambridge University Press, 1975), p. 21.

5. Michael Gallagher, *Laws of Heaven: Catholic Activists Today* (New York: Ticknor and Fields, 1992), chronicles the civil disobedience of the Berrigans and other peace activists, but also writes movingly about Joan Andrews and other anti-abortion activists.

ACKNOWLEDGMENTS

I wish first of all to thank the Lilly Endowment for its support of this project and of my research projects for the last several years. Jeanne Knoerle and Fred Hofheinz have been gracious foundation officers and steady supporters of the mapping project, and Jeanne has been a good friend to me as well. It is a small mark of gratitude and a great pleasure to dedicate this book to her.

My colleagues at Indiana University and friends at other universities have read part of the manuscript and given me the kind of critical support I needed along the way. I am particularly indebted to R. Scott Appleby, my canoe partner in this mapping exploration for almost a decade. He is a brilliant reader and editor, an old friend, and a good companion even when we find that we are not exactly on the same journey. I have been helped in my thinking about liberalism and other issues by my Indiana University colleague Richard Miller, whose sage advice got me through more than one tangle of ideas. Robyn Wiegman at the University of California at Irvine, Joan Huber at Ohio State, and John McGreevy at the University of Notre Dame helped me to shape the introduction. I am particularly thankful to John for stepping in at the last minute to write the fine historical introduction to the race/ethnicity section. I am also hugely indebted to Mary Ann Hinsdale of Holy Cross for her work on the theology section. She and John Boyle have drafted and redrafted and refined that impossibly large area and made it sing.

My graduate assistants, Jason Bivins and Doug Winiarski, were extraordinary. Doug was especially energetic in tracking down footnotes, formatting manuscripts, and supplying me with references. Jason is always good to talk to about religion and politics, and he has been a steady support for several years. John Haas at the Cushwa Center at Notre Dame has been a reliable and cordial helper when I needed information I could not find in my own library. Barbara Lockwood, also at the Cushwa Center, is amazing and, at many stages along the way, graciously took on tasks that added extra work to an already crowded agenda. She has been a great support throughout the years of this project. Jenny Louis, our departmental secretary, and Kris Cain, my financial officer at Indiana University, have helped me through the mazes of financial reality in this grant and did chores that I thought impossible as if they were easy. I've been grateful for their cheerful countenances as I asked the same questions year after year.

I am honored and pleased to have been part of a project that gave me three chances a year to spend time with the core group of this book. Susan Ross, Rosemary Ruether, John Boyle, David O'Brien, Gene Burns, Sheila Briggs, Diana Hayes, Tim Matovina, Gary Riebe-Estrella, Anne Patrick, and Bernard Cooke have taken on their share of this large project with good will and intelligence and have endured my editorial quibbling and sometimes demanding interpersonal style. They have been fun to work with and have acquitted themselves very well in this book.

Because of the core group, I also got to work with a fabulous group of consultants over the past three years. Ada María Isasi-Díaz, Mary Hunt, and Toinette Eugene helped us craft the section on feminist theology and practice. Fred Perella, Tom Fox, Elizabeth McKeown, and Anne Klejment were wonderful resources for the public Catholicism section. Joann Wolski Conn, Barbara J. Fleischer, and Anthony Padavano guided us through the complex issues of ministry, liturgy, and spirituality. Frances Kissling, Margaret Farley, and John McNeill were excellent critics and resources for the sexuality chapters. John McGreevy, Beverly Carroll, and David Fukuzawa made the race/ethnicity section a great learning experience and were marvelously helpful. Finally, Mary Ann Hinsdale, Francis Schüssler Fiorenza, and Robert Schreiter contributed a great deal to our understanding of the enormous issues embedded in the theological section. It is not hard to imagine the dynamism and creative agitation that the core group received from this splendid group of consultants, and this book owes a great deal to their wisdom.

Finally, a word of thanks to my community of intimacy and support, who were compassionate witnesses to my frustrations, ministering angels to my weariness, and smart critics when I needed them to be. To Susan Gubar, Jean Alice McGoff, Julie Bloom, David Brakke, and Gena DiLabio I owe my greatest thanks. They make my life, and by extension, this book, possible.

WHAT'S LEFT?

INTRODUCTION

MARY JO WEAVER

Those familiar with controversial themes in American Catholic history in the twentieth century will recognize the major themes of this volume and not be surprised to find feminist theology, selective dissent, and ecclesiastical pluralism among them. Even those whose knowledge of contemporary American Catholicism is limited to what they read in popular news magazines will not be shocked to learn that there is a significant group of Catholics who are at odds with the pope over one issue or another.[1] In this volume about liberal American Catholics, disagreements over the nature of the Church—its ministry, teachings, policies—underlie many of the essays. If conservative Catholics can be gathered together under the theme of resistance to change,[2] liberals can be characterized by their willingness to welcome it. Their reaction to newness—usually interpreted as an openness to the workings of the Holy Spirit or fidelity to the example of Jesus— puts them in a position to welcome experimentation and so puts them at odds with the present pope.

In the summer of 1998, the Vatican published an apostolic letter introducing changes in the Code of Canon Law.[3] In order to "defend the faith of the Catholic Church against errors that arise on the part of some of the faithful," the pope specified penalties to be imposed on Catholics who do not "firmly accept and hold" certain doctrinal and moral teachings. The accompanying commentary gave several examples of those teachings, including the exclusion of women from ordination to the priesthood and the condemnation of pre-marital sexual intercourse. Taken together, these two documents are the strongest expressions to date of the pope's twenty-year campaign to stifle dissent and contain the spread of theological pluralism that began before the Second Vatican Council (1962–65) and accelerated rapidly thereafter.

Although the documents were focused on erring theologians, I notice that the pope seemed particularly worried about two clusters of contemporary issues: those related to the women's movement and those that involve personal sexual morality, two sites on which the battles between conservative and liberal Catholics occur. Generally speaking, the essays in this book describe liberals as those who oppose the papal desire to restore the magisterium to its pre-conciliar, pre-*Humanae Vitae* status[4] as the uncontested source not only of Roman Catholic moral and doctrinal teachings, but also of their theological interpretations and pastoral applications.

Liberal Catholic Identity

Liberal Catholicism may be most clear when contrasted to traditional perspectives. Conservative Catholics believe that they have held steady while the world around them has moved and are distressed that the markers that identified their Catholicism have shifted since the council. Liberal Catholics tend to move with the world and to welcome the changes that have occurred in the last thirty years. One of the divisions between them has to do with the way each group remembers the past, especially the years immediately preceding the Second Vatican Council (1962–65). Conservative Catholics may recall pre-conciliar Catholicism as Pat Buchanan does: a time when "we already had the truth . . . and began our education with the answers." The Church then had a "magnetism of certitude" he says: "Men seek certitude. That is what the Catholic church of the midcentury offered—and the modern Church in America does not seem to understand. We had the Way, the Truth, and the Light. Other ways were not equally valid; they were false."[5] In contrast, liberal Catholics may remember the same time period as it was described by Garry Wills: a ghetto in "isolation from the intellectual currents of this country." Progressive Catholics in the fifties, he said, remember 1957 as "the year when liberal complaints about the American church—that it was intellectually and culturally stagnant—were finally voiced in a respectable Catholic journal (*Thought*) by a loyal priest-scholar, Monsignor John Tracy Ellis." The most acutely experienced urge of fifties Catholic liberals, according to Wills, "was to prove that something recognizably Catholic need not be as cramped, ugly, and anti-intellectual as they found at the corner church."[6] Memories of the fifties often serve as the contextual setting in which Catholics understand Vatican II and its aftermath. If the 1950s were a golden age, then many of the changes of the past thirty years look odious. If the 1950s were as cramped as Wills described them to be, then post-conciliar life is a decided improvement.

It is fair to say that most American Catholics welcomed the council, but found themselves in disagreement about events that followed it. Although changes in the liturgy, in some disciplinary matters (Friday abstinence from meat, for example), and in devotional life distressed some of the faithful, those issues, in themselves, did not constitute an indelible dividing line between conservatives and liberals in the Church. That division occurred in the summer of 1968 when the public outcry over *Humanae Vitae* appalled conservatives and galvanized liberals. For the first time in memory and in American Catholic history, a group of prominent American Catholics publicly—and with impunity—dissented from papal teaching. They criticized the Church on academic and secular grounds, pointed to its failure to embody the ecclesiology of Vatican II, and asserted their rights to form their own opinions on a variety of matters. Their action emboldened others to open themselves to some of the many new directions in the Catholic atmosphere after the council.

In the religious climate of the late 1960s and the 1970s, theologies of experience and immanence that had been around since the nineteenth century took hold of the liberal Catholic imagination and propelled Catholicism toward a more egalitarian self-understanding. The openness of these theologies to personal experience eventually meant that lay people acquired some confidence about interpreting Scripture and making moral decisions for themselves. When Catholics learned from the documents of Vatican II that the Holy Spirit, continually at work in the Church, was also actively disclosing God's presence in their own lives, they embraced that dynamism in a particularly American fashion. Put another way, they conflated the conciliar definition of the Church as the "people of God," with the American national creed of "we the people." As they saw it, the conciliar acceptance of religious freedom echoed American pluralism.[7] The sense of empowerment felt by many lay people after Vatican II was almost palpable, and the enthusiastic acceptance of a concept of Church as the people of God manifested itself in discussions about the election of bishops and the power of parish councils.

In the decades following the council, experienced-based theologies from Latin America (liberation theology) and the women's movement (feminist theology) took root in Catholic popular consciousness. For the first time in history, a significant number of lay people and nuns began to get degrees in theology and to bring the "new theology" into religious education programs, Catholic school classrooms, and parish discussion groups. A generation of seminarians learned to see the Church as the "people of God" in dialogue with the modern world, and a generation of Catholic students was encouraged to reflect upon their own experience as they sought to understand the meaning of Catholicism in their lives. Those whose identities were formed in the decade after the council, along with an older generation of liberal

Catholics, imagined themselves as a pilgrim people accompanied on their journey by members of other religious traditions.

Liberal Catholics tended to embrace dialogue and to find unity in diversity. They also learned what it meant to dissent from official Church teaching without leaving the Church as they practiced artificial birth control and remained members in good standing. These experiences of dialogue, diversity, and dissent helped many Catholics to change the way they understood themselves *as Catholics*, and their new self-understanding was accompanied by major shifts in their ordinary religious lives. Their liturgical experience welcomed musical idioms that reflected popular culture rather than the medieval cathedral. They preferred active participation in the Mass to passive attendance at it, and developed an understanding of Eucharist as rooted in the assembly rather than in the power of the priest. Young Catholics might not know the answers to questions from *The Baltimore Catechism*, but many of them accompanied their teachers to Appalachia or urban slums in order to put social justice into action. If devotions to Mary —the rosary and novenas—waned, new interpretations of Mary by feminist theologians and ecumenically minded Catholics tried to make her more accessible as a woman of profound courage and an image of salvation that could appeal beyond traditional Catholic doctrine. As middle-aged liberal Catholics found themselves at odds with the pope, younger Catholics, enthralled with such a charismatic presence, adopted him as a cultural icon. Yet, neither group was willing to accept his teaching in areas of personal sexual morality. When an enthusiastic young Catholic attending a papal rally in Denver in 1993 was reminded that the pope was against pre-marital sex, she continued to wave her "Long live the Pope" banner as she said, "Well, he's entitled to his opinion."

Liberal American Catholics are probably more interested in new forms of spirituality than their conservative counterparts. Today, spirituality is a best-selling business in bookstores and seems remarkably diverse and syncretistic. A liberal Catholic version of renewed spiritual interest is exemplified by the great number of people who now seek and find spiritual directors and by those who are willing to learn new ways to pray that are sometimes traditional (the Catholic mystical heritage) and sometimes based in the practices of other religions (Buddhism, for example). Because spiritual direction is very much based in the experience of those seeking direction, it can be subversive of hierarchical authority. Put another way, those on spiritual journeys pay attention to God's presence within them and are sensitive to those places where their spiritual lives conflict with their experience in a local parish. That very sensitivity tends to privilege their interior lives.

Many liberal Catholics, especially those who support the renewed

Call to Action[8] agenda, spend considerable energy on an international Catholic referendum called "We Are the Church," a document that has been signed by more than two and a half million Catholics in Austria and Germany. Similar initiatives have been undertaken across Western Europe and in Canada, Latin America, and Australia. The referendum seeks to implement five major goals: (1) participation of the laity in the selection of bishops and pastors; (2) equal rights for women in all ministries, including priesthood; (3) optional celibacy for priests; (4) an affirmation of the goodness of sexuality, the primacy of conscience in sexual issues, the human rights of all persons regardless of sexual orientation, along with an acknowledgment of the importance and urgency of issues other than sexual morality; and (5) a church that affirms rather than condemns its members, and welcomes those who are divorced and remarried, married priests, theologians and others who exercise freedom of speech.[9]

The essays in this book seek to make these issues clear in an effort to describe the sensibility of liberal American Catholics. Liberal aspects of American Catholicism can be found in feminism and in issues that touch upon personal sexual morality. They are also a part of academic theology and take shape in those parts of ministry, liturgy, and spirituality that stand to the left of traditional embodiments. We have included sections on race / ethnicity and social justice, not because they are necessarily left-wing or liberal, but because liberal Catholics are generally sensitive to those issues and have found ways to combine those interests with their progressive proclivities.

General Organization

In September 1996 the core group of authors for *What's Left?* met in Indianapolis to discuss the shape of a book on liberal American Catholicism. That brainstorming meeting began with an imaginary group portrait of left-wing Catholics and ended with a plan of action. Although we argued about terms like left wing, liberal, and progressive, we agreed to proceed without a need to define them *a priori* and concentrated instead on how we might embody the issues that made up our composite understanding. We believed then that we needed to include a variety of peace and social justice groups, clusters of academic theology, feminist theology and activism, ecological consciousness, spirituality, race and class issues, groups of liberal or radical sisters, clergy, and laity, and a representative selection of publications and publishers. Ultimately, we listed nearly fifty groups that fit somewhere on a liberal Catholic spectrum. Although we have not included every group on our list, most of them managed to find a spot in this volume.

I originally believed that *What's Left?* should mirror the structure of *Being Right,* the book Scott Appleby and I edited about conservative American Catholics. I thought it should have a set of contextual essays followed by insider and outsider perspectives on a variety of issues, but I was persuaded by the group that we should develop our own schema. Accordingly, we identified six critical areas of discussion that eventually became the major sections of this book: each unit was to include both context for and liberal exemplars of that area of Catholicism. We agreed to limit our essays to the last thirty-five years and to be sensitive to the divergences (in social action, location, and origins) of the people and movements about which we were writing. Although we have not been as perfectly attuned to this model as we originally hoped, most sections have addressed context and outlined specific progressive activities. Because we all identified ourselves as, in some way, liberal Catholics, the insider/outsider paradigm that was used to organize *Being Right* did not work in this volume. Some of the essays in this book are clearly written from an insider's perspective, others with some critical distance. Each time we met, we focused on a specific section of the book, and those responsible for the essays invited consultants to join us as we discussed the papers produced and distributed in advance. We met several times over a two-day period, and after the meeting authors solicited feedback from colleagues, revised their papers, and then submitted them in final form. Each time we met, we used our final two-hour session to review the shape of the book and refine our plans.

As I mentioned in the Preface, I was concerned about how to fit our various exemplars of left-wing Catholicism into some coherent understanding of liberalism within the Church. As we worked together on the major sections of this book, it was clear that some of the exemplars were clearly liberal and that others needed some explanation. Feminist theology, the Women-Church movement, dissent around *Humanae Vitae,* gay and lesbian rights groups, and pro-choice advocacy are undoubtedly liberal, perhaps occupying the far left end of the liberal Catholic bell curve. Academic theology is more troublesome: although conservative Catholics often imagine the Catholic Theological Society of America (CTSA) and the College Theology Society (CTS) as wildly liberal, most of the theologians in those groups are professionals employed by (mostly) Catholic institutions and imagine themselves to be mainstream. Some areas of interest to us were shared by all American Catholics: liturgy, spirituality, and ministry; in the section on those topics, authors wrote about explicitly liberal aspects of these common parish experiences. The inclusion of race and ethnicity in a volume on liberal American Catholics raised many questions for us, as did the inclusion of public Catholicism, because they are mainstream issues that do not necessarily fit into a liberal/conservative dichotomy. At the same time, it is possible to identify liberal Catholics within these large areas and to include them in this book.

Feminist Theology and the Women-Church Movement

Feminist theology (Susan Ross) and the Women-Church movement (Rosemary Ruether) open the book because they are perhaps the most widely recognized expressions of liberal belief and practice in the American Church. In some respects, the issues embedded in the women's movement in Catholicism embrace the very things that the pope fears the most. The Women-Church movement is thoroughly feminist, accepts experience as a more authentic source of religious authority than the hierarchy, and is often radically ecumenical as women celebrate liturgy together without benefit of clergy and with no attention to the affiliations of the participants. Feminist theology is an experience-based discipline with a variety of contemporary expressions.

When we met to discuss this part of the book, three consultants assisted us: Mary Hunt, Toinette Eugene, and Ada María Isasi-Díaz. Hunt is the founder and co-director of the Women's Alliance for Theology, Ethics, and Ritual (WATER) in Washington, D.C.; Eugene, then a professor of ethics at Garrett Evangelical seminary, is now the director of African-American ministries for the diocese of Oakland, California; and Isasi-Díaz is a professor of theology at Drew University and one of the founders and shapers of mujerista theology. Susan Ross's chapter on Catholic women theologians of the left provides a contextual map of this complicated territory. Ross shows us that feminist theologies are historically and methodologically diverse, sensitive to issues of racial and gender justice, committed to radical transformation of Church structures and theology. Since her essay is about a contemporary and new kind of theology, she explains some of the hallmarks of modern theological investigation, for example, the importance of experience as a theological source and the role of embodiment in spirituality. She also outlines some ethical considerations and ends with a reflection on the critique of power and the reformulation of doctrine. Rosemary Ruether writes as a feminist theologian and from her long experience in Women-Church. Since this movement includes more than fifty women's organizations and since most of those organizations have embraced—not without dispute and never without extensive discussion—a variety of justice issues, including the ordination of women, this chapter pays homage to the energy of Catholic women as they attempt to transform a recalcitrant church.

Sexuality, Homosexuality, and Abortion

Anyone familiar with papal documents or speeches in the last twenty years knows that there have been repeated references to sexual morality. The pope continues to insist that Catholics may not use artificial birth control, have pre-marital sexual intercourse, or get divorced and remarried and hope to remain in good standing in the Church. Since most American Catholics practice artificial birth control and since we can imagine that unmarried Catholics are as sexually active as others in their cohort, and since many Catholics *have* been divorced and re-married yet continue to attend church, sing in the choir, and partici-pate in parish activities, we cannot argue that these matters make lib-erals out of American Catholics. Yet, although the birth control debate is over in practical terms, the issue of *public dissent* from official Church teaching is a marker of liberal Catholicism. In addition, groups like Dignity (which affirms the goodness of homosexual sex in the same terms Vatican II used to describe married love) and Catholics for a Free Choice (which advocates a pro-choice position on abortion) are undoubtedly liberal expressions of American Catholicism. Some crit-ics would deny these groups the right to call themselves Catholic, which means that these issues raise questions of Catholic identity and naming.

Gene Burns and I were joined for the meeting on this topic by Frances Kissling, Margaret Farley, and John McNeill. Kissling is the director of Catholics for a Free Choice (CFFC); Farley is the Gilbert L. Stark Professor of Christian Ethics at Yale University; and John McNeill, a psychotherapist and former Jesuit, is a pioneer in ministry to and acceptance of homosexuals in the Church. Much of the discus-sion at that meeting centered on the ways in which dissent, homo-sexuality, and abortion are *political* issues within the Church. In his chapter, Burns asks why the question of sexuality has become so im-portant in the Church and analyzes the reasons the Vatican stakes its institutional authority on the enforcement of its view of sexual ortho-doxy. He focuses on the political power surrounding sexual issues in the Church. My chapter on CFFC and Dignity explains why many Catholics resist Catholic teaching, finding it rooted in a "contracep-tive logic" that narrows and betrays sexuality and divine/human in-teraction.[10] Groups that resist or protest official Catholic sexual teach-ing underscore the radical importance of experience in the minds of liberal Catholics. Put another way, many of us who dissent from traditional Catholic sexual teaching believe that God's design is unfolding in the present moment in our experience. Taken together, these chapters focus on questions of power, identity, experience, and the politics of dissent as they play out in the arena of personal sexual morality.

Academic Theologians and Liberal Theologies

Like other areas of Catholic life since Vatican II, theology has been informed by the kinds of reformist energies that animate the work being done in liturgy, feminism, and social justice. Theology is not merely "academic," but is a discipline that contributes to and draws from work done in other areas. We have chosen to focus on theology as it is done in the academy, particularly the ways it has changed in the last thirty years. As an area, academic theology is not clearly or necessarily liberal: obviously, much academic theology is mainstream and acceptable to most Catholics, including bishops. At the same time, there are explosive new directions and disputes within academic theology that place some of it on the liberal side of the spectrum. Although Susan Ross's essay at the beginning of this book is a tour de force of contemporary theological practice, it confines itself to feminism and to women theologians. The essay by Mary Ann Hinsdale and John Boyle is a more general look at academic theology, setting its context, describing its practitioners, and focusing on some of the work of its professional societies. John Boyle, now emeritus professor in the School of Religion at the University of Iowa, drafted the original version of this chapter as a detailed look at the historical background of contemporary theology. Mary Ann Hinsdale, associate professor of religious studies at the College of the Holy Cross, revised the original essay to focus it more directly on the contemporary scene.

When we met to discuss the original draft of this chapter, we were joined by Hinsdale, Francis Schüssler Fiorenza, and Robert Schreiter. Fiorenza is the Charles Chauncy Stillman Professor of Roman Catholic Theological Studies in the Harvard Divinity School; and Robert Schreiter is a professor in the Catholic Theological Union in Chicago. This chapter describes how academic theology has changed since the Second Vatican Council, especially the ways in which new social locations of theologians have led to the creation of competing theological cultures within the American Church. Liberal academic theology has responded favorably to three major intellectual challenges in the last thirty years: it has rooted theology in historical consciousness, accepted experience as a legitimate source for theological reflection, and adopted critical theory as a methodological tool. Since many Catholic theologians have academic appointments in non-Catholic universities, they are not readily subject to Church authority and sometimes find themselves in tension with the Vatican. That tension is characteristic of scholars on the liberal end of the Catholic theological spectrum.

Liberal Approaches to Liturgy, Ministry, and Spirituality

The lives of nearly all American Catholics are shaped by their experience of liturgy, spirituality, and ministry in a local parish. These components of religious identity and life, with long histories and complex heritages, are inherently neither conservative nor liberal, but can take on those descriptions in practice. In this section we chose to write about the aspects of liturgy, spirituality, and ministry that are recognizably left-wing, and to augment those perceptions with insider accounts of two organizations that embody liberal Catholic activism in these areas. It might be useful to remember that liturgy was the first area that Vatican II addressed; that is, it had a privileged place among the architects of the council, indicating their sense that liturgical reform would have the most pervasive impact on the Church. Liturgy, therefore, was a critical vehicle for institutionalizing liberalizing changes in the Church, and liberal Catholics have continued to support it. Bernard Cooke's chapter on liturgy is supplemented with his account of the new Call to Action movement, an undoubtedly liberal collection of groups and initiatives in the American Church. The chapter on ministry and spirituality, collectively written by Anne Patrick, Bernard Cooke, and Diana Hayes, is accompanied by Anne Patrick's chapter on the National Assembly of Religious Women, a case study in liberal ministry and spirituality.

Three consultants joined us for the meeting about this section of the book: Joann Wolski Conn, Anthony Padavano, and Barbara Fleischer. Conn is professor of spirituality at Neumann College in Aston, Pennsylvania; Padavano is the president of CORPUS, an organization of married former priests; and Fleischer is the director of and associate professor in the Institute of Ministry at Loyola University in New Orleans. Cooke's chapter on progressive approaches to ministry sets the context for this section by reviewing the history of ministry and the changes in Catholic understandings of ministry wrought by the Second Vatican Council. He discusses the new roles of the laity in ministry and describes some liberal ministerial organizations. Writing from a dedicated insider's perspective, Cooke also captures the spirit of the renewed Call to Action (CTA) movement, which he calls an "engine of lay ministry." The CTA chapter is an illustration of ministry in action from someone who has been a highly visible and active member of the group.

The chapter written by Anne Patrick, Bernard Cooke, and Diana Hayes takes on the enormous area of liturgy and spirituality in ways that are historical and contemporary. Beginning and ending with references to the controversial television program *Nothing Sacred*, this chapter discusses patterns of change in Catholic understandings of liturgy and spirituality in the last thirty years and illustrates some of its liberal examples. The authors conclude this chapter by noting a range—from moderate to radical—of progressive approaches to liturgy and spirituality. Anne Patrick's insider account of the twenty-five-year pilgrimage of the National Assembly of Religious Women punctuates this section with a dramatic case in point.

Race and Ethnicity

The inclusion of race/ethnicity as a category of analysis in this volume poses some thorny questions. The first is semantic: what does "race" mean in a Catholic context? The second concerns the relationship between one's membership in a racial group and left-wing Catholicism. John McGreevy's introduction to this section sets the historical context of American Catholicism and diversity. Diana Hayes's essay on the revival of the Black Catholic Congress movement and Tim Matovina's chapter on the contrasting histories of Latino organizations (PADRES, a clerical group, and Las Hermanas, originally a group of Hispanic sisters, now a movement of Hispanic women) note that many African Americans and Latinos can be conservative on social and doctrinal issues. At the same time, they find seams of liberal Catholicism in each group and speak to the intuitive sense that Catholics who are interested in racial issues tend to be on the left. Gary Riebe-Estrella's assessment of left-wing strategies on racial issues revolves around identity politics. His emphasis on the Black Catholic Theological Symposium and the American Academy of Catholic Hispanic Theologians highlights a new spirit in the 1970s and shows how distinct social experience (being a member of a racial group) requires a specific kind of theological reflection.

A particular problem raised by the race/ethnicity section is one of mainstreaming. If we put race/ethnicity chapters into a separate section, we idealize those groups and suggest that they are left-wing simply by virtue of their social location. If, however, we distribute these chapters throughout the book to create a more neutral categorization, they tend to disappear into an array of issues capable of obliterating their specific interests. There is no easy solution to this problem, and gallons of ink have been used to argue the rightness of standpoint theory or critical race studies. When we weighed the options, we finally decided to look at race and ethnicity questions as a unit of their own.

When we met to discuss these issues, we were joined by John T. McGreevy, Beverly Carroll, and David Fukuzawa. McGreevy is an associate professor of history at the University of Notre Dame, Carroll is the executive director of the Secretariat of African American Catholics for the National Conference of Catholic Bishops; and Fukuzawa had been a member of the board of the National Catholic Council for Interracial Justice. Sheila Briggs, a member of the core group, was an important part of this discussion as well. When we looked at the papers as a whole, we thought they might benefit from an introductory essay that sets the historical context. Accordingly, we asked John McGreevy to join the project in its last stages and to provide such an essay for the book. His chapter tells a complicated story of racial diversity in American Catholicism and nuances the race/ethnicity issue with historical ironies. Riebe-Estrella's essay is a contextual analysis of some liberal strategies within Catholic racial and ethnic groups that raises questions about the commitment of American Catholics in general to eliminate racism within the Church. Hayes explains the energy behind the Black Catholic Congress movement of the nineteenth century and shows how its revival in the twentieth century exhibits a spirit of assertive self-determination. Matovina compares two Hispanic groups —one clerical and one originally devised to respond to the needs of Hispanic sisters—and shows how the exclusivity of the priests led to the decline of their organization while the inclusivity of the sisters eventually led to a vibrant group of Hispanic religious and lay women united in a new strategy of empowerment for women in the Church. Taken together, these essays serve to illustrate the complexity of race and ethnicity within the American Catholic Church and highlight some aspects of liberal activism.

Public Catholicism

Our final organization problem coalesced around public Catholicism or social justice. Those who lived through the revolutions and uproar of the 1960s know intuitively that social justice is a left-wing issue. Yet, David O'Brien, who drafted this chapter, wondered throughout these meetings about the disappearance of the "Catholic left," meaning the kinds of radical activism that characterized the Catholic Worker, Berrigan-style civil disobedience, and other such earlier initiatives. Is it possible that social justice has moved to the center of American Catholicism? Does the fact that the institutional Church takes social justice as a mandate mean that there is no liberal version of public Catholicism? The present pope is usually applauded by liberals when he speaks on justice issues, and the National Conference of Catholic Bishops has irritated the right and delighted the left with its letters on nuclear war and economics.

David O'Brien, whose chapter constitutes this section, invited Tom Fox, Fred Perella, Elizabeth McKeown, and Anne Klejment to join us for a discussion of his paper. Fox is the editor of the liberal weekly *The National Catholic Reporter*; Perella, now with the Raskob Foundation, has experience as a community organizer for the Campaign for Human Development; McKeown, an associate professor of theology at Georgetown University, specializes in Catholic social welfare; and Klejment is an expert on the peace movement at the University of St. Thomas in St. Paul, Minnesota. If everything that constitutes the Church must be oriented toward social transformation, this chapter is an appropriate way to summarize the history of the Catholic left and to gather the various aspects of this project together. O'Brien summarizes the contexts that form American Catholicism and describes three styles of public Catholicism that are used by American Catholics across the political spectrum. Whereas the "republican" style (favored by bishops) is interested in the public good, the "immigrant" style is self-interested, and the "evangelical" style appeals to Gospel values to criticize both the religious and the secular order. Using these contexts and styles, O'Brien proposes an answer to the question, "What ever happened to the Catholic left?" As he muses on this question, he notes that "liberal Catholics among the hierarchy and clergy, and among church employees generally, found it increasingly difficult to negotiate their way through an organization whose leaders required acceptance, or at least silence, on theological and ecclesiastical issues of growing importance and great moral force, particularly those dealing with women and with the use of power."

Conclusion

As this book goes to press, John Paul II celebrates his twentieth anniversary as pope. The Paris newspaper *Le Monde* marked the anniversary with an opinion poll showing that 53 percent of the French people think he should resign. American Catholics, however much they might disagree with some of the policies of the pope, would probably not be so harsh with their judgment. At the same time, there is widespread disagreement over official Catholic policies within the American Church. This pope has distinguished himself as a great champion of freedom of conscience in places like Eastern Europe while being a fierce opponent of any dissent in the Church. As such, he is a paradoxical combination of fearlessness and fearfulness: he confronts communism, capitalism, and the consumer culture heroically yet approaches members of his church in a fearful, controlling manner. His style suggests that he believes his job requires him to carry the burden of the Church on his shoulders. Liberal Catholics like the ones described in this book believe that his job is to trust the dynamism of the Holy Spirit as it moves through the Church. Liberals tend to have a profound trust in the "people of God" and the workings of the spirit, whereas the Vatican shows the face of profound distrust for anything that is uncontrollable, like feminism, sexuality, some theologians, and even some bishops.

In the judgment of Reinhold Stecher, bishop of Innsbruck, Austria, the desire for control has blinded the Vatican to the actual pastoral situation of the Church in many countries.[11] In America as in other parts of the world, Catholicism faces a severe priest shortage, which means a limited availability of the sacraments for its people. The failure to recognize the vocations of women to the priesthood or to reinstate priests who were forced to abandon their vocations when they married seems more an effort to control the Church than to minister to it. While there has been more than a 20 percent decline in active priests in the United States in the last fifteen years, there has been a steady increase in support for women's ordination. Yet the Church is so nervous about women's issues in general and women's ordination in particular that the Vatican (in 1997) issued an instruction to limit ministry by the non-ordained. The key word seems to be "ministry": lay people may not even *call themselves* pastoral coordinators, or moderators, let alone chaplains. Significantly, women compose more than 85 percent of the 20,000 non-ordained people functioning as parish ministers and more than 80 percent of those administering priestless parishes.

Whereas the present pope holds a brief against dialogue, liberal American Catholics welcome it. Significantly, many of those condemned by the Vatican or fired from their academic posts in the last twenty years have not denied faith, or God, or revelation, but have asked for dialogue about how these great mysteries relate to human experience in a variety of cultural locations. Liberal Catholics, therefore, raise the perennial problem of unity versus pluralism, stagnancy versus creativity, orthodoxy versus chaos. Where one stands in relation to those dichotomies differs since American Catholics have a widely diverse set of approaches to an enormously complex set of issues. Conservatives welcome or yearn for a world of unchanging doctrine, clear lines of command, and good order, the religious analogue of the Newtonian universe. Liberals believe that experience and scientific evidence have undermined the principle of unchangeableness and challenged the view that revelation is closed or that authority is fixed. They are more comfortable with ambiguity, spontaneity, and chaos, with the world of disconcerting chance that has replaced the

Newtonian universe in modern science. The liberal world is messier than the conservative one: it can accept a God and a world in process and in partnership. A complete picture of American Catholicism is framed by both conservative and liberal views. As the Church enters the next millennium, it will have to recognize that order and chaos are not enemies; they are partners in the creative enterprise.

NOTES

1. In the last eight years, *Time* magazine has carried more than half a dozen stories of conflict between the pope and the American Church (16 April 1990, 7 July 1993, 16 August 1993, 26 December 1994, 9 October 1995, 27 May 1996, and 25 May 1998). *Newsweek* and *U.S. News and World Report* have not had as many, but, like *Time*, tend to focus on conflicts between the Vatican and American Catholics. Daily newspapers, including the *New York Times*, the *Chicago Tribune*, and the *Los Angeles Times* have published many more such stories.

2. Mary Jo Weaver, "Introduction: Who Are the Conservative Catholics?" in Mary Jo Weaver and R. Scott Appleby, eds., *Being Right: Conservative American Catholics* (Bloomington: Indiana University Press, 1995), pp. 1–14.

3. *Ad Tuendam Fidem* ("To Defend the Faith") was published on June 30, 1998, accompanied by a "doctrinal commentary" by Cardinal Joseph Ratzinger, Prefect of the Congregation for the Doctrine of Faith.

4. *Humanae Vitae*, issued in July 1968, is the papal encyclical condemning all forms of artificial birth control.

5. *Right from the Beginning* (Washington, D.C.: Regnery Gateway, 1990), pp. 70–72.

6. *Bare Ruined Choirs: Doubt, Prophecy, and Radical Religion* (New York: Doubleday, 1971), pp. 38, 46, and 45.

7. *Dignitatis Humanae*, the Declaration on Religious Freedom, is widely interpreted as an American victory at the council, the place where the council fathers accepted the freedoms associated with the founding of the United States.

8. See the essay "Call to Action" in this volume, by Bernard Cooke.

9. Copies of the referendum can be obtained from We Are the Church Coalition, P.O. Box 2548, Fairfax, Virginia, 22031. Some Catholics who have tried to collect signatures on the referendum have been cautioned by their pastors not to do so on Church property.

10. Rowan Williams, "The Body's Grace," in Charles Hefling, ed., *Our Selves, Our Souls and Bodies: Sexuality and the Household of God* (Boston: Cowley Press, 1996), pp. 58–68, is brilliant on this issue.

11. See the *National Catholic Reporter* 34 (26 December 1997), p. 28. Bishop Stecher delivered his critical remarks before he retired from his see.

Part I

FEMINIST THEOLOGY AND PRACTICE

1

CATHOLIC WOMEN
THEOLOGIANS OF THE LEFT

SUSAN A. ROSS

In her 1990 Presidential Address to the Catholic Theological Society of
America (CTSA), Anne E. Patrick reported on two articles that contained the mistaken perception that clergy no longer constituted a majority of the Society. She "set the record straight" by noting that "anyone counting the women's names in the present membership lists will
not get past 250, and probably not that far, and the numbers of laymen
are certainly fewer."[1] Nevertheless, the fact that these 250 women had
attained the doctoral degree and had become members in the 26 years
since women were first admitted to the Society in 1964 (membership
being previously restricted to clergy) says something important about
the growth in influence of women theologians. To be sure, the ranks
of women theologians, especially those "on the left," are not by any
means restricted to those who hold membership in the CTSA.[2] But
many of the CTSA's women members do place themselves on the left,
and they, along with their colleagues in various academic and activist
organizations, have been exerting their influence in these groups, as
well as in colleges, universities, and seminaries. The face of contemporary Catholic theology has been deeply affected by the work of these
women.

This chapter is intended to provide a "map" of Catholic women's
theology "of the left." But before I attend to the topography, two important issues relating to identity need to be addressed. The first is the
diversity and pluralism of these theologies, their resistance to easy labeling, and the important questions, tensions, and dynamics that they
surface. The second is a definition of what constitutes a "left" position
for Catholic women theologians. I will turn first to the diversity of
Catholic women's theology. The work of the first Catholic woman to
publish a book on women's role in theology can help to illustrate what
is involved.

Mary Daly's first book, *The Church and the Second Sex*, published in 1968, concluded with these hopeful words: "Men and women, using their best talents, forgetful of self and intent upon the work, will with God's help mount together toward a higher order of consciousness and being, in which the alienating projections will have been defeated and wholeness, psychic integrity, achieved."[3] In the immediate aftermath of Vatican II, such hope was shared by many, who anticipated great changes in the Church. Seven years later, the book was reissued, with a "New Feminist Postchristian Introduction" in which Daly repudiated her Catholicism, and her optimistic conclusion, as being fundamentally incompatible with her feminism. Her next two books— *Beyond God the Father: Toward a Philosophy of Women's Liberation* (1973)[4] and *Gyn/Ecology: the Metaethics of Radical Feminism* (1978)[5]—furthered her agenda of uncovering the sexism and misogyny of human history and providing an alternative language for women. But Daly's conception of her task raised serious problems for some of her readers. In 1979, the African-American poet and writer Audre Lorde responded to *Gyn/Ecology* in "An Open Letter to Mary Daly." While appreciative of Daly's work, Lorde was disturbed by her focus on Euro-American women's experiences, her failure to explore the richness of African cultures, and her assumptions of the universality of women's experiences. Lorde wrote to Daly: "But to imply, however, that all women suffer the same oppression simply because we are women, is to lose sight of the many varied tools of patriarchy. It is to ignore how these tools are used by women without awareness against each other."[6]

Lorde's words opened up issues that had been churning beneath the surface of the emerging body of work that had come to be known as "feminist theology": that is, that women do not constitute a uniform group; that differences of race, ethnicity, and class cannot be ignored; and that the tendency of white feminist theologians to generalize on the basis of their own experiences compounds the multiple forms of oppression faced by racial-ethnic women.

Daly's work has been an important source for Catholic women's theology. While some of her conclusions are not shared by "Catholic feminists" (e.g., her separatism and repudiation of traditional religions), her ability to name the outrages perpetuated against women over the centuries, as well as her reclaiming of language, remain influential. Yet her failure to recognize the reality of differences in women's lives is also illustrative of the pluralism, and attendant tensions, within theology done by Catholic women, as well as in other Christian denominations and in other religious traditions. Thus the term "feminist" does not describe adequately what critical theology done by women is; indeed, two groups of women have rejected the term as inadequate for their own self-descriptions. African-American women theologians have taken up Alice Walker's term "womanist" to describe a position that is self-consciously from Black women's perspective and experiences.[7] Some U.S. Hispanic women have coined the term *"mujerista"* to describe the position of women of Hispanic/Latina heritage in the U.S.[8] "Feminist," at least in the U.S. context, generally refers to the theology of white, Euro-American women. The question of what to call theology done by Catholic women "on the left," then, is only the tip of the iceberg in terms of the diversity and pluralism beneath.[9] Feminist theology has tended to emerge from the academic sector; mujerista and womanist theologies, while also related to academia, tend to have a more activist base. Thus it is more accurate to describe a pluralism of theologies by women, all concerned in some way with structural change, but with differing foci.

This leads to the second issue of the identity of the "left." The term "left," as it is conceived in this volume, constitutes a position over and against the "right" and, as well, distinct from the "center." What, then, constitutes a "left-wing" position for Catholic women theologians? Most of the theologians whose work is considered here would probably not use the term "left" to describe themselves. Some might term themselves "radical," while others would prefer the term "reformist." But I think it is possible to identify a set of positions that would be taken by this diverse group of theologians, that would constitute something roughly like this: Christianity, like the other religious and social institutions of human history, has been deeply infected with sexism—that is, the systematic denigration of women—as well as other destructive hierarchical dualisms such as racism and classism. Thus, what is needed is not mere inclusion into the prevailing patriarchal structures of theology—sometimes described as the "add women and stir" solution. Rather, what is necessary is the systemic transformation of theology itself. I will focus on five dimensions of this transformation. *First*, it involves the method and purpose of theology. Feminist, womanist, and mujerista theologians turn to experience, rather than the inherited tradition, as the starting point for theology and see theology's purpose as liberation. *Second*, the transformation means a renaming and reclaiming of the past. This task reveals both the historical forces that worked to silence women's voices and the retrieval of women's active involvement and significant achievements. *Third*, feminist theology advocates a holistic understanding of embodiment, which includes a concrete focus on how persons act, express, and celebrate themselves and their communities. *Fourth*, all of these women-developed theologies recognize the interconnection of multiple forms of oppression (sexism, heterosexism, racism, classism, anti-Semitism) and argue for the need to develop strategies to overcome them as well as to rethink what it means to be a moral person. *Fifth*, and not least,

Catholic feminist theology contains a strong critique of power relations in theology, the Church, and society and advocates a reformulation of the major doctrines of the tradition.

For labeling purposes, it might be more accurate to label this position "radical," although the term is sometimes used to label both post-
traditionalist and separatist women. But the term "radical" is also
used by some Church officials to separate "good" women theologians
from "bad" ones.[10] Those who would prefer "radical" over "left"
would argue that radical means "to the roots"—that is, that change is
not cosmetic or superficial, but structural and transformative. In general, "liberal" and "moderate" feminists seek inclusion into prevailing
structures on equal grounds with men. A "conservative" feminist approach (which many feminists on the left would see as a contradiction
in terms) would see the Catholic tradition as having an inherent "feminism," which simply needs more explicit attention. The "radical" position I am outlining here seeks the transformation of Church structures and theological method without departing from fidelity to the
message of Jesus. For example, on the issue of ordination of women, a
conservative feminist would oppose it; a moderate feminist would argue that women should be ordained alongside men; and a radical, or
left-wing, feminist would argue for a transformation of all ministries
in the Church.

My "mapping" of Catholic women "of the left" assumes this
shared commitment to radical transformation and the conviction that
this transformation is the only way to be authentically faithful to the
message of Jesus and to the tradition. I will explore the work of Catholic women theologians of the left using the five-part task outlined
above.

Theological Method and Experience

"Experience" is a very slippery concept, having many different meanings and applications. The idea that one's theology is contextualized
by one's experience is a major contention of contemporary theology,
but its roots go back at least to the Enlightenment. As I shall use the
term in this chapter, it refers to the complex of feelings, actions, judgments, histories, and perceptions of persons and groups that both con-
tribute to and result in self-conscious reflection. "Experience" itself is
never unmediated; yet there can be levels of awareness of the impact
of one's experience on one's thought and action.[11] On the whole, liberation theologies—Latin American, African-American, women's—
give experience a central place, arguing that all theologies, at least in
part, are the result of the experiences of their practitioners. That is to
say, all theologies are, to some extent, particular, and their claims to

universality are, minimally, suspect. It is necessary for theologians to acknowledge this fact and to begin their theological reflections from this explicit vantage point.[12]

Moreover, liberation theologies—again, I include women's liberation theologies as one variety of this theological genre—argue that experience and revelation are not, in principle, separable. Revelation occurs *within human experience,* and so it is critical to be attentive to the varieties of experience, so as not to privilege the experience of only some.[13] Thus the traditional sources of revelation—in Roman Catholicism, Scripture and tradition—are historically limited because they too arise out of human experience and are open to interpretation and critique from the vantage point of experience. But liberation theologies do not abandon the concept of revelation. It is reformulated to reflect the conviction that God's word is a liberating one, that Jesus' message explicitly rejects all forms of domination, calls for overcoming all structures of oppression and domination, and establishes God's reign in the present. Women's liberation theologies have as their main focus the liberation of women from all forms of oppression but may focus on or begin with those based on sex. They are concerned as well with the interrelation of sexism with other forms of domination and oppression. These oppressions are identified by liberation theologies as sinful.

Valerie Saiving first made the connection between theology and the experience of women in a 1960 article, arguing that the traditional formulations of such doctrines as sin and grace have overwhelmingly represented the experiences of men.[14] But the charge that there is no such singular reality as "women's experience" that can be applied to all women has been one of the most important criticisms emerging from Catholic women theologians of the left. The aim of feminist, especially womanist and mujerista, theologies is to name the *particular* and *diverse* experiences of women—cultural, physical, psychological, economic—that have been ignored or seen as unimportant by the tradition, as well as by dominant men and women, so that they can be identified and addressed. In this way, experience operates critically so as to reveal the gaps and erasures in tradition. This is a claim that is made by all feminist perspectives on traditional disciplines: that is, the absence of women, the silencing of women's voices, has been a part of the disciplines' own formation. One dimension of the theological task, then, is to see how traditional teachings have been implicated in the perpetuation of injustices directed at women. Thus, such issues as domestic violence, sexist language, and stereotyped images of women are relevant to theology insofar as they represent its failure to recognize and to offer hope to the lived reality of women's lives.

The experiences of women in relation to the traditional sources of theology—especially the Bible—are mixed. On the one hand, the scriptural narratives themselves are filled with stories that one scholar refers to as "texts of terror"—the rape of Tamar, the sacrifice of Jephthah's unnamed daughter—as well as stories of women who have been neglected, absent from lectionaries, and denied their rightful place in the tradition.[15] Thus the experiences of women in relation to the Bible can be profoundly negative ones, leading some to reject the Bible and the Jewish and Christian traditions as hopelessly oppressive to women.

But the Bible can also be a source of hope and inspiration to women, with the prophetic tradition, the teachings of Jesus, and the community of the early church representative of the Bible's liberating potential for women. The key point here is to underscore the nature of tradition (both scriptural and doctrinal) as deeply intertwined with human experience, and consequently, as *both* oppressive and liberating. As one feminist theologian puts it, "[f]eminist theologians. . . rely on multiple sources of revelation, drawn from the religious experience of traditions beyond Christianity and from human experience."[16] The "useable canon" is, in fact, much larger than the traditional canon.[17] This focus on experience has led to charges from the right that feminist theology is profoundly anti-Christian by rejecting the traditional sources.[18]

Indeed, the focus on experience is one of the crucial dividing lines between the left and right. Conservatives reject the centrality of experience in contemporary theology, and feminist theology is no exception. The dangers of such a focus, according to conservatives, are relativism and subjectivism, without reference to an objective moral order. And while some feminist theologians would not entirely reject the concept of an objective moral order, their point is that it is essentially ambiguous, open to and capable of bearing and even enriching multiple perspectives and interpretations.[19]

Further, the plurality of women's experiences works against "universalizing" tendencies in theology. That is, the *particularity and distinctness* of diverse groups of women is important to identify so that one group—usually dominant, white, middle-class women—does not claim that its experience describes that of all women. Unintentionally, perhaps, but nevertheless in reality, feminist discourse has for some functioned as a language of *domination*, muting and even silencing the many voices that have not yet been "heard into speech."[20] For all women, gender is not the only issue, but women of color are more conscious of their experiences as members of particular racial or ethnic groups. Race, socio-economic status, and ethnicity are at least as much a concern as is gender. Indeed, the failure of white women to recognize the role of race in their own thinking needs much greater attention.[21] Race, class, and heterosexual privilege can blind women to different dimensions of oppression. For feminist theologies, then, the task is not simply to acknowledge diversity but to embrace it, to incorporate it methodologically and practically, and especially to be attentive to those who have been voiceless.

For these theologies, then, women's experience is used negatively as a *critique of tradition*. But experience is also used positively as a source for constructive theological work: for new understandings of God, of the Church, of ministry, of the nature of being human. Such examples as women's experiences of their own sexuality—in marriage, in other committed relationships, and in motherhood—women's affective lives, communities, and "women's ways of knowing"[22] have all pushed the limits of the tradition's language, images, and ways of life. The point is that women's reflective understandings of their own situations are, in feminist, mujerista, and womanist theologies, brought explicitly into theological language and used both to critique and to reconstruct Christian theology. The methodological criterion of "adequacy to women's experience" functions throughout this movement.

History and Tradition

As noted above, one of the first steps of a theology that is informed by women's experiences is a critical examination of the tradition. In this regard, feminist biblical criticism has emerged as one of the most fruitful areas of scholarship. This discipline has as one of its goals a more adequate understanding of the historical situation of biblical and historical texts. Thus, feminist biblical scholars rely on historical-critical method, as well as literary, archeological, and linguistic scholarship, so as better to understand what the biblical and historical texts meant in their original context.

But this does not exhaust the task of feminist biblical scholarship, as its most prominent and prolific proponent has shown. Elisabeth Schüssler Fiorenza, a biblical theologian, has argued consistently for an understanding of biblical interpretation that is self-consciously political: that is, an interpretation that recognizes the importance of the Bible as a text that still has an important function in the contemporary world (both positive and negative) and that can be used to inspire women and men to live out the Bible's liberating message. Schüssler Fiorenza has developed a four-step hermeneutical process of feminist biblical interpretation that I will describe here.[23] Underlying her (and others') hermeneutics are the convictions that the revelatory message of the Bible is one of liberation from all forms of oppression, that the message of Jesus was a radically inclusive and egalitarian one, and that the early Christian community, with its diversity of ministries shared by women and men, can serve as a prototype for the future.[24]

How does one approach these ancient, sacred, and normative texts? Schüssler Fiorenza's first step is to develop a *hermeneutics of suspicion*. Feminist interpreters approach historical texts (as well as many contemporary ones) with this critical attitude. That is, one begins by questioning the androcentrism of the text as well as its function in supporting a patriarchal understanding of the tradition. One cannot assume that the texts have been adequately translated or interpreted. Thus a feminist hermeneutics of suspicion takes the task of translation very seriously, and attempts to put texts into a broad social and historical context. This suspicion is not directed solely, however, to the writers of the past. Contemporary biblical interpretation is also taken to task for claiming "objectivity" while ignoring its own political biases.

But an approach of suspicion does not exhaust the interpretive task, since the Bible can function as a liberative as well as an oppressive text. Thus a *hermeneutics of proclamation* is necessary to highlight its liberating message, as well as to reveal its potential for oppression. Indeed, as Schüssler Fiorenza writes in *In Memory of Her:* "Biblical revelation and truth are given only in those texts and interpretive models that transcend critically their patriarchal frameworks and allow for a vision of Christian women as historical and theological subjects and actors."[25] Thus all feminist critical approaches to historical texts, including the Bible, scrutinize them carefully for their coherence with the liberating message of Jesus. In addition, the ways in which biblical texts are used within the tradition are also subject to criticism. Which readings are chosen for the lectionary (which, for most Catholics, is their main encounter with the Bible)?[26] Which texts are used to justify doctrinal positions (such as the prohibition of women's ordination)?[27] Yet there is also an appreciative dimension to a hermeneutics of proclamation, in that the perduring liberating power of these texts is affirmed. A hermeneutics of proclamation is both critical and constructive, seeking to use the biblical tradition in the ways most conducive to the liberation of women.

The third step is what Schüssler Fiorenza terms a *hermeneutics of remembrance*. Relying on Johannes Metz's conception of the "dangerous memory" of the sufferings of those in the past, Schüssler Fiorenza calls for remembering the forgotten women of the Bible and of the historical tradition. In remembering them, Christians keep alive their witness and example. Perhaps most importantly, remembering the witness of the past encourages a solidarity with those who have suffered in the past and in the present, and helps to reclaim the scriptural tradition as a history of struggle.

Fourth, Schüssler Fiorenza proposes a *hermeneutics of creative actualization* in which the biblical tradition is brought alive again in ritual and in practice. This allows an "active engagement in liberation," and the potential for the Bible's liberating power in the present is unleashed for contemporary women. Retelling the biblical stories and developing new forms of ritual are ways to continue the struggle against oppression witnessed to by biblical and historical women and continuing in the present.

While Schüssler Fiorenza's work is the most prolific and detailed among Catholic feminist biblical interpreters, other feminist theologians have made analogous arguments for an attitude of suspicion toward the Bible and toward the major texts of the tradition, and for critical reinterpretation. Rosemary Radford Ruether's work deserves mention here. Her argument that the prophetic tradition of the Bible provides one key biblical theme of liberation, even though the prophets tolerated the unjust treatment of women, suggests as well that the Bible has been in the past and still functions in the present as a text to inspire liberation. Although Schüssler Fiorenza has been critical of Ruether for her "neo-orthodoxy," both scholars would concur that the Bible cannot be ignored by feminist theologians, that a liberative hermeneutics is necessary to begin to undo the damage of centuries of androcentric (mis)translation and (mis)interpretation, and that the role of the Bible in the present is to serve as a prototype for the future.[28]

The hermeneutical task continues into the post-biblical traditions. Some of the most creative work in feminist theology has been in the reinterpretation of the historical tradition. The roles of women in the early church, as well as the work of medieval women nuns and mystics, have been discovered and rediscovered by contemporary scholars seeking to understand the complex history of Christianity. The use of "feminine" imagery in the writings of medieval women (and men), for example, has enriched the understanding of such issues as naming God,[29] Eucharistic piety,[30] and the role of Mary.[31]

The histories of congregations of women religious are also being rewritten, revealing the struggles that many of these orders faced with male religious authorities and the monumental work that was accomplished in helping to build a system of social support in the U.S.[32] And the ambiguities of U.S. Catholic history, including not only sexism, but also racism and ethnic prejudice, are coming to light with the work of a new generation of scholars.[33] The history of women is thus being rewritten as a history of struggle.

In short, what this historical and textual work reveals is that the tradition has been largely shaped by men and continues to show this

androcentric imprint. Feminist theologians are thus not only rein-
terpreting the past, but challenging its authority. If all of history is
vulnerable to the charge of androcentrism if not sexism, then the normative role of tradition, for Roman Catholicism, is very much shaken.
This is proving to be the case with the issue of women's ordination,
as recent polls show a majority of Roman Catholics in the U.S. favoring the ordination of women and of married men.[34] The magisterium's recent action of declaring the teaching on ordination to be part
of the infallible "ordinary magisterium" of the Church reveals the fra-
gility of this authority, as the experiences of women and men, and a
more critical attitude toward the tradition, erode the old attitude of
obedience.

Embodiment and Spirituality

Feminist spirituality begins with the conviction that religious faith involves the entire person—physical, spiritual, and emotional dimensions—and it resists the dualism that, it claims, has plagued western
thought since the Greeks and that was accentuated in the Enlightenment elevation of reason over emotion. Thus a crucial dimension of
feminist, mujerista, and womanist spiritualities is their reclaiming of
the wholeness and goodness of the body. Further, these theologians
have also pointed out how devalued groups of people—women, racial
minorities, Jews—have been traditionally associated with the body
while elite men have been understood to be more "spiritual" and intellectual.[35] This dualistic split reveals both a deep suspicion of the
body and of sexuality and a fear and hatred of women on the part of
many influential thinkers that has pervaded the tradition.

Feminist spirituality seeks to reclaim the body as one medium of
revelation as well as to question the ways in which "spiritual development" has been defined. First, women's bodies—as well as the bodies
of the most vulnerable, including children, the poor, and the disabled
—are seen as holy. In the tradition, women's bodies have been seen as
impure (e.g., the "churching" of women after childbirth and the prohibition of menstruating Orthodox women from receiving communion), as in need of covering (especially the head; women religious were
praised for disguising their femaleness), and as sources of temptation.
Church practice has been that spiritual, ecclesial, and liturgical leadership is inappropriate for women, that contact with women is threaten-
ing to clerical piety,[36] and that male language and images for both God
and humanity are the norm. The message, feminist theologians argue,
could not be clearer: men are closer to God than are women.

Yet women have never accepted this message unquestioningly.
Women in the early Christian communities served in leadership ca-

pacities and suffered martyrdom alongside their brothers. Medieval women focused especially on the connection between their own bodiliness and that of Jesus as expressive of the wonder of the incarnation.[37] Contemporary women have (re)discovered their own "beauty of body," and have developed a storehouse of images, rituals, and literature expressive of its sacrality.[38]

Alongside this reclaiming of women's bodily beauty and integrity has been a strong critique of the ways in which religious and secular culture have denigrated women's bodiliness. Such a denigration is inexorably connected with the global epidemics of sex-tourism, prostitution, domestic violence, and such practices as genital mutilation, bride-burning, and sex-selective abortion.[39] The distinction between feminist spirituality and ethics breaks down because the attitudes that underlie these atrocities are revealed to be rooted, in part, in both secular and religious conceptions of women's lesser worth.

Moreover, Roman Catholic spirituality long emphasized a withdrawal from "the world" and, consequently, from the concerns of women, children, the poor.[40] Traditionally, to be "spiritual" was to be concerned with the higher things of life—prayer, biblical study, contemplation—suggesting that caring for children or preparing meals was of lower value. "Folk religion"—i.e., the practices of the people, largely outside the positions of power—was considered worthy of study only by anthropologists. Mujerista theologians point out that folk religion is where Christianity has been kept alive, in the everyday traditions of the people, such as veneration of the saints and of Mary, processions, and oral traditions, and that such religion has largely been in the hands of women.[41] Womanist theologians make a similar claim that African-American spirituality places a high value on "persons, relationships, and values," and rejects dualistic sacred/secular and mind/body splits.[42] Especially for mujerista and womanist theologies, spirituality is not conceived solely in terms of the individual task of "growing closer to God," but is intrinsically related to the well-being of their communities.

An important dimension of these spiritualities is a broader conception of embodiment and sexuality that moves beyond narrow conceptions of "correct" sexual practices. All of these theologies reject the Catholic magisterium's focus on sexuality as the litmus test of Catholic orthodoxy and argue that Catholicism has long been suspicious of bodily pleasures. Prohibitions against gay and lesbian relationships and masturbation (not to mention nonprocreative heterosexual intercourse) have been based on a conception of sexuality as primarily oriented toward procreation, a conception that, these theologians observe, is androcentric in its understanding. A fuller understanding of women's sexuality might, even on natural law grounds, take a very different view as to the "telos" of one's genital organs and of the ultimate purpose of committed relationships. Women's sexuality, with its greater relational orientation, diffuseness, and cyclicality, suggests an attitude toward the body and sexuality that is more closely integrated with one's relationships and with nature and that emphasizes more fully its potential for passion and joy.[43]

It is here that there is some congruence between conservatives and feminists, although they disagree on the conclusions of these themes. Where conservative theologians also describe women's embodiment as unique and revelatory of the sacred, and celebrate the sacrality of sexuality, it is most often in the language of the spousal relationship with God. This relationship is decidedly heterosexual in its use of metaphors, and also understands women as fundamentally receptive, nurturing, and essentially maternal.[44]

Women's reclaiming of experience, tradition, and embodiment has also led to new and creative approaches to ritual and celebration. In part because of the exclusion of women from ordination, left-wing Catholic women have not sought primarily to be included in established Church structures, as has been largely the case for women in Protestant denominations that do ordain women. Catholic women have used this situation as the opportunity for imagining egalitarian Church structures and for developing new forms of ritual that draw explicitly on women's experiences. The movement that has come to be known as "Women-Church" has been largely, though not exclusively, a movement of Catholic women who find in it a place for alternative community and celebrations, a safe place on the margins that does not replace the institutional Church but is in process toward the transformation of the entire Christian community.[45]

One noted theorist of liturgy has recently described five principles that can be identified as basic to intentional feminist liturgy:

> First, feminist liturgies ritualize relationships that emancipate and empower women. Second, feminist liturgy is the production of the community of worshipers, not of special experts or authorities. Third, feminist liturgies critique patriarchal liturgies. Fourth, feminist liturgists have begun to develop a distinctive repertoire of ritual symbols and strategies. Fifth, feminist liturgies produce liturgical events, not liturgical texts.[46]

These five principles are both critical and constructive. In focusing on emancipation and empowerment, feminist liturgies arise directly from women's lives and concerns. They are distinctive: not replacements for patriarchal liturgies, but rather women-centered alternatives.

As one woman phrased it, "There is an increasing need for me to become actively involved with a group of women for ritual, prayer, discussion, support, and social action. . . . It's time for women to develop their own rituals using language and symbols that are meaningful to us, while drawing on the rich depths of our spirituality."[47] Ranging from international to local, such groups for women are meeting the needs of those alienated by the institutional churches. While not all feminist women regularly participate in such unofficial liturgies, the liturgies nevertheless stand as an alternative to the standard parish fare.

Ethics and Social Justice

As is probably already evident to the reader, the main themes of feminist, mujerista, and womanist theology overlap considerably. Experience is a crucial factor in biblical interpretation as well as in spirituality and theology; similarly, to discuss "ethics and social justice" as a discrete category is, for feminists, to make a distinction that obscures more than it illumines. In an article on feminist ethics in 1990, Lisa Sowle Cahill remarked that "[v]irtually by definition, feminist theology is moral theology or ethics. It emerges from a practical situation of injustice and aims at social and political change."[48] The task in this section is to focus on the particular ways in which feminist, mujerista, and womanist theologies challenge the traditions of Roman Catholic moral theology and social ethics and propose more adequate criteria for moral thinking and action.

The Roman Catholic tradition has long prided itself on its progressive, and at times prophetic, positions in areas related to social justice—the just wage, economic equality, war-and-peace issues—and Catholic women's liberation theologies have worked to extend this concern for social justice to women. With the emphasis of Vatican II, especially in *Gaudium et Spes*, on issues concerning the wider world, feminist theologies have challenged the Church on its understanding of justice, arguing that the justice due to women in marriage, to all human beings regardless of sex, and to workers within the Church (especially women) has not even come close to full realization. Social justice cannot come about, these theologies argue, in a situation in which women's and men's humanities are understood as essentially different—thus understandings of social justice are necessarily tied to theological anthropology.

In addition, the striking fact that the U.S. Catholic bishops were able to develop strong statements on economic justice and on war and peace but were unable to agree on a pastoral statement on women's issues says much about the problematic position women find themselves in, in relation to U.S. Catholic social justice concerns. Women on the left charged that a pastoral letter ought to deal not with "women's issues," as if they were a "problem," but rather with sexism. Women on the right denied the need for any kind of statement at all.[49] Social justice also connects with the issue of ordination in that feminist, mujerista, and womanist theologies argue that women will lack any decision-making power in the Church as long as such power is tied to ordination. The Church's failure to address this issue continues seriously to undermine its credibility as it speaks of the equality of women and of social justice "in the world," but fails to act on it *ad intra*. The traditional distinctions between the public and private arenas are challenged by feminists, expressed in the phrase "the personal is the political." The realms of the private and public reflect and reinforce each other, feminist theorists have long observed. Nevertheless, Catholic organizations that tie social justice, ordination, and women's concerns (such as Call to Action, Las Hermanas, the former National Assembly of Religious Women, and the Association for the Rights of Catholics in the Church) continue to press this issue, sometimes with serious theological and ecclesiological consequences (as in the case of Mercy Sister Carmel McEnroy).[50]

In terms of moral theology's understanding of the human person, and of sin and grace, feminist, mujerista, and womanist theologies have challenged traditional norms and have developed new criteria, again drawing on women's experiences. Critical of the "act-centered" conception of morality so characteristic of manualist Catholic moral theology, women ethicists have sought to establish morality in the context of the person and her community and to challenge the centrality of sexual morality as the litmus test for Christian behavior. Thus, such concerns as relationality, mutuality, conscience, embodiment, and nature have emerged as central to an ethics informed by women's critical interpretation of the Christian tradition.

Relationality and mutuality refer to a restructuring of human relationships according to egalitarian and mutual principles.[51] Feminist theologies are critical of all forms of domination and subjugation, especially those based on sex, and they challenge Christians to establish relationships with each other that are mutual, that recognize the full humanity of the other person, and that are egalitarian. Such norms apply not only to basic human relationships such as marriage and friendship, but also to societal structures, especially including the Church. Hierarchical structures are special objects of criticism, since, feminist theologians claim, they tend to be self-serving and self-perpetuating. Elisabeth Schüssler Fiorenza's term for the church, "discipleship of equals," serves as the guiding image of Christian community, where "[c]onversion and solidarity but not patriarchal control, obedience, or submission . . . characterize our discipleship and commitment today."[52]

Conscience has always played a crucial role in Roman Catholic moral thinking. Mujerista, feminist, and womanist theologies extend and transform the understanding of conscience so as to stress women's autonomy and right to make moral decisions.[53] Along with liberation theology's stress on the importance of "conscientization," these theologies stress the need to develop a critical sense of one's worth as a person, one's obligations, and one's position in society.[54] "Conscience" is thus seen in developmental terms (an emphasis shared with left-wing Catholic moral theology in general) and in a broader social context than has traditionally been the case. "Acting on one's conscience" is seen not as an isolated act, but rather as a process in which the person becomes aware of the multiple dimensions of the human situation, becomes informed, reflects, and acts.[55] While it might be claimed that this understanding of conscience does not reflect anything radically new in Catholic moral theology, what *is* new is that women are claiming moral authority for themselves, relying and reflecting on their own distinct experiences as women in a context that has not sufficiently encouraged this. Including women's moral agency does not merely "spice up" the pot of moral theology but, to change metaphors, adds new harmonies, instruments, and themes to the chorus of moral reflection.

As a moral principle, embodiment draws on what has already been said about the importance of an expanded understanding of human being. Embodiment incorporates sexuality, but sexuality hardly exhausts its meaning. Feminist theologians argue that the Catholic moral tradition, while claiming to take the body and nature seriously, has in its particular emphasis on natural law taken the body and sexuality out of the lived contexts of people's lives. It has failed to be attentive to the challenges arising from scientific research that are potentially relevant to natural law, as well as to women's embodied experiences that suggest alternative ways of construing "natural law."[56] What has resulted, feminist theologians argue, is a theology that emphasizes "acts," takes them out of the continuity of one's life as a whole, freezes certain "faculties," and unduly stresses the sexual dimensions of one's life at the expense of economic, social, or psychological well-being.[57] Some observers of Catholic moral theology have pointed out that the Catholic tradition tolerates a plurality of views on some very serious moral issues, such as war and economic justice, but insists on uniformity on issues relating to personal morality.[58] It is not a coincidence, feminists argue, that such an emphasis on issues relating to personal morality and sexuality has a disproportionate effect on women and diminishes women's full moral agency.

The issue of women's reproductive rights is probably the issue that most illustrates the challenges that feminism presents to the institutional Church and that most marks the division between "right" and "left" forms of Catholicism. The publication of *Humanae Vitae* in July of 1968, maintaining the Church's prohibition of "artificial" forms of contraception, disappointed many women (and men) who felt that the Church failed to respond to the experiences of many who could not, in good conscience, follow Church teaching. But the issue of contraception as a symbol of traditional Roman Catholic morality has really given way to the issue of abortion.[59] When the U.S. Supreme Court upheld abortion as part of a woman's right to privacy in 1973, feminists, including many religious feminists, hailed the decision as a positive one for women. For Roman Catholic women of the left, there is no unanimity on the issue of abortion. The more left-wing organizations, such as Catholics for a Free Choice (CFFC), emphasize the tradition's ambiguous history on the issue and advocate greater reproductive planning for women as a means to lower abortion rates.[60] Other groups, such as Feminists for Life, stress the connections with the Church's social teachings, and argue against abortion.[61] But even theologians who are uneasy with CFFC's stance argue that the Church's position fails to see women as fully mature moral agents who are able to make difficult moral decisions, in good conscience. The issue of abortion, all these theologians argue, needs to be seen in the wider context of women's lives: in how Church and society support children, in the Church's failure to support programs for population planning, and especially in the context of a church that accords to women no voice in institutional decision making.[62]

Connected to this issue is a continuing concern with the ecological well-being of the world. Over twenty years ago, Rosemary Ruether connected ecological and feminist issues as she observed how women, Jews, racial minorities, and the earth have all been seen as wild and untamed and thus subject to patriarchal control.[63] A transformation of attitudes is in order, she and others have argued, if the earth itself is to survive. This transformation involves a new and interdependent way of seeing oneself in relationship to other forms of life as well as to God.

In Catholic moral theology, the issue at stake in the present is the ability simply to *discuss* issues relating to women, and in particular the issue of abortion. Archbishop Rembert Weakland of Milwaukee resolved a few years back simply to *hear* the experiences of women on this issue. He scheduled a series of "listening sessions" in his archdiocese so that women could come and express their experiences and concerns on the issue. But the response from Catholics on the right was overwhelmingly negative, and a subsequent invitation to receive an honorary degree from a European university was withdrawn at the Vatican's insistence.[64] Feminist theologies, while not necessarily of one voice in regard to the morality of abortion, nevertheless are concerned that the "single-issue" focus of the Vatican, and especially on the part of the U.S. bishops, on matters of sexual morality, has been detrimental to the discipline of moral theology and has had particularly damaging effects on women. But Catholic women of the left are far from silent in the area of moral theology, and their contributions to the literature are transforming the discipline.[65]

Critique of Power/Reformulation of Doctrine

It is nearly impossible to separate the critique of power structures and the reformulation of doctrine in Roman Catholicism. Because the structure of Church governance places the oversight of theology under clerical control, challenges to traditional doctrines are, in effect, challenges to Church structure. Recent events concerning Catholics of a more liberal bent confirm this connection: e.g., Rev. Richard McBrien's struggles with the U.S. Catholic bishops over his book *Catholicism*,[66] the Vatican directive to Brazilian feminist theologian Ivonne Gebara to undertake two years of "study" in Europe,[67] liberation theologian Leonardo Boff's "silencing" and subsequent resignation from the Franciscans,[68] the termination of a woman professor at an Ohio pontifical seminary.[69] While an exhaustive treatment of feminist, womanist, and mujerista theologies on doctrines is impossible in this survey, some highlights will give the reader a sense of the directions that these theologies are taking.

Before getting to doctrines *per se*, the issue of language deserves consideration. One of the major efforts of the contemporary feminist critique in all disciplines is a heightened awareness of the power of language. We are shaped by language; it is not so much an instrument we control but rather a "house" in which we dwell, as Heidegger observed. Thus the recognition of the power of language, and especially the effect that androcentric language has on the imagination, is a key step in woman-centered theological transformation. As the concern over naming women's theologies (e.g., as feminist, womanist, mujerista) evidences, how we name reality is an immensely important issue.

The issue of "inclusive language," that is, language that does not use the generic masculine to refer to humanity, has emerged as one very real division between right and left Catholicism. Catholics on the right are, on the whole, opposed to the use of inclusive language.[70] Catholics on the left, and particularly feminist Catholics, argue not only that "horizontal" language for humanity is in need of inclusivity, but that "vertical" language for God in all-male terms impoverishes the human imagination and understanding of God.[71]

Thus the issue of inclusive language leads to the doctrine of God.

Feminist theologies have turned their attention not only to naming God but also to the ways in which God's being (the Trinity) is conceived and to how God is related to the world. In terms of naming God, feminist theologians Elisabeth Schüssler Fiorenza and Rosemary Radford Ruether have proposed that the term for the divine be written in alternative ways: as G*d (for the former) and as God/ess (for the latter).[72] Both terms are meant to "visibly destabilize" the largely patriarchal ways in which human beings think about the divine. Thus God's "Fatherhood" is challenged as the primary "name" for God (as it is in liturgical language); this particular point is another issue that sharply divides the Catholic right from the left, leading to charges from the right that feminist theology inevitably involves "goddess worship."[73]

As in reformulations of moral theology, the category of relationality is key. The traditional monarchial conceptions of God as unchanging, all-knowing, and all-powerful have given way, in feminist theologies, to a conception of God as Being-in-Relation and Being-For-Us.[74] Drawing on themes developed by process theologians earlier in this century, feminists stress God's dynamic relationship with humanity, God's special concern for the poor, God's compassion in suffering alongside humanity, God's identification with the lowest of the low.

Christology has raised a number of critical issues for feminist, mujerista, and womanist theologians: the theological significance of Jesus' maleness and his death on the cross and the continuing meaning of his ministry. Rosemary Ruether put the first issue bluntly in her *Sexism and God-Talk*: "Can a Male Savior Save Women?"[75] In other words, is Jesus' maleness intrinsic to his role as savior? The overwhelming answer on the part of women's liberation theologies is "No." Jesus' maleness is an inescapable dimension of his humanity and social location, but, these theologians argue, "it reveals nothing about the nature or gender of God, nor about the appropriateness or necessity of male images or language for the divine. Neither does the maleness of Jesus establish any 'essential distinctions' between the sexes in terms of status, vocation, ability to image God or Christ, or appropriate ministerial roles."[76] As generations of theologians before them have done, feminist, mujerista, and womanist theologians have found in Jesus the exemplar of God's saving and mysterious love. Jesus is understood as a prophet of liberation, as the prophet of Sophia (God's Wisdom), as fellow-sufferer, as minister to the *anawim*, the least of the least.[77] These are "Christologies from below," in the sense that they arise out of feminist interpretations of the life and message of Jesus, and not "from above," in that they avoid conceptualizing Jesus in ways that accentuate traditional ways of conceiving the divine (e.g., as knowing his divine status, as establishing the institutional Church). In all of these theologies, Jesus is understood to have condemned structures of domination ("kyriarchy" is Elisabeth Schüssler Fiorenza's term) and to have encouraged radically egalitarian forms of community. These Christologies have obvious significance for a number of disputed issues between the right and the left, most notably the ordination of women and the hierarchical structure of the Church.

The other Christological issue of importance to women's liberation theologies is the significance of the Cross. Here, Catholic theologians join with their Protestant sisters in challenging traditional interpretations of the atoning death of Jesus. Probably the earliest critic of this from a feminist perspective was Mary Daly, who, in *Beyond God the Father*, condemned the "scapegoat syndrome," which glorified Christ the victim.[78] More traditional formulations of the doctrine of the Cross, based in Anselm's theology of satisfaction, are "widely criticized, if not totally rejected, by feminists"[79] as they are by some theologians in the "malestream" tradition. In particular, the connection of the sacrificial death of Jesus with an ethics of self-sacrifice has been challenged both as a misinterpretation of Jesus' death and as having especially destructive effects on women.[80] On the whole, for these theologies, the death of Jesus is placed into its social and historical context as the consequence of Jesus' commitment to his ministry and his refusal to compromise with authorities. His suffering and death can be understood to be in solidarity with the sufferings and death of those who have struggled for justice, and his resurrection is interpreted to mean that he was not, nor will we be, abandoned by God in our trials and deaths.

Feminist, mujerista, and womanist theologies draw on the life of Jesus and the early Christian community as inspiration for the church in the present. Jesus' critical attitude toward hierarchical structures, his inclusive table fellowship and forgiving love, the egalitarian character of the early Christian community, are all raised up so as to contrast with the contemporary Roman Catholic Church's hierarchical nature, structures of inequality, and adherence to legalism. Thus, as language leads to God, and God's dynamic relationality leads to a new Christology, so Christology leads to a transformed ecclesiology.

As the contributors to *Being Right* have observed, much of the contemporary division in the Catholic Church today arises from differing interpretations of Vatican II. While feminist theologies do not, as a rule, look to the conciliar documents as one of their main sources of inspiration, the understanding of Church as "People of God," and a sense that "*We* are the Church" is very strong among those who continue to locate themselves within the Catholic tradition.[81] A commitment to democratizing the governing structures of the Church, advocacy of the ordination of women and of a married clergy, and demands for greater openness on financial matters are the bare-bones minimum for women-centered theologies, as they are for nearly all left Roman Catholic groups. But womanist, feminist, and mujerista theologians are not necessarily in agreement on the best strategy for a more inclusive and liberating Church. Some are opposed to advocating the ordination of women, convinced that the present structures are too corrupt; ordaining women into these structures would only corrupt women.[82] Rather, a completely transformed Church—in structures and ministry—is called for: one that is radically egalitarian and inclusive, in which women and men minister together, and where authority is shared with the people.

Conclusion

The claim has been made, both by U.S. Catholics on the right and by the leadership of the Church, that feminist theology does not represent the majority of Catholic women nor is it faithful to the tradition. However one judges the diversity and sheer volume of these developing theologies, it is clear that they are here to stay. A few concluding comments on the impact of these theologies is in order.

First, the exclusion of women from ordination in Roman Catholicism has, ironically, led to many women entering the field of academic theology. Theology is one of the few avenues open to women in the Church where something like "full equality" can be achieved.[83] While women in Roman Catholic seminaries take the same courses as their male colleagues, they part ways at graduation. But women theologians work alongside their male colleagues in departments of theology in colleges, universities, and seminaries, publish in the same theological journals, and, increasingly, hold positions of authority: as chairs of departments, as deans, and as officers of theological societies. Women-centered theologies are no longer entirely marginal to the theological enterprise. This is not to say that academia is free from sexism, tokenism, or marginalization, but the increasing numbers of women theologians are beginning to make a difference in the discipline of theology.

Second, the issue of reproductive choice, while significant, is only one issue, and tends to be isolated from its wider context in much theological rhetoric. Arguably, not enough ambiguity is recognized by either side, at least publicly. But abortion is symbolic of women's real lack of voice in Church structures and in decision making. This lack of voice is shared by lay people. As long as women lack a significant role in decision making in the Church, and as long as the magisterium focuses on sexuality as the litmus test for "true" Catholicism, there will be serious divisions over the issues of sexuality and reproduction.

Third, these theologies are having a significant impact outside of academia. Many women who are not professionally trained but are interested in women's issues in religion read these books written by these theologians. Women's parish groups, discussion groups, diocesan women's commissions are filled with women familiar with the major names in feminist theology, and turn to these books for inspiration for spirituality, language about God, biblical study, and new understandings of the tradition.[84]

Fourth, these theologies are having an impact on Catholic parish life. Issues such as inclusive language, female altar servers, women-led parishes, which increasingly are unavoidable in the U.S., open up larger issues that are addressed by women-centered theologies. The dominance of women in parish leadership roles is only beginning to be taken seriously. Those who are being trained for such parish leadership are studying with and about feminist, mujerista, and womanist theologians, and as the numbers of "priestless" parishes increase, such issues will become more significant.

Finally, the Vatican, the right wing of Catholicism, and many U.S. bishops are right to feel threatened by feminist theologies: they do challenge some of the most basic components of the Roman Catholic tradition: e.g., the hierarchical structure of the Church, the celibate and all-male priesthood, the clerical domination of theological training. Some theologians have suggested that the changes involved in women's full participation in the Church are analogous to the changes involved in the early church's decision to admit Gentiles without adherence to Jewish law: a major shift in direction and decision. Depending on one's vantage point, they represent either a serious threat to tradition (the right) or the vanguard of the future, inclusive, non-hierarchical Church (the left). While some wishful-thinking conservatives believe that these theologies will be proven to be short-lived, and are working assiduously to ensure this outcome, the momentum of history—including educational culture and demographics—is clearly against them.

NOTES

This chapter benefited greatly from the contributions of many others. Toinette M. Eugene, Mary E. Hunt, and Ada María Isasi-Díaz were consultants for the initial discussion on a very early version of this chapter. They were also generous in their comments on later outlines of the chapter and on some particular questions. The members of the What's Left core group, especially R. Scott Appleby and Anne E. Patrick, also made helpful suggestions. My graduate assistant, Marcia Kurzynski, did a great deal of leg-work in looking up books, articles, and references. William P. George and Patricia Beattie

Jung read drafts of the chapter and made helpful suggestions, comments, and criticisms. I am grateful to all of these consultants for their time and expertise.

1. Anne E. Patrick, "Catholicity, Inculturation, and Social Justice," *Proceedings of the Catholic Theological Society of America* 45 (1990), p. 45. Membership in the entire Society, in 1990, was estimated to be approximately 1450.

2. One would need also to look at women's membership in the College Theology Society, which was established as a lay counterpart to the then all-clerical CTSA in 1954, as well as Catholic women involved in societies such as the American Academy of Religion, the Society of Biblical Literature, the Society of Christian Ethics, and the North American Academy of Liturgy, to name only some of the major organizations of theologians. Other organizations, such as the Women's Ordination Conference, would also be important sources. Moreover, the number of women active in leadership positions is also significant, often out of proportion to their numbers.

3. Mary Daly, *The Church and the Second Sex, With the Feminist Postchristian Introduction and New Archaic Afterwords by the Author* (Boston: Beacon Press, 1985 [1968, 1975]), p. 223.

4. Mary Daly, *Beyond God the Father: Toward a Philosophy of Women's Liberation* (Boston: Beacon Press, 1973).

5. Mary Daly, *Gyn/Ecology: The Metaethics of Radical Feminism* (Boston: Beacon Press, 1978).

6. Audre Lorde, "An Open Letter to Mary Daly," in *This Bridge Called My Back: Writings by Radical Women of Color*, ed. Cheríe Moraga and Gloria Anzaldúa (New York: Kitchen Table: Women of Color Press, 1981, 1983), p. 95.

7. See "Roundtable Discussion: Christian Ethics and Theology in Womanist Perspective," *Journal of Feminist Studies in Religion* 5, no. 2 (Summer 1990), pp. 83–112. The term "womanist" is used largely by African-American women theologians in the U.S.

8. See "Roundtable Discussion: *Mujeristas*: Who We Are and What We Are About," *Journal of Feminist Studies in Religion* 8, no. 1 (Spring 1992), pp. 105–125. It is important to note, however, that not all Hispanic/Latina theologians have adopted this term. Maria Pilar Aquino, for example, retains the term "feminist" because of its connection with the feminist movement worldwide and especially in Latin America.

9. For a helpful discussion of the category of "difference," see Cynthia S. W. Crysdale, "Horizons That Differ: Women and Men and the Flight from Understanding," *Cross Currents* 44 (1994), pp. 345–361.

10. See *Origins* 22, no. 3 (10 September 1992), p. 223. A sidebar comment on the third draft of the pastoral letter on women's concerns reports that some bishops were concerned ". . . that the third draft failed to consider the evil of radical feminism and other movements today that do not correspond to the Christian understanding of women." "Good" feminists are those who do not challenge Church teaching, and would be labeled conservative by the theologians I discuss in this chapter.

11. For a helpful discussion of experience, see David Tracy, *Blessed Rage for Order: The New Pluralism in Theology* (New York: Seabury, 1975), pp. 64–71. For a more critical approach to the use of experience in theology, see George Lindbeck, *The Nature of Doctrine: Religion and Theology in a Postliberal Age* (Louisville: The Westminster Press, 1984), esp. ch. 2, "Religion and Experience: A Pretheological Inquiry," pp. 30–45. For two feminist reflections on experience, see Ann O'Hara Graff, "The Struggle to Name Women's Experience," in *In the Embrace of God: Feminist Approaches to Theological Anthropology*, ed. Ann O'Hara Graff (New York: Orbis, 1995), pp. 71–89; Ada María Isasi-Díaz, "Experi-

ences," s.v., *Dictionary of Feminist Theologies*, ed. Letty M. Russell and J. Shannon Clarkson (Louisville: Westminster/John Knox, 1996), pp. 95–96.

12. See, e.g., Gustavo Gutiérrez, *A Theology of Liberation: History, Politics and Salvation*, trans. and ed. Sister Caridad Inda and John Eagleson (Maryknoll: Orbis Books, 1971, 1988).

13. For a very helpful discussion of revelation and experience in feminist theology, see Mary Catherine Hilkert, "Experience and Tradition—Can the Center Hold?" in *Freeing Theology: The Essentials of Theology in Feminist Perspective*, ed. Catherine M. LaCugna (San Francisco: HarperSanFrancisco, 1993), pp. 59–82.

14. Valerie Saiving, "The Human Situation: A Feminine View," *The Journal of Religion* 40 (1960), pp. 100–112; reprinted in *Womanspirit Rising: A Feminist Reader in Religion*, ed. Carol Christ and Judith Plaskow (San Francisco: Harper and Row, 1979); for liberation theology, see Gutiérrez, *A Theology of Liberation*.

15. See Phyllis Trible, *Texts of Terror: Literary-Feminist Readings of Biblical Narratives* (Philadelphia: Fortress, 1984).

16. Hilkert, "Experience and Tradition," p. 65.

17. See Rosemary Radford Ruether, *Sexism and God-Talk: Toward a Feminist Theology* (Boston: Beacon Press, 1983), pp. 21–22, where Ruether draws on five sources, including the Bible and Christian teachings, but also including "heretical" traditions, non-Christian religion and philosophy, and "critical post-Christian worldviews."

18. For two highly critical perspectives on feminist theology, see Francis Martin, *The Feminist Question: Feminist Theology in the Light of Christian Tradition* (Grand Rapids: Eerdmans, 1994); Donna Steichen, *Ungodly Rage: The Hidden Face of Catholic Feminism* (San Francisco: Ignatius Press, 1991). See, e.g., Steichen, p. 309: "'Feminist theology' is corrupted by ideological bias on every level; it lacks not only faith but also scholarly integrity."

19. For a good example of one such theologian, see Lisa Sowle Cahill, *Sex, Gender and Christian Ethics* (Cambridge: Cambridge University Press, 1996).

20. The phrase is taken from Nelle Morton, *The Journey is Home* (Boston: Beacon Press, 1985), p. 99. See also Diana L. Hayes's comment: "This failure to include or acknowledge the existence of other women's voices leads to the masking of specific differences among women in this country, in an effort, albeit unconscious perhaps, to present a united face to the oppressor." "Feminist Theology, Womanist Theology: A Black Catholic Perspective," in *Black Theology: A Documentary History*, vol. 2: *1980–1992*, ed. James H. Cone and Gayraud S. Wilmore (Maryknoll: Orbis, 1993). Part IV, "Womanist Theology," pp. 257–351, includes some significant articles by womanist theologians.

21. See Ruth Frankenberg, *White Women, Race Matters: The Social Construction of Whiteness* (Minneapolis: University of Minnesota Press, 1993); "Roundtable Discussion: Racism in the Women's Movement," *Journal of Feminist Studies in Religion* 4 (Spring 1988), pp. 93–114.

22. See Mary Field Belenky, Blythe McVicker Clinchy, Nancy Rule Goldberger, and Jill Mattuck Tarule, *Women's Ways of Knowing: The Development of Self, Voice and Mind* (New York: Basic Books, 1986).

23. This is taken from Elisabeth Schüssler Fiorenza, *Bread Not Stone: The Challenge of Feminist Biblical Interpretation* (Boston: Beacon Press, 1984), pp. 15–22.

24. For a full development of these ideas, see Elisabeth Schüssler Fiorenza, *In Memory of Her: A Feminist Theological Reconstruction of Christian Origins* (New York: Crossroad, 1983). The issue of whether feminist theology seeks a "neo-orthodox" or "transcendent" ground of truth beyond history has been

the subject of discussion among feminist theologians. See Sheila Greeve Davaney, "Problems with Feminist Theory: Historicity and the Search for Sure Foundations," in *Embodied Love: Sensuality and Relationship as Feminist Values*, ed. Paula M. Cooey, Sharon A. Farmer, and Mary Ellen Ross (San Francisco: Harper and Row, 1987), pp. 79–95.

25. Schüssler Fiorenza, *In Memory of Her*, p. 30.

26. See Regina A. Boisclair, "Amnesia in the Catholic Sunday Lectionary: Women—Silenced from the Memories of Salvation History," in *Women and Theology*, vol. 40 of the Annual Publication of the College Theology Society, ed. Mary Ann Hinsdale and Phyllis H. Kaminski (Maryknoll: Orbis Books, 1995), pp. 109–135; see also Marjorie Procter-Smith, "Liturgical Anamnesis and Women's Memory: 'Something Missing,'" *Worship* 61 (1987), pp. 405–424; Ann Patrick Ware, "The Easter Vigil: A Theological and Liturgical Critique," in *Women at Worship: Interpretations of North American Diversity*, ed. Marjorie Procter-Smith and Janet R. Walton (Louisville: Westminster/John Knox Press, 1993), pp. 83–106.

27. See the report of the Pontifical Biblical Commission on the biblical arguments for and against the ordination of women. The Commission concluded that there was no firm support for either position on biblical grounds. See "Biblical Commission Report: Can Women Be Priests?" in *Women Priests: A Catholic Commentary on the Vatican Declaration*, ed. Leonard Swidler and Arlene Swidler (New York: Paulist, 1977).

28. See Schüssler Fiorenza, *In Memory of Her*, pp. 16–19, for her critique of Ruether's position.

29. See Joan Nuth, *Wisdom's Daughter: The Theology of Julian of Norwich* (New York: Crossroad, 1991).

30. See, e.g., Carolyn Walker Bynum, *Holy Feast and Holy Fast: The Religious Significance of Food for Medieval Women* (New York: Columbia University Press, 1987).

31. Elizabeth A. Johnson, "Mary and the Female Face of God," *Theological Studies* 50 (1989), pp. 500–526.

32. See Mary Jo Weaver, *New Catholic Women: A Contemporary Challenge to Traditional Religious Authority* (Bloomington: Indiana University Press, 1995); see also "Journey into Freedom: Mary Ward: Essays in Honor of the Fourth Centenary of Her Birth," *The Way*, Supplement 52 (1985).

33. See M. Shawn Copeland, "African American Catholics and Black Theology: An Interpretation," in Cone and Wilmore, eds., *Black Theology*, pp. 99–115; Barbara Hilkert Andolsen, *Daughters of Jefferson, Daughters of Bootblacks*, (Macon, Ga.: Mercer University Press, 1986).

34. See the statistics cited in Miriam Therese Winter, Adair Lummis, and Allison Stokes, *Defecting in Place: Women Claiming Responsibility for Their Own Spiritual Lives* (New York: Crossroad, 1995), p. 111: ". . . a 1992 Gallup survey of Catholic opinion . . . found that 67 per cent of the Catholic population at large supports women priests. It also compares favorably with a 1993 ABC News poll taken prior to the visit of Pope John Paul II, which puts the figure of those wanting women priests at 62 per cent."

35. For some classic statements on this theme, see Rosemary Radford Ruether, *New Woman, New Earth: Sexist Ideologies and Human Liberation* (New York: Seabury, 1975); Toinette M. Eugene, "While Love Is Unfashionable: Ethical Implications of Black Spirituality and Sexuality," in *Women's Consciousness, Women's Conscience: A Reader in Feminist Ethics*, ed. Barbara Hilkert Andolsen, Christine E. Gudorf, and Mary D. Pellauer (San Francisco: Harper and Row, 1985), pp. 121–141.

36. For some explicit examples of such attitudes, see Clara Maria Henning, "Canon Law and the Battle of the Sexes," in *Religion and Sexism: Images of Women in the Jewish and Christian Traditions*, ed. Rosemary Radford Ruether (New York: Simon and Schuster, 1974), pp. 267–291.

37. See Bynum, *Holy Feast*; idem., *Fragmentation and Redemption: Essays on the Human Body in Medieval Religion* (New York: Zone Books, 1991), esp. ch. 5: ". . . and Woman His Humanity: Female Imagery in the Religious Writings of the Later Middle Ages," pp. 151–238.

38. Penelope Washbourne, *Becoming Woman: The Quest for Wholeness in Female Experience* (San Francisco: Harper and Row, 1977), was one of the first to do this; see also Ruether, *Women-Church: Theology and Practice* (San Francisco: Harper and Row, 1985) for examples of such rituals; Meinrad Craighead, *The Mother's Songs: Images of God the Mother* (New York: Paulist, 1986) is an example of artistic work; Diann L. Neu and Mary E. Hunt, *Women-Church Sourcebook* (Silver Spring, Md.: WATERworks Press, 1993).

39. See the *Concilium* issue "Violence against Women," ed. M. Shawn Copeland and Elisabeth Schüssler Fiorenza (Maryknoll: Orbis, 1994); see also *Violence against Women and Children: A Christian Theological Sourcebook*, ed. Carol J. Adams and Marie M. Fortune (New York: Concilium, 1995); Rita Nakashima Brock and Susan Brooks Thistlethwaite, *Casting Stones: Prostitution and Liberation in Asia and the United States* (Minneapolis: Fortress, 1996).

40. Martin Luther and the Reformation deserve credit for helping to break down the distinction between lay and religious piety. I am grateful to Patricia Jung for reminding me of this.

41. See Maria Pilar Aquino, *Our Cry for Life: Feminist Theology from Latin America* (Maryknoll: Orbis, 1993), and Ada María Isasi-Díaz, *En la Lucha/In the Struggle: Elaborating a Mujerista Theology* (Philadelphia: Fortress Press, 1993).

42. Toinette Eugene, "While Love Is Unfashionable."

43. See Lisa Sowle Cahill, *Sex, Gender and Christian Ethics*, p. 85.

44. See, e.g., John Paul II, *Mulieris Dignitatem* (On the Dignity and Vocation of Women), *Origins* 18, no. 17 (6 October 1988); Donald Keefe, "Sacramental Sexuality and the Ordination of Women," *Communio* 5 (Fall 1978), pp. 228–251; Paul Quay, S.J., *The Christian Meaning of Sexuality* (San Francisco: Ignatius Press, 1985).

45. Ruether, *Women-Church*.

46. Mary Collins, "Principles of Feminist Liturgy," in *Women at Worship: Interpretations of North American Diversity* (Louisville: Westminster/John Knox Press, 1993), p. 11.

47. From Winter, Lummis, and Stokes, *Defecting in Place*, p. 121.

48. Lisa Sowle Cahill, "Notes on Moral Theology: Feminist Ethics," *Theological Studies* 51 (1990), pp. 49–64.

49. See Helen Hull Hitchcock, "Women for Faith and Family," in *Being Right: Conservative Catholics in America*, ed. Mary Jo Weaver and R. Scott Appleby (Bloomington: Indiana University Press, 1996), pp. 163–185.

50. See "Bishops Want Feminist Professor Fired," *National Catholic Reporter* 31, no. 3 (31 March 1995). See also *Proceedings of the Catholic Theological Society of America* 1995, pp. 321–322 for the CTSA's response.

51. See Margaret Farley, *Personal Commitments: Making, Keeping, Breaking* (San Francisco: Harper and Row, 1985); Mary Hunt, *Fierce Tenderness: A Feminist Theology of Friendship* (New York: Crossroad, 1992).

52. Elisabeth Schüssler Fiorenza, "Patriarchal Structures and the Discipleship of Equals," in *Discipleship of Equals: A Critical Feminist Ekklesia-logy of Liberation* (New York: Crossroad, 1993), p. 231.

53. See Isasi-Díaz, *En la Lucha*; Anne E. Patrick, *Liberating Conscience: Feminist Explorations in Catholic Moral Theology* (New York: Continuum, 1996).

54. See Isasi-Díaz, *En la Lucha*, ch. 5: "Conscience, Conscientization and Moral Agency in *Mujerista* Theology," pp. 141–165.

55. Patrick, *Liberating Conscience*, ch. 3: "Changing Paradigms of Virtue: the Good Life Reconsidered," pp. 72–101.

56. Cahill, *Sex, Gender and Christian Ethics* is one such effort; see also Susan Frank Parsons, *Feminism and Christian Ethics* (Cambridge: Cambridge University Press, 1996), which helpfully lays out liberal, social-constructivist, and naturalist approaches in feminist theory and theology.

57. Cahill, *Sex, Gender and Christian Ethics*.

58. See Christine E. Gudorf, "To Make a Seamless Garment, Use a Single Piece of Cloth," in *The Public Vocation of Christian Ethics*, ed. Beverly W. Harrison and Robert L. Stivers (New York: Pilgrim Press, 1986); also William P. George, "Catholic Moral Pluralism: War and Other Issues," Core Nine unpublished lecture, St. Joseph College, Renssalaer, Ind., March 1994.

59. Although the Pope still condemns all forms of artificial contraception as intrinsically immoral. See *Veritatis Splendor* (The Splendor of Truth), *Origins* 23, no. 18 (14 October 1993), paras. 42–44, 79–83.

60. CFFC says in its promotional literature that it is not "pro-abortion" but believes that abortion must be legal for women to even begin to make moral choices with real freedom. See http://www.cath4choice.org

61. This is where it is difficult to distinguish between the center and left wings of Catholicism. Pro-life feminists (such as Sydney Callahan) line up with the left on almost all social justice issues, but part company with other feminists on the issue of abortion. See her "Abortion and the Sexual Agenda: A Case for Prolife Feminism," in *Feminist Ethics and the Catholic Moral Tradition*, ed. Charles E. Curran, Margaret A. Farley, and Richard A. McCormick (New York: Paulist, 1996), pp. 422–439.

62. See Patricia Beattie Jung and Thomas Shannon, eds., *Abortion and the American Catholic Conscience* (New York: Crossroad, 1988).

63. See Ruether, *New Woman*; Ruether continues this concern in *Gaia and God: An Ecofeminist Theology of Earth Healing* (San Francisco: HarperSanFrancisco, 1992).

64. "Weakland Remarks Set off a Firestorm in Milwaukee," *National Catholic Register* 66, no. 1 (24 June 1990); "Weakland on Abortion: Who's Confusing Whom?" *National Catholic Reporter* 27, no. 7 (23 November 1990); "Vatican Bars Honorary Degree for Archbishop Weakland," *Origins* 20 (22 November 1990), pp. 387–389.

65. See *Feminist Ethics and the Catholic Moral Tradition*, ed. Curran, Farley, and McCormick.

66. "Prelates Revoke Theologian's *Catholicism*," *National Catholic Reporter* 21, no. 7 (19 July 1985); and *Proceeedings of the Catholic Theological Society of America* 1996.

67. "Rome Moves to Silence Brazil's Gebara," *National Catholic Reporter* 31, no. 5 (26 May 1995).

68. "Fr. Leonardo Boff Silenced Again for Views," *Our Sunday Visitor* 78, no. 4 (22 October 1989); Harvey G. Cox, "The Silencing of Leonardo Boff: The Vatican and the Future of World Christianity," *Ecumenical Trends* 23, no. 572 (Summer 1989).

69. "Seminary Ousts Fiand after Push from Right," *National Catholic Reporter* 34, no. 26 (1 May 1998).

70. See Helen Hull Hitchcock, "Women for Faith and Family," in *Being*

Right, pp. 175, 181. Note also that the distribution of *The New Catholic Cat-echism* in the U.S. was delayed so that the inclusive-language translation, ap-proved by the U.S. Bishops, could be retranslated in language that used the generic masculine. Note also the continuing and neuralgic issue between U.S. bishops and the Vatican on biblical translations. See, e.g., James Gaffney, "She Who Laughs Last: The Gender-Inclusive Language Debate," *America* 173, no. 5 (26 August 1995), pp. 8–12; Joseph Jensen, "Inclusive Language and the Bible," *America* 171, no. 14 (5 November 1994), pp. 14–18; Richard J. Clifford, "The Bishops, the Bible and Liturgical Language," *America* 172, no. 19 (27 May 1995), pp. 12–16.

71. Elizabeth A. Johnson, *SHE WHO IS: The Mystery of God in Feminist Theo-logical Discourse* (New York: Crossroad, 1992).

72. For Schüssler Fiorenza, see *Jesus: Miriam's Child, Sophia's Prophet: Criti-cal Issues in Feminist Christology* (New York: Continuum, 1994); for Ruether, see *Sexism and God-Talk*.

73. See, for example, Monica Migliorino Miller, *Sexuality and Authority in the Catholic Church* (Scranton: University of Scranton Press, 1994), p. 83: "Femi-nine images of God are aberrations that serve a particular crisis moment."

74. See Catherine M. LaCugna, *God for Us: The Trinity and Christian Life* (San Francisco: HarperCollins, 1991).

75. Ruether, *Sexism and God-Talk*, ch. 5, pp. 116–138.

76. Mary Catherine Hilkert, "Key Religious Symbols: Christ and God," *Theological Studies* 56, no. 2 (June 1995), p. 342.

77. See Hilkert's article (n. 75) for a full and helpful description of feminist Christologies.

78. Daly, *Beyond God the Father*, pp. 75–77.

79. Hilkert, "Symbols," p. 344.

80. Barbara Hilkert Andolsen, "Agape in Feminist Ethics," *Journal of Reli-gious Ethics* 9 (1981), pp. 69–83.

81. See Anne E. Patrick, "Toward Renewing 'The Life and Culture of Fallen Man': *Gaudium et Spes* as Catalyst for Catholic Feminist Theology," in *Feminist Ethics and the Catholic Moral Tradition*, ed. Curran et al., pp. 483–510.

82. The 20th anniversary meeting of the Women's Ordination Conference in November 1995 witnessed real disagreement between those who wanted to continue the organization's original mandate and those who advocated a more radical stance.

83. See Catherine M. LaCugna, "Catholic Women as Ministers and Theolo-gians," *America*, 10 October 1992.

84. In my own experience of giving presentations at parishes, I have yet to encounter a woman interested in feminist theologies who has not read Eliza-beth Johnson's *SHE WHO IS*. The question I am most frequently asked is what to read next.

2

WOMEN-CHURCH

An American Catholic Feminist Movement

ROSEMARY RADFORD RUETHER

The Women-Church movement in American Roman Catholicism expresses a number of characteristics of American culture and the American Catholic Church. It reflects the volunteerism and democratic impulse of Americans to organize movements to oppose perceived injustices, rather than passively accept them. It also reflects the new wave of feminism that began in American society in the late 1960s, inspired by the civil rights movement. The feminist movement had its expression in the Protestant churches with the call for women's ordination (where that had not yet taken place),[1] and for an end to sexual discrimination in church practice. Feminists were beginning to take a critical look at the supports for sexism in the Bible and theology and to reshape the ministry and theological education. Women from many religious traditions also began to organize their own worship groups related to their heritage but independent of its official leadership.

For American Catholics this new wave of feminism in society and the churches coincided with the call for Church renewal by the Second Vatican Council. Catholic women began to shape their own feminist movement, with the expectations that the kinds of changes going on in Protestant churches and theological schools—the ordination of women, feminist theology, inclusive language in liturgy, and recognition of women's reproductive rights—would reshape Roman Catholicism as well.

Many American Catholics appropriated the ideas of Church renewal of the Second Vatican Council with particular zeal, connecting the new ecclesiology of the "People of God" with a democratic concept of the Church as "we, the people."[2] Vatican II Catholics became disappointed by the resistance of the Catholic hierarchy to applying this vision to structural reform to create a more participatory Church. They began to experiment with "house churches" as expressions of more egalitarian forms of liturgical community. At the same time the liberation theology movement in Latin American, also inspired by post–Vatican II Church renewal and the call for justice in society, was developing "base communities" as small, egalitarian Christian gatherings for Bible study and worship to ground social action.[3]

American Catholic women, inspired by Church renewal, feminism, and social justice movements, began to shape groups with a feminist perspective in the late 1960s. Some of the leaders in the development of Catholic feminism were women religious who connected the call of the Vatican Council for renewal of their congregations with a feminist view of their identity and mission. In 1968 the National Assembly of Women Religious (later renamed the National Assembly of Religious Women) was formed by several sisters, such as Marjorie Tuite, to commit women in religious orders to grassroots social justice ministry, including issues of women. A parallel organization with women's concerns on their agenda, the National Coalition of American Nuns, was founded by Margaret Traxler in 1969.

In the same period the Grail, a movement of lay women that originated in Holland, began to adopt the feminist agenda and to explore its meaning for their identity and work. Beginning in 1970 the Grail offered feminist conferences to the general public. Recognizing the growing number of women, Catholic and Protestant, who were studying theology in seminaries for either ordained ministry or teaching, the Grail brought this rising generation of women teachers and students in seminaries together to discuss what feminist theology might mean.[4]

Other Catholic feminist organizations arose in the early 1970s. In Chicago Donna Quinn founded Chicago Catholic Women in 1974 to organize around justice for women in the Church, including the demand for ordination. In 1972 in New York City, a small group of pro-choice Catholics formed Catholics for a Free Choice to counteract the Catholic Church's campaign against legalized abortion, which had just been won by the Supreme Court decision, *Roe v. Wade,* of that year. In 1976 CFFC founded a second branch to do lobbying on abortion in Washington, D.C. This lobbying group received its first major funding (from the Unitarians) in 1979. By 1982 CFFC became well enough funded to hire Frances Kissling as its executive director.[5] By 1998 it had grown into an organization with a twenty-member staff in Washington, a two-million-dollar budget, and three affiliated organizations in Latin America, as well as contact groups in Poland, the Philippines, and elsewhere.

A key turning point for Catholic feminist organizing took place in 1975. The struggle for women's ordination in the American Episcopal Church broke open in 1974 when a group of eleven women seminary graduates were ordained "irregularly" by three retired bishops. Four more women were irregularly ordained a year later. This event created a crisis in the Episcopal Church that was resolved in the fall of 1976 when the national convention of the Episcopal Church voted to approve the ordination of women.[6] Catholic women responded to this struggle in the Episcopal Church. In December 1974 Mary B. Lynch, a lay woman studying at the Catholic Theological Union in Chicago, called a meeting of thirty-one women, from which a task force emerged to organize a conference on the ordination of Catholic women. In November of 1975 a conference titled "Women in Future Priesthood Now—a Call for Action" was held in Detroit, Michigan, mostly sponsored by women's religious orders. The planners had expected a maximum attendance of 600. When the applications moved past 1000 they finally cut off registration at 1200. The conference was organized around a two-sided demand: the admission of women to all ordained ministries and the renewal of the Church and its ministry.

By this emphasis on women's ordination in the context of Church renewal the conference organizers wished to signal that they wanted not simply to include women in the present model of patriarchal clericalism, but to transform the Church into a more democratic, participatory community in which the clergy would be animators of the ministry of the people, rather than rule over them as a superior caste. Only within such renewal of ministry in community could or should women assume their place in ordained ministry. How to understand the relation between these two demands for ordination and Church renewal would remain an area of tension within the Women's Ordination Conference to the present.

The speakers at the Detroit WOC conference reflected a new generation of Catholic theologically trained feminists, such as Anne Carr, Margaret Farley, Elisabeth Schüssler Fiorenza, Marie Augusta Neal, Rosemary Ruether, and Arlene Swidler, who continue to shape Catholic feminism to the present.[7] Rosalie Muschal-Reinhardt read a statement from women who felt themselves called to priestly ministry. After this successful conference it was decided to established the Women's Ordination Conference (WOC) as a national organization.

WOC was first headquartered in the Washington, D.C., area, with Ruth McDonough Fitzpatrick as national coordinator (who also led WOC from 1984 to 1995). For several years its office was located in Rochester, New York, where second national coordinator Rosalie Muschal-Reinhardt was joined by Ada María Isasi-Díaz and Joan Sabala as national team. This team spent much of their time networking with Catholic women across the United States and putting WOC chapters in place in different cities.

Another important turning point for the Women-Church movement took place in May of 1977. In November of 1976 the Catholic bishops had organized the Call to Action, envisioned as a national synod of Church renewal, in Detroit. To their alarm, the delegates who had assembled at the meeting to represent the laity, priests, and religious of each diocese voted for various demands the bishops found unacceptable; e.g., the ordination of women, the end to sexism in the Church, married priests, the acceptance of contraception and of divorce. In May the National Conference of Catholic Bishops met in Chicago for their biannual meeting. One item on their agenda was the recommendations on women from this Detroit conference.

Donna Quinn, Rosalie Muschal-Reinhardt, and Delores Brooks mobilized a number of other Catholic pro-women groups—LCWR (the Leadership Conference of Women Religious), NCAN (the National Coalition of American Nuns), NAWR (the National Assembly of Women Religious), WOC (the Women's Ordination Conference), St. Joan's Alliance, the Institute for Women Today, Christian Feminists, Las Hermanas, the National Black Sisters Conference, the National Sisters Vocation Conference, and Priests for Equality—to come together to lobby the bishops on these issues. This group rented a room in the Palmer House, where the bishops were meeting. Calling themselves the Women of the Church Coalition, they invited the bishops to dialogue with them on justice for women. Only two bishops, Raymond Lucker of New Ulm, Minnesota, and Charles Buswell of Pueblo, Colorado, responded to this invitation.[8]

In November of 1978 the Women's Ordination Conference held its Second National Conference in Baltimore, Maryland. This meeting was timed so that those women who wished to go to Washington for the NCCB meeting to lobby the bishops on women's ordination could do so after the conference. As a result of this effort the bishops voted to enter into a formal dialogue with the Women's Ordination Conference. This dialogue would take place in a series of weekend meetings from 1979 to 1982. (One result of this dialogue was the decision of the American bishops to undertake what was to prove an abortive effort to write a pastoral letter on women.)[9] Already the Vatican was hardening against the demands of Catholic women for ordination. On October 15, 1976, in response to the American Episcopal Church's decision to ordain women, the Vatican released a Pastoral Letter on Women's Ordination, which contained the startling statement that women could not be ordained because they were unable by their very nature as women to "image Christ." The theology of this statement was widely criticized by progressive male theologians, as well as by women,[10] and the support for women's ordination actually rose among American Catholics in response to this letter. Clearly the issue was not going to go away easily, as the American bishops recognized in deciding in 1978 to hold a formal dialogue with the Women's Ordination Conference.

By 1982 it appeared that this dialogue was unlikely to bear any real potential for change. Some Catholic feminists, such as Mary Hunt, were suggesting that ordination was not the primary goal for women, but rather the organization of autonomous women's liturgical communities, feminist base communities, where renewal of ministry in egalitarian participatory communities could take place directly. Some leaders of the loose coalition of groups that had come together as the Women of the Church Coalition decided to organize another major national conference, this time with the focus on building feminist communities of faith and praxis, rather than on ordination to institutional Church ministry.

This conference, called Woman Church Speaks, was held in Chicago in November of 1983. The conference was sponsored by Chicago Catholic Women, the Institute for Women Today, Las Hermanas, the NARW, NCAN, WOC, and the newly founded groups in Washington, D.C.—the Quixote Center and WATER (the Women's Alliance for Theology, Ethics and Ritual). It was organized out of the Chicago Catholic Women's offices. This conference would set the pattern for subsequent Women-Church national conventions, with a combination of festive Mass liturgies and intense workshops on a variety of feminist issues, ranging from women's spirituality to justice for women in the Church and society to questions of sexuality and reproductive rights.[11]

In the aftermath of this first Women-Church gathering, which drew over 2500 participants, the sponsoring groups formally constituted a network of Catholic feminist organizations, naming it the Women-Church Convergence. Recognizing that women belonged to many ethnic and class contexts, the earlier term "woman-church" was later changed to the plural in order to avoid the racist, classist implication that there was one group of women (white, middle-class women) who represented normative "woman."[12]

Subsequent national Women-Church conferences took place in Cincinnati in October of 1987 and in Albuquerque in April of 1993. The network of members of the Women-Church Convergence continually expanded, with the addition of new local groups and women's-interest offices of religious orders. Also the national conferences inspired the founding of new local groups. After each national conference a surge of new Women-Church groups were founded by participants. The national meetings continued to be festive events with growing attendance. But intense conflicts took place in the planning meetings of the Convergence over how best to promote greater racial and ethnic inclusivity. Power relations between different types of groups in different regions also proved a problem.

The member-groups of WCC represent quite different kinds of constituencies and organizational resources. Some, like NARW and NCAN, the Quixote Center, CFFC, WATER, and WOC, were/are national groups with a full-time paid staff. Others are the women's office of a religious order or institute, such as the Women's Task Force of the

Sisters of Loretto, the BVM Network for Women's Issues, the Feminist Interest Group, SSSF, and the Women's Office of the Sisters of Charity; although the women running the group might be few, they had some part of the membership and resources of their order behind them. Others are local feminist base community groups, such as Boston Women-Church, the Community of the Anawin-Denver, and the San Antonio Women-Church network, that have no office or paid staff and are volunteer gatherings of lay women with other full-time jobs.[13] The member groups had decided that they did not want to create another centralized institution, so the Convergence was constituted as a network or coalition without any national office or staff, although there is a national coordinator (the first was Donna Quinn and the second Rosalie Muschal-Reinhardt). No ground rules were set up as to how to negotiate differences of power and resources. Also there was an idealistic expectation that feminist women gathered apart from the hierarchy on their own ground would automatically engage in a democratic, participatory style of relationship. Thus when turf wars broke out between Chicago- and Washington-based groups, when some national groups with paid staff and budgets assumed the right to greater influence than small local groups with no staff or budget, the anger and pain of these conflicts was exacerbated by the expectation that "this shouldn't be happening among us."

One long-time member of the Convergence wrote of these meetings, "for me personally the great puzzle has been the difficult dynamics within the WCC. Some of the most destructive dynamics I have ever experienced—manipulation, power-grabbing, projecting, guilt-tripping, ego-tripping, using racism as a weapon—have occurred around the WCC table. It is a mystery how a process so filled with misery has produced conferences full of energy and inspiration."[14]

Another woman representing a religious order wrote, "I had attended the Women-Church Convergence Board meetings. I found that because I did not have a large membership and did not have an office inside the Belt-way I had little, if any, voice. I often said that I could go to a bishop's meeting for this kind of treatment. The struggle for a patterned relationship that would allow decision-making was not even being addressed. We needed that discussion in order to make meetings productive and non-abusive. My motto was anarchy is not a solution to patriarchy."[15] This organizational vacuum and power differences between groups in the WCC have been addressed by a sliding scale of dues and the use of process facilitators. In 1996 the WCC had thirty-one member groups and met twice a year. No new national conference is planned. Rather the group is focusing on developing itself as a network that can work together productively and take official public positions together. Connecting the WCC with other networks of Catholic progressive groups, such as CORE and Call to Action, is being discussed, although there is also fear of being "swallowed up" by these groups.[16]

Although no new national Women-Church conference is currently planned, the September 1995 WOC convention celebrating the twenty-year anniversary of its founding served as a gathering of much of the same network. With the Vatican's continued hardening of its stand against women's ordination, even suggesting that its teaching was "infallible,"[17] many women seriously doubted whether ordination should be pursued as a goal. The WOC commitment to women's ordination in Church renewal seemed unlikely to ever come about. If ordination is ever allowed in Catholicism, it is likely to be only for those women who will fit themselves into the lowest level of patriarchal hierarchy.

The WOC conference's theme of "the discipleship of equals" suggested to many that ordination as a goal was being rejected in favor of Women-Church. Yet many women, lay and religious, who attended the conference were already working in parish ministry and chaplaincies and wanted the legitimation of ordination. At a time when the Vatican was seeking to silence the discussion of women's ordination, it did not seem appropriate for women to silence themselves by withdrawing their demand. This question of ordination or Women-Church also reflected a growing uncertainty about whether the impulse for Church reform could be held in tandem with creating autonomous groups increasingly uninterested in any relation with institutional Catholicism.

In the resulting shake-up of WOC after this conference, new leadership took over to redevelop its financial base and commitments. The historical demand for women's ordination within the context of Church renewal was reaffirmed. In addition there was a decision to expand its base through the development of an international network of women's ordination groups. The new leaders believe that the struggle for women's ordination in a world Church must take place across nations, and not be seen merely as something "American."[18] The beginning of this international women's ordination network was founded at the European Women's Synod, held in Gmunden, Austria, in July 1996.

A survey of the existing membership of the Women-Church Convergence conducted in the late spring and summer of 1996 showed a considerable diversity of understandings of the religious identity and purpose of these member groups.[19] Although all who responded saw themselves as arising from "Catholic roots," the meaning of this had evolved over time as they were joined by new members from other Christian or secular backgrounds and also as they experienced increasing despair of any real democratic reform and inclusion of women in ministry in institutional Catholicism.

Catholic identity obviously has a different meaning for groups that are women's offices of canonical orders than for groups with no ties to institutional Catholicism. But even while acknowledging this relation to a canonical order, the women leading these offices or networks expressed considerable doubt about their relation to the hierarchical male Church. One respondent said of her religious order:

> Our religious identity is that of Roman Catholic women who are committed to a community that is also a papal institution. For some time we talked about pushing to become non-canonical, but now we do not think it is worth the effort. We see ourselves as proof that persons can be identified as Roman Catholic outside the structure of the parish. We are a large small faith community, if you will.

But this same woman went on to express profound burn-out with efforts at Church reform:

> Also we are old. We have fought for the vernacular in the liturgy and we have been fired. We have fought not to wear the habit and we have had priests who said they respect us deride us. We have fought to keep schools open and have had parents call us money-grabbers. We fight to give our old sick sisters decent living and we are called middle-class. We fight for women's rights and we have women call us obsolete. Perhaps now our most significant struggle is to find a way to die well, with dignity and grace.[20]

A representative of the Loretto's Women's Network responded to the question about religious identity: Catholic, ecumenical, or post-Christian, by saying:

> I find this an intriguing question. We have never really discussed this as a network and I'm not sure how we'd respond to it. The Sisters of Loretto are, as you know, a canonical community of the Catholic Church. At the same time, we have some co-members who are members of other faith communities, some who do not belong to any church and Sisters of Loretto who are totally disenchanted with the Roman Catholic hierarchical structure. . . . At the same time I know we see ourselves sufficiently rooted in Catholicism to choose to be in dialogue with the bishops (or one or two bishops) on any given subject—those that have to do especially with women, such as our God-given right and ability to make moral decisions; how some decisions of the hierarchy cannot stand because of their ignoring (not accepting) of this principle.[21]

The Grail had moved farther along the lines of broadening its membership to include non-Catholics and developing religious outreach that goes beyond Christianity. Janet Kalven, speaking of the Grail Women's Task Force, responded to the question of religious identity by saying:

The make-up of the GWTF is ecumenical Christian, including several Protestants and seven Catholics who range from faithful Sunday Mass-goers to some who would describe themselves as post-Christian. We draw on resource persons from various traditions, Catholic, Protestant, Jewish, native American, Wiccan, etc. The women who participate in our programs come from various traditions and no tradition. Our roots are in the Roman Catholic Church, although we are exceeding critical of the tradition and of the current institutional practices. Some of us have given up on the institutional church altogether, some are loath to break the tie completely, one person still does some work in her parish.[22]

Some local Women-Church groups described themselves as consisting of a diverse group: mostly of Catholic background, some of whom continued to relate to local parishes and others of whom saw the Women-Church liturgy as their sole church, with still others of non-Catholic background. Some saw themselves as adhering to post-Christian or "Goddess" spirituality. One such local group described their identity in this way: "Some members say Roman Catholic, some post-Catholic/goddess-centered, some spiritualist, not connected with any religion." Another group leader responded by saying: "ecumenical Christian, the Catholics in the group still see ourselves as R.C., dissenting, but not leaving."

Yet not all Women-Church groups see themselves as moving away from concern with Catholic Church reform to an ecumenical and/or post-Christian identity. Massachusetts Women-Church, which has grown to being itself a network of groups in the greater Boston area meeting for worship, discussion, and interpersonal support, made the decision to affirm its identity as Catholic, with the result that some members who wanted the group to become ecumenical departed:

> We see ourselves as Catholic but not dependent on the institutional church which is sinful and dysfunctional. We choose to follow our informed conscience and "defect in place." We come from the Catholic faith tradition and work to make change within the church toward a discipleship of equals.

Massachusetts Women-Church has entered into dialogue with the New England Province of the Jesuits "to see how we can work together to implement their document (the decree of the Jesuit General Congregation, 'Jesuits and the Situation of Women in Church and Civil Society') and work toward a discipleship of equals."[23]

Although there is a range of identity along the spectrum of Catholic, ecumenical, and post-Christian, with some groups combining all three, most Women-Church groups have assumed the right and power to do their own liturgical celebrations "without benefit of clergy." The occasions for doing liturgy vary among groups. Some local groups, such as Chicago Women-Church and the Community of the Anawin, have a monthly or bimonthly get-together for liturgy and mutual support as their primary activity. Others, such as Chicago Catholic Women, have a variety of activities, which include liturgies twice a month. Others, particularly national groups, do not offer regular local liturgies, but have a feminist liturgy as part of national conferences.

Although some of these liturgies focus on blessing and sharing bread and wine, together with prayers, readings, and reflection that follow the general format of a Eucharistic liturgy, others have developed a variety of symbolic expressions as the occasion may suggest. One group, WATER, has as one of its purposes the development and dissemination of new forms of feminist liturgy for Women-Church groups.[24] Others, such as the Grail, report that

> we create a lot of our own rituals and liturgies drawing from a variety of sources, scriptural, official Roman Catholic, Jewish, other Christian traditions, African, Asian, native American, contemporary (especially contemporary women writers). Holy Week remains a central celebration with an intergenerational community of members, friends and neighbors who come from near and far. We do a very free adaptation of the official liturgy.[25]

These liturgies are usually done by non-ordained women, but at more formal meetings of the Grail there is a nod to the role of the ordained:

> We may have a liturgy with a priest who writes his own Eucharistic prayers, or with an ordained woman. At national meetings we usually try to have both a Mass celebrated by a priest and a Eucharistic liturgy celebrated by an ordained woman or else a concelebration, male and female presiders. In a movement that now spans half a century, individuals are in different places in their views of ordination. Some of us are comfortable with a Eucharist celebrated together by women, without an ordained celebrant; others are not.[26]

The activities of Women-Church groups also vary across a spectrum of options. Almost all do their own creative feminist liturgies either regularly or on special occasions, with the exception of Catholics for a Free Choice, which is strictly an educational and advocacy organization. One representative of a religious order said their community had tried a number of types of alternative liturgies but had recently given up on this, more from the sense that it wasn't worth the effort than from any rejection of the right to do independent liturgies:

> After several years of struggling with non-eucharistic liturgies, no liturgies, non-institutional Eucharistic liturgies, we attend any liturgy than the local church provides. Local church is defined as the group of believers that is geographically close to where we are meeting.[27]

In addition to regular or occasional liturgies some groups offer an annual retreat to their members. These retreats provide both a time for more intensive spiritual renewal and also an opportunity to renew their vision of their purpose as a group and to plan activities for the coming year. Both the Eight Day Center for Justice and Chicago Catholic Women have such yearly retreats for spiritual renewal and for future planning.

Another typical activity of many Women-Church groups is public protests, often related to issues at conflict in the Church. Several groups concerned with women's ordination have a regular event held on particular occasions, such as Mother's Day or the yearly ordination of men from the local diocesan seminary, in which the group and its supporters picket the church to protest the Church's refusal to ordain women. These public protests can take the form of counter-liturgies, such as a footwashing of women in front of a cathedral of a bishop who has banned women from participating in the Holy Thursday footwashing ceremony.

In addition to liturgy, the most common activity of Women-Church groups is educational events: public lectures, conferences, and workshops. These events serve to stimulate their own members through having outside speakers and resource people on particular topics and also function to help educate the larger community on women's issues in the Church and society. Some national groups, such as the Grail and WATER, are constituted to provide regular conferences open to the public and partly support themselves economically by registrations for such educational events.

Publications are another outreach to the larger public, as well as a way of networking with their own constituencies. One group, Catholics for Free Choice, has a large array of publications, such as its regular magazine, *Conscience;* an international newsletter on ethical issues of reproductive choice, *In-Fire* (International Network of Feminists Interested in Reproductive Ethics); and a variety of special pamphlets. CFFC also does research on special issues, such as the membership of the Catholic right, research on the medical services relative to reproduction offered by Catholic hospitals, and polls of Catholic views on birth control and abortion; it distributes the results of these studies to members of Congress and other groups concerned about these issues.[28]

The CFFC-affiliated Latin American groups in Brazil, Mexico, and Uruguay also have their own Spanish *Conciencia* (with independent articles, not translations of the articles in the English-language magazine), books, and pamphlets.[29] The IN-FIRE group also has a Spanish version of its newsletter. CFFC and its three Latin American sister-groups recently have challenged the Vatican's views internationally by attending major United Nations meetings concerned with women's issues, such as the meeting on population and development in Cairo,

Egypt, in 1994 and the Fourth Conference on Women in Beijing, China, in 1995.

Other member groups of the Convergence also have nationally circulated magazines. WOC publishes *Women-Church Speaks*, while NARW, before it went out of existence, had a major newspaper, *Probe*, that combined issues of women's rights in the Church and in society with questions of class, poverty, and U.S. military intervention. Other groups, such as the Lorettos and WATER, have a subscription newsletter, and create occasional resource packets on particular issues.

Women-Church groups also engage in public protest in relation to Church or political events through press releases. CFFC regularly issues press releases in response to official statements of the Roman Catholic hierarchy on reproductive and sexual issues. It has become skilled at seeing that these press releases are in the hands of the media immediately after the release of an official Church statement and providing speakers who can respond to the issues on television.

Press releases in response to statements of the Church or the American government that are seen as violating women's rights and other issues of social justice are also typical of groups such as NAWR, NCAN, and WOC. Over its more than twenty-five-year history NCAN has spoken out on a great variety of issues, from protesting the attempted firing of Dr. Mary Daly by Boston College in 1969, to condemning white racism in Cairo, Illinois (1969), condemning the ownership of war stocks and the B-1 bomber program, opposing the MX missile, and opposing the "Family Protection Act," to supporting various state initiatives on gay rights.[30] The Women-Church Convergence as a total body is presently organized so it can respond even between its biannual meetings with press releases on areas of disagreement with the Catholic hierarchy or American government policy.

Social justice is a concern broadly shared by all Women-Church groups, although there has been division between academics concerned to have more intellectual analysis and those who want to focus on grassroots activism. But only a few have the means to organize particular social justice ministries as a group. NCAN has a prison ministry and halfway houses for women ex-prisoners, which it has conducted for many years. Chicago Catholic Women has a program in Southside Chicago of job training for homeless women in a shelter. It also connects these women with elderly women living alone. The shelter women obtain training as nurses and caretakers, while the elderly play roles as surrogate mothers and grandmothers. In 1996 CCW was working with forty-five shelter women, about one hundred and twenty-five children, and about thirty seniors. It also ran a storefront center for advocacy and counseling open to anyone who dropped in.

Other Women-Church groups also are involved in direct political action or legal advocacy of victims. The Women's Office of the Sisters of Charity maintains a database on women prisoners and runs a Women's Quick Action hot line that responds to particular cases of abuse. The Loretto Network has filed amicus briefs on social issues, for example, against the Colorado law that sought to forbid affirmative action for homosexuals. NARW engaged in a number of direct-action campaigns, such as aid to Central America and a national pilgrimage of protest against the Gulf War January–March 1991. Those Women-Church groups who do not have their own projects promote social justice through educational programs and support their members who are engaged in community work.

Generally Women-Church groups support the range of feminist issues in the Church and in society. All would favor overcoming discrimination against women and gays in ordination and Church employment and making the Church a democratic, participatory community, although there are differences on whether particular groups still want to give "energy" to Church reform issues. Socially, most groups support reproductive rights, including legalized abortion, and gay/lesbian rights in society. Some are involved particularly in anti-racism work and issues of poverty of women and children. Anti-militarism and concern with U.S. intervention are broadly shared in principle.

These shared social/moral principles, however, do not make the activities of Women-Church groups tension-free, either within or between groups in the Convergence. There are a number of issues that have been a source of tension within local groups and between groups over the years. One important cause of conflict has been over racial/ethnic diversity. Although all groups would endorse the principle of more racial/ethnic inclusivity, and some are involved in community work across racial lines, making the Women-Church Convergence itself more racially and ethnically diverse has been difficult. This conflict was brought to a head by the NARW leadership in 1992.

In 1988 NARW committed itself to two priorities: (1) racism and (2) injustice and discrimination in the Roman Catholic Church. For several years NARW came to Convergence meetings with the insistence that these gatherings, and the national conferences, be more racially and ethnically inclusive and give priority to empowering the leadership of women from Black, Hispanic, Asian, Pacific Islander, and Native American backgrounds. In November of 1991 it issued an ultimatum to the members of the Women-Church Convergence that either they make concerted efforts to make their meetings more racially/ethnically inclusive or else it would sever its membership in WCC by the Fall 1992 meeting.

The other members of the WCC objected to this approach to the issue by NARW. Several pointed out that NARW was in a position, as a national organization with a paid staff, to hire people of different racial/ethnic backgrounds, even though its actual membership was mostly Euro-American (membership was 3% ethnic in 1980, but became 18% by 1993, with a fifty-fifty representation on the national board). Other groups that had no paid staff and represented local groups were not in the position to do this. Other national groups, such as CFFC, objected that they had already hired African-American and Latina staff, but the priorities of these women were with other CFFC programs directly related to their ethnic communities. These women were not interested in being the CFFC representative to Women-Church, and it would not be a good use of their time to make them do this.

WCC leaders claimed they wanted to work on greater ethnic inclusivity, but felt that this was a long-term process. It was not helpful to make it into an ultimatum to be acted out by NARW leaving the WCC if there was no movement within a year. NARW was not satisfied with these responses. Terry Hamilton and Ida Galvan, speaking for the NARW board, voiced their objections to these views in a letter to the WCC in February 1992.[31] NARW withdrew from the WCC that fall, although it did participate unofficially in the 1993 Women-Church conference in Albuquerque, New Mexico, as well as holding a dinner event in a nearby Indian pueblo.

Although the issue of NARW's membership in WCC soon became moot, since NARW itself fell into difficulties of staff leadership and funding and folded as an organization in the spring of 1994,[32] the issue of racial/ethnic inclusivity remains a concern of the members of the Convergence in 1996. Although racial/ethnic inclusivity remains a goal, the WCC board generally feels that it is not adequate simply to hire on staffs non-Euro-American racial/ethnic people who then come to represent a group at a WCC board meeting, if this is not rooted organically in the ethnic composition of that group.

Only if the idea of Women-Church expands into the Black, Latina, and other non-Euro-American communities, so that there arise organically in these communities groups that could be represented on the board, would there be authentic diversity. So far this has not happened. In fact, WCC was more mono-cultural in 1996 than it was at the beginning of its predecessor group in 1977, when the Black Sisters Conference and Las Hermanas were members. The Black Sisters Conference ceased to connect to the Coalition early in the 1980s. Las Hermanas dropped out of the WCC in 1992, along with NAWR and for the same reasons.

The 1993 national conference in Albuquerque made a concerted effort to present itself as a movement of many strands of ethnic and other kinds of diversity: African-American, Asian-American, Native American, Hispanic, Lesbian, and Euro-American. But because the numbers of various groups of "non-Euros" were small, these women felt exploited and overworked, trying to provide parallel workshops on an equal-time basis, while some Euro-American women who had worked hard for inclusivity felt they were being trashed for their efforts. A glance around the assembly hall where several thousand participants in the conference gathered quickly revealed that the vast majority were older (white-haired) white women. The "age factor" as well as the racial/ethnic factor were evident. As the spokeswoman for the women's office of her religious order so poignantly stated above, "also we are old."

In addition to the issue of racial/ethnic inclusivity, the greatest issue that has divided the WCC has been the disparity of power between large and small groups and the difficulty of finding an appropriate group process to make meetings productive. It appears as if this issue is beginning to be addressed more satisfactorily, although the fact that each group is responsible for funding the travel of a member to the biannual meetings still points up the differences between groups with funding and those without funding. This means that only about two-thirds of the member groups attend any one board meeting. These meetings move around the country to East Coast, West Coast, Midwest, and South to equalize expenses. While larger, better-funded groups can send a representative regularly, smaller groups tend to attend when it is in their region.

While some of the members of the WCC now have a twenty-year history and are in no danger of disappearing soon, smaller local groups often come and go, merge, split, or disappear. The Boston Women-Church group was active from 1984 to the early 1990s but now has become a part of the Massachusetts Women-Church.[33] In January of 1995 one of the liturgical groups developed by Chicago Catholic Women separated from CCW to operate independently as Chicago Women-Church.[34]

Another disputed issue for WCC, as well as member groups, has been an explicit pro-choice position. CFFC has urged all Convergence members to sign on to the pro-choice position, but some groups, particularly those related to religious orders, have hesitated to do so. The issue of abortion has also divided the women's offices of religious orders from some of their constituency in the order. The Loretto Women's Network took a pro-choice position and sought to educate the Sisters of Loretto on this issue, but some members of the order did not agree. Significantly, there was less controversy between the Loretto Women's Network and the order over homosexuality and homophobia. After an educational event on the subject, there was a unanimous "yes" from the assembly to the project of opposing the Colorado law that sought to ban non-discrimination laws against homosexuals.[35]

There have also been a number of issues that are points of tension within particular groups. These have to do with the identity and focus of particular groups. One group reported that there were differences over whether the group should function primarily as a support community for its members or whether it should put its energy into social action. For others the question of whether to remain focused on Catholic reform or whether to become ecumenical was an issue. Some groups had differences over whether they should be all women or should include men.

For WOC, a key issue, as mentioned above, was under what conditions it would be appropriate to accept the ordination of women. Yet the discussion of this issue is something of a luxury during this time when ordination is being categorically rejected by the Vatican. Many realize that the moment when the Catholic Church accepts women's ordination, even if this is only to the diaconate, the issue will become moot. Some Catholic women will gratefully accept such ordination, even in a hierarchical Church. Then the question will become how to continue a relationship of positive dialogue between such ordained women and those who might feel that ordination should be rejected under such circumstances.

The experience of ordained Protestant women should be studied in this regard. Significantly, as more Protestant women are being ordained, they have found that such official ministry does not fully solve the problems of real inclusion of women. Some ordained Protestant women have started Women-Church groups as support groups to nourish and sustain them alongside their participation in ordained ministry in the institutional Church.[36] The dialectic between inclusion of women in present structures and the need to nourish a more transformative vision of a non-sexist Church continues after ordination has been won.

Some groups have areas of tension related to their particular constituency. For example, Las Hermanas (no longer a member of the WCC, but surveyed for its long-term relation to the Women-Church movement) reported that a major area of discussion for them relates to both non-Hispanic and non-Catholic membership. Should the group be only Latinas or should it include an occasional Spanish-speaking woman of Euro-American background with long-term commitments to the Latina community? Also what about Protestants, particularly Latinas who have become Evangelicals? Since the outreach of many evangelical churches to Latino/a Catholics has an anti-Catholic bias, this problem is particularly difficult. At this point Las Hermanas does have on their board one Latina who is an ordained Episcopalian.[37]

Another area of significant conflict for some groups lies in differences of spirituality among members, particularly the differences between Women-Church members who see their identity as Catholic or Christian and those who relate to a post-Christian/goddess perspective. The liturgical celebrations of the National Women-Church conferences could be described as post-Christian, in the sense of evoking symbols of life without particular references to Christ or Scripture.

Significantly it is often the few Protestant women attending these events who have had the greatest problem with this 'celebration-of-life' approach, without reference to Christ.[38]

In 1994 I attended a Eucharistic liturgy of a local Women-Church group in which bread and wine were blessed and shared among the participants without any Christian references at all. The two women of Protestant background attending the service were shocked by this and raised critical questions about it. It was evident that the Catholic women, including a member of a religious order who planned the service, were surprised by this objection and were not really able to discuss theologically what they were doing. Many Women-Church liturgies are actually engaged in shaping a post-Christian spirituality in which the sacrality of the natural is primary. If Jesus is mentioned at all, it is likely to be as one prophetic figure among others, rather than as the exclusive means of redemption and relation to the divine.

In conclusion one can say that the Women-Church movement exhibits the expected tensions of Catholics "between the times." Catholic feminists are seeking to transform an existing tradition to be inclusive of women and shape a new spirituality that transcends the limits of that historical tradition. As one respondent put it: "I perceive the greatest difficulty to be retaining one foot in Catholicism and one foot in creating the new. The ambiguity and the need to stay in dynamic tension is too hard for some."[39] Perhaps what is most significant about the now more than twenty-year history of the American Women-Church movement is the extent to which most of its members are determined to remain with both sides of these ambiguities, without acceding to an either-or solution on one side or the other.

NOTES

1. Women's ordination was already accepted by Congregationalists, Unitarians, Universalists, Methodist Protestants, and some other Christian groups in America in the 19th century. After World War II, women's ordination was accepted by the Lutheran and Reformed Churches in Europe, and by the Methodist Church and the Presbyterian Church in the United States in 1956. Some Lutherans in the United States accepted it in the mid-1960s, so by 1974 the main struggles over this issue in American Protestant churches were in the Episcopal Church and in the more fundamentalist churches.

2. See Rosemary Ruether, "Spirituality and Justice: Popular Church Movements in the United States," in *A Democratic Catholic Church: The Reconstruction of Roman Catholicism,* Rosemary Radford Ruether and Eugene C. Bianchi, eds. (New York: Crossroad, 1992), pp. 189–193.

3. See Sergio Torres and John Eagleson, eds., *The Challenge of Basic Christian Communities* (Maryknoll, N.Y.: Orbis Press, 1980).

4. See Janet Kalven, "Women Breaking Boundaries: The Grail and Feminism," in *The Journal of Feminist Studies in Religion,* no. 1 (Spring 1989), pp. 119–142.

5. See Mary C. Seegers, "The Loyal Opposition: Catholics for a Free Choice," in *The Catholic Church and the Politics of Abortion: A View from the States*, ed. Timothy A. Byrnes and Mary C. Seegers (Boulder, Colo.: Westview Press, 1992), pp. 169–187.

6. See Norene Carter, "Entering the Sanctuary: The Episcopalian Story," in *Women of Spirit: Female Leadership in the Jewish and Christian Traditions*, ed. Rosemary R. Ruether and Eleanor McLaughlin (New York: Simon and Schuster, 1979), pp. 356–372.

7. See *Women and Catholic Priesthood: An Expanded Vision: Proceedings of the Detroit Ordination Conference*, ed. Anne Marie Gardiner (New York: Paulist, 1976).

8. Donna Quinn, founder of Chicago Catholic Women, provided me with the information on this history.

9. The WOC dialogue team strongly opposed the bishops' decision to write a pastoral letter on women. Marjorie Tuite, one of the WOC team, suggested to the bishops that it would be better if women did a pastoral letter on bishops.

10. See *Women Priests: A Catholic Commentary on the Vatican Declaration*, ed. Leonard Swidler and Arlene Swidler (New York: Paulist Press, 1977).

11. The papers of the three national Women-Church conferences are in the archives of the Gannon Center on Women and Leadership of Mundelein College, Loyola University, in Chicago.

12. This is written from personal recollections. After the 1983 conference Convergence members discussed the name in Chicago. I wrote one of the position papers arguing for the plural spelling on the grounds of recognizing diversity among women, and this was accepted. I do not currently have any copy of this paper and am not aware if it has been preserved anyplace else.

13. This reflects the membership list of the Women-Church Convergence as of December 1995.

14. These remarks are in the survey response sent to me by Janet Kalven of the Grail Women's Task Force, based on her attendance of the Convergence meetings over ten years.

15. Remarks sent to me by Felicia Wolf, of the Feminist Interest Group of the School Sisters of St. Francis, as part of her response to my survey.

16. Reported to me by Carol Cook, Eighth Day Center for Justice, by phone, August 16, 1996.

17. The Vatican statement claiming that the teaching against women's ordination was "infallible" and could not be changed appeared October 28, 1995. See discussion in early November 1995 issues of the *National Catholic Reporter*.

18. These remarks are based on my own attendance at the November 1995 WOC conference in Crystal City, Virginia, and on conversations before and after the conference with Maureen Fiedler of the Quixote Center, who undertook to reorganize WOC after WOC suffered a large debt caused by poor financial management of the conference.

19. In April 1996 I sent out a questionnaire to the list of thirty-one members of the Women-Church Convergence as of December 1995. I received a response from eighteen of these groups. The survey asked the following questions: (1) When was your organization founded? When did it become associated with the Women-Church Convergence? (2) What is the approximate membership (or if this question is not applicable) about how many people attend its events? (3) What sort of events do you sponsor? How frequently? (4) How would you define your religious identity—Roman Catholic, Ecumenical Christian, Post-Christian? (5) How do you see your relation to the Roman Catholic church or to the historical institutional churches? (6) If your

group does liturgy, how does your liturgy define Eucharistic leadership? (7) What is the organizational structure of your group? What kind of leadership does it have and how is leadership developed? (8) What issues have been most important for your group in its history? What issues have been most important in terms of discussion, practice, commitments? What issues have been most divisive; i.e., in terms of disagreements and tensions in the group? How have these tensions been resolved or not resolved? (9) What issues have been most important in your relation with (or tension with) the Women-Church Convergence? 10) If your group has disassociated itself from the Women-Church Convergence, what issues were critical to the making of this decision? The survey was also sent to two groups who left the Women-Church Convergence, NARW and Las Hermanas, both of whom responded.

20. Survey response: Feminist Interest Group of the School Sisters of St. Francis.

21. Survey response: Ginny Williams, Loretto Women's Network.

22. Survey response: Janet Kalven for the Grail Women's Network.

23. Survey response: Massachusetts Women-Church.

24. For example, *Women-Church Source Book*, ed. Mary E. Hunt and Diann Neu (Silver Spring, Md.: WATER, 1993), available from the WATER office in Silver Spring, Maryland.

25. Survey response: Janet Kalven for the Grail Women's Network.

26. Ibid.

27. Survey response: Feminist Interest Group, School Sisters of St. Francis.

28. These publications are available from the CFFC office in Washington, D.C.

29. These publications are available from the CCD office, CC Central 1326, Montevideo, Uruguay.

30. See the publication *If Anyone Can, NCAN: Twenty Years of Speaking Out* (NCAN: 1307 S. Wabash, Chicago, IL 60605).

31. A packet of correspondence between the NARW board and the members of the Convergence between November 1991 and February 1992 was supplied to me by Judy Vaughan, former director of NARW.

32. After the April 1993 Women-Church Conference in Albuquerque, Judy Vaughan turned over the leadership of NAWR to a new leadership team. Some of these individuals lacked adequate administrative and fund-raising skills, and there was ethnic/racial struggle on the staff. By spring of 1994 the reserve funds of NARW were used up and the organization closed.

33. Survey response: Boston Women-Church.

34. Survey response: Chicago Women-Church.

35. Survey response: Loretto Women's Network.

36. In Chicago a Women-Church liturgical group has been founded by Protestant women, many of them ordained, for feminist support. In Gelnhausen, Germany, a group of ordained Protestant women has developed a center for Women-Church liturgy and Bible drama.

37. Survey response: Las Hermanas.

38. These remarks are drawn from my experience at the national Women-Church conferences. The focus on natural sacrality rather than Christian references in these liturgies reflects both the theological perspective of the liturgical organizers and also their concern to be inclusive of non-Christians attending the conferences.

39. Survey response: Loretto Women's Network.

Part 2

PERSONAL SEXUAL MORALITY

3

ABANDONING SUSPICION

The Catholic Left and Sexuality

GENE BURNS

This chapter aims primarily to highlight some of the central developments that gave birth to Catholic left perspectives on sexuality. (In
discussing "sexuality," I also mean to include Catholic views of reproduction, as the two are inextricably intertwined. The hierarchy's
opposition to abortion and to contraception, for example, both ultimately depend on the sacred status of procreation.) Especially important is noting why sexuality has become such a matter of division
within the Church. I make the argument that the contemporary conflict is understandable only if we understand that secular changes in
the church-state relationship have led the hierarchy increasingly to
stake its institutional authority on enforcing its view of sexual orthodoxy. But, in recent decades, Catholic laity and theologians often treat
Rome's approach to sexuality as simply irrelevant.

Before continuing with the substance of the chapter, I should note
briefly the intended scope of the paper. The point of this essay, as noted
above, is to provide some historical context for the discussion of sexuality from what many Catholics would consider a left perspective. The
author is a historical sociologist; discussions of the history of theological understandings of sexuality, therefore, are not from the point of
view of a theological expert.

There are a number of additional discussions that one might include in this essay, but that I did not, such as a detailed history of
Catholic views of marriage, or the relationship between views of sexuality and opposition to women's ordination. The particular compro-
mises embodied in the essay below result from the facts that, first, I
thought it sensible to focus on those issues that are at the heart of today's Catholic left and, second, some related topics are covered in
other chapters in this book.

This essay benefited a great deal from the comments of consultants Margaret Farley, Frances Kissling, and John J. McNeill, and from the many insights provided by other contributors to this volume. Especially helpful were the comments of Mary Jo Weaver, Scott Appleby, and Susan Ross.

Introduction

THE VATICAN, SEXUALITY, AND PROGRESSIVE CATHOLICS

One of the more interesting, and for many Catholics frustrating, realities of the institutional Catholic Church in the late twentieth century is that the Vatican has based its authority so prominently on its own version of sexual orthodoxy. When it comes to issues of sexuality and reproduction, the Vatican takes a position so intolerant of dissent that is quite difficult to distinguish, say, a "reformist" or "moderate" position from a "left" position. The Vatican sees everyone to its left as a dangerous moral relativist, but one can be to the left of the Vatican on sexual matters and yet, from many other mainstream perspectives, still be quite conservative. While there are, for example, Catholics who call only for an easing of the ban on contraception, but otherwise would leave Vatican doctrine on sexuality intact, even that position has, over the last few decades, become inextricably tied to a critique of the power structure of the Church. That is, Rome has exerted its authority to treat even a position mildly in favor of contraception—let alone one sanctioning homosexuality or legal abortion—as a fundamental assault on Catholicism. And so an attempt to push even an apparently moderate position easily escalates into a struggle over Vatican authority.

Still, it is a mistake to see Catholic positions on sexuality and reproductive issues only in terms of a battle between Rome and the myriad of dissenters. Quite independently of Rome or of the hierarchy as a whole, many Catholics have developed their own more positive, less suspicious view of sexuality. Perhaps the most significant fact of such developments is that a large majority of American Catholics— most of whom certainly do not think of themselves as involved in politicized discussions in the Church—do not follow the hierarchy's pronouncements on sexuality. But it is also the case that there have been more organized alternatives to the hierarchy's approach. While partly spurred by Rome's intransigence on such matters, there has developed extended Catholic exploration of the ethical and theological aspects of sexuality, a discussion that has to a great extent gone on regardless of the hierarchy.

This chapter examines the history of institutional Catholic suspicion of the morality of sexuality, Rome's turn toward basing its authority on a conservative view of sexuality, and the development of an American lay and theological rejection of Rome's approach to sexuality.

CATHOLICISM AND SEXUALITY: A HISTORY OF SUSPICION

The particular suspicion of sexuality, viewed as a realm of lustful, sinful temptation, has a considerable history within Catholic theology. It goes back at least to Augustine, who is credited to a considerable extent with the view that intercourse is morally permissible only with procreative intentions. From a historical perspective, then, on the one hand it does not seem surprising that the hierarchy's discussions of sex and reproduction would emphasize sex as a legitimate activity only in the context of a marriage open to procreation, nor that it would intertwine discussions of sexuality with a focus on the moral status of the fetus. In that sense, the hierarchy's view of contraception, homosexuality, and abortion is continuous with centuries of officially sanctioned theology.[1]

On the other hand, the particular emphasis that the hierarchy currently places on sexual issues, so much that sexuality becomes a primary focus of Church discipline and dissent, is a relatively recent phenomenon. This particular emphasis of the late twentieth century has origins, in the United States, from about the 1920s but has intensified in the last few decades. Since Vatican II, Rome has dug in its heels so fervently on sexual orthodoxy that it has come to center its own authority in terms of doctrine on sexuality, more than any other area of doctrine. I argue below that there are two primary reasons for this development: first, there has emerged a much greater pluralism of views of sexuality and family arrangements in Western society in general. The Vatican, like the rest of society, cannot avoid facing new social arrangements and new cultural assumptions. The Vatican maintains views it held a century ago, views that were then uncontroversial within at least mainstream, publicly voiced Western discussions of gender and sexuality. And so, while the Vatican's views paralleled the secular mainstream a century ago, the Catholic left parallels the secular mainstream today. Second, the relationship of the papacy to secular society has changed so dramatically in the last century and a half that sexuality is one of the few sets of issues where the Vatican can attempt to defend centralized Church authority in the wake of Vatican II.

Below, I will first discuss the liberalization of secular views of sexuality that emerged in twentieth-century American society. I will then return to a discussion of how the Church hierarchy has responded to those changes, why defending conservative views of sexuality has become so central to the Vatican's maintenance of authority, and what alternative, less suspicious views of sexuality the Catholic left has offered.

Secular Changes: The Liberalization of Sexuality in Twentieth-Century America

There was some American discussion of the supposed evils of contraception before the Catholic Church was much of a player in American public life, and so Catholics certainly did not frame that initial discussion. Central to the legal restriction was the 1873 federal Comstock law, which greatly limited access to birth control, officially defining such information as "obscene." The federal law enforced such restrictions primarily by forbidding use of the mails to circulate contraceptive information, while most states passed similar laws that further restricted access to such information and sometimes declared birth control information and technology entirely illegal. Usually physicians were directly or indirectly permitted to share such information with their patients, but even the legality of physicians supplying contraceptive information or supplies was dubious enough in many states that most physicians avoided dealing with the issue (and many doctors were hostile to birth control anyway).

Initially public opposition to contraception in this country, in the late nineteenth and early twentieth centuries, was associated primarily with Protestant moralists, anti-feminists of various stripes, and intellectuals and politicians influenced by eugenic worries that white, native-born Protestants were not sufficiently reproducing themselves. Indeed, one of the central concerns of those who decried white Protestant "race suicide" was that, along with African Americans, immigrant Catholics with high fertility would overwhelm the supposedly superior "race" of native-born white Protestants.

Another strike against contraception was that, in the late nineteenth century, it was essentially impossible to argue publicly that sex had any positive value outside of procreation. To do so was scandalous. Note, for example, the late-nineteenth-century movement for "voluntary motherhood." This movement was radical for its times in the sense that it argued that women had a right to decide when they wanted to have children. But many advocates of voluntary motherhood still assumed that sex legitimately occurred only within heterosexual marriage and that one voluntarily controlled pregnancy simply via abstention. Thus, if the intent was to limit family size, then the only and obvious answer was for the woman to limit sex.[2]

However, demographic changes and changes in the American economy ultimately contributed to the liberalization of views of contraception and sexuality. For urban and suburban couples, children were no longer the economic asset that they had been for farm families, so that American urbanization effected a decrease in fertility rates. As some historians and sociologists have put it, the emotional value of children increased while their economic value decreased. With the beginning of a movement in favor of birth control in the 1910s came arguments that limiting the number of children allowed parents to focus more on the quality of their children's lives rather than coping (or failing to cope), economically and physically, with the quantity of children typical in a family that used no birth control.[3]

In the early decades of the twentieth century, it also gradually became possible to argue that married couples could engage in sex without always intending to have children. Now, at this time, for many families birth control meant an attempt to have perhaps three or four children, instead of eight or nine. There was still the assumption that women were primarily defined by their role as potential mothers. There was, then, for example, no advocacy of legal abortion; indeed, activists in favor of contraception typically argued that legal, accessible contraception would reduce the need for desperate women to resort to the horrors of abortion.[4]

A number of activists, including Emma Goldman and Mary Ware Dennett, had advocated for birth control along with other causes of the American left, but it was Margaret Sanger who expanded and took control of the movement in the 1910s. Sanger, an Irish American, had a pious Catholic mother and an atheist, socialist father. While often stating that Catholic women were avid clients of her birth control clinics, she saw Catholic clerics as her chief enemy. Her criticism of Catholicism, on the one hand, was based on a realistic assessment of clerical opposition to birth control and, on the other, bordered occasionally on the paranoid.

Between the two world wars contraception gradually became an acceptable, middle-class cause in the U.S. After World War II, in the United States and internationally, promotion of birth control became linked to concerns about rising world populations, so that promoting birth control was by the 1960s part of U.S. foreign policy.[5] And so it hardly had radical connotations. Catholic opposition to birth control, then, had early in the century been in line with dominant viewpoints of the day. But by the 1960s such opposition was considered in many circles to be reactionary, perhaps even a bit bizarre.

Abortion, on the other hand, was rarely discussed through most of American history, though illegal abortion was widely practiced. As noted above, advocates for contraception in the early twentieth century explicitly opposed abortion; for the most part the idea of liberalizing abortion laws did not emerge until the 1960s. Until then, legal abortion was available only for such reasons as rape, incest, and danger to the pregnant woman's life. But as a result of a quiet, elite movement mostly led by physicians, a minority of states liberalized their abortion laws in the late 1960s. The issue became more of a public concern in the 1970s, especially as a result of the U.S. Supreme Court's *Roe v. Wade* and *Doe v. Bolton* decisions in 1973, which made legal abortion much more widely available throughout the country.[6]

Like abortion until the 1960s, sexual orientation was generally off the radar screen of Catholic or even secular politics for much of the twentieth century. However, the issue emerged as part of what is sometimes called "the sexual revolution" of the 1960s and 1970s, which was really a series of partly discrete changes and innovations.

One of those changes was the emergence of an explicit U.S. gay liberation movement, often dated to the June 1969 Stonewall incident. Stonewall was a Greenwich Village gay bar that police raided, in the type of "vice" action that had become periodic and even routine for many police forces. But, contrary to past reactions, patrons of the bar strongly resisted, in what became a weekend-long physical struggle between police and gay New Yorkers. There had been some New Left discussion of gay liberation before this time, but a more sustained movement developed after Stonewall.[7]

While not as much in the public eye as was abortion in the 1970s, with the emergence of the AIDS crisis in the 1980s, homosexuality became more of a topic of public debate. Gallup polls suggest that (depending on exactly how the survey question is asked), at most only about half of the American public thinks homosexuality is an acceptable lifestyle, a proportion essentially unchanged since the early 1980s.[8] Groups like the Moral Majority and the Christian Coalition, and prominent public figures like Senator Jesse Helms and Cardinal John O'Connor of New York, have of course been in the forefront of attempts to keep homosexuality in the closet. However, despite the anti-gay rhetoric of such prominent public figures, public tolerance of homosexuality (for example, the right of gays to serve in the military) is also much more visible today than it was twenty years ago. It also appears to be the case that Catholics have been more tolerant of homosexuality than have Protestants, given the strong moral objection to homosexuality among many evangelical Protestants.[9]

The Catholic Church Faces Secular Liberalization

SEXUAL ORTHODOXY AND VATICAN AUTHORITY

By the time of the Second Vatican Council, then, contraception had become uncontroversial in American society, and soon afterward it became possible to advocate openly for the legitimacy of homosexuality and legal abortion, though these two issues certainly remained controversial. In the meantime, as addressed below, Rome had come to guard jealously its authority to define Catholic sexual and reproductive orthodoxy.

As I noted earlier, the Vatican's sexual conservatism itself is not new. However, this particular view of sexuality has gained increasing prominence partly as a result of the papacy's loss of its position in European geopolitics.[10] Especially since the loss of the Papal States (which became part of a unified Italy) in the second half of the nineteenth century, the papacy found it problematic to make detailed pronouncements on matters of macroeconomic and macropolitical policy that states considered their own realm of authority. One result was that social doctrine—which concerned precisely such matters—become a more distinct category of papal teaching, one that generally avoided the kind of specific prohibitions and directives common to Vatican pronouncements on matters it considers fundamental matters of faith and morals. Thus, while a central point of Pope Gregory XVI's *Syllabus of Errors* (1864) was condemnation of the idea of church-state separation, in fact by the early twentieth century the papacy came to define its authority primarily over matters that did not directly interfere with the authority claims of European states.

The papacy received certain political benefits in return; control over internal Church affairs actually increased. For example, during this period, Catholic states gradually gave up the right to name bishops or to veto candidates in papal conclaves. And such states thus came to pay less attention to papal pronouncements on doctrinal matters, including the papacy's patriarchal views of sex roles, which were, in any case, thoroughly conventional within late-nineteenth- and early-twentieth-century European society. It is rare for Rome to identify and condemn specific violations of social doctrine, and excommunication for such violations seems not to be in the realm of consideration. Thus, for example, when American bishops addressed the ethics of U.S. government economic and nuclear policy in the 1980s, they made clear (partly at the Vatican's insistence) that binding moral *principles* (which were general in nature—e.g., that one cannot target innocents in warfare) did not imply approval or condemnation of specific economic or defense *policies*. On matters such as artificial insemination, birth control, abortion, or homosexuality, however, the Catholic hierarchy (whether in Rome or in the U.S.) does not hesitate to condemn or endorse particular government policies and particular behaviors. And Catholic politicians have occasionally been threatened with excommunication for being pro-choice.[11]

Rome's approach to sexual issues not only attempts to police conservative doctrine on sexuality but also necessarily turns disagreements over such matters into fundamental battles over authority. The entire struggle is reminiscent of Rome's anti-modernist crusade earlier in the twentieth century, as described by Lester R. Kurtz, in which Rome came to identify its own authority with the attack on modernism.[12] And by defining what beliefs were unacceptable, Rome was simultaneously rallying its troops around a particular position and clarifying, and concentrating attention upon, what it considered orthodoxy. Kurtz notes that it is easier to point out and enforce what is acceptable when one can demarcate a clear group of opponents whose views are defined as unacceptable. In the process, then, determination to identify and punish heretics helps create a clear identity of heresy that might not otherwise exist. Before being identified as heretics, dissenters might have thought of themselves as perhaps inquisitive or innovative, but ultimately faithful; they might not have thought of their views as necessarily implying a direct challenge to Roman authority.

In the case of both modernism in the early twentieth century and sexuality in the late twentieth century, Rome has chosen not only to defend doctrine but to assure that its authority remains intact. Disagreement with Rome is treated as a direct, unacceptable rejection of papal authority. Today it is rare for the actual term "heresy" to be invoked in debates over sexual orthodoxy, and Rome's attack on opponents within the Church does not quite match the ferocity of Pius X's crusade against modernism. Nevertheless, in both cases Rome created a situation in which identifying and condemning diversions from orthodoxy on a particular set of issues—theological modernism early this century, and sexuality today—became the central means by which Rome defines and maintains its authority. Given that Rome learned to avoid many issues of state policy as it lost its role in European geopolitics, sexuality is one of the few areas of doctrine where Rome can pursue a strategy of centralized institutional authority.

MAKING AN ISSUE OF BIRTH CONTROL

The European Catholic hierarchy had made an issue of birth control and declining European birth rates in the late nineteenth century. The U.S. hierarchy had long followed standard Catholic sexual puritanism, but it made more of a public issue of the matter starting in the 1910s and 1920s. It was only in the twentieth century that sexual conservatism became a distinctive feature of American Catholicism, partly because mainstream Protestantism then began to liberalize on the matter of birth control. In the nineteenth century, it had not been any distinctive Catholic sexual conservatism that had caught Protestants' attention, as Protestants shared similar views.

By the 1920s, Catholic bishops and some other prominent Catholic clerics (most notably John Ryan) had become the central organized opponents of the American pro–birth control movement. Their position on contraception had considerable precedent within Catholic theology and was a response to the growth of a pro–birth control movement in the U.S. in the 1910s. But their prominence was partly a result of the fact that Protestant and other opposition to birth control largely faded from view by the 1920s; as there was some Protestant liberalization, Margaret Sanger effectively built new alliances in support of birth control.

But Catholic opposition to contraception, if anything, only increased, reinforced by Pius XI's *Casti Connubii* (On Christian Marriage),[13] probably written in reaction to the Lambeth Conference of 1929, at which the Anglican Church accepted contraception in the context of loving marriages.[14] The encyclical addressed in as much or greater detail such issues as the dangers of marrying outside the Catholic faith, but its place in history is primarily based upon its prohibition of birth control. There was a widespread perception that *Casti Connubii* had endorsed the rhythm method and Pius XII officially approved rhythm (via an interpretation of a cryptic passage in *Casti Connubii*) in 1951. But, since about the 1950s, American Catholics have favored "artificial" birth control in roughly the same proportion as the rest of the American population.[15] It appears that, by 1960, slightly less than half of American Catholics practicing birth control restricted themselves to the rhythm method, and a few years before *Humanae Vitae* about three-quarters of Catholics favored wider availability of birth control services.[16]

And so by the time of Vatican II, it was clear that many Catholics found the hierarchy's perspective on birth control to be inadequate. There emerged among theologians and some members of the hierarchy, especially in Europe, discussion of possibly retracting the ban on contraception. The development of the birth control pill (which became available in the early 1960s) helped spur such discussions. Indeed, some theologians argued that, because the pill regulated a woman's cycle and did not involve a physical barrier to conception, its role in married sexuality was similar to rhythm, and thus morally acceptable.[17]

In the mid-1960s, it began to appear that the ban on contraception might be overturned. In March 1963, John XXIII set up a commission to study the issue of birth control. John died in June 1963, before the commission ever met, but his successor, Paul VI, expanded the commission, ultimately to include lay members. Among the lay members was a Chicago couple, Patrick and Patty Crowley, who had been leaders in a national organization, the Catholic Family Movement.[18] The commission made its recommendations to Paul in the summer of 1966, splitting into a large majority that favored acceptance of the legitimacy of contraception and a minority that did not. The majority report favored "responsible parenthood" that allowed "correctly formed" consciences to make a responsible choice about contraception. In this majority report, use of contraception in the context of responsible parenthood "is altogether distinguished from a mentality and way of married life which in its totality is egoistically and irrationally opposed to fruitfulness."[19]

The fact that *Humanae Vitae*'s reaffirmation of the ban on contraception (in July 1968) came as a shock to many Catholics is quite understandable if we look at the context. First, Vatican II had put reform, and the idea of collaboration of different parts of the Church, very much in the air; the papal birth control mission seemed a perfect example of such collaboration and openness to the experiences of the laity. The very composition of the commission seemed to suggest that the pope would make a decision based on consultation with different elements of "the people of God," not just a close circle of theological advisers and Curial officials. Lay members like the Crowleys were part of the large majority of the commission that argued that rhythm was a barrier, more than a contributor, to a loving, spiritual marriage. Second, there had been international media speculation that the Catholic Church was going to change its position for more than two years before the encyclical was issued, and the majority report appeared in the press more than a year before the encyclical.[20]

And so *Humanae Vitae* was a shock; its significance cannot be overstated. Rome had dug in its heels, in a way that progressive Catholics experienced as a betrayal of the spirit of the Second Vatican Council. For many, that encyclical threw ice water on the conciliar mood in a way that no other event has matched.[21]

SEXUAL MORALITY AND VATICAN AUTHORITY AFTER VATICAN II

I would argue that *Humanae Vitae* must be understood as a defining moment of the Vatican's attempt to assert and clarify its authority within the institutional Church, in the wake of Vatican II. I am not saying that the encyclical was issued only as a grab for power; I have every reason to believe that the theologians and curates behind *Humanae Vitae*, including Paul VI, sincerely felt that they were arguing a proper Christian morality. But once the Vatican had been forced out of European geopolitics in the nineteenth century, attempting to regulate the sexual morality of Catholics was one of the few areas where Rome could claim absolute authority. There are a number of areas where Rome feels it knows what is right and what is wrong but cannot ultimately enforce those positions, especially if they conflict with secular state authority. But when it comes to (at least the public declaration of) sexual morality within the Church, Rome can, if it so chooses, use its institutional power to define and enforce orthodoxy. Indeed, if Rome relinquishes the authority to regulate the consciences of Catholics, it loses much of its centralized authority and thus would have to redefine its relationship to the Church as a whole. That is precisely what it does not want to do, and what much of the Catholic left does want it to do. Thus in discussing sexuality, Rome talks of unchanging magisterial authority rooted in unchanging natural law; the Catholic left, in contrast, talks about the moral agency of Christians, and a theology based in Christians' everyday lived experience.

The strategy Rome has chosen on sexual morality must be understood in the context of Vatican II. Had Rome ultimately decided to treat Vatican II as a truly revolutionary reassessment of Church authority, then *Humanae Vitae* would not have made sense. And if Rome had decided to treat sexual morality the way it does issues of state diplomacy—that is, as matters where the hierarchy attempts to provide moral guidance but does not condemn specific policies, nor define and discipline heresy—then *Humanae Vitae* would not have made sense. But, instead of following the collegial approach to decision making that the existence of the birth control commission initially seemed to imply, Paul VI and John Paul II ultimately decided that Vatican II would not inaugurate a revolutionary redefinition of Church authority. Compatible with a centralized view of authority, then, has been an approach to Catholic doctrine emphasizing an unyielding view of natural law, in which any deviation from sexual orthodoxy defeats the intended purpose of sexuality (the purpose being procreation) and thus is specifically, unambiguously, and mortally sinful. Thus Rome, in enforcing this view of sexuality, can claim unambiguously that anyone who disagrees in any way with this view of natural law is unambiguously and seriously immoral.

In retrospect, then, we can see *Humanae Vitae* as the beginning of a series of stern Vatican pronouncements on matters of sexuality, as well as gender, along with a series of disciplinary actions meant to silence dissenters.[22] Among the more celebrated have been forcing Seattle Archbishop Raymond Hunthausen, in 1986, to share authority in his diocese temporarily because of his permissive views toward sterilization in Catholic hospitals, homosexuality, and a number of other issues.[23] Also in 1986 was the removal of Rev. Charles E. Curran from his tenured faculty position in theology at Catholic University of America because of his views on sexual morality. Curran had been under investigation for two decades and had almost been removed from his post quite a bit earlier, in 1967.[24] Reflecting the strong link between sexual orthodoxy and Church authority, Curran framed his official responses to Rome's investigation of him in terms of an inquiry about what were the legitimate boundaries of dissent within the Church. According to Curran, Rome never responded to that, his principal concern. Soon after he was removed from Catholic University's faculty, the university's chancellor, Archbishop James A. Hickey, declared, "there is no right to public dissent."[25]

The lack of any right to public dissent on sexual morality and gender roles has been made clear in Vatican pronouncements over the last few decades, which if anything seem to emerge with increasing rapidity. In 1976 Paul VI explicitly ruled out the possibility of women's ordination, and in 1983 John Paul II went further by prohibiting even discussion of the issue. In 1975, the Vatican issued a "Declaration on Certain Questions Concerning Sexual Ethics," which discussed homosexuality as a pathological condition that, however, was not in itself sinful because it was beyond the control of the individual. Homosexual acts, however, were prohibited because they were "intrinsically disordered."[26] As in all Vatican discussions of sexuality, the natural law argument that sex was intrinsically meant for reproduction was implicit in the discussion.

Nevertheless, some bishops and bishops' conferences, especially in the United States, had in the late 1970s and early 1980s edged toward an ever more tolerant view of homosexuality.[27] Such changes were partly spurred by the 1976 publication of *The Church and the Homosexual*, by the American Jesuit John McNeill, who was ultimately driven out of the priesthood.

In response, the Congregation for the Doctrine of the Faith, headed by Cardinal Joseph Ratzinger, issued in 1986 a "Letter to the Bishops of the Catholic Church on the Pastoral Care of Homosexual Persons." The 1986 letter was written in English and apparently directed primarily toward American Catholics. It aimed to correct "an overly benign interpretation . . . given to the homosexual condition itself" since the publication of the 1975 Declaration.[28] The letter declared: "Although the particular inclination of the homosexual person is not a sin, it is more or less a strong tendency ordered toward an intrinsic moral evil. . . ."[29] Following the letter was pressure for Catholic churches to disassociate themselves from any groups that did not toe the Vatican line on homosexuality.

Rome went even further in 1992, releasing a document titled "Some Considerations Concerning the Catholic Response to Legislate Proposals on the Non-discrimination of Homosexual Persons." This document explicitly endorsed discrimination against homosexuals in certain contexts, "for example, in the consignment of children to adoption or foster care, in employment of teachers or coaches, and in military recruitment. . . ."[30] Even a number of bishops made clear that they thought Rome had gone too far.[31]

Still, Rome maintains its strongest condemnation for abortion and pro-choice Catholics. For Rome, abortion is a particularly frightening example of a secular, relativist "culture of death." Making clear how much he sees liberal views of sexuality to be a threat to his vision of the Church, John Paul II issued in 1993 *Veritatis Splendor*, a document that portrayed the Church as under siege from a secular, relativist culture that threatened the foundations of society and the authority of the Church. Ronald R. Burke, among many others, critiqued the encyclical's obsession with sexuality, noting that "*the only intrinsically evil acts that the Pope discusses in this encyclical are sexual acts.*"[32]

What the Catholic Left Says about Sexuality and Ecclesiology

CHALLENGING ROMAN AUTHORITY

Ever since *Humanae Vitae* in 1968, both Rome and progressives have linked the attempt to hold the line on sexuality with a defense of centralized Roman authority. Not only in the United States,[33] the reaction against *Humanae Vitae* became almost immediately a matter of dissent not just against a particular teaching, but against the power politics of the Vatican in general. A storm of protest quickly emerged in Catholic circles late in the summer of 1968. One of the more significant acts of protest was that year's statement of dissent signed by hundreds of Catholic theologians, which appeared in numerous publications.[34] The statement criticized the ecclesiology implied in the encyclical as inconsistent with Vatican II, and criticized the implication that there was only one competent view of natural law as it applied to birth control. It also emphasized that the ban on contraception was not an infallible teaching. Thus Catholics had the right to form their own consciences on the matter.

This statement indicates the typical dynamic of Catholic discussions, in the last three decades, of sexual and reproductive ethics. That is, because the hierarchy attempts to prohibit almost any independent inquiry into Catholic teaching on sexuality, beginning with *Humanae Vitae* almost any discussion of alternative approaches to sexuality is inseparable from a challenge to hierarchical authority and support for a theology appealing to pluralism and experience.[35]

A central theme of many of the writings likely to be identified as examples of a Catholic left approach to sexuality is the image of a plural people of God, with explicit reference to a progressive interpretation of Vatican II. For example, in 1984, pro-choice Catholics placed an ad in the *New York Times* challenging the hierarchy's approach to abortion. The central message of the ad was that there was no single Catholic position on abortion, implicitly meaning that the hierarchy does not in itself constitute the Church. If Catholics—that is, all members of the Church—have different views on the ethics of abortion, then by definition there is not a single Catholic position on abortion.[36] Paired with a more permissive view of reproductive choice was a progressive view of ecclesiology.

It is ironic that, while the Vatican is particularly intolerant of dissenter on sexual orthodoxy, it is here where the American Catholic left is arguably closest to the laity in general and thus, from the laity's perspective, not necessarily at all radical. While the typical Catholic may not even be aware of Catholic debates about poverty, race, pacifism, or collegiality, such a Catholic would probably find completely familiar the idea that contraception is normal and reasonable and that upstanding citizens have diverse views on abortion and homosexuality.[37] About a decade ago, a book examining public opinion surveys of Catholics conducted by the Gallup organization described Catholics in a way highly reminiscent of progressive theologians who emphasize a need to base theology on the everyday experience of the people of God:

> The simple fact is that the Catholic Church has not merely lost its credibility on birth control—it has lost much of its credibility on everything related to sex. American Catholics do not disregard Church teaching on every issue, but birth control clearly established the pattern that they accept Church teaching only when it makes sense in terms of their own situations and their own consciences. When it comes to sex, Church leaders are preaching to an audience that is simply not paying any attention.[38]

ABANDONING SUSPICION OF SEXUALITY

The struggles over the papal birth control commission strongly suggest, within the Catholic clerical tradition, an ingrained discomfort with sexuality. Opponents of change within the commission emphasized a slippery slope argument that accepting contraception would lead to all kinds of other evils, like abortion, masturbation, homosexuality, and adultery. This was despite the fact that the proposal was only that the Church accept contraception within the context of a marriage that, as a whole, was open to procreation. Thus contraception was not to be used at all times. Given that even advocates of change proposed such a limited acceptance of contraception, the slippery slope argument assumes that any free expression of sexuality poses the danger of temptation into sin.

Two central points of the large majority of the commission in favor of change were that sexuality is an expression of love, not just a means of procreation, and that, while marriage as a whole should be open to procreation, this need not be true of every conjugal act. While *Humanae Vitae* did accept that sexuality was an expression of love and that love, like procreation, was a central component of marriage, it rejected the idea of any sexual act that was not open to procreation. And so, even if one were to accept that the Vatican really did believe that love within marriage was not secondary to procreation within marriage, this could only be true with the corollary that sexual love cannot be expressed independently of reproductive sex. Since there are other ways to express love, the distinguishing and primary feature of sexuality, from the Vatican's point of view, remains not the fact that the Church accepts it as a legitimate expression of married love, but that it (unlike other expressions of love) is concerned with procreation.

In contrast, the left, following the path of many American Catholics in general, has developed in recent decades a strikingly different approach to sexual morality. This new approach has abandoned the essentially suspicious view of sexuality associated with Catholicism, that is, the view that the most salient feature of sexuality was its location at the brink of temptation and sin. Within theological circles, justifying this more open approach to sexuality was an appeal to the experiences of the Catholic laity. Given the diversity of the Catholic laity, at times one might question the legitimacy of proliferating claims that nearly every theological innovation is truly rooted in the experience of the laity. But on matters of sexuality, especially in regard to the role of sex and birth control within marriage, it truly is the case that the American Catholic laity largely ignores the restrictions that Rome wants to enforce. And so the left is almost certainly much closer to the laity than is Rome.

I do not mean to imply here that there is unanimity on the Catholic left on sexual issues. First, I remind the reader that I discuss in this chapter only that segment of the Catholic left concerned primarily with sexual issues; other elements of the Catholic left (e.g., some groups concerned primarily with peace and economic justice issues) are not willing to reject the hierarchy's view of abortion, especially. And there are some theologians, for example, who consider themselves progressive on gender and sexuality issues in general but are critical of pro-choice Catholics.[39]

Still, for the most part (even among pro-life feminists), the American Catholic left that focuses on sexuality has turned away from a rule-bound model of morality concerned with defining exactly which actions constitute transgressions. The left is more likely to discuss morality as a call to full Christian love. With such an emphasis, morality becomes less a focus on whether specific acts are unambiguously good or bad, as the meaning of specific acts cannot simply be isolated from their context within Christian life and love.[40] As Timothy E. O'Connell argues, sin is not defined by the performance of specific acts but must be understood in terms of whether people, as full persons, are alienated from God. Sin is more the rejection of God through and in acts; it is not the acts themselves that are so central, but one's stance toward God and revelation.[41] "Humanity in the Bible is never seen as autonomous. It is always in relationship to God that people are viewed, their actions judged, and achievements evaluated."[42]

Charles E. Curran cites European writings in the 1950s, by theologians such as Josef Fuchs and Bernard Häring of the neo-Thomist school of theology, as the source of such a changed perspective within Catholic morality.[43]

This less suspicious view of sexuality, then, began in theological writings before Vatican II. When applied to specific sexual matters, before the 1970s the central focus was the ban on contraception. But ultimately, acceptance of birth control opened the door for a more positive view of sexuality in general, as evidenced, for example, in the career of Charles Curran. In a 1966 book, Curran noted that he recently had become convinced, via exposure to the experiences of married Catholics, that allowing only rhythm caused difficulties within loving marriages. While he had previously written of the dangers to marriage of "artificial" contraception and had touted the virtues of rhythm and the wisdom of the prohibition of other forms of birth control,[44] by 1964 he justified the need to alter the birth control teaching[45] on the basis of the development of doctrine. That is, doctrine based on false assumptions requires a rejection of the false assumptions, to reveal what has always been the truth.[46]

Thus by the mid-1960s we see in an influential moral theologian such as Curran the view that sexual morality should not be just a series of rigid prohibitions and that it should learn from the lived experience of the laity. Traveling further down this path, we see within the Catholic left today arguments that on such matters as abortion one has to trust the moral agency of Christians, meaning that it is legitimate for different Catholics to come to different moral conclusions. Thus, rigid application of natural law, with unambiguous condemnations of particular sexual acts, is inconsistent with this entire perspective.

Such a perspective—opposed simply to handing down one natural law interpretation of every sexual act, and appealing instead partly to the experiences of Catholics in diverse circumstances—has strongly influenced American Catholic theologians.[47] Thus, one of the first points that Timothy E. O'Connell makes in his survey of Catholic moral theology—one that draws upon the intellectual currents that have influenced the left's moral theology—is that biblical exegesis necessarily requires understanding the context within which Scripture was written, the prevailing literary symbols and conventions of the time, and so forth. Because people exist only in particular historical and cultural contexts, understanding what Scriptures mean necessarily means interpreting the context in which they were written and interpreting how they might apply to a very different context[48] in which, for example, the literal words of the Scriptures (which necessarily includes linguistic translation) have a different meaning and suggest different nuances than was true a century ago, or two millennia ago.

And because we are simply human beings, almost necessarily there will be some uncertainty and disagreement. "The one truly tragic thing would be to claim or exhibit unanimity before it is actually discovered, to accept common ways of speaking before they are truly understood, to proclaim common convictions before they are really affirmed."[49]

It is not difficult to see the way that conflicts with the Catholic right would emerge on questions of morality; one of the central targets of the American religious right, whether in Catholicism or another faith, is "situational ethics." From the point of view of the right, the significant feature of progressive Catholic sexual morality is that it is relativist and in conflict with Catholic orthodoxy as defined by the hierarchy: the right would argue that the left has indeed fallen down the slippery slope that began with rejection of *Humanae Vitae*. But while the very existence of a Catholic left ultimately owes a great deal to the hierarchy's rigid approach to sexual morality, the Catholic left does not see itself simply as dissenters. Amongst themselves, Catholics who emphasize a more contextually rich, less rule-bound view of morality have for several decades seen themselves as offering primarily a positive program of moral theology. Seeing their own intellectual origins in Thomism, they see themselves as continuing, not breaking with, Catholic moral tradition. But instead of emphasizing the external authority of the hierarchy, they emphasize the moral agency of Christians. Moral theology, or any theology, is not simply the province of magisterial experts. Thus, for example, Timothy O'Connell defines theology as the task of "reconstituting the inner meaning of revelation for successive audiences."[50] It follows from this definition "that all Christian believers are theologians. Inasmuch as all the members of the Church must, of human necessity, express to themselves the meaning of their inner experience of faith, they are involved in the theological enterprise."[51]

Morality, then, is not just a matter of avoiding specific, prohibited acts, but a positive Christian approach that includes, as O'Connell puts it, the active process of going the extra mile.[52] O'Connell notes, for example, that the concept of mortal sin should also be discussed in terms of what he calls "mortal acts of virtue." But he notes that, while the term "sin" is well known, "it is interesting that the Christian tradition has never generated a clear vocabulary for positive acts. . . ."[53] A central aim of this component of the Catholic left—that is, those Catholics objecting to the hierarchy's approach to sexuality—has, then, been to reject suspicion as a defining feature of Catholic views of sexuality. Instead they emphasize that part of the Christian tradition that sees sexuality as a divine creation, as something that is fundamentally good.[54]

NOTES

1. Not to say there have been no changes. For example, the prohibition of abortion from conception (rather than later in the pregnancy), implying certainty that ensoulment occurs at conception, is historically relatively recent. See Kristin Luker, *Abortion and the Politics of Motherhood* (Berkeley: University of California Press, 1984), pp. 12–13, 58–59. John T. Noonan, Jr., "An Almost Absolute Value in History" (pp. 1–59 in *The Morality of Abortion*, ed. Noonan [Cambridge, Mass.: Harvard University Press, 1970]), claims that there is long-standing precedent for Christian pro-life values, that is, that early Christians believed that killing of a fetus was sinful at any stage of gestation (pp. 10, 12, 15, 17). But, as Luker implies (pp. 12–13), Noonan also demonstrates that for most of Christian history it was assumed that a fetus did not at first have a soul, and thus early abortion was of lesser moral consequence, or perhaps even morally acceptable (Noonan, pp. 18, 20, 22–23, 26, 28–32, 34–36). In modern history, then, Catholic conviction that the soul begins with conception emerged in the nineteenth century, and was influenced by the mid-nineteenth-century proclamation of the immaculate *conception* of Mary (Noonan, pp. 38–40). Given that the immaculate conception was ultimately proclaimed as an infallible doctrine, this is an interesting, early example of doctrine on sexuality and reproduction being indirectly tied to ultramontanism.

2. Linda Gordon, *Woman's Body, Woman's Right: Birth Control in America*, rev. ed. (Harmondsworth, England: Penguin, 1990), pp. 93–96, 100–101, 107–109, 114.

3. Ibid., p. 479; James Reed, *The Birth Control Movement and American Society: From Private Vice to Public Virtue* (Princeton, N.J.: Princeton University Press, 1983), pp. 21–23; Viviana A. Zelizer, *Pricing the Priceless Child: The Changing Social Value of Children* (New York: Basic Books, 1985).

4. Carole R. McCann, *Birth Control Politics in the United States, 1916–1945* (Ithaca, N.Y., and London: Cornell University Press, 1994), pp. 43–44.

5. Gordon, *Woman's Body, Woman's Right*, pp. 387–388, 390–391.

6. Luker, *Abortion and the Politics of Motherhood*, pp. 54–94, 142–143; Raymond Tatalovich and Byron W. Daynes, *The Politics of Abortion: A Study of Community Conflict in Public Policy Making* (New York: Praeger, 1981), pp. 16–146.

7. Barry D. Adam, *The Rise of a Gay and Lesbian Movement* (Boston: Twayne, 1987), pp. 75–77.

8. From questions 26 and 27 of a CNN/USA Today/Gallup poll conducted in April 1997, and compared to data from March 1996 and June 1982. My thanks to Maura A. Strausberg, research librarian for The Gallup Poll, who kindly provided me with these data.

9. George Gallup, Jr., and Jim Castelli, *The American Catholic People: Their Beliefs, Practices, and Values* (Garden City, N.Y.: Doubleday, 1987), pp. 60, 63–64. Still, it seems Catholics might be more willing to accept someone's sexual orientation than the fact that they engage in homosexual acts. For example, a 1993 poll indicated that 66% of American Catholics thought one could vote for a candidate favoring legal abortion and still be a good Catholic; 51% thought one could have an abortion and be a good Catholic; but only 35% thought one could engage in homosexual acts and still be a good Catholic. This despite the fact that a majority of Catholics think homosexual acts should be legal and that homosexuals should have equal job rights.

Among Americans generally (regardless of religion), Gallup poll data suggest that acceptance of homosexuality has gradually increased over the last couple decades, but again with definite reservations. For example, in 1977 poll data found 56% of Americans supporting equal job rights for homosexuals; the figure went up gradually, reaching 80% in 1993. But, for example, also in 1993 a clear majority thought leaders of homosexual rights movements were pushing for change too fast. David Moore, "Public Polarized on Gay Issue," *The Gallup Poll Monthly*, no. 331 (April 1993), pp. 30–31.

10. I have made related, more detailed arguments in Burns, *The Frontiers of Catholicism: The Politics of Ideology in a Liberal World* (Berkeley: University of California Press, 1992).

11. Ibid., pp. 54–55, 63–65, 118, 120–122.

12. Lester R. Kurtz, *The Politics of Heresy: The Modernist Crisis in Roman Catholicism* (Berkeley: University of California Press, 1986).

13. The date for this encyclical is variously given as 1930 or 1931, the confusion perhaps following from the fact that its official date of issue was December 31, 1930.

14. Robert Blair Kaiser, *The Politics of Sex and Religion: A Case History in the Development of Doctrine, 1962–1984* (Kansas City: Leaven Press, 1985), p. 4.

15. Gallup and Castelli, *The American Catholic People*, p. 6.

16. C. Thomas Dienes, *Law, Politics, and Birth Control* (Urbana: University of Illinois Press, 1972), p. 151.

17. Kaiser, *The Politics of Sex and Religion*, pp. 17–30; Thomas C. Fox, *Sexuality and Catholicism* (New York: George Braziller, 1995), pp. 48–52.

18. On the commission, see Robert McClory, *Turning Point: The Inside Story of the Papal Birth Control Commission and How Humanae Vitae Changed the Life of Patty Crowley and the Future of the Church* (New York: Crossroad, 1995); and Kaiser, *The Politics of Sex and Religion*.

19. The report is reproduced in Daniel Callahan, ed., *The Catholic Case for Contraception* (New York: Macmillan, 1969), pp. 149–173; quotation, p. 159.

20. Fox, *Sexuality and Catholicism*, pp. 52–63.

21. Even a more recent supporter of the encyclical concedes that it "has unquestionably received more opposition than support." Janet E. Smith, *Humanae Vitae: A Generation Later* (Washington, D.C.: Catholic University of America Press, 1991), p. xiv.

22. For numerous examples of the disciplining of dissenters from *Humanae Vitae*, see John Seidler and Katherine Meyer, *Conflict and Change in the Catholic Church* (New Brunswick: Rutgers University Press, 1989), pp. 92–108.

23. See the Vatican's public chronology of the Hunthausen case and Hunthausen's response in *Origins*, 6 November 1986, pp. 361, 363–365; and the *New York Times*, 28 October 1986, 10, 11, and 15 November 1986, 30 January 1987, 28 May 1986, 13 and 25 April 1989.

24. Charles E. Curran, *Faithful Dissent* (Kansas City: Sheed and Ward, 1986), pp. 14–16, 33–35, 46–47.

25. Ibid., pp. 3, 30–36, 40–44, 46–47; Hickey quoted on p. 47.

26. Richard L. Smith, *AIDS, Gays, and the American Catholic Church* (Cleveland: Pilgrim Press, 1994), p. 45.

27. Jeannine Gramick and Pat Furey, "Introduction," in *The Vatican and Homosexuality*, ed. Gramick and Furey (New York: Crossroad, 1988), pp. xiii–xxi.

28. The "Letter to the Bishops of the Catholic Church on the Pastoral Care of Homosexual Persons" is reproduced in Gramick and Furey, eds., *The Vatican and Homosexuality*. Quotation here from p. 2.

29. Ibid., p. 2.

30. Quoted in Smith, *AIDS, Gays, and the American Catholic Church*, p. 51.

31. Ibid., pp. 51–52.

32. Ronald R. Burke, "*Veritatis Splendor*: Papal Authority and the Sovereignty of Reason," in *Veritatis Splendor: American Responses*, ed. Michael E. Allsopp and John J. O'Keefe (Kansas City: Sheed and Ward, 1995), pp. 119–136, quotation from p. 127. The emphasis is Burke's. For a more general discussion of the long-standing assumption that sexual sins were always grave sins, see Charles E. Curran, "Sexuality and Sin: A Current Appraisal," in *Readings in Moral Theology no. 8: Dialogue about Catholic Sexual Teaching*, ed. Curran and Richard A. McCormick (New York/Mahway, N.J.: Paulist Press, 1993), pp. 405–417.

33. See, e.g., *The Bitter Pill: Worldwide Reaction to the Encyclical Humanae Vitae*, ed. F. V. Joannes of IDO-C, trans. IDO-C (Philadelphia and Boston: Pilgrim Press, 1970), pp. 45–46.

34. Reproduced in *The Catholic Case for Contraception*, pp. 67–70.

35. See, for example, Rosemary Radford Ruether, "Catholics and Abortion: Authority vs. Dissent," in *Abortion and Catholicism: The American Debate*, ed. Patricia Beattie Jung and Thomas A. Shannon (New York: Crossroad, 1988), pp. 320–326; and various writings of Charles Curran, including *Faithful Dissent* and "Public Dissent in the Church," in *Abortion and Catholicism*, pp. 301–319.

36. It is interesting to note, for example, that a *National Catholic Reporter* editorial of 28 December 1984, p. 10, misinterpreted what the ad was actually claiming, not seeing the implicit point about ecclesiology. See also Burns, *The Frontiers of Catholicism*, pp. 153–154.

37. Since the time of *Roe v. Wade*, support for legal abortion among Catholics has increased a bit. According to Gallup polls, the proportion of American Catholics who support legal abortion under some but not all circumstances has stayed fairly constant at about half, while the proportion who support legal abortion no matter what the circumstances went from 21% in 1975 to 32% in 1993. Thus a large majority favors an abortion policy that the hierarchy condemns. Leslie McAneny and Lydia Saad, "Strong Ties between Religious Commitment and Abortion Views," *The Gallup Poll Monthly*, no. 331 (April 1993), p. 38.

It also interesting to note that in 1974 29% of American Catholics agreed that it would be a good thing to allow women to be ordained as priests; the figure has gradually increased so that, in 1993, it stood at 63%. George Gallup, Jr., *The Gallup Poll: Public Opinion 1993* (Wilmington, Del.: Scholarly Resources, 1994), p. 144.

38. Gallup and Castelli, *The American Catholic People*, p. 183.

39. See Sidney Callahan, "Abortion and the Sexual Agenda: A Case for Prolife Feminism," in *Abortion and Catholicism*, pp. 128–140; Lisa Sowle Cahill, "Abortion, Autonomy, and Community," in *Abortion and Catholicism*, pp. 85–97; and Denise Lardner Carmody, *The Double Cross: Ordination, Abortion, and Catholic Feminism* (New York: Crossroad, 1986).

40. Charles E. Curran, "Foreword" to Timothy E. O'Connell, *Principles for a Catholic Morality* (New York: Crossroad/Seabury, 1976), pp. ix–xii; Charles E. Curran, *Christian Morality Today: The Renewal of Moral Theology* (Notre Dame, Ind.: Fides Publishers, 1966), pp. 79–80.

41. O'Connell, *Principles for a Catholic Morality*, pp. 68–69.

42. Anthony Kosnik, William Carroll, Agnes Cunningham, Ronald Modras, and James Schulte, *Human Sexuality: New Directions in American Catholic Thought* (New York: Paulist Press, 1977), p. 2.

43. Curran, "Foreword" to O'Connell, *Principles for a Catholic Morality*, pp. ix–xi. See also O'Connell, pp. 18–19.

44. Curran, *Christian Morality Today*, pp. 51–53, 67.

45. Ibid., pp. 47, 57–59, 68–69; Curran, *Faithful Dissent*, pp. 10–11.

46. Curran, *Christian Morality Today*, pp. 73, 87–88.

47. For example, a 1977 volume very much reflecting this more open view of sexuality was published by the Catholic Theological Society of America (CTSA), the main professional organization of American Catholic theologians. The CTSA had commissioned a study of the topic in 1972, resulting in *Human Sexuality: New Directions in American Catholic Thought* (see note 42). CTSA officially "received" rather than endorsed the committee's report, but the organization did publish and hold the copyright for *Human Sexuality*, and so it is reasonable to presume that the report reflected views held by at least a substantial portion of the organization.

48. O'Connell, *Principles for a Catholic Morality*, p. 4.

49. Ibid., p. 211.

50. Ibid., p. 4.

51. Ibid., p. 5. O'Connell defines moral theology, specifically, as that part of theology that inquires how we ought to live, given God's gift of revelation (p. 6).

52. Ibid., p. 13.

53. Ibid., p. 71.

54. Curran, *Christian Morality Today*, p. 50; Kosnik et al., *Human Sexuality*, pp. 1, 4, 37, 80–81.

4

RESISTING TRADITIONAL
CATHOLIC SEXUAL TEACHING

Pro-Choice Advocacy and Homosexual
Support Groups

MARY JO WEAVER

Introduction

Roman Catholicism in a pluralistic world is continually tossed on the
horns of the assimilation dilemma: becoming too much like the surrounding culture threatens to erase Catholic distinctiveness, yet
continual stress on particularity can result in protective isolation and
social retardation. The Church—in both its institutional and congregational incarnations—has had to confront this conundrum throughout
its history, sometimes paying a high price for its specific views (per-
secutions) and other times diplomatically accepting the art of the
possible (church-state separation in the modern world). Whereas medieval popes could enforce uniformity of doctrine, practice, and behavior,[1] modern Church leaders have more often had to bend to a surrounding culture. In the Middle Ages, ecclesiastical authority virtually
covered the known world, and until the middle of the twentieth century, it was generally accepted by the faithful without dissent. David
Schultenover, writing about the Church's reaction to the turn-of-the-
century modernist crisis, argues that the Church exercises a "Mediterranean concept of authority . . . almost entirely defined in terms of the
right and power to command, enforce laws, exact obedience, deter-
mine and judge."[2]

Today, faithful Catholics disagree openly with Church teaching
against artificial contraception and raise questions about divorce,
abortion, and homosexuality.[3] The late twentieth century has been
characterized, in part, by open, public dissent against the magisterium

on these issues, which in turn has led to the serious disagreements that
have divided conservative and liberal Catholics, and also have sometimes divided left-wing Catholics from one another. Whatever their
disagreements, it is clear that left-wing Catholics experience two different forms of Church leadership (quasi-democratic and authoritarian), depending on whether the issues cluster around social justice or
sexuality. When the American bishops wrote pastoral letters about
nuclear war and economics, for example, they used a listening method
and a democratic style. They identified themselves as dialogue partners within a broad spectrum of cultural opinion, willing to work toward common ground. When the Church speaks on homosexuality or
abortion, however, its leaders tend to invoke an authoritarian style
that does not welcome differences of opinion. In matters of sexual politics, Church leaders see themselves as heralds of the truth.[4] Left-wing
Catholics tend to identify more readily with democratic process, dialogue, and a willingness to change, whereas right-wing Catholics are
more at home *as Catholics* in an authoritarian Church that guards and
preaches eternal truth. Perhaps those who dissent from Church teaching read the Vatican II phrase "people of God" through the eyes of
democracy as "we the people," whereas those who eschew dissent
understand "people of God" to define a set of believers who are in
obedient harmony with Church authority.

There are a number of contexts in which the differences between
progressive and conservative Catholics get articulated (the American
experience, feminism, Vatican II), none of which need to be rehearsed
here.[5] Suffice it to say, as Susan Ross points out in her essay, that they
tend to cluster around the role of experience in discerning and following Church teaching. There is an identifiable Catholic left on issues of
sexuality because, as Margaret Farley puts it, "here is perhaps a para-
digmatic instance of experience conflicting with received teaching in a
way that experience (one's own and others') calls tradition into serious question. Over time, critical reflection on experience has led many
Catholics not only to question but to dissent from and even to protest
traditional teaching regarding sexual moral possibilities."[6]

Dissent and Cultural Change

In the pre-conciliar Church, American Catholics accepted their roles in
a hierarchical system, neither desiring nor expecting a church structure that gave them any voice in its decisions. Since most of those decisions were doctrinal or, if political, usually aimed at European situations, there was no need to question them. At the same time, as
Catholics were assimilated into American society, they found themselves in a cultural environment where issues of sexual morality were

changing at a rather disconcerting pace. The birth control movement, for example, was a nineteenth-century phenomenon championed by feminists, labor leaders, and those concerned with overpopulation, but increasingly appealed to those aiming at upward social mobility. Urbanization, one outcome of immigration and economic growth, gave those with same-sex preference opportunities for anonymity and stimulated the emergence of social movements that would eventually become gay rights protests. The presence of women in the labor force gave lesbians freedom and mobility they had not previously enjoyed, and gave heterosexual women some power to lobby for safe and legal abortion. Although Catholics were part of these cultural shifts, they were slow to make the connections between those changes and their personal sexual lives. They were, after all, members of a church that celebrated consecrated virginity and celibacy as superior to marriage. It is fair to say that in official Church teaching sex was a problem to be avoided through either virginity or marriage, where marriage was understood as a remedy for concupiscence.

The first encounter between Catholics and the changing sexual climate of American culture was over birth control. We have already seen that Catholic hopes for a change in official policy about artificial birth control were squelched by *Humanae Vitae*, a papal encyclical that stimulated the largest and most serious movement of public dissent from Catholic teaching in the modern period. It is worth remembering that the statement of protest drafted by Charles Curran and originally signed by 87 (later 600) theologians took special aim at its underlying ecclesiology:

> The encyclical consistently assumes that the church is identical with the hierarchical office. No real importance is afforded the witness of the life of the church in its totality; the special witness of many Catholic couples is neglected; it fails to acknowledge the witness of the separated Christian churches and ecclesial communities; it is insensitive to the witness of many men and women of good will; it pays insufficient attention to the ethical import of modern science.[7]

According to protesters, therefore, in addition to the verdict of the pope and the methods used to arrive at that verdict, the major underlying issue was an ecclesiological one: the post-conciliar Church could not be identified with the pope or the hierarchy. In this reading, acceptance of the encyclical would have meant a rejection of the major thrust of the council.

Accepting the encyclical also would have meant accepting a patriarchal view of women, thereby rejecting their moral agency. Marie Vianney Bilgrien, expanding on Richard McCormick's judgment that the emergence of feminism is one of the revolutionary developments in moral theology in the last fifty years, summarized the feminist position. She noted that there are differences between men's and women's experience, that these differences are theologically and morally significant, and that the theological tradition has mainly been shaped by men's experience. "Women are expected to be the repositories and safeguards of morality. Yet when women try to extend their moral consciousness into the wider political or religious world, their femaleness becomes a detriment. The drafters of Church policy, in their teaching authority, assume that they know what is good for women because they assume that they know what is good for the human person always and everywhere."[8] Addressing the feminist point, Richard Miller took the birth control encyclical to task for its grammar of gender relations. Ironically, argues Miller, Paul VI's patriarchal ideology is most blatant in his paternalistic attempts to protect women. "Warnings against harming women trade on language in which *harm finds ideological legitimation,* namely, the idiom of male-as-culture, the center of creative power over instrumental feminine processes. . . . Paul VI's argument thus implodes by simultaneously seeking to protect the female while underwriting the cultural ideology with which sexual exploitation and violence find legitimation."[9]

These two issues—the ecclesiological one and the feminist one—are the grounds on which dissent over sexual issues began. Left-wing Catholics who challenge the Church's sexual teachings on homosexuality and abortion are not unanimous in their acceptance of feminism, nor do they all accept a progressive reading of the documents of the Second Vatican Council. At the same time, like feminists and progressives, they agree that dissent from Catholic sexual teaching is a necessary (if often painful) part of their Catholic identity. Reporters, students, and interested observers outside the Catholic Church often ask those who actively protest the Church's teaching on birth control, homosexuality, divorce, and abortion how they can claim to be Catholics in good standing. Why don't they just leave the Church? Although there are many answers to that question, the bottom line is usually an ability on the part of protesters to see a larger picture and to find life within it. They do not abandon the Church because they believe it to be more than its sexual teachings and hope to find within the tradition itself the grounds for their challenge. They believe that the moral life ought to make sense and that it can do so within the Catholic tradition.[10]

Catholic Dissent and Sexual Issues

Although a majority of American Catholics take a dissenting position in relation to Church teaching against artificial birth control, they are often not willing to accept the dissenting claims of homosexuals and pro-choice activists. What divides Catholics from one another in these matters is often the very thing that divides them from the hierarchy, the relative weight they give to their belief that God's revelation continues to unfold in human experience. This tenet of the Second Vatican Council[11] underlies the hope that Catholic tradition can change in the very areas that are presently most strenuously defended by the Vatican, i.e., on women's ordination, clerical celibacy, and a variety of sexual issues. In an article about homosexuality, New Testament scholar Luke Johnson suggested a method to confront the hermeneutical problem presented to the Church by same-sex relations. Accepting the traditional framework of ecclesial self-definition (the canon of Scripture, the rule of faith, and the teaching authority of the bishops), he argues that hermeneutics involves "the complex task of negotiating normative texts and continuing human experiences. Within the faith community, this means an openness to the ways in which God's revelation continues in human experience." This call to the discernment of human experience is not a call to carelessness. On the contrary, Johnson says, discerning God's revelation in human experience takes the "rigorous asceticism" of attentiveness. "An appeal to some populist claim . . . is theologically meaningless. What counts is whether *God* is up to something in human lives." The Catholic tradition discloses an astonishing God. As Johnson puts it: "God *does* act in surprising and unanticipated ways and upsets human perceptions of God's scriptural precedents."[12]

Margaret Farley argues that when the Church speaks on sexual issues, it uses a "contraceptive logic" that precludes change in Church teaching not only regarding contraception, but also about abortion, homosexuality, and even divorce and remarriage. Contraceptive logic means that there is a procreative ethic underlying Catholic sexual teaching: the Church can neither understand nor countenance venereal pleasure that is not open to procreation. If ordinary Catholics have rejected this logic in their own married lives, it continues to reside in their psyches. To put it another way, there is a strong link in the minds of many Catholics between sexuality and reproduction, or between sexuality and marriage. It is possible that negative reactions to homosexuality are rooted in the fear that homosexuals enjoy sexual pleasure with no possibility of procreation. Whatever the psychic links among these issues, the two clearest examples of left-wing Catholic dissent over sexual matters are abortion and homosexuality, and the main illustrative groups are Catholics for a Free Choice (CFFC) and Dignity.

CFFC challenges the magisterium on the contested points of sexual experience: they argue for the goodness of sexual pleasure apart from procreation; question the right of a celibate clergy to speak on issues about which they have no experience; highlight the complete eclipse of women's experience in Church teaching; and contest the territorial imperative of the word "Catholic." The newfound space for public activism since the middle of this century has opened a space for groups like CFFC, and tensions within the Catholic Church have led to a widening understanding of the word "Catholic": it is no longer the exclusive preserve of the Catholic bishops as it was before the council. Dignity is geared to a specific advocacy within the Catholic Church that, perforce, challenges the contraceptive mentality that lies behind church teaching on sexual issues.

Catholics for a Free Choice: Dissent in Feminist Terms

Catholics for a Free Choice (CFFC) was founded in the early 1970s, in a climate of women's rights, to defend the New York policy of legalized abortion. It grew into a national movement after *Roe v. Wade* made abortion a national option. In its early years, CFFC participated in some guerilla theater publicity-generating events and understood itself largely as a reactive group responding to episcopal initiatives. The existence of CFFC as an alternative was almost its whole story, and until 1976 CFFC operated from New York with no staff, no programs, and only periodic contact with other pro-choice organizations. It was "a national organization of Catholics dedicated to the principle that women have the right and the duty to follow their consciences regarding decisions on contraception and termination of pregnancy."[13]

In 1976, CFFC moved to Washington, secured a small grant, hired a part-time lobbyist, and initiated a publications program called "Abortion in Good Faith." By 1979, deciding that its strength lay in the power of ideas rather than in numbers, CFFC shifted its status from a lobbying group to that of an educational organization, a move that made it eligible for foundation grants. Frances Kissling, then director of the National Abortion Federation, became the executive director of CFFC in 1982. She brought three dimensions to the job: a strong support for women's rights (the ground on which the pro-choice movement stands); experience in women's health issues; and lifelong Catholicism with a strong interest in institutional change. Her staff and board of directors bring expertise in law, national politics, feminism, theology, and labor relations. Today, CFFC describes itself as a social justice organization that stands for the rights of women in both Church and society (nationally and internationally). It aims to shape and advance sexual and reproductive choices, women's well-being, and a respect for the moral capacity of women and men to make sound decisions about their lives. Though education and advocacy, it attempts to insert these values into public policy, community life, and Catholic social thinking and teaching.

With headquarters in Washington, D.C., CFFC is a non-profit, tax-exempt organization funded primarily by foundations. Its 1991 budget was $750,000 (compared to $15,000 twelve years earlier). Although it began as a one-issue organization rooted in freedom of conscience and feminist consciousness, CFFC has become a multi-issue organization interested in a nexus of women's questions, usually those related to control and power in the political arena. According to Kissling, abortion has "staying power" in the public arena because it is a significant political issue in health care, hospital mergers, elections, war (where rape and its aftermath seldom come to public attention), and foreign policy (questions of population and the environment). The last five United Nations conferences, whatever their main focus (the environment, for example), eventually dealt with abortion as a major issue. CFFC has been an articulate and annoying presence to the Vatican (a non-member state, permanent observer in the United Nations) at these conferences. CFFC has held national and international conferences—in Mexico City in 1992, for example—where it addressed the concrete situations of poverty and illiteracy faced by many of the world's women. Lisa Sowle Cahill, professor of theology at Boston College and a moderate on the abortion question, attended the Mexico City conference because she had detected "a growing reflectiveness about the complexity of abortion" in the leadership and publications of CFFC. The conference, she says, "began from a perspective of compassion toward women, especially poor women whose lack of options is compounded by culturally entrenched sexism."[14]

Because CFFC perceives abortion as a *political* issue, it is interested in the role of the Church in the political process. It should not be surprising, therefore, that its publication projects often aim at political confrontation. CFFC publishes a quarterly review, *Conscience: A Newsjournal of Prochoice Catholic Opinion,* with a mailing list of just over 10,000. Articles usually address abortion politics and practice, Vatican publications and actions, current books of interest, and feminist theology. As a feminist organization, CFFC focuses on how religious groups treat women and where they stand in the struggle for women's autonomy. Because many women struggle to maintain their feminism and their faith, CFFC believes the link between feminism and religion to be a critical one. Accordingly, *Conscience* publishes articles on feminist theology by Catholics, other Christians, Buddhists, Muslims, and Jews.

In the last few years, CFFC has increased its criticism of Vatican politics. In 1995, for example, it began a coordinated drive among international women's groups petitioning the United Nations to revoke the non-member state/permanent observer status of the Vatican. According to CFFC, the intractability of the Holy See on birth control, its attempts to hinder access to all family planning for all the peoples of the world (Catholic or not), its claim to represent a single Catholic voice, and its identity as a religious rather than a political organization disqualify it for voting membership in United Nations conferences. Determined to expose the links between the Vatican and right-wing groups, especially in Europe, CFFC has recently turned its attention to conservative Catholic groups in Europe: *Conservative Catholic Influence in Europe* (1997) was an investigative report about Opus Dei; *A New Rite: Conservative Catholic Organizations and their Allies* (1994) was written to expose a number of Church organizations linked with Vatican policies that CFFC considers repressive to women and reproductive rights.

As an educational organization interested in political issues, CFFC has published a number of small books (or booklets) addressing particular political issues from a perspective directly opposed to that of the Vatican. The CFFC *Guide for Prochoice Catholics* (1990) and *Everything You Always Wanted to Know about the Catholic Vote* (1996) were both aimed to bring pro-choice information to Catholic readers. According to these publications, poll after poll shows that most Catholics are pro-choice and that as voters, they do not follow their bishops. Using Time/CNN nationwide polls, Pew Research Center religious surveys, CBS/New York Times polling data, ABC/Washington Post polling results, and other survey data, CFFC claims to tell Catholics what their bishops will not tell them, namely that (1) most Catholics say that abortion should be legal; (2) this finding holds true across polls and over time; (3) Catholics believe abortion can be moral; (4) Catholic women have abortions; (5) Catholics follow their own consciences on birth control and abortion; (6) Catholics vote and believe that religion should not dictate politics; and (7) Catholics vote pro-choice.

The relationship between CFFC and women's groups inside and outside the Church identifies it as primarily a feminist organization. Kissling's tenure at CFFC began at a time when feminist consciousness had begun to be a fundamental part of many women's groups in the American Catholic Church. As Rosemary Ruether has shown in her chapter on Women-Church, groups like the National Coalition of American Nuns (NCAN), the Women's Ordination Conference (WOC), and the National Assembly of Religious Women (NARW), along with others, began to organize in order to be more effective agents of change within the Catholic Church. In 1982, CFFC and the Conference of Catholic Lesbians (CCL) were invited to Women-Church, but, because some groups in the convergence did not want to be associated with them, CFFC and CCL were asked to leave. They agreed to "go home" if the directors would allow them to address the board. After that executive meeting, CFFC and CCL were admitted to

Women-Church on the principle that all groups should be allowed to bring their perspectives into the discussion. The acceptance of CFFC into Women-Church compromised (or enraged) some member groups like the National Council of Catholic Women (NCCW) and the Women's Auxiliary of the Knights of St. Peter Claver, who themselves dropped out of Women-Church over this issue. As CFFC was progressively more "acceptable" to organizations of Catholic women, it began to put more of its own energy into the Catholic community. It sees itself, therefore, as a Catholic, feminist, pro-choice organization with a mission to oppose the latent anti-Catholicism of the secular pro-choice movement.

Although CFFC prides itself on being a *Catholic* alternative, it has been denounced by the National Conference of Catholic Bishops as having no official status within the Church. Nevertheless, CFFC continues to call itself Catholic, claiming not to represent Catholicism, but to address Catholics with alternatives to traditional teaching on sexual issues. CFFC has a history of having Catholic-trained, Catholic ethicists on its board in order to provide a thoughtful alternative to official Church teaching. For all its interest in theological education, however, CFFC is predominantly interested in politics, specifically, in confronting the role of the Church in the political process.

When asked to address the role of CFFC in the Catholic left, Kissling listed seven components of the Catholic left: *academic* (theologians); *establishment* (the old *Commonweal* crowd); *social justice and peace activists; feminists; Church reform groups* (usually those found in the new Call to Action); *spirituality groups; and left-wing bishops.* CFFC's firmest connections are with feminists and Church reform groups. In typical confrontational style, Kissling claimed that "the establishment crowd is the most conservative about abortion; they are no longer major players with national media or politicians because they have been replaced by CFFC and feminist organizations."[15]

One example of CFFC's ability to get a share of the national spotlight was its most famous media event: "A Catholic Statement on Pluralism and Abortion" was signed by 97 Catholic activists and theologians and published in the *New York Times* as a full-page ad on 7 October 1984. In its educational mission, CFFC had held a briefing, sponsored by Geraldine Ferraro and later published as a booklet, for Catholic members of the House of Representatives in 1982. That event set the stage for the 1984 public condemnation of Ferraro by New York archbishop John O'Connor when Ferraro ran for vice-president of the United States. The controversy between Ferraro and O'Connor was the immediate context for the *New York Times* ad, which generated an enormous controversy within the Church. Since twenty-six women belonging to fourteen different canonical groups signed the ad, it generated a maelstrom within many religious orders as well. The result of the ad and its aftermath gave CFFC a higher status level within pro-choice circles and within some segments of progressive Catholicism as well.[16]

In sum, CFFC is part of a pro-choice coalition that is increasingly involved in reproductive rights at the national and international level. It appeals to and is supported by progressive Catholics who believe that reproductive questions are moral decisions to be made by those involved in them. It is feminist dissent because it insists on women's moral agency and is willing to confront religious authorities in a variety of venues to press this point.

Dignity: Dissent around Sexual Pleasure

Homosexuals suffer discrimination in the face of the gospel, human decency, the American sense of equality, and the Church's teaching on justice. Before the Second Vatican Council, homosexuality was largely a silent subject in the Catholic Church. Although one can find material on "particular friendships" in the rules of religious orders, there was little official teaching about it. Like the gay/lesbian/bisexual subculture (GLB), itself, Church teaching was closeted.[17] The coming of the gay liberation movement in the summer of 1969 stimulated major changes in the ways in which GLB persons were perceived and led to initiatives that began to petition for their civil rights. In 1973 the American Psychiatric Association removed homosexuality from its list of pathological disturbances, followed in 1975 by a similar action on the part of the American Psychological Association. As homosexuality came out of the closet, it became a topic of scholarly concern, and religious thinkers began to reconsider its ethical and moral dimensions.[18]

In Catholicism as in other religious groups, one can usually find four different approaches to homosexuality: (1) based on natural law, Scripture, and the tradition of the Church, homosexual acts are always wrong; (2) homosexual acts are wrong, but homosexuals are often not fully responsible for their condition and sometimes for their behavior; (3) sexual acts ought to be judged on the basis of their relational significance; and (4) homosexual acts are natural and good. Each of these positions can be found in the Catholic Church, the first in official Church teaching, and the last in the mission statements of Dignity, a national Catholic lay movement for gay, lesbian, bisexual and trans-gendered Catholics (with their friends and families).

Several events stimulated Church leaders to publish a series of documents on homosexuality. In 1976, Jesuit priest John McNeill published his book *The Church and the Homosexual*, with the permission of his superiors. Nevertheless, he was told by the Vatican to remain silent on the issue, and complied with that directive for nearly a decade. In 1985, he spoke to a national meeting of Dignity about freedom of conscience. The Vatican again silenced him and told him that he might be asked to cease his ministry to gays and lesbians. When he refused to obey, he was expelled from the Jesuits and lost his right to exercise his priesthood.[19] Through the 1970s and into the 1980s, a group of Catholic activists in San Francisco argued that gay Catholic experience was a social justice issue.[20] In many areas of the country, priests were dealing with homosexuality in pastoral situations and asking for some compassionate guidance from their bishops.

Four documents can narrate the essence of the conflict between Catholic homosexuals and their church, two being moderate approaches by the American Catholic bishops, and two "clarifications" by the Vatican, written by Josef Cardinal Ratzinger. The relatively accepting language of the American bishops can be understood as a pastoral attempt to address an anguished situation, whereas the hard-line position of the Vatican can be understood as a reaction to the ways homosexual love opens the question of the meaning and morality of non-procreative sexual activity.

In 1976 the NCCB published a document to condemn prejudice against homosexuals: *To Live in Jesus Christ* distinguished between homosexual orientation (present at birth) and homosexual conduct (a responsible moral choice). According to the bishops, a homosexual orientation, in itself, is not sinful. This teaching, profoundly Catholic —insofar as it understood sinfulness in terms of actions rather than attitudes or inclinations—and genuinely pastoral fostered some cautious optimism among GLB Catholics because it seemed to open a discussion. As John McNeill had shown in his books, many Catholic homosexuals lived in despair, fearing exposure, feeling abandoned by God, and often drawn to suicide. *To Live in Jesus Christ*, not an endorsement of homosexuality by any means, was a pastoral outreach affirming the dignity of homosexuals.

One pastoral initiative that followed the bishops' letter was New Ways Ministry, founded in 1977 by Robert Nugent and Jeannine Gramick, a diocesan priest and a Sister of St. Joseph, both from Philadelphia and both interested in pastoral care for gays and lesbians. They began by speaking and writing about pastoral care for gays and lesbians, but soon became involved in political issues like gay rights bills, where they found their views opposed by local ordinaries. As Tom Fox summarized the situation, "what was emerging was a conflict between two components of the Catholic faith: a gospel-based call to compassion and a call to uphold traditional church teachings."[21] Conflicts between New Ways and official teaching led to reprimands. When New Ways sponsored a retreat for homosexual religious women in 1978, for example, and when it held a national symposium on homosexuality and the Catholic Church in 1981, Rome intervened. By 1985, Nugent and Gramick had been directed through their religious superiors to cease all clear and public association with New Ways Ministry. Although New Ways Ministry was not the specific stimulus for the Vatican document of 1986, it illustrates, perhaps, why Rome believed it necessary to write a document to clarify its position.[22]

Letter to the Bishops of the Catholic Church on the Pastoral Care of Homosexual Persons was signed by Joseph Cardinal Ratzinger on the first of October, 1986, nearly ten years after the document of the American Catholic bishops. If the earlier document had inspired a cautious optimism about dialogue or hope for change in the Church's understanding of homosexuality, the Vatican letter made it clear that nothing had changed and nothing would. Since homosexuality has become a matter of public debate, often advancing "arguments inconsistent with the teaching of the Catholic church," says Ratzinger, this letter will address those concerns. He reminds the bishops of a Vatican document of 1975 and notes that although it drew a distinction between homosexual orientation and homosexual activity, it insisted then (as it repeats now) that homosexual acts are "intrinsically disordered and able in no case to be approved of." In the discussion following the Vatican declaration of 1975, he notes, an "overly benign interpretation was given to the homosexual condition itself, some going so far as to call it neutral, or even good. Although the particular inclination of the homosexual person is not a sin, it is a more or less strong tendency ordered toward an intrinsic moral evil: and thus the inclination itself must be seen as an objective disorder." He explains this position in the light of creation (normative, married heterosexual love), and cites scriptural passages that appear to condemn it. He recognizes that this teaching may cause suffering, but appeals to the cross of Christ as a model of patient suffering. He urges the bishops to be caring of homosexual persons, but "cautious of any programmes which may seek to pressure the church to change her teaching. . . . Some of these groups will use the word 'Catholic,' . . . yet they do not defend and promote the teaching of the Magisterium . . . and should not have the support of the bishops in any way." Finally, he urges the bishops to "withdraw all support from organizations which seek to undermine the teaching of the Church . . . scheduling religious services . . . the use of church buildings . . . permission to use church property . . . is contradictory to the purpose for which these institutions were founded."[23]

In his discussion of the pastoral care of homosexuals, Ratzinger says that there can be "no organization in which homosexual persons associate with each other without clearly stating that homosexual activity is immoral." The general effect of this Vatican directive was the radicalization of groups like Dignity. This national Catholic lay movement was founded in Los Angeles under the leadership of Father Patrick Nidorf, and achieved national status in 1973. With offices in Washington, D.C., Dignity is the largest support group of its kind in the American Catholic Church, with approximately 3,000 paid members and nearly 10,000 people attending various liturgies, programs, meetings, and conventions. Like other protest groups within the Church, Dignity members originally hoped that they could effect change from within the Church if they maintained a non-confrontational profile. Accordingly, they kept a delicate balance: they met quietly in Catholic churches, celebrated liturgy together, worked on social justice and outreach issues, and served as an education forum and support system for homosexual Catholics.

After the 1986 letter from Cardinal Ratzinger to the bishops, Dignity changed its strategy in at least two ways. In a strong dissenting voice it began to affirm the goodness of same-sex relations (non-procreative sexual pleasure as a good thing) and it began to be more active as a protest group. The Ratzinger letter and a higher dissenting profile from Dignity members resulted in the expulsion of many local chapters from church property: Dignity members were forbidden to use Catholic retreat facilities and priests were forbidden to preside at Dignity Masses. Some priests began to refuse to give communion to known Dignity members. Timothy Healy, president of Georgetown University from 1976 to 1990, remembers the formal order he received from the archbishop in 1987 forbidding the Sunday Dignity Mass that had been celebrated for Georgetown's gay students for fifteen years. Looking back on that event, he says: "As I stood at the Georgetown altar and told 400 Catholics that the modality under which they gathered made it impossible for us to welcome them to a Sunday Mass, I had no knowledge of any sins, and the church does not define homosexual orientation as sinful. I also for the first time in my life as a priest felt that what I was doing at that altar was obscene."[24]

If the Vatican clarification of 1986 stimulated GLB Catholic protest, the Vatican clarification of 1992 galvanized a much broader community. The Ratzinger letter of 1986 was predicated on the Catholic tradition against any and all non-procreative sexual activity: the letter of 1992 seemed to rewrite the Catholic tradition.[25] In 1991, the American Catholic bishops published a pastoral letter, *Human Sexuality: A Catholic Perspective for Education and Lifelong Learning,* in which they said that homosexuals, like others, should not suffer from prejudice against their basic human rights. The bishops called upon Christians and citizens of goodwill "to confront their own fears about homosexuality and to curb the humor and discrimination that offends homosexual persons." Although features of this approach were echoed in a subsequent Vatican document, Cardinal Ratzinger again sought to clarify official teaching in a particularly negative way. As non-discrimination legislation was considered in state legislatures, the Vatican responded with *Some Considerations Concerning the Catholic Response to Legislative Proposals on the Non-Discrimination of Homosexual Persons* (1992), which encourages discrimination. "In some cities, municipal authorities have made public housing, otherwise reserved for families, available to homosexuals (and unmarried heterosexual) couples." Such initiatives condone the homosexual lifestyle, and "may in fact have a negative impact on the family and society," says Ratzinger. His fears were echoed two years later in the nervous hostility of the Ramsey Colloquium, an ecumenical group of conservative religious thinkers whose views were published in *First Things*, the American vanguard of Ratzinger's positions.[26] Since, Ratzinger argues, "the homosexual orientation is an objective disorder . . . there are areas in which is it not unjust discrimination to take [it] into account, for example, in the placement of children for adoption or foster care, in employment of teachers or athletic coaches, and in military recruitment." States can restrict the exercise of rights by homosexuals for the same reasons that they can do so in the case of "contagious or mentally ill persons, in order to protect the common good."

The groundswell of reaction to the 1992 Vatican document came not so much from gay activists as from the general Catholic community.[27] Critics noted the pejorative stereotyping of homosexuals and said that the Congregation for the Doctrine of Faith (CDF) was "guilty of encouraging the violence of injustice."[28] Writers raised pastoral issues, especially about gay adolescents; noted that the Church's traditional arguments for the absolute immorality of all gay sexuality are increasingly unconvincing to many people; defended gay politics on a pastoral basis; urged the Church to take the role of a dialogue partner; and called for Catholic clergy and laity to come out of the closet. Bishops, priests, theologians, pastoral counselors, and others rejected the document as unfair, counterproductive, and lacking in compassion. One bishop, Thomas Gumbleton, rejected it altogether.

One of the most interesting responses to Church teaching on homosexuality came from Andrew Sullivan, a young, theologically conservative Englishman who became the editor of *The New Republic*. In his book, *Virtually Normal*, he says that he saw the Vatican making some concessions in the 1986 letter, concessions that led him to hope for dialogue. His book, an outline of a new politics to deal with the homosexual question as a public policy issue, argues for inclusion of gays in the military and the homosexual marriage.[29] His argument turns, as do many of the ones cited above, on the dissonance between his experience and official Church teaching. "As soon as I allowed myself to love someone—all the constructs the church had taught me about the inherent disorder seemed just so self-evidently wrong . . . my own moral sense was overwhelming." He says that many homosexuals "want desperately to have a life that can be spiritually and morally whole. The church as presently constituted refuses to grapple with this desire."[30] Sullivan's love for Catholicism and his acceptance of his homosexuality force him to twist himself into a pretzel in order to fit into the Church.

Homosexuality has become a topic of national dialogue for mainstream theologians and Catholic thinkers. The Fourth National Symposium held in 1997 by New Ways Ministry featured distinguished moral theologians (Margaret Farley), bishops (Thomas Gumbleton and Matthew Clark), Catholic columnists (Sydney Callahan), and religious leaders (Joan Chittister). New Ways Ministry has the endorsement and support of national and regional groups of American priests, sisters, brothers, social justice ministries, and educational associations. This support says something about the way homosexuality is perceived in progressive sectors of American Catholicism, i.e., as a cause for justice and as a moral issue on which there is a wide-ranging disparity between Church teaching and personal experience.

Paradoxically, although New Ways Ministry gathered a distinguished group of Catholics to talk about homosexuality, it did not feature many homosexuals on the program. To find groups that speak *for* GLB Catholics, one must turn to Dignity and the Conference of Catholic Lesbians (CCL). Once gay groups were no longer permitted to use Church facilities (after the 1986 Ratzinger letter), Dignity started working more assiduously with grassroots organizations, finding issues where they could pool resources and work together with other GLB groups. Meetings and profiles of regional Dignity groups differ, but it is safe to say that for many years Dignity has been a locus of transitional ministry: GLB people who are coming out, or are in need of help integrating sexuality and spirituality, turn to Dignity chapters to help them. Once comfortable with themselves as GLB Catholics, they often move on. Others stay around, finding in Dignity, itself, a place of spiritual sustenance and vital ministry.[31] Dignity, a predominantly male group, has a counterpart in the Conference of Catholic Lesbians, founded in 1983. CCL publishes a quarterly newsletter, *Images*, and is informed by a feminist perspective that is generally invisible in Dignity. Since most CCL members believe the feminist issues are as important as GLB ones, they are more inclined than Dignity to make common cause with CFFC.[32]

GLB protest groups in American Catholicism share with CFFC a profile of dissent against certain parts of Catholic sexual teaching. Dignity distinguishes itself from other GLB groups within the Catholic

Church by its understanding of the essential goodness of sexually active homosexual relationships.[33] "Our experience and our faith tell us that sex is good and that our unions are as holy as other unions," says Dignity's president, Mary Ann Duddy. "This is pretty radical: we marry people, baptize their kids, mourn their break-ups. Sometimes with priests. Sometimes with the blessing of the community."[34]

Dignity makes a radical move in its positive acknowledgment of non-procreative sex. When it began to protest Vatican teaching and policy, Dignity consciously used the words Vatican II used about marriage, and claimed that gay people can be physically active in a way that is "unitive, live-giving, and life-affirming." Many fair-minded people in contemporary American Catholicism protest Vatican teaching about homosexuality in justice terms. Dignity dissents on those grounds and adds a voice about sexual pleasure, thus challenging the bottom line of Catholic sexual ethics, that there can be no sexual pleasure that is not open to reproduction.

Conclusion

Mapping progressive Catholic responses to official sexual teaching is most effective in relation to controversies around abortion and homosexuality. Birth control and, increasingly, divorce and remarriage are pastorally acceptable choices in American Catholicism. When survey data indicate overwhelming rejection of official Church teaching against artificial birth control and growing support for an option for divorce within Catholicism, it suggests that American Catholics trust their experience more than Church teaching in these matters. Abortion and homosexuality may have less popular support because they are typically vicarious experiences: most Catholics have not had an abortion, but they know someone who has; and most Catholics are not homosexuals, but they know someone who is. These "someones" are often friends or members of their families whose struggles have disclosed painful choices and called for compassionate response.

It is clear, as evidenced by the presence of conventional writers in mainstream Catholic journals of opinion, that there is a significant and growing protest against official Catholic teaching even in these sensitive areas. One does not have to be a homosexual to find the Vatican documents on homosexuality reactionary and mean-spirited. Neither does one have to have had an abortion to appreciate the ways in which CFFC challenges Catholic sexual teachings by paying particular attention to the voices of women, especially poor women. Abortion and homosexuality, as locations of protest against traditional Church teaching on sexuality, highlight the crucial nature of experience in the minds of liberal Catholics.

Why have CFFC and Dignity been able to attract the attention of contemporary theologians and commentators who, with them, are willing to work toward pragmatic strategies for legal and moral consensus within American pluralistic society? Why are abortion and homosexuality the two most active venues of Catholic protest against traditional Catholic sexual teaching? It is reasonable to conclude that liberal Catholics, with their understanding of experience as a location of continuing revelation and discernment, see the Church in terms of larger possibilities than those defined by CDF. In their efforts to make some common cause with CFFC and Dignity, and in their willingness to accept those groups as "Catholic," liberal Catholics show a willingness to accept the claims of people whose experience is, in key areas, unlike their own. Their openness to God's design unfolding in the present moment makes them idealists whose reading of the Second Vatican Council is more hopeful and less self-interested than that of the Vatican.

NOTES

1. R. I. Moore, *The Making of a Persecuting Society* (Oxford: Blackwell, 1987), shows that the period from 950 to 1250, when the Church consolidated its power, was also the time when the isolation, repression, exile, and attempted extinction of Jews, heretics, lepers, and homosexuals were perfected as policy.

2. *A View from Rome: On the Eve of the Modernist Crisis* (Bronx: Fordham University Press, 1993). For a short presentation of this argument see his article "The Church as Mediterranean Family" in *America* (8 October 1994), pp. 9–13.

3. James D. Davidson, et al., *The Search for Common Ground: What Unites and Divides Catholic Americans* (Fort Wayne, Ind.: Our Sunday Visitor Press, 1997), suggests that the major fault line running through the American Catholic Church is age: the beliefs and attitudes of the younger (under 50) generation differ significantly from those of older Catholics. Although there is no division about doctrine and creed, there are serious disagreements with the Church over leadership, priesthood, and moral teaching about sexual issues.

4. Richard L. Smith, "Gays and Bishops: Searching for Common Ground," *America* 171 (24 September 1994), pp. 12–17, identifies these two modes of hierarchical operation and asks how the Church is to conduct itself within a post-modern, pluralistic United States. Should Church leaders take the role of a dialogue partner or become the herald of truth? Smith's question is one way to look at the assimilation dilemma: dialogue presupposes a willingness to change one's mind, whereas the herald modality preaches to the choir. Each is risky.

5. Jay Dolan, *The American Catholic Experience* (New York: Doubleday, 1985), argues that there is a discernible *American* Catholic tradition that ran parallel to Romanism in the colonial period, was supplanted largely during the nineteenth century by Romanization, but stayed alive in the Americanist/modernist controversies at the turn of the century and re-emerged in the years

leading to the Second Vatican Council. In my book *New Catholic Women: A Contemporary Challenge to Traditional Religious Authority*, rev. ed. (Bloomington: Indiana University Press, 1995), I chart the movements that galvanized around the historical coalescence of the Second Vatican Council and a re-emerging women's movement in the second half of the twentieth century. Giuseppe Alberigo, Jean-Pierre Jossua, and Joseph A. Komonchak, in *The Reception of Vatican II* (Washington, D.C.: Catholic University Press, 1987), look at Catholicism twenty years after the council as a search for identity in a post-Tridentine Church. Americanism, feminism, and the reception of Vatican II are all issues that tend to divide Catholics along a conservative/progressive spectrum.

6. Unpublished "Response Statement" prepared by Margaret A. Farley for discussion at the Lilly Conference on Catholicism and Issues of Sexuality, February 1997.

7. "Statement by Catholic Theologians, Washington, D.C., July 30, 1968," in Charles Curran and Richard McCormick, eds., *Readings in Moral Theology, No. 8* (New York: Paulist Press, 1993), p. 135.

8. "The Voice of Women in Moral Theology," *America* 173 (16 December 1995), pp. 13–20, quotation from p. 19. For a feminist theological analysis of Catholic sexual teaching and women's bodies see Susan A. Ross, "The Bride of Christ and the Body Politic: Body and Gender in Pre–Vatican II Marriage Theology," *The Journal of Religion* 71 (1990), pp. 345–361.

9. "Popular Catholicism, *Humanae Vitae* and Ideology in Casuistry," in *Casuistry and Modern Ethics: A Poetics of Practical Reasoning* (Chicago: University of Chicago Press, 1996), pp. 129–153, quotation from p. 145. Miller says that the real flaw of the encyclical is that it lacks the self-reflexivity necessary to resist a patriarchal ideology, i.e., it rejects the notion that women are moral agents.

10. When Catholic natural law tradition, for example, is understood as a *method* based on some optimism about human reason and a commitment to take account of new scientific knowledge, people's experience, and other data, it can accommodate change. In addition, some moral theologians have questioned the body/soul dualism on which traditional sexual teachings are based. For example, Christian Gudorf has reconstructed sexual ethics in terms of mutuality, perceiving pleasure as a grace. See *Body, Sex, and Pleasure: Reconstructing Christian Sexual Ethics* (Cleveland: Pilgrim Press, 1994). In chapter two, "Ending Procreationism," she argues that the procreative mentality is the real problem in contemporary sexual ethics.

11. "Dei Verbum," the Dogmatic Constitution on Divine Revelation, can be interpreted in this way. Although no new "public" revelation is to be expected before the return of Christ, the spirit leads us into all truth. In paragraph six it says, "By divine revelation God wishes to manifest and communicate himself and the eternal decrees of his will." Those words suggest that God's self-communication is not just propositions or decrees, i.e., there may well be an unknown or at least not yet pinned-down dimension to revelation. In paragraph eight, it says, "the tradition that comes from the apostles makes progress in the church with the help of the Holy Spirit. There is a growth in insight into the realities and words that are being passed on. . . . the church is always advancing toward the plentitude of divine truth." Our response to the living God, and the continuing presence of the Spirit in the Church make it possible to speak of a continuing revelation.

12. "Debate & Discernment, Scripture & The Spirit," *Commonweal* (28 January 1994). Pursuing the demand to negotiate normative texts in light of con-

tinuing human experiences, Johnson says, shows us that "for many persons the acceptance of their homosexuality *is* an acceptance of creation as it applies to them."

13. Some of my information on the history of CFFC comes from Mary Segars, "The Loyal Opposition: Catholics for a Free Choice," in Timothy A. Byrnes and Mary C. Segars, *The Catholic Church and the Politics of Abortion* (Boulder, Colo.: Westview Press, 1992), pp. 169–184.

14. "Abortion, Sex and Gender: The Church's Public Voice," *America* 168 (22 May 1993), pp. 6–11. Cahill was invited to Mexico City as a token "pro-life" presence. Several months later she was invited to an abortion debate at St. Louis University where she was the token "feminist" and on the "far left" end of the group spectrum. Her paper in St. Louis, she says, "was the only one to build considerations of equality for women into the moral picture of abortion."

15. Interview with Frances Kissling in the context of the "What's Left" seminar on sexuality issues, 14 February 1997.

16. For more on the controversies over this ad, especially in the lives of the twenty-four sisters who were told by the Vatican to recant or leave their religious communities, see Mary Hunt and Frances Kissling, "The New York Times Ad: A Case Study in Religious Feminism," *Journal of Feminist Studies in Religion* 3 (1987), pp. 115–127. For a first-person account of that drama, see Barbara Ferraro and Patricia Hussey, *Two Nuns Battle with the Vatican over Women's Right to Choose* (New York: Poseidon Press, 1990). For a thoughtful analysis of this issue in the lives of many of the other sister signers, see Anne E. Patrick, *Liberating Conscience: Feminist Explorations in Catholic Moral Theology* (New York: Continuum, 1996), pp. 102–133.

17. The first attempt to change societal attitudes in Anglo-Saxon countries took place because an Anglican priest, Derrick Sherwin Bailey, a member of the Church of England Moral Welfare Council in 1950, got people interested in legal reform for homosexuals. In 1955 he published *Homosexuality and the Western Christian Tradition*, which, along with his political work, led to the formation of the Wolfenden Committee in Parliament. Their report (1957) recommending decriminalization of private homosexual conduct was finally passed into law in 1967.

18. The most comprehensive historical study was that of John Boswell, *Christianity, Social Tolerance, and Homosexuality: Gay People in Western Europe from the Beginning of the Christian Era to the Fourteenth Century* (Chicago: University of Chicago Press, 1980). For a sense of the early literature on this issue, see Tom Horner, *Homosexuality and the Judeo-Christian Tradition: An Annotated Bibliography*, American Theological Library Association Bibliography Series 5 (London: Scarecrow Press, 1981), which contains 459 entries of books, articles, and pamphlets, along with eleven other bibliographies containing thousands of entries.

19. *The Church and the Homosexual* (Boston: Beacon Press, 1976) is now in a fourth edition and considered a classic. *Taking a Chance on God* (Boston: Beacon Press, 1988) is a pastoral approach to homosexuality that shows GLBs how they can have lives of integrity (and sexual lives) in the Catholic tradition. *Freedom, Glorious Freedom* (Boston: Beacon Press, 1995) is the most recent statement of (now, former priest) McNeill's "good news" of God's love for homosexuals. In this book he makes an explicit appeal to "freedom in the spirit," a tenet of mature spirituality.

20. *Homosexuality and Social Justice: Reissue of the Report of the Task Force on Gay/Lesbian Issues, San Francisco*, rev. ed. (San Francisco: The Consultation on

Homosexuality, Social Justice, and Roman Catholic Theology, 1986). This document was originally published in 1982. In the 1980s, several books appeared raising questions about traditional Catholic (and Christian) teaching about homosexuality, notably *Homosexuality and Ethics*, ed. Edward Batchelor, Jr. (New York: Pilgrim Press, 1980); *Homosexuality and Religion*, ed. Richard Hansby (New York: Harrington Park Press, 1989); and *Homosexuality in the Church: Both Sides of the Debate*, ed. Jeffrey S. Siker (Louisville: John Knox/ Westminster Press, 1994).

21. *Sexuality and Catholicism* (New York: George Braziller, 1995), p. 137. Fox's thesis is that the primary right-left spectrum in the American Catholic Church is shaped by sexual morality. His book deals with abortion, homosexuality, women and the Church, birth control, clergy and sex abuse, carnal love, celibacy, and population control, all neuralgic issues within contemporary American Catholicism.

22. In 1975 the Vatican had published a "Declaration on Certain Questions Concerning Sexual Ethics," in which it stressed the duty of trying to understand homosexual persons. That document noted the distinction between homosexual orientation and homosexual acts, but described homosexual acts as "intrinsically disordered," something the American bishops did not say in *To Live in Jesus Christ*.

23. Sacred Congregation for the Doctrine of the Faith, "Letter to the Bishops of the Catholic Church on the Pastoral Care of Homosexual Persons" (London: The Catholic Truth Society, 1986). For a response to this letter see *The Vatican and Homosexuality*, ed. Jeannine Gramick and Pat Furey (New York: Crossroad, 1988).

24. "Probity and Freedom on the Border: Learning and Belief in the Catholic University," *America* 163 (7 July 1990), pp. 5–11, quotation from p. 11.

25. John F. Tuohey, "The C.D.F. and Homosexuals: Rewriting the Moral Tradition," *America* 167 (12 September 1992), pp. 136–138. Tuohey says that the document calls for direct discrimination without presenting any proportionate reason that might justify it.

26. "The Homosexual Movement: A Response by the Ramsey Colloquium," which appeared in *First Things* 41(March 1994), pp. 15–20, is a statement signed by twenty-one Jewish and Christian men asserting the "heterosexual norm" and explaining the logic of "a reflexive recoil from what is wrong." The statement was excerpted and published in *The Wall Street Journal* on 24 February 1994, p. A20. The general impression one gets about homosexuality from this statement is that homosexuals are predatory, sinful people who prey upon the young and whose very existence is a threat to the common good. The future of the family requires protection from such people.

27. See Paul Giurlanda, "What About Our Church's Children?" *America* 168 (8 May 1993), pp. 12–14; James L. Nash, "A Monologue on Dialogue," *Commonweal* (24 March 1995), pp. 22ff; David S. Toolan, "In Defense of Gay Politics: Confessions of a Pastoralist," *America* 173 (23 September 1995), pp. 18–21; Richard L. Smith, "Gays and the Bishops: Searching for Common Ground," *America* 171 (24 September 1994), pp. 12–17; Tom Roberts, "Bishop Wants Clergy, Laity Out of the Closet," *National Catholic Reporter*, 21 March 1997, p. 9. For a comprehensive look at these and other writings, see *Voices of Hope: A Collection of Positive Catholic Writings on Gay and Lesbian Issues*, ed. Jeannine Gramick and Robert Nugent (New York: Center for Homophobia Education, 1995).

28. Tuohey, "The C.D.F. and Homosexuals," p. 138.

29. New York: Alfred A. Knopf, 1995.

30. "I'm Here: An Interview with Andrew Sullivan," *America* 168 (8 May 1993), pp. 5– 11, quotations from p. 6.

31. My information about Dignity comes from an interview with its president, Mary Ann Duddy (November 1996). Some early Dignity groups tended to remain at the navel-gazing stage, she said, but increasingly there are chapters that are also very involved in local social justice issues. The Boston chapter, for example, has been running a Friday night food program for the homeless for the past fifteen years.

32. My information about CCL comes from an interview with Christine Nusse, one of the founders. In addition to CCL and Dignity, there are groups like Communications Ministry Inc. (CMI), which is for gay and lesbian members of religious orders, who must be more protective about their homosexual identity and therefore less visible than they would be in Dignity or CCL. Sisters in Gay Ministry Associated (SIGMA) is another such group. It should be noted that the Vatican distinction between a homosexual orientation and a choice on whether to act on it does not always describe lesbian experience. "God made me gay" is only one perspective on this complex issue. What emerges from lesbian feminists is the thought that maybe God made human beings a good deal more unprogrammed than previously imagined, able to be responsive to sexual delight in a number of situations. Lesbians tend to believe there is a *choice* in the matter.

33. I am ignoring the ethical issues that gather around sexual relationships (homosexual and heterosexual), specifically around the tension between mutuality and "natural and good" understandings of sex. Controversies about normative sexual ethics have a place within a discussion of homosexuality. See Lisa Sowle Cahill, *Sex, Gender and Christian Ethics* (Cambridge, U.K.: Cambridge University Press, 1996). Also, *Feminist Ethics and the Catholic Moral Tradition*, ed. Charles E. Curran, Margaret E. Farley, and Richard A. McCormick (New York: Paulist Press, 1996). Finally, Christien E. Gudorf, *Body, Sex, and Pleasure: Reconstructing Christian Sexual Ethics* (Cleveland: Pilgrim Press, 1994).

34. Interview with Mary Ann Duddy; see note 31.

Part 3

ACADEMIC THEOLOGY

5

ACADEMIC THEOLOGY

Why We Are Not What We Were

MARY ANN HINSDALE AND JOHN BOYLE

Academic theology, distinct from its popular counterpart, embraces the work of professional theologians who teach and write in a variety of institutional settings. As is the case with American Catholicism in general, its theologians occupy a spectrum of widely diverse opinions. Since pluralism—a word used disparagingly by conservatives and proudly by liberals—is a hallmark of left-wing Catholic theology, this chapter will describe the major factors that contributed to its dominance, and describe the ways in which theology has changed since the Second Vatican Council. In many ways, new social locations of theologians have led to the creation of competing theological cultures within the American Church. We will describe some of the groups of theologians that are either liberal or perceived by conservatives to be on the left wing of Catholic thought.

Liberal Catholic theology has experienced three significant shifts in the post-conciliar period, changes that have rooted academic theology in historical consciousness, in the acceptance of experience as a legitimate source for theological reflection, and in the use of critical theory. In shifting from a classical consciousness to a historical one, liberal Catholic theologians bring a modern sensibility, including a "hermeneutics of suspicion," to the sources and questions of theology.

Historical Consciousness

The development of historical consciousness among liberal theologians can be generally attributed to a felicitous combination of factors. The Enlightenment's philosophical "turn to the subject" undermined the notion of a divine, supernatural revelation operating independently of human reason. German Protestant attention to biblical texts

using methods and insights derived from philology, literary criticism, and archeology made it impossible to read a scriptural text or a
traditional teaching literally or in a simplistic way. The application of
Darwin's evolutionary hypothesis to the development of doctrine
suggested that traditional measures of truth—as ubiquitous and constantly held positions—needed some revision. Finally, the explicit rejection of monarchies in favor of republican or democratic governments put the Vatican in a politically awkward position. Frightened
by these events, which they believed led directly to the excesses of the
French revolution, nineteenth-century popes—Pius IX and Leo XIII—
staunchly resisted these currents and anchored the Church in a rigidly
apologetic and ahistorical neoscholasticism. And yet, despite blanket
condemnations of modern thought in Pius IX's *Syllabus of Errors* (1864)
and the anti-modernist statements of Pius X in *Lamentabili sane exitu*
(1907) and *Pascendi dominici gregis* (1907), theological research continued—albeit in an underground fashion—in the guise of historical research, or philosophy. Ironically, the very neo-Thomism that Leo XIII
trusted to ward off modernity and pluralism may have contained the
seeds of pluralism within itself.

In *Being Right,* Benedict Ashley described three schools of Thomistic thought operative in the early twentieth century.[1] He identified
the existentialist school with Etienne Gilson (who still influences contemporary conservative Catholic theology), the transcendental school
with Joseph Maréchal (who influenced the work of Karl Rahner, Bernard Lonergan, and their students), and the Aristotelian school with
Jacques Maritain. Ashley argued that although this variety among
Thomistic scholars was not censured by the Church, we should not
conclude that all their interpretive trajectories have equal validity. Indeed, in Ashley's judgment, precisely because the "more reliable"
Thomists failed to respond to the needs of contemporary culture, theology inherited the deplorable pluralism that has become a hallmark
of post-conciliar Catholic thought. If the fractures within Thomism
were the culprits in this adventure, they were also the victims: pluralism replaced neoscholasticism with such speed and completeness that
Thomism virtually disappeared as a staple of academic theology.

But if Ashley attributes the collapse of a supposed unitary system
in Catholic theology to the fact that Thomism was badly served by its
own proponents, Gerald McCool, S.J., believes that tensions internal
to Thomism itself inexorably led from unity to pluralism.[2] According
to McCool, the tensions within the overall system of Thomism—represented by the work of Pierre Rouselot and Joseph Maréchal—eventually led to the "transcendental Thomism" of Rahner and Lonergan.
Likewise, Jacques Maritain developed the Thomist tradition in a manner that exercised great influence for a time, but eventually proved

inadequate to the theological needs of the post–World War II period. Finally, the historical research of Etienne Gilson also revealed that the philosophy and theology of the scholastics was not as uniform as had been thought.

Whether theological pluralism can be found along the fault lines of early-twentieth-century Thomism or not, historical consciousness has become one of the hallmarks of contemporary academic theology. Those who approach texts, traditions, doctrines, or ethics typically enlist the help of contextual, philological, political, and historical critics to understand the embedded complexities of a specific teaching. When theologians ask to whom a text or teaching was addressed, or ask what it was supposed to accomplish when it was written, they relativize that text or teaching: it may be true, but not categorically true. Put another way, texts and traditions were shaped by a complex set of circumstances including ethnicity, politics, gender, economics, language, and rhetorical intention. Historical consciousness, therefore, disturbs conservatives because of its power to de-essentialize doctrines, credal formulas, or moral teachings.

Experience as a Source for Theology

In a reflection she used for one of the first meetings of the What's Left group, Susan Ross explained experience as a theological source. It is, she said, a source in the sense in which authority is found in the self-understanding of an individual or a community as it relates to the texts and traditions of the faith, but also as it places those sources in critical dialogue with contemporary events. Experience tests the relevance of the texts and traditions to the present. Although this stress on experience is grounded theologically in *Gaudium et spes* (with its emphasis on the integrity of the modern world) and in *Dignitatis humanae* (which recognized the integrity of other religious traditions) it did not originate at Vatican II. One needs, for example, to review the influence of the neo-Thomists and their stress on the relative autonomy of the world and of academic disciplines. Still, to put it quite broadly, *Gaudium et spes* suggested that the faithful could "trust their experience" and that their knowledge of the world was a positive resource for the Church.

Ross's assessment suggests both the power and the legitimacy of experience as a theological source. Although it is not possible here to pursue in detail the implications of this move in modern theology,[3] it is clear that the appeal to experience is a hallmark of liberal Catholic theology. Such a claim seems to ignore the Church's objections against modernism that were made at the beginning of the twentieth century. Indeed, one of the chief criticisms of liberal theology by conservative

Catholics is that it has capitulated to modernism or reinvented it in a host of contemporary theologies. Since conservatives seem to have history on their side, they appeal to it to argue that ascetical theology has always cautioned against trusting personal experience. The Church, in other words, has never taken kindly to experience as a datum of theology. Liberal theologians, however, argue that revelation and the inspiration of the Holy Spirit can be discerned *only* from within human experience. Their position is grounded on Vatican II's definition of the Church as the people of God (*Lumen Gentium*), and it is consonant with an empowered laity whose experience, according to the council, must be considered along with that of the ordained as the Church moves forward in history.

In stressing the charismatic as well as the institutional element of the Church, liberal theologians point to the Church's own realization of the need to reflect on lived experience as a source for the renewal and strengthening of the Church.[4] For example, we can point to the appeal made to the experience of married Christians in the discussion of acceptable ways of preventing pregnancy prior to *Humanae vitae* and in the critical way in which the encyclical was received by many lay men and women. The experience of marriage became an ingredient of the decisions of conscience made by married couples in the light of the papal teaching. In the decades since 1968 other issues of sexual morality, such as abortion and homosexuality, have been dealt with in Church teaching documents, to be met with similar appeals to the experience of Christians in the formation of the believer's conscience. Another example of the conflicts that can arise from using experience as a starting point for theological reflection comes from women who feel a clear call to priestly ordination. Although the discipline of the Church—indeed, a teaching that has been declared to reside in the deposit of faith—holds that the Church has no authority to ordain women as priests,[5] the experience of women with vocations and the experience of a Church with a severe priest shortage push toward changes in Church teaching.

Appeals to experience raise serious theological questions involving the nature and authority of revelation, the nature and rules of biblical interpretation, and the status of tradition and authoritative Church teaching. The questions are not new, but they remain unresolved and so remain as a continual irritant. As the questions raised by John Henry Newman more than a century ago (in his book *On Consulting the Faithful in Matters of Doctrine*[6]) remain open, theologians willing to accept the value of experience are in a stand-off with Vatican officials who believe in unchanging doctrine, clear lines of authority, and control.

The refusal of those in authority to attend to the experience of

Christian believers raises questions about the fundamental fairness of the Church's processes in dealing with disputes over doctrine or moral teaching. In addition, when the official Church ignores the experience of its members, it tends to impoverish the perspectives available to enrich the theological task. When the American bishops, who published important pastoral letters on war and on the American economy, tried to write a pastoral letter on women in the Church, they faltered. Although reasons for the failure to publish such a letter are many, a key one was located in the serious disagreements about the place and importance of the experience of women.

The Development of Critical Theology

When political and liberation theologians look for those elements in dominant cultures that legitimate oppression, they draw upon critical social theory. The principles of critical theory have helped theologians to uncover the emancipatory meaning of the gospel. Nearly twenty-five years ago, Gregory Baum coined the term "critical theology" to designate a common feature of European political theologies, Latin American liberation theology, and other contextual approaches, such as feminist and black theologies.[7] Although the term has not been widely used until recently, Baum argues that the preferential option for the poor—a term used by liberation theologies to describe the form of discipleship demanded by Jesus—has a certain affinity with the critical theory of the Frankfurt School. Moreover, the discourse of critical theology, despite the cautions articulated by Congregation for the Doctrine of the Faith (CDF), has entered the official discourse of the Church in a positive way.[8] For example, the Latin American bishops at Medellín (1968) and Puebla (1979) officially adopted the terminology of "the preferential option for the poor." In addition, Pope John Paul II's encyclical *Laborem exercens* (1981) and several pastoral statements of national episcopal conferences also support the hallmarks of critical theology. Briefly, these hallmarks include:

1. being present with and listening to the experiences of the poor, the marginalized, the oppressed in our society,

2. developing a critical analysis of the economic, political, and social structures that cause human suffering,

3. making judgments in the light of Christian principles concerning social values and priorities,

4. stimulating creative thought and action regarding alternative visions and models for social and economic development, and

5. acting in solidarity with popular groups in their struggles to transform economic, political, and social structures that cause social and economic injustice.[9]

Feminist theologians, whether or not they use the name "libera-tion theology" to describe their method, criticize structures that sup-port androcentric and patriarchal practices that disadvantage and ex-ploit women. From biblical practices too long defended as normative to the issue of women's ordination or other forms of power sharing in the Church today, no authority escapes examination by critical theol-ogy, and no office or practice is defensible that impedes the flourishing of women.

Increasingly, liberation and feminist theologians who employ the insights of critical theory are referring to their works as "postmodern theology."[10] These theologians use the work of critical social theor-ists such as Jürgen Habermas, who stresses that modernity is a project awaiting completion. Without attention to praxis, such theologians argue, particularly to those practices and commitments that consti-tute shared religious life, the modern project cannot be finished and religious communities (including their institutions) will wither and die. "True belief is, for them, not the foundation of religious life, but its result," says Terrence Tilley.[11] Postmodern Catholic theologies not only revise and reinterpret the classical sources of Catholic theology, but also address the problem of religious pluralism and diversity and the challenges they raise to the exclusivist claims of Christianity.[12]

In sum, not only have historical consciousness, the validation of experience in theological reflection, and the employment of critical theory in theology brought about the collapse of the unitary philo-sophical and theological system that held Catholicism together from the time of Leo XIII to that of Pius XII, but these shifts have enabled Catholic theologians from a variety of backgrounds and social loca-tions to develop new ways of doing theology and to apply their re-flection method to urgent concerns. In short, the era of pluralism in theology has arrived.[13]

Theologians and Theologies

Because Susan Ross has dealt extensively with feminist theology, the most prominent Catholic women theologians on the left, and the is-sues that most concern them, we will not deal with those matters here. Instead, we will feature a brief introduction to some of the key pe-sonalities and issues in contemporary theology. Not surprisingly, fun-damental theology has been a preoccupation of many prominent Catholic theologians in the twentieth century. The early works of Karl Rahner (d. 1984), *Spirit in the World* and *Hearers of the Word,* both dating from just before World War II, have been a major influence on much later work by others. Although *Hearers of the Word* was presented origi-nally as a work in philosophy of religion, Rahner later relabeled his concerns as "formal and fundamental theology." Because Rahner is the single most important and influential Catholic theologian of the twentieth century, it is not surprising that students of his work have been prominent among theologians of the left since the council. Bernard Lonergan (d. 1984) was another member of the transcendental Thomist school whose writing and teaching continue to exert much influence. Lonergan's *Insight* and *Method in Theology*, along with his essays, helped to change the face of contemporary theology. A fuller account would pay more attention to the difference both of personal style and of substance between the German Rahner and Canadian Lonergan, but for present purposes the convergences in their thought on fundamental theology are most important.

Post-conciliar theologians who continue to maintain that the revelation of God is disclosed in human experience, but are more cautious about identifying revelation with human experience, include Rahner's former student and colleague in Münster, Johannes Baptist Metz,[14] and the Dutch theologian Edward Schillebeeckx. Both go beyond Rahner's and Lonergan's "turn to the subject" and critically examine history as the arena of God's presence and activity. Their theology is another example of critical theology in its acknowledgment that power struggles and manipulation are often involved in the transmission of religious traditions (including Christianity), and represents an important stream in post-conciliar theology emanating from the left.[15] Critical theology argues that an authentic retrieval of Christian tradition must include ideology critique as well as appropriation for new circumstances.[16]

Among the next generation of Catholic theologians David Tracy and Francis Schüssler Fiorenza are, perhaps, the best-known fundamental theologians. Tracy's *Blessed Rage for Order* (1975), *The Analogical Imagination* (1981), and *Plurality and Ambiguity: Hermeneutics, Religion, Hope* (1987) have been widely influential among Catholic theologians. Schüssler Fiorenza's *Foundational Theology* (1984) and his two-volume *Systematic Theology* (edited with John Galvin, 1991) make important contributions to our theological understanding. The latter volume includes a valuable introductory essay, "Systematic Theology: Tasks and Methods," which describes three classic paradigms of theology and five contemporary approaches to theology as well as a constructive proposal for their implementation. Even though the work of Tracy and Schüssler Fiorenza is rooted in the ancient theological tradition of Catholic theology, the fact that they make space for plurality and ambiguity in their constructive proposals clearly sets them apart from conservative theologians. Indeed, the term "constructive theology" has gained ascendancy as a description for this kind of theology.

The question of God has always been of great concern to theologians, and in the past thirty years, has been a particular interest of feminist theologians. Mary Daly's *Beyond God the Father* (1972) announced her departure from Catholicism and positioned her as a radical feminist. Elizabeth Johnson's *She Who Is* and the late Catherine Mowry LaCugna's *God for Us: The Trinity and Christian Life* are revisionist in approach and attempt to retrieve the liberating aspects of the tradition that have been made invisible by patriarchy. Among European theologians Hans Küng has addressed contemporary questions of belief in God in his massive book *Does God Exist? An Answer for Today* (1980) and his earlier volume *On Being a Christian*. In Christology, Edward Schillebeeckx brought contemporary biblical scholarship to bear on Christological dogma in a much more nuanced way than previous Catholic systematic theologians had done. Schillebeeckx, a founding editor of *Concilium*, has consistently related theology to culture. Mary Catherine Hilkert describes his tomes, *Jesus: An Experiment in Christology* (1979) and *Christ: The Experience of Jesus as Lord* (1980), as "an ambitious project of rethinking the Christian claim that Jesus is universal savior in the face of radical human suffering, structural injustice, and the devastation of the earth."[17] Among the most recent attempts to address Christology in the light of contemporary religious pluralism is Roger Haight's *Jesus, Symbol of God* (1999). The controversial biblical studies of the Jesus Seminar, perhaps best represented by John Dominic Crossan's *The Historical Jesus: The Life of a Mediterranean Peasant*, have yet to be critically addressed by systematic theologians. At the same time, Elizabeth Johnson's *Consider Jesus* (1990) provides a good summary of post-conciliar developments in Christology from the left.

The theology of the Church, important before Vatican II, received a strong further impetus from the work of the council. Biblical and historical studies, already numerous before the council, continue to appear as questions of Church governance, the ordination of women, roles of clergy and laity in Church and world, the universal call to holiness, and other issues arise for reflection. Contentious issues such as the ordination of women raise significant issues of method and authority in the Church. As feminists and revisionist theologians address such issues, they sometimes find themselves in conflict with Church authorities. Although the issue of dissent is more of a fundamental theological issue than an ecclesiological one, since it concerns whether and how Church teaching develops, many of the recent books on the Church from the left have been concerned with the issue of the Church's teaching authority.[18] Many liberal theologians who have attempted to write ecclesiologies from a critical and experiential point of view have paid a price for their efforts. For example, Leonardo Boff, a Brazilian liberation theologian who taught at the Franciscan seminary in Petropolis, was silenced and lost his teaching position for his books

Ecclesiogenesis: The Base Communties Reinvent the Church (1986) and *The Church: Charism and Power* (1992).[19] In the United States, ecclesiologist Richard McBrien also came under fire for a revised edition of his widely used comprehensive text, *Catholicism* (1994). Indeed, feminist theologian Mary Hines, writing in *Freeing Theology,* notes that "ecclesiology is perhaps the most difficult area of systematic theology to treat from a feminist perspective within the Roman Catholic tradition. Church traditions and structures seem intractably patriarchal and hierarchical. Church documents continue to legitimize the exclusion of women from important areas in Church life, especially from leadership roles simply because they are women."[20]

Issues of sexual morality, particularly, are often addressed in controversial terms. Despite the strenuous efforts of Pope John Paul II to stifle dissent, theologians in the last thirty years have raised questions about every facet of moral theology. They question sources, the authority of various teachings, and the assent owed to moral teaching. While some of these questions are not new, recent historical and theological studies shed new life on their complexities. The clashes between theologians and Church authorities over matters of sexual ethics has led to the disciplining of theologians in the past twenty years. Significantly, many of the theologians who have drawn Vatican opprobrium have not denied essential doctrines, but have tried to stimulate discussion in areas that the institutional Church has closed to dialogue. Clashes between theologians and the Vatican, or between religious orders and the Vatican, raise questions about the role of conscience and the formation of conscience in this era of pluralism and ambiguity, as Anne Patrick has pointed out in her recent book *Liberating Conscience: Feminist Explorations in Catholic Moral Theology* (1996).

New Social Locations for Theology

These various agents of change in contemporary theology have collectively produced an important response to the question posed to liberals by many conservative and traditionalist Catholics. "We are who you were," a traditionalist Catholic told sociologist of religion Bill Dinges. The unspoken question suggested by that statement is: "Why have you changed?" [21] The answer represented in the identities and works of the "agents of change" just surveyed is simple and direct: because the "other" has become the "we." Theologians today include all those people who were not part of the theological enterprise before the council: lay people, women, Black, Hispanic, and Asian Catholics, gays and lesbians, feminists, and pro-choice activists. The truth of this explanation is perhaps nowhere so evident as in the way theology has come to be practiced as an academic discipline in the Catholic and non-Catholic universities and colleges of the United States.

The first new group produced by the changes in theology during the post-conciliar period comprises women, Latin American, Third World, and lay theologians. Their presence is especially significant in theology that takes experience as its point of departure. Until recently teachers and most students of theology were clerics. Today the change that is taking place is a shift to non-clerics as the agents, subjects, and professors of theology. This change produces new methods of doing theology even as it brings new perspectives to theological inquiry. Since the new *we* of non-clerical theology includes women, theology is now forced to address a new set of questions, as Ross showed in the opening chapter of this book. Feminist theologians point to the *androcentric* use of language but also emphasize that the *patriarchal* use of language, images, and symbols has structured Christian religious culture and institutions in quite specific ways that limit the God-symbol and stifle the development of the church community.

Close to feminist theologians in their privileging of experience are theologians from Latin America and the Third World who have a liberationist approach that combines spiritual questions with practical politics. Their appeal to the experience of base communities and to Third World realities challenges modern Western and Enlightenment modes of thought. As the Roman Catholic Church becomes a world church in a much more radical way than in previous centuries, it is increasingly aware that white Europeans are a minority group. Issues being raised by African and Asian cultures not only question the medieval intertwining of Christianity and Western European culture; they also raise important issues about the identity of Christianity and its tolerance for syncretism in its practices. Events like the 1998 Synod for Asia produced blunt criticism of Western ways by the Asian bishops, making clear that theologians and Third World Catholics bring a new set of questions for theological reflection.[22]

Academic theology has also been challenged by the presence of scholars of different religious convictions. The collegium of scholars is not simply a group of Catholics but includes Protestants, Jews, Hindus, Buddhists, Muslims, Confucians, Native Americans, Wiccans, and others. Many academic institutions today consider the representation of such scholars on their faculties as a necessary component of religious understanding. Undergraduates in Catholic colleges and secular universities may experience their first academic study of religion in a religiously diverse setting in which several religions—not just one—are studied. The American Academy of Religion's publications and role in job placement make it an important location for Roman Catholic scholars. The scholarly peers of Catholic theologians, therefore, are not just Catholics, but include scholars of differing theological persuasions and diverse institutional settings.

Finally, since theologians have to be responsive to the needs of their students, we can say that graduate students in theology constitute a new group as well. Many of them were educated within the pluralistic context of a liberal arts college, where disputation was an integral part of their studies, and so bring a different set of questions and expectations to their graduate study. Although conflicts of interpretation have always existed, today's students are often introduced to a bewildering array of methods and perspectives. Few Catholic students today enter the graduate study of religion with the background in Thomistic philosophy that once was required of undergraduates from Catholic institutions. Graduate students today may come from a background where they took courses with postmodern structuralists or textual critics, courses that introduced them to functionalism or positivism or critical theory. In a word, today's students are exposed to a diversity of philosophical, methodological, and intellectual perspectives and present a different set of pedagogical needs than did those students who entered graduate theology programs twenty years ago. Late-twentieth-century theologians—indeed, all people of faith studying or teaching in this setting—have been required to respond to the critique of religion in modern philosophy, psychology, and social analysis.

Theologians are required to respond to these and other profound shifts in the cultural and intellectual climate in which theology is produced. The enormous variety of academic perspectives and interests outlined above is sometimes complicated by a surrounding climate of dissent. The Vatican response to all this diversity and dissent has been defensive. A web of controls over theologians and their teaching and publications has been put in place.[23] Proceedings against dissenters, the best known of which resulted in the removal of Charles Curran from his teaching post at the Catholic University of America, grated against American notions of academic freedom and due process. Though the National Conference of Catholic Bishops (NCCB) approved a policy formulated by a joint committee of the Catholic Theological Society of America and the Canon Law Society of America and amended by the NCCB Committee on Doctrine, there is little evidence of its being widely used.[24] Clearly the Vatican does not support such dialogical processes as a means of settling disputes. It returned an American episcopal draft of ordinances for the implementation of *Ex corde ecclesiae*, without approval, asking for greater attention to the mission or mandate to teach, a topic of constant friction between the bishops and the presidents of Catholic colleges and universities in the United States.

In the past thirty years there have been many dissenting issues within American Catholicism—as other essays in this volume attest— but they all began in the public dissent over *Humanae vitae*, and it is at that source that the Vatican often chooses to make its own stand. The issue of contraception has proved to be the first of many in dispute between moralists on the right and left, but it is also a litmus test used when determining the position of individual moralists vis-à-vis the teaching authority of the Church. Pope John Paul II has not hesitated to make the acceptance of the teaching of *Humanae vitae* a decisive consideration in choosing among candidates for the episcopacy or among theologians being considered for promotion or tenure on pontifical faculties.

Professional Theological Organizations

In the last thirty years, as indicated above, academic theology in North America has moved from being taught principally by clergy in seminaries and houses of study for religious to being an academic discipline taught by faculty who are increasingly lay persons and increasingly women. Those changes are reflected in the profiles of theological organizations, like the Catholic Theological Society of America (CTSA), the College Theology Society (CTS), the Catholic Biblical Association (CBA), and the Society of Christian Ethics (SCE). As two of the larger theological societies in North America, the CTSA and CTS serve as interesting case studies.[25] CTSA, formerly a clerical society of Catholic theologians, has changed both in its membership and in the regard of some members of the hierarchy. Even though it is sometimes perceived as a liberal organization, it is fundamentally moderate in its membership and intentions. CTS, because of its history, is perceived to be somewhat more liberal in its approaches to contemporary issues, but it, too, is a relatively moderate group of professional theologians.

CTSA

The Catholic Theological Society of America was established in 1946 as a society of priest-teachers of theology. "Within the context of the Roman Catholic tradition," its statement of purpose reads, the purpose of the CTSA is "to promote studies and research in theology, to relate theological science to current problems, and to foster a more effective theological education, by providing a forum for an exchange of views among theologians and with scholars in other disciplines."[26] The society publishes the *Proceedings* of its annual meeting and, from time to time, a *Directory* of its membership. As the occasion warrants, CTSA publishes reports of its research teams. These have included *The Problem of Second Marriages* (1972); *Catholic Hospital Ethics* (1972); *Re-*

newal of the Sacrament of Penance (1975); *Human Sexuality* (1977); *Women in Church and Society* (1978); *Catholic Perspectives on Baptism, Eucharist and Ministry* (1986); *Profession of Faith and the Oath of Fidelity* (1990); two reports on the ecumenical Bilateral Consultations (1972, 1979); two joint reports of the CTSA and the Canon Law Society of America: *Cooperation between Theologians and the Ecclesiastical Magisterium* (1982) and *Doctrinal Responsibilities* (1984); and the report of a joint commission of the CTSA, the Canon Law Society of America, the College Theology Society, and the National Conference of Diocesan Directors of Religious Education: *The Approval of Catechisms and Catechetical Materials* (1986).

In its organizational year (1946) the CTSA had 104 members, all of them Roman Catholic priests. By 1992 the membership totaled 1471, of whom 17 percent were female.[27] Today, membership steadily hovers around 1400 with the number of women around 300 (just over 20 percent). The modest number of women may be explained in part by the fact that the CTSA has admitted women only since 1964.[28] At the same time, participation and attendance of women members at conventions is very high, creating a misleading impression that women constitute a much larger proportion of the membership than they actually do. Also, over the last several years, the CTSA board has been sensitive to the issue of representation of women and minorities both among the organization's leadership and on its convention program. Thus, the number of women active in conventions and in elected leadership or appointed committee roles is disproportionate to their total number in the society.

The increase in the number of women active in the society was not the only significant change in its composition. The era of improved relations between Catholics and other religions or Christian groups opened the doors of distinguished theological faculties in non-Catholic or even tax-supported institutions to large numbers of Catholics in the United States and Canada. Members trained in non-Catholic institutions and ecumenical theological consortia were exposed to more non-Catholic and secular authors than was the case for those trained in Catholic seminaries and religious houses and homogeneously Catholic universities. The expanded cast of thinkers—whose number include Paul Ricoeur, Michel Foucault, Jürgen Habermas, Jacques Derrida, Hans Frei, James Gustafson, Sallie McFague, George Lindbeck, Richard Rorty, Richard Bernstein, Eberhard Jüngel, Thomas Torrance, Gordon Kauffman, and John Hick—as dialogue partners has moved well beyond the "usual suspects" considered controversial during the years immediately following the council.[29] This phenomenon is considered to be dangerous by some members of the hierarchy as well as by some members of the CTSA.

Such increasing diversification within the Catholic academy has engendered criticism and expressions of fear from the Catholic Church. For example, in the summer of 1997, Cardinal Bernard Law, archbishop of Boston, claimed that the CTSA "has become an association of advocacy for theological dissent" and "a wasteland."[30] Law, writing in *The Pilot,* Boston's archdiocesan newspaper, was reacting to the publication of a study produced and published by the CTSA. The study dealt with the doctrinal authority of the grounds offered for the Church's teaching that it is not authorized to ordain women to the priesthood. (Of the six members of the committee that had drafted the report, five hold doctorates from Catholic institutions.)

CTSA's diversity, as Cardinal Law complained, includes a significant number of members who are now teachers of Catholic theology though trained themselves in non-Catholic institutions.[31] To many CTSA members, Law's article sounded like an endorsement of a refrain that CTSA member Matthew Lamb had been echoing since 1990. Six months after Law's column, Lamb published another article in the conservative journal *Crisis,* lamenting this issue.[32] Another CTSA member who supports Cardinal Law's accusations is Avery Dulles. In a 1998 issue of *Commonweal,* Dulles described the major addresses at the 1997 CTSA convention as "an orchestrated chorus" that "rejected fundamental articles of Catholic belief regarding priesthood and Eucharist as expressed by the Council of Trent, the Second Vatican Council, the synods of bishops, Paul VI, John Paul II, and the Congregation for the Doctrine of the Faith." These dissenting views, he complained, "were set forth with a certain display of historical erudition, as though doctrines could be invalidated by tagging them chronologically." Unfortunately, Dulles, who did not attend the convention but relied upon the CTSA Proceedings, injected a certain polemical tone into his critique. CTSA President Mary Ann Donovan pointed out "how mistaken are the terms he uses to establish attitudes: for example, one speaker 'sarcastically' declared, the priest who spoke 'meekly' was 'sharply' reminded, the chorus was 'orchestrated.'" Peter Steinfels, former religion editor of the *New York Times,* found the society's task force on women's ordination "not only respectful and responsible but actually conservative" in its response to the Congregation for the Doctrine of the Faith's *responsum* on the "infallibility" of Pope John Paul II's letter rejecting the ordination of women (*Ordinatio sacerdatolis*).[33]

CTS

Originally called the Society of Catholic College Teachers of Sacred Doctrine, the College Theology Society (CTS) was founded in 1953 as an organization of lay and religious teachers of undergraduate theology.[34] It took its present name in the 1960s. Today, CTS is a "professional society of college and university professors" with its roots in the Roman Catholic tradition, but with an increasingly ecumenical membership list. In its publications and its annual meetings it focuses on developing the academic disciplines of theology and religious studies by assisting college and university teachers in their pedagogical lives and with their religious concerns.

Membership in CTS is open to those who teach theology or religious studies on the college level and who hold advanced degrees in these areas. Associate membership is open to those pursuing advanced degrees in theology or religious studies, to those engaged in pastoral work, to retired members, and to friends (those who may not be part of the academic enterprise directly, but are supportive of it). Current membership in the United States and Canada is approximately 800. The annual convention is a forum for the exchange of ideas, usually held on a college campus in the first week of June. Awards are given for outstanding books and articles by members, and an annual prize is given to a student essay. Members receive *Horizons*, the society's journal published semiannually, and they receive copies of the annual volume of selected papers from the conventions.

Conclusions

Changes in the discipline of theology, its teachers, and its students have been ingredients in the professionalization of theological teaching in the United States. Teachers of theology now expect to make teaching their full-time job and to work at that job under conditions and with the freedoms customary in American academic life. Those expectations apply particularly for teachers in universities and colleges, but are expected to operate for seminary teachers as well. Recent experience has shown, however, that seminary teachers are subject to summary dismissal in spite of institutional statements that seem to assure faculty members of academic freedom and due process in cases of dispute.[35] The role of women as faculty members in seminaries has become especially problematic.[36]

Their academic appointments to non-Catholic or independent Catholic universities means that many professional theologians are not readily subject to Church authority in spite of the controls that have been put in place under Pope John Paul II. But the tension with Church authorities remains, and the experience of that tension is characteristic of scholars on the left of the Catholic theological spectrum. Some critics attribute to this lack of ecclesiastical control their increasing concern about the "Catholic identity" of historically Catholic institutions at a time of declining numbers of clergy and religious from the sponsoring religious group. Another unfortunate result is an increasing separation of Catholic academic theology from pastoral caregivers and social activists. Unless they are invited to be plenary speaker, academic theologians are rarely seen at liberal Catholic reform movement gatherings such as Call to Action, Pax Christi, or the Women's Ordination Conference.

The mental universe of left-wing theologians in relations with Church authorities is described theologically by the Vatican II definition of the Church as the people of God endowed with the gifts of the Spirit, sharing a common priesthood. It is reinforced by contemporary problems such as the shortage of clergy and religious and its impact on parishes, schools, and other Church institutions, which results in increasing dependence on lay ministries. Debate also continues on the appropriate roles for clergy and laity in the world.[37]

When one thinks of the future in light of the broad sweep of theological change that has just been presented, it is natural to ask "what's left" on the liberal theological agenda as we move into the twenty-first century. If the hallmarks of liberal theology continue to be historical consciousness, experience as a starting point for theological reflection, and the use of critical theory both in retrieving the authentic Christian past and in constructing significantly new ways to understand and live the message of Jesus, then one can predict that the challenges of a postmodern world will be the subject matter for liberal theology. To the extent that the poor, women, persons of color, and gays and lesbians continue to be marginalized as "the other," a variety of liberationist perspectives (including feminist theology) will be necessary. In addition, theologians will add our planet to the ranks of the powerless and voiceless: some segments of liberal theology have already begun to include ecological concerns in their agenda.[38] New partnership with science and scientific theory is necessary if theology is to have an environment in which to exist.

The creation of a global economic system and the challenge of religious pluralism present competing and often contradictory challenges. The praxis element and the prophetic-critical task will continue to be important aspects of liberal theology. Religious pluralism challenges theologians to devise criteria for dialogue that allow the maintenance of the real diversity of religious traditions even while striving to find some "common ground" among them. This may well mean that consensus always remains, in some sense, partial.[39]

On a practical note, whatever one may think of the possible dissolution of Catholic theology due to Catholics studying in secular institutions, it has become evident that the new social location of theology (in the laity as well as in the clergy) means that more theologians (especially lay men and women) have to pay their own way. Today's Catholic theological students not only seek the best programs at the best universities, but are drawn to those programs that can support them financially with fellowships and grants. In many respects, the future of liberal Catholic theology will depend to some degree upon financial support from the community that shares its vision.

NOTES

1. See B. Ashley, O.P., "The Loss of Theological Unity: Pluralism, Thomism, and Catholic Morality," in Mary Jo Weaver and R. Scott Appleby, eds., *Being Right: Conservative Catholics in America* (Bloomington: Indiana University Press, 1995). See also Gerald McCool, S.J., *From Unity to Pluralism: The Internal Evolution of Thomism* (New York: Fordham University Press, 1989).

2. See McCool, *From Unity to Pluralism*, and his *The Neo-Thomists*, Marquette Studies in Philosophy, III (Milwaukee: Marquette University Press, 1994).

3. See Ellen Leonard, "Experience as a Source for Theology: A Canadian and Feminist Perspective," *Studies in Religion* 19 (1990), pp. 143–162; and Ann Graff, "The Struggle to Name Women's Experience: Assessment and Implications for Theological Construction," *Horizons* 20 (1993), pp. 215–233.

4. "The body of the faithful as a whole anointed as they are by the Holy One (Cf Jn. 2:20) cannot err in matters of belief. Thanks to a supernatural sense of the faith which characterizes the People as a whole, it manifests this unerring quality when, 'from the bishops down to the last member of the laity,' it shows universal agreement in matters of faith and morals." *Lumen Gentium*, #12. The document goes on to discuss the distribution of charisms by the Holy Spirit: "He distributes special graces among the faithful of every rank. By these gifts He makes them fit and ready to undertake the various tasks or offices advantageous for the renewal and upbuilding of the church. . . . These charismatic gifts, whether they be the most outstanding or the more simple and widely diffused are to be received with thanksgiving and consolation, for they are exceedingly suitable and useful for the needs of the church" (ibid.).

5. See Paul VI, *Humanae vitae* (1968) on the regulation of births [Text in A. Flannery, *Vatican Council II: More Postconciliar Documents* (Northport, N.Y.: Costello, 1982), pp. 397–416]; the Congregation for the Doctrine of the Faith (hereafter CDF), Instruction *Personae humanae* (1975) on certain questions in sexual ethics [Text in Flannery, *Vatican Council II*, pp. 486–500]; and John Paul II, the apostolic letter *Ordinatio sacerdotalis* (1994) on the ordination of women [Text in *Origins* 24 (1994), pp. 49–52]; together with the 1995 response of the CDF affirming the pope's teaching as pertaining to the deposit of faith [Text in *Origins* 25 (1995), pp. 401–403].

6. See John Henry Newman, *On Consulting the Faithful in Matters of Doctrine*, ed. John Coulson (1859; reprint, Kansas City, Mo.: Sheed and Ward, 1961).

7. Gregory Baum, *Religion and Alienation* (New York: Paulist Press, 1975), pp. 193–223. See also *Essays in Critical Theology* (Kansas City: Sheed and Ward, 1994), pp. 3–34.

8. See CDF, "Instruction on Certain Themes in Liberation Theology," *Origins* 14 (1984), pp. 194–204, and "Instruction on Christian Freedom and Liberation," *Origins* 15 (1986), pp. 115–128.

9. This pastoral methodology, which also represents the key elements of critical theology, is distilled from the Canadian bishops' statement "Ethical Reflections of Canada's Socio-Economic Order." In *Do Justice! The Social Teaching of the Canadian Bishops*, ed. E. F. Sheridan (Toronto: Jesuit Centre for Faith and Justice, 1987), pp. 411–432.

10. For an introduction to these theologies, see Terrence W. Tilley, et al., *Postmodern Theologies: The Challenge of Religious Diversity* (Maryknoll, N.Y.: Orbis Books, 1995); Paul Lakeland, *Theology and Critical Theory: The Discourse of the Church* (Nashville, Tenn.: Abingdon Press, 1990); and *Postmodernity: Christian Identity in a Fragmented Age* (Minneapolis: Fortress Press, 1997).

11. Tilley, et al., *Postmodern Theologies*, p. viii.

12. The major theological positions vis-à-vis religious diversity are exclusivism, inclusivism, and pluralism, all of which are basically soteriological positions about who can be saved or who has "the truth." Exclusivism holds the doctrine of *extra ecclesiam nulla salus* (outside the Church there is no salvation) in its most narrow sense. Inclusivism represents a modern broadening of the concept of church so that even those who are not aware of it can be saved (for example, in the "anonymous Christian" theology of Karl Rahner). Pluralism claims that there are many paths and that we cannot know for sure which one is the best. See Tilley, et al., *Postmodern Theologies*, p. 158.

13. A more detailed description of the options open to contemporary theology and a proposal for a "revisionist theology" is David Tracy's *Blessed Rage for Order: The New Pluralism in Theology* (New York: Seabury, 1975).

14. See Metz's *Theology of the World* (New York: Seabury Press, 1972), *Faith in History and Society* (New York: Crossroad, 1980), and *The Emerging Church: The Future of Christianity in a Post Bourgeois World* (London: SCM Press, 1981).

15. Matthew Lamb's *Solidarity with Victims: Toward a Theology of Social Transformation* (New York: Crossroad, 1982) should also be mentioned here. Since the early 1990s, however, Lamb has taken a curious turn to the right, and his ideological lens appears to exempt the hierarchical magisterium from such scrutiny.

16. Schillebeeckx's work on ordained ministry provides good examples of his critical theology. See *The Church with a Human Face: A New and Expanded Theology of Ministry* (New York: Crossroad, 1985). An earlier version of this book appeared as *Ministry: Leadership in the Community of Jesus Christ* (New York: Crossroad, 1981). Both books analyze the history of ordained ministry in Catholicism with attention to the question of whose interests are being served.

17. "Edward Schillebeeckx," in Donald W. Musser and Joseph L. Price, eds., *A New Handbook of Christian Theologians* (Nashville: Abingdon Press, 1996), p. 415. See also Robert J. Schreiter and Mary Catherine Hilkert, eds., *The Praxis of Christianity Experience: An Introduction to the Theology of Edward Schillebeeckx* (New York: Crossroad, 1986).

18. See John Boyle, *Church Teaching Authority: Historical and Theological Studies* (Notre Dame: University of Notre Dame Press, 1995); Richard Gaillardetz, *Teaching with Authority: A Theology of the Magisterium in the Church* (Collegeville, Minn.: Liturgical Press, 1997); and Francis A. Sullivan, *Creative Fidelity: Weighing and Interpreting Documents of the Magisterium* (New York: Paulist Press, 1996).

19. See Otto Maduro, "Leonardo Boff," in Musser and Price, *New Handbook*. See also Harvey Cox, *The Silencing of Leonardo Boff: The Vatican and the Future of World Christianity* (Oak Park, Ill.: Meyer Stone Books, 1988).

20. "Community for Liberation: Church," in Catherine M. LaCugna, ed., *Freeing Theology: Essentials of Theology in a Feminist Perspective* (San Francisco: Harper and Row, 1993), p. 161.

21. William P. Dinges, "We Are Who You Were: Traditionalist Catholics in America," in Weaver and Appleby, *Being Right*, pp. 241–270.

22. Documentation on the Synod for Asia appears in *Origins* 27, nos. 45 and 46 (30 April and 7 May 1998) and 28, no. 2 (28 May 1998).

23. See the constitution *Sapientia Christiana*, which deals with pontifical faculties, Canon 812 of the 1983 *Code of Canon Law*, and the constitution *Ex Corde Ecclesiae*, which deals with the whole range of Catholic institutions of higher learning. All require theologians to have a formal mission or mandate to teach in the institutions to which the documents pertain. See J. P. Boyle, *Church Teaching Authority: Historical and Theological Studies* (Notre Dame: University of Notre Dame Press, 1995). See also *Cooperation between Theologians and the Ecclesiastical Magisterium*, ed. Leo O'Donovan, S.J. (Washington: CLSA, 1982), especially the canonical study by John Alessandro, pp. 76–116.

The CDF Instruction *Donum veritatis* summarizes the official view of the ecclesial role of the theologian. See *Origins* 20 (1990), 118–26.

24. In an ironic turn, Cardinal Roger Mahoney of Los Angeles recommended to the CTSA that it might use the policy itself to settle disputes with society members critical of the members' approval in 1997 of a committee report that raised questions about the CDF response, which asserted that the inability of the Church to ordain women pertains to the deposit of faith. See *Commonweal* 125, no. 10 (22 May 1998), p. 4.

25. The Ecumenical Association of Third World Theologians (EATWOT) and the Association of Catholic Hispanic Theologians in the U.S. (ACHTUS) should also be mentioned here. The creation of these societies reflects the marginalization that so-called Third World or minority theologians have experienced in the societies of theologians from the dominant culture. Ironically, the women theologians of EATWOT have experienced the same kind of marginalization among their liberationist colleagues as have their sisters in the mainstream theological societies. See Ursula King, ed., *Feminist Theology from the Third World* (Maryknoll, N.Y.: Orbis Books, 1994). Recently, as part of a need to maintain solidarity among theologians on the left, an international network of Catholic theologians was formed. Known as the International Network of Societies of Catholic Theologians (INSeCT), this umbrella organization includes Catholic theological societies from Brazil, Colombia, Chile, Argentina, Europe, the United States, Canada, and the Ecumenical Association of African Theologians.

26. The society seeks "to assist those entrusted with a teaching ministry of the Church, to develop in the Christian people a more mature understanding of their faith, and to further the cause of unity among all people through a better appreciation of the role of religious faith in the life of human beings and society" (CTSA Constitution, article 1). Active membership is open to those who possess the doctoral degree in theological or related studies or who have been actively engaged in teaching or research in the sacred sciences. Associate membership is open to those who have completed at least the course requirements for a doctoral degree in theology or religious studies.

In 1964 membership was opened to "all who are professionally competent in Sacred Theology and who are or have been actively engaged in the promotion and research in the sacred sciences. Professional competence in this instance is understood to mean the possession of the Licentiate degree in any of the sacred sciences from a Pontifical University or a Doctorate in any of the sacred sciences from a non-Pontifical institution of higher learning" (CTSAP, 1964: 236). Prior to that time membership had been limited to priests and religious brothers.

27. As evidence of further moves toward equality in status, the fiftieth anniversary issue of the *CTSA Proceedings* notes that "the Proceedings from 1964–1971 distinguish among priests, laymen, sisters, and laywomen. Subsequent lists of new members do not make these distinctions although the 1972 and 1977 issues of the Directory continue to use religious titles." *CTSA Proceedings* 50 (1995), pp. 301f.

28. See *PCTSA* 50 (1995), p. 296.

29. One thinks of Rudolph Bultmann, Karl Barth, Dietrich Bonhoefer, Martin Buber, the so-called God-is-dead theologians (e.g. Thomas Altizer, or Friedrich Gogarten), process thinkers (Alfred North Whitehead, Charles Hartshorne, Schubert Ogden, John Cobb), Paul Tillich, Langdon Gilkey. Pierre Teilhard de Chardin and Raimundo Panikkar are both Catholic thinkers, but they too would have been considered avant garde in Catholic schools in the 1960s and 1970s.

30. *The Pilot* (June 20, 1997). Cardinal Law was responding to CTSA's statement on women's ordination. The text of the report is in *Proceedings of the Catholic Theological Society of America* 51 (1997), pp. 197–204. The resolution voted on by the members is on pp. 19–94. See also the text of the resolution and study paper in *Origins* 27 (1997–98), pp. 75–79. CTSA members sometimes publish their disagreements in more popular media. See Thomas F. O'Meara, "Doctoral Programs in Theology at U.S. Catholic Universities," in *America* 162 (1990), pp. 79–84, 101–103; and Matthew L. Lamb, "Will There Be Catholic Theology in the United States?" in *America* 162 (1990), pp. 523–525, 531–534. Recent proceedings of CTSA meetings have also included the report of a "developing group" on the topic "criteria for Catholic theology," in which Lamb and Avery Dulles and others have taken part.

31. Although an accurate profile of the history of the degree-granting institutions of CTSA members is difficult to obtain (because of the overlap in reporting categories), of 1348 active members in 1992, 489 (36 percent) earned doctorates at Catholic institutions in the U.S., 89 (7 percent) earned degrees from Canadian institutions, 321 (24 percent) held doctorates from Roman universities, 183 (14 percent) held degrees from other European universities, and 195 (14 percent) earned doctorates from non-Catholic universities in the U.S. By contrast, in 1963, 39 percent of the members held degrees from American Catholic universities, 44 percent had degrees from Roman universities, 6 percent had degrees from other European universities, 4 percent had degrees from Canadian universities, and 1 percent had degrees from U.S. non-Catholic universities. By 1998 this number had increased to 277, nearly 20 percent.

The place of employment of the membership in 1992 is also of interest: 553 (41 percent) taught in Catholic colleges and universities, 269 (19 percent) taught in seminaries and theological unions, and 85 (6 percent) taught in non-Catholic universities and seminaries. In 1963 only three members of the CTSA taught in non-Catholic universities and seminaries and in 1982 35 members (3 percent) taught in such institutions.

32. "Catholic Theological Society of America: Theologians Unbound," in *Crisis* (December 1997), pp. 36–37.

33. Avery Dulles, Mary Ann Donovan, and Peter Steinfels, "How Catholic Is the CTSA?" *Commonweal,* 27 March 1998, pp. 13, 17.

34. It was the inspiration of Sister Rose Eileen Masterman, C.S.C. See Rosemary Rogers, *A History of the College Theology Society* (Villanova, Penn.: Villanova University Press, 1983).

35. See the CTSA statement on the dismissal of Sister M. Carmel McEnroy, R.S.M., in 1995 at St. Meinrad Seminary and the demotion leading to the resignation of Sister Barbara Fiand in 1998 from the Atheneum of Ohio.

The CTSA statement on Sister McEnroy is published in the *PCTSA* 50 (1995), pp. 326–329. Sister Fiand's resignation is reported in *The National Catholic Reporter* 34, no. 31 (5 June 1998), p. 11.

36. See the comments of Sister Fiand's religious community in the *NCR* cited in note 35.

37. See *Instruction on Certain Questions Regarding the Collaboration of the Non-Ordained Faithful in the Sacred Ministry of Priests*, dated August 15, 1997, and published jointly by the Congregation for the Clergy, the Pontifical Council on the Laity, the Congregation for the Doctrine of the Faith, the Congregation for Divine Worship and the Discipline of the Sacraments, the Congregation for Bishops, the Congregation for the Evangelization of Peoples, the Congregation for the Institutes of Consecrated Life and Societies of Apostolic Life, and the Pontifical Council for the Interpretation of Legislative Texts. The text was approved *in forma specifica* by Pope John Paul II, who ordered its promulgation. (Washington: USCC, 1998.)

38. See, for example, Mary Evelyn Tucker and John A Grim, eds., *Worldview and Ecology: Religion, Philosophy, and the Environment* (Maryknoll, N.Y.: Orbis Books, 1994); Stephen Scharper, *Redeeming the Time: A Political Theology of the Environment* (New York: Continuum, 1997); Leonardo Boff, *Cry of the Earth, Cry of the Poor* (Maryknoll N.Y.: Orbis Books, 1977); Rosemary Ruether, ed., *Women Healing Earth: Third World Women on Ecology, Feminism, and Religion* (Maryknoll, N.Y.: Orbis Books, 1996).

39. David Tracy, *Dialogue with the Other: The Inter-Religions Dialogue* (Grand Rapids: Eerdmans, 1990). Also his article "Theology and the Many Faces of Postmodernity," *Theology Today* 51 (1994), pp. 104–144.

Part 4

LITURGY,
MINISTRY,
AND
SPIRITUALITY

6

PROGRESSIVE APPROACHES
TO MINISTRY

BERNARD J. COOKE

Three decades ago, Peter Drucker pointed to the radical shifts that characterize the present time: things change so rapidly that people may have a sense of disorientation.[1] In this situation, one usually finds that people have strong tendencies either to hold on to the past or to move toward the future quickly. The Catholic Church in the United States is no stranger to this conflict. Catholics have defined and practiced ministry much differently in the last thirty years than they had for several centuries prior to Vatican II. Not surprisingly, therefore, Catholics are divided on this issue, some stressing continuity and others discontinuity with the past. The range of opinions that falls between these two poles provides a key vantage point from which to assess the differences between conservatives and liberals in the American Catholic community.

The complex nature of ministry—its definitions, history, practice—along with the theology behind it and the structures that support it require a wide-ranging approach to the topic. Because the Second Vatican Council played a major role in the reconfiguration of ministry in the Church, I will describe the ways in which the council approved extensions of ministry beyond the ordained clergy and vowed religious, and will rehearse the history of ministerial roles for the laity. Since most Catholics experience ministry at the parish level, I will concentrate on the ministries being exercised in this context, by ordained pastors, non-ordained professional ministers, and other non-ordained persons. In this context, I will also describe the ministerial outreach to the world and some of the ministerial structures and supporting organizations that embody a progressive approach to ministry.

Vatican II, Ministry, and the Laity

Although there is a widespread tendency to attribute contemporary changes in Catholicism to the Second Vatican Council, and although there is considerable justification for this attribution, the council did not so much initiate change as it recognized and cautiously accepted modifications that were already underway. We can see, in the compromised nature of the documents themselves, that there were divisions among the bishops,[2] and we can acknowledge that the bishops had a relatively conservative outlook. At the same time, it is clear that the position taken by the council with respect to Christian ministry represents a basic reversal of attitudes that had prevailed for centuries.

At the council, the theological advisors (*periti*) of the bishops brought them up to speed on the biblical and historical scholarship that was critical in influencing their decisions. Historians, Scripture scholars, and liturgical scholars made it clear to the bishops that Christian ministry had not always taken the shape with which they were familiar. Tridentine Catholicism was part of the story of Christian ministry, but not all of it. When we begin with the public ministry of Jesus and note that he chose both women and men to work with him in a mission characterized as "service," we can see, as the council fathers did, that members of the early Christian community understood ministry as something to be shared by all the baptized. Paul's letters to the Christians of Corinth reflected a basic responsibility of discipleship and explained the range of distinctive ministries as grounded in the gifts (charisms) of the Spirit. Christianity in its early years had no sense of ministerial office. Rather, all members, both women and men, were invited to participate in ministries of teaching, healing, governing, evangelizing, and prophecy, as gifted by the Holy Spirit. All Christians were expected to be of service, to care for one another.[3]

For a number of complex reasons, and rather quickly, however, a narrowing of ministerial involvement took place that reduced the ministerial status of the laity to relative inactivity and to second- or third-class status behind those ordained for official leadership or those who pursued vocations in monastic life. On the part of the ordained, while serving the reign of God through evangelization remained an important element in their ministry, the focus of official activity shifted to administering the internal life of the Church.[4] Over the centuries a few lay persons, especially those civil rulers who felt an overall Christian responsibility for their subjects, did exercise some ministerial initiative in teaching or caring for the disadvantaged or providing religious guidance, but it was only in modern times that "ordinary folk" became more engaged in active ministry. This modern development had three phases. It began with the rapid growth in the last three centuries of active congregations of women and non-ordained men. Technically, these sisters and brothers were members of the laity, but they quickly lost social identification as such. It was supplemented in the eighteenth and nineteenth centuries by "pious associations" of laity who gathered to pray for the work of priests, sisters, and brothers. Finally, in the twentieth century, it grew into various forms of Catholic Action, organized social and educational activity through which the laity could extend the apostolate of the hierarchy. Events leading up to and surrounding World War II hastened the growth of lay activity and responsibility and prepared the ground for the stance taken by the Second Vatican Council.

The bishops at Vatican II, in the "Dogmatic Constitution on the Church" *(Lumen gentium)*, the "Pastoral Constitution on the Church in the Modern World" *(Gaudium et spes)*, and the "Pastoral Constitution on the Apostolate of Lay People" *(Apostolicam actuositatem)*, finally gave full recognition to the active role of all the baptized. No longer appropriating the term "the Church" for themselves (as they had done at Vatican I), the bishops defined the Church as the entire people of God and said that all members, in diverse ways, are meant to participate actively in the Church's mission in history.[5] Even though it was viewed by many of the council's bishops as an unfinished document, the constitution on the Church in the modern world went far beyond a generic shift in the direction of the laity. Indeed, it fleshed out in considerable detail the vast ministerial goal of transforming human life in such areas as war and peace, economic and social justice, nurture of family life, and cultural advance through education.

In the years since the council, the interpretation and implementation of the conciliar decrees has been uneven.[6] For example, there is still some ambivalence in official circles about designating lay activity as "ministry" and some argument about the extent to which bishops should share responsibility with the laity. At the 1987 Synod of the Bishops that dealt with the role of the laity, there was much debate about the demarcation of roles and responsibilities. It is instructive to compare the interventions made at that synod by two of the U.S. representatives. On one hand, then Archbishop (now Cardinal) Roger Mahony stressed the differences in ministerial autonomy of clergy and laity: "While taking nothing away from the contribution made by religious and laity who have joined parish staffs to work on religious education and liturgical development in parishes, we have probably been mistaken in developing specialties for these ministerial works distinct from the role of the priest." On the other hand, the then president of the U.S. hierarchy, Archbishop John May of St. Louis, encouraged the bishops to enable the laity "to fulfill whatever ministry God has for them." As he summarized it, "they [the laity] recognize clearly the essentially unique role of the ordained ministry, but they have a strong sense of their share in the mission of Jesus Christ and the Church by virtue of their baptism."[7]

On the part of lay people in the Church the invitation to ministerial involvement received widespread positive response. There has been a veritable explosion of ministerial activity by the laity as they either step into roles vacated by priest and religious, significantly diminished in numbers, or create new ministries that enable them to serve both the Church and human society.[8] "About 20,000 lay people and religious are employed at least twenty hours a week as parish ministers in half of the 19,000 Catholic parishes in the United States," and 80 percent of these are women.[9] Far greater in number are those who, though not employed by their parish, assist in a wide variety of roles to further the internal life of the Church or have committed themselves as Catholics to active ministries "in the world." For the time being, however, much of the progressive leadership in ministry, particularly in the parish context, is provided by ordained clergy or vowed religious sisters or brothers who encourage the initiative of parishioners and work collegially with them.

Ministerial activity in itself does not distinguish conservative from progressive Catholics. When Archbishop May said that "the laity of the United States see the development of lay ministry as integral to their faith,"[10] he was talking about Catholics generally. Both liberals and conservatives have accepted the invitation to greater participation in ministry and both now take for granted new roles within the parish, such as lector or Eucharistic minister. What does distinguish them to some extent is the attitude toward further change, especially change initiated by the laity themselves. Progressive Catholics are more inclined to develop ministries on their own, whereas more conservative Catholics generally prefer to work under clerical direction in established Church structures, provided, of course, that the supervising clergy are not too liberal. Conservative activists generally have a stake in shoring up "traditional" structures and practices of Catholicism and are often very active in devotions like the recitation of the rosary or Benediction. Liberal Catholics are often more inclined to experiment with new prayer forms and ideas and to imagine how they can work to help create a somewhat different future Church.[11] When it comes to the Church's relationship to the surrounding society, progressive Catholics are more likely than conservatives to contest the justice of economic or political policies that appear to threaten the disadvantaged. The reaction to the U.S. bishops' pastoral letter on the economy reflected that.[12] The distinguishing characteristics of "conservative" and "liberal" apply not only to the dominant Euro-American Catholic population, but to African-American, Latino-American,

Asian-American and Native-American Catholics as well. The same range of attitudes that divide Catholics in general probably marks those groups.

Ministry at the Parish Level

Most Catholics experience ministerial activity in the context of their local parish. In studying the nature and extent of change in the patterns of parish ministry and of lay people's role in this change, three types of lay involvement must be distinguished: professionally trained lay men and women acting in ministerial capacities, volunteers for parish work, and those engaged in more global ministries.[13] The first group constitutes a new phenomenon in the history of the Church, selected and (usually) professionally trained lay women and men who occupy positions as directors of religious education (DREs) or facilitators of liturgy, and do so as full-time employees of the parish. These professional lay ministers by "official" appointment fill positions formerly considered part of the clergy's role, and their ministries are close to the heart of parish life. They act as part of the parish leadership team, almost always under the direction of the ordained pastor. Because their roles necessitate interaction with the entire parish, they must bridge conservative/progressive divisions, and the approach to the ministry they exercise is influential in shaping outlooks in the parish. This means that they are key players in the conservative/progressive dialectic in the U.S. Catholic Church.

It would be difficult to substantiate a characterization of these professional ministers as "progressive," especially since many of them must mute their personal outlooks in order to work effectively in a parish situation. At the same time, since a good proportion of them have been trained in progressive graduate-level programs—such as the Institute of Religious Education and Pastoral Ministry at Boston College—we may surmise that many of them are on the progressive end of the spectrum of Catholic opinion. Anecdotal evidence can offer some confirmation of this observation.[14]

The second group, more numerous by far than full-time professional ministers, are the scores of Catholics who are engaged as volunteers in the various programs of an active parish, activities that range from Bible study groups to managing food banks for the poor. It makes no sense to claim that a particular group of Catholics—liberals or conservatives—are more active as parish volunteers. At the same time, we can speak of progressive parishes—the Pax Christi community in Eden Prairie, Minnesota, or St. Mary's in Colt's Neck, New Jersey—and notice that they tend to be more social-minded in the kinds of ministries they foster. Such parishes are usually known for their creative approach to liturgy. The third group of Catholics active in ministry directs its attention more to the world outside the Church than to the internal life of the Church. This sense of ministry is one that is organized for a particular purpose that goes beyond the parish. Network, a Catholic social justice lobby in Washington, D.C. (see Appendix), and the Center of Concern, an educational and activist organization for national and international justice, are examples of such ministry.

Both Vatican II and recent statements by the popes and bishops have stressed that ministry to the world in which we live is the special responsibility of lay men and women in the Church. There is every indication that Catholics in the U.S. have responded to this urging; but there are deep divisions of opinion regarding the appropriate "interventions" of Catholicism in the society outside the Church. This area may be the one in which progressive and conservative Catholic most often disagree with one another. Differences between conservative and progressive Catholics does not mean that only progressive Catholics are interested in overcoming injustice and caring for society's disadvantaged. Rather, it is a question of means: in general, while conservative Catholics look to traditional volunteer efforts, like those of the Vincent de Paul Society, to deal with social ills, progressive Catholics are more likely to criticize the status quo and advocate systemic changes in economic and political life. On public policy issues such as immigration, reform of the welfare system, or affirmative action, progressive Catholics are more often associated with the "liberal" camp. The linkage of religious and social views is so close that one needs to ask whether for many Catholics the posture of either conservative or progressive is more basically religious or political.[15]

Progressive Catholic Structures and Organizations

With the changed teaching on the role of the laity that resulted from Vatican II and the rapidly increasing participation of lay women and men in the ministry of the Church, a number of new structures are emerging to give shape to this activity. Since both conservative and progressive Catholics participate in the new lay involvement, new forms structure both approaches to Catholic life and ministry. Though the following examples do not exhaust the instances of progressive structures, they illustrate some of the diversity involved in liberal approaches to ministry in both form and function.

Perhaps the most widespread and potentially most influential of these new forms are the small Christian communities that have sprung up across the country. Many of these are parish-based: a parish (often the pastor) encourages the development of such smaller groups within the parish, which then becomes a community of communities.[16] As Archbishop May noted nearly a decade ago, "most lay people . . . regard small communities within the parish as vital in deepening their life of faith and enabling them to fulfill whatever ministry God has for them."[17] Generally, though not in all cases, such a development takes place within a parish that can be considered progressive, and attracts the participation of more progressively inclined parishioners. More obviously part of the progressive wing of U.S. Catholicism are the small communities that are formed independent of—though not necessarily opposed to—parish structures. These small Christian communities are not organized formally into any overarching structure, but informal links have been created by networking that is facilitated by groups such as Call to Action (see Appendix) or Women-Church (see chapter 2).

Another prominent structure, not new but increasingly prominent in progressive developments, is the professional society. In the early decades of its existence, the Catholic Theological Society of America (CTSA) was composed almost exclusively of seminary professors, and the seminary, controlled by the bishop, was the structure within which the teaching of theology occurred. As the location of theological research and teaching moved to universities, both Catholic and "secular," as women along with men became active in the CTSA, and as the ministry of theologians came to be understood as more than service to the official Church, the function of the society has changed. Increasingly, this society, as well as other such groups, like the College Theology Society (CTS) or the Catholic Biblical Association (CBA), has become the community of scholarship where the ministry of theology is carried on and with which individual theologians most identify. One of the clearest indications of the progressive character of this shift has been the leadership provided by the Canon Law Society of America (CLSA) in fostering reflection on the changed ecclesiology demanded by Vatican II.[18]

Though not large in numbers, the Association for the Rights of Catholics in the Church (ARCC) has been a prominent catalyst among progressive Catholics. With its membership embracing both clergy and laity, many of them prominent in other circles of Church reform, ARCC has consistently advocated a basic shift in official Church policies and the procedures that implement them. In conjunction with similar groups in Europe, ARCC agitates for structural reform in the Church, working for adoption of a constitution it has drafted to guarantee justice within the Catholic Church.

As lay involvement becomes a recognized phenomenon in Catholic ministry, a number of autonomous organizations have arisen to structure and facilitate ministries. To mention only two prominent ones: The Chicago-based National Association of Lay Catholics has directed the interests and energies of Catholic activists to the concrete needs and potential of "the marketplace." Its quarterly publication reflects the broad span of interventions in business, professional, and political life that the organization has encouraged. On the East Coast, the National Center for Pastoral Leadership has played a somewhat different role. Under the guidance of Timothy Ragan, the Center had for twenty years staged large regional conventions for religious educators and national gatherings to discuss the future of the U.S. Church. In 1996, after a year of targeting and consulting prominent Catholic leaders across the U.S., the Center set up a national program for coordinating Catholic ministry leadership, and called it the Ministry Renewal Network. An annual conference plus informational and networking services are intended to keep ministerial leaders throughout the country, clerical and lay, in contact with one another. The goal of NCPL, as stated in its promotional literature, is "to provide the highest quality of resources, programs, research, and planning strategies in fostering visionary and competent leadership to sustain and enrich the Church's ministry."[19]

Very clearly part of the progressive wing of U.S. Catholicism are organizations of former clergy, CORPUS and the Fellowship for Christian Ministry (FCM). Though formed with the goals of providing support for resigned and married priests and their families and working for optional celibacy in the Catholic Church, they have increasingly become structures of organized ministry apart from the official Church, though still identified as Catholic. Members of these two groups—membership is open to both former priests and their wives—are engaged in a range of ministries like hospital chaplaincies, pastoral counseling, and teaching. To facilitate the ministries of its members, FCM has initiated a program of formal certification for ministry to make it possible for members to function in roles, such as officiating at weddings, that require public recognition and civic credentials.

Finally, though not commonly thought of in the context of ministry, I want to mention that a key role in progressive Catholic circles has been played by publications like the *National Catholic Reporter* and *America* and by publishing houses like Twenty Third Publications, Paulist Press, and Orbis Press. One of the principal causes for the emergence of the progressive wing of U.S. Catholicism has been the raised level of information about the Church, and Catholic publications have been a major factor in this. With the advent of the Internet and unimaginable technical communication in the future, with globalization of economy and culture, there will undoubtedly be many other new structures of ministry within the Church and in its ministerial outreach to the outside world.

Concluding Reflections

What will be the pattern of Catholic ministry in the years ahead? This question could be recast by asking how men and women are today being prepared for ministries. Since the Council of Trent, when for the most part ministry was reserved to the ordained, the standard preparation of priests has been provided by seminaries, a system that remains in place today to prepare men for ordination. Today, however, many lay people are enrolled in seminaries, studying theology and ministry. In addition to those seminaries that are open to lay students, many Catholic universities have ministry-training programs that are open to lay men and women as well as to priests, nuns, and seminarians. "Today there are about three times as many men and women in graduate programs in religion, theology, and ministry who are not on an ordination track as there are seminarians in the four years of theology before ordination."[20]

A measure of the new context for ministerial preparation is the large number of graduate programs aimed specifically at lay women and men who intend to work in one or another form of ministry. More than fifty such programs, all of them Catholic, are now linked in the Association of Graduate Programs in Ministry (AGPIM) and in 1992 had an enrollment of more than six thousand students. In their curricula, they emphasize a contextual approach that is grounded on biblical and historical understanding. In their specific training orientations, they emphasize practical theology, described in the AGPIM position statement as "a mutually interpretive, critical and transforming conversation between the Christian tradition and contemporary experience . . . [which] takes place in a community of faith, implies a spirituality that is both personal and liturgical, and is directed towards individual and social transformation in Christ."

Whether programs aimed at preparing persons for ministry can be considered progressive or conservative depends basically on the theological approach they use. Since progressives and traditionalists have significantly different understandings of theology, it is little wonder that much of the controversy, official and non-official, between the two wings of the Catholic Church focuses on the activity of theologians.[21] A subsequent chapter of this book will deal in more detail with present developments in theology; but I want to pay some particular attention to theology in the context of ministry.

At the root of any social change, whether it be in the secular realm or in religion, lies a shift in the dominant ideology, the controlling explanation of reality. In the Catholic Church, theology has traditionally provided explanations for doctrine. When Anselm described theology as faith seeking understanding (*fides quaerens intellectum*), he defined its parameters. Traditional theology presumes faith (in the Church, in its teaching authority, in its doctrines) and seeks to deepen it through intelligent reflection. Yet, historically, theologians have continually widened these parameters so that there have been fundamental shifts in the ways theologians understand themselves and their task. In the recent past, and even today in some circles, the task of theology has been and continues to be much like Anselm's: theology provides explanations and defenses of official Church teaching. The starting point of theological reflection in this system is the doctrinal teaching of popes and the hierarchy. Most modern theologians, however, begin from a different place. Slowly over the last fifty years, a paradigm shift in theological method and outlook has occurred, which stresses shared faith experience and memory as a starting point. As biblical and historical scholarship have been taken seriously and used as tools by reflective theology, and as professional theology has increasingly interacted with other disciplines of knowledge, the purpose of theological reflection has been understood anew. Today, theology is not primarily a means of explaining doctrine. It understands itself as a ministry to the intellectual life, mature faith, and informed pastoral practice of the Church. In broader terms, theology can be seen as a service to contemporary thought and culture.[22] Once we understand theology in these terms, as a ministry in service to contemporary thought, we can see why conservatives resist this change. One of the characteristics of progressive Catholics as they face the future, perhaps their most distinguishing characteristic, is their belief that Vatican II pointed to the transforming role of God's spirit in the world. They view change, despite its uncertainties, dangers, and pains, as something to be welcomed, fostered, and managed.

NOTES

1. Peter F. Drucker, *The Age of Discontinuity: Guidelines to Our Changing Society* (New York: Harper and Row, 1969).

2. Xavier Rynne, *Vatican Council II* (New York: Farrar, Strauss, and Giroux, 1968). His vivid account of the strongly opposing views aired during the council helps to explain the compromise nature of major documents like *Lumen gentium*.

3. Bernard Cooke, *Ministry to Word and Sacraments: History and Theology* (Philadephia: Fortress Press, 1976), pp. 343–348.

4. Paul Bernier, *Ministry in the Church: A Historical and Pastoral Approach* (Mystic, Conn.: Twenty-Third Publications, 1992), pp. 1–81. See also William J. Rademacher, *Lay Ministry* (New York: St. Paul, 1991).

5. *Lumen gentium*, ch. 2.

6. Giuseppe Alberigo, Jean-Pierre Jossua, and Joseph A. Komonchak,

eds., *The Reception of Vatican II* (Washington, D.C.: Catholic University of America Press, 1987).

7. This discussion and the quotations from it can be found in Archbishop Roger Mahoney, "The Relationship of Priests and Laity," *Origins* 17, no. 19 (22 October 1987), pp. 349–355, and Archbishop John May, "The Laity and Parish Life," *Origins* 17, no. 20 (29 October 1987), pp. 353–356. Mahoney's quotation on p. 351, May's on p. 355.

8. In his remarks at the synod, Archbishop May pointed to a survey of the United States laity conducted for the synod. "Very few persons mention the lack of ordained priests as the primary reason for lay ministry," he said, "collaborative ministry is their high priority—co-discipleship" (Mahoney, "The Relationship of Priests and Laity," p. 355). At the same time, it is clear that the increasing shortage of ordained clergy is without question a major influence on the greater involvement of the laity in the conduct of the Church's life. The exact character of this new phenomenon is debated and demands more clarification than space here allows. See Richard A. Schoenherr, *Full Pews and Empty Altars: Demographics of the Priest Shortage in United States Catholic Dioceses* (Madison: University of Wisconsin Press, 1993). He gives a detailed sociological study of the situation.

9. Philip Murnion, ed., *New Parish Ministers: Laity and Religious on Parish Staffs* (New York: National Pastoral Life Center, 1992), p. v.

10. May, "The Laity and Parish Life," p. 355.

11. For a progressive view of desired changes in the Church, see Gerald A. Arbuckle, *Refounding the Church: Dissent for Leadership* (Maryknoll, N.Y.: Orbis Books, 1993).

12. For a recent appraisal of the letter and reaction to it see Archbishop Rembert Weakland, "Economic Justice for All: Ten Years Later," *America* (22 March 1998), pp. 8–22.

13. Jay P. Dolan, et al., *Transforming Parish Ministry: The Changing Roles of Catholic Clergy, Laity, and Women Religious* (New York: Crossroad, 1989).

14. On the role of religious educators in the parish see Maria Harris, ed., *Parish Religious Education* (New York: Paulist Press, 1978), and the more recent study of Donald G. Emler, *Revisioning the DRE* (Birmingham, Ala.: Religious Education Press, 1989).

15. Patrick M. Arnold, S.J., "The Reemergence of Fundamentalism in the Catholic Church," in Norman J. Cohen, ed., *The Fundamentalist Phenomenon: A View from Within; A Response from Without* (Grand Rapids: William B. Eerdmans, 1990), p. 174. Arnold sees fundamentalism (which he does not identify with conservatism) in the Catholic Church as having a political-religious link. "I would define modern fundamentalism as an aggressive and marginalized religious movement which, in reaction to the perceived threat of modernity, seeks to return its home religion and nation to traditional orthodox principles, values, and text through the co-option of the central executive and legislative power of both the religion itself and the modern national state. . . . [F]undamentalism is much more than a purely religious movement; rather, it involves social and political forces as well."

16. John Paul Vandenakker, *Small Christian Communities and the Parish: An Ecclesiological Analysis of the North American Experience* (Kansas City: Sheed and Ward, 1994).

17. Archbishop May's intervention at the synod. See n. 7.

18. See the special issues of *The Jurist* beginning in 1976 that contain the papers from the sessions of the permanent seminar of the CLSA (directed by James Provost). These seminars dealt with topics such as the Church as com-

munion, the Church as mission, and official ministry in the post-conciliar period.

19. For further information about NCPL and its Ministry Renewal Network, contact its office at 2661 Riva Road, Suite 1042, Annapolis, MD 21401.

20. Bernard J. Lee, *The Future Church of 140 BCE* (New York: Crossroad, 1995), p. 4.

21. At the heart of the controversy lies the issue of authority, both the extent and the nature of authority attached to statements of the magisterium, particularly to papal pronouncements. Most recently this controversy has focused on Pope John Paul II's authoritative claims in his 1993 encyclical, *Veritatis splendor* (see *Origins* 23, no. 18 [14 October 1993], pp. 297–334 for text). For two recent reactions, see Francis A. Sullivan's study of magisterial pronouncements, *Creative Fidelity: Weighing and Interpreting Documents of the Magisterium* (New York: Paulist Press, 1996), and Michael E. Allsopp and John J. O'Keefe, eds., *Veritatis Splendor: American Responses* (Kansas City: Sheed and Ward, 1995), especially the essay of Ronald R. Burke, "Veritatis Splendor: Papal Authority and the Sovereignty of Reason," pp. 119–136.

22. Hans Kung and David Tracy, eds., *Paradigm Change in Theology* (New York: Crossroad, 1989).

7
CALL TO ACTION
Engine of Lay Ministry

BERNARD J. COOKE

On October 21, 1976, 1340 women and men representing Catholics from all parts of the United States and of diverse backgrounds and views came together in Cobo Hall, Detroit, for what promised to be the most important gathering in the history of the U.S. Catholic Church. As part of the 1976 nationwide bicentennial celebration of the Revolutionary War and the country's foundation as a free republic, the Catholic bishops of the country had initiated the "Call to Action," a conference intended to stimulate American Catholics to become more involved in their religious lives. Because the bishops hoped that this meeting would help Catholics to translate the vision of Vatican II into action, thereby strengthening the mission of the Church, they had devised a process to identify the basic challenges facing Catholics in the United States as the country moved into its third century.

Starting at the local level—in parishes and religious communities—throughout the country, Catholics gathered to discuss the issues they found most crucial in their own lives. More than 800,000 responses were received from all parts of the nation and every segment of society. As people saw their ideas and suggestions moving from the parish to the diocesan level and finally to a culminating meeting in Detroit's Cobo Hall, excitement grew. Many anticipated a shift in the Church's approach to the issues that people considered of greatest interest and importance, namely methods of family planning, optional celibacy for the clergy, the morality of disarmament, capital punishment, and the ordination of women. There was widespread enthusiasm when John Cardinal Dearden, the "father of the process" and archbishop of Detroit, said, "We are trying to begin a new way of doing the work of the Church in America."[1]

During those three days in October, the excitement intensified and the candor of discussion increased as the delegates debated and then formulated a set of decidedly progressive proposals, advocating, among other things, optional clerical celibacy and the ordination of women. At that point, however, the bishops, who until then had been supportive of the process, were startled by it and, probably because they found "more action than they called for," felt the need to halt the momentum of the Detroit meeting. Despite episcopal statements to the contrary, the more progressive conclusions of the Call to Action were effectively tabled.[2] This action by the bishops generated considerable disappointment, even cynicism, in many participants. Many of the lay people who had committed time and energy to what they considered a chance to shape the ministry of the Church concluded that their role in implementing the spirit of Vatican II would be a minor one. Some of them were so demoralized that they abandoned involvement with the Church's activities.[3]

Despite the disappointment that many people experienced in Detroit, not all gave in to disappointment. Some Catholics in Chicago formed themselves into a local Call to Action group (CTA) and continued to work for change in the Church according to the guidelines of Vatican II and the conclusions of the 1976 Detroit meeting. For the next ten years, this group met for discussions in small groups and held a monthly gathering to sustain their energy and the movement begun in Detroit. They made no attempt to form a national organization. In 1987, however, along with about two hundred others, the Chicago CTA went to Rome to observe the synod of the bishops as they discussed the "role of the laity" in the Church. Both stimulated and disappointed by the synod, the Chicago CTA, now supported by some Catholics activists from around the country and led by co-directors Dan and Sheila Daley, started to move toward national status.

National recognition came in 1990 with the Ash Wednesday publication of an advertisement in the *New York Times*. "A Call for Reform in the Catholic Church" laid out a vision of a renewed Catholic community, taking up many of the issues that had been tabled in Detroit fourteen years earlier. Shortly after this advertisement, a renewed, lay-led Call to Action held a national conference on "The Future of the U.S. Church" in the Shoreham Hotel in Washington, D.C. At that meeting, a "Manifesto" of the goals and future plans of CTA, which had been prepared as a handout for convention-goers, was unexpectedly read to the assembly by Hans Küng at the end of his keynote address. This action and this meeting gave CTA a new visibility among leading Catholic activists and stimulated interest across the country.

Later that same year, CTA held its first national convention (in Chicago). Though it drew only 400 participants, attendance was no longer limited to the Chicago area, and it was clear that there was national interest in the issues and enthusiasm for going ahead with an

agenda for change. Call to Action as a national movement of progressive Catholics desirous of realizing the promise of Vatican II and of
Detroit 1976 was launched at that convention. The story since then has
been one of steady growth: attendance at national conventions in Chicago grew to more than 4000 by 1995. Conventions in Detroit in 1996
and 1997 drew similar crowds from all parts of the United States and
Canada, with a few participants from Australia and Europe.

Who attends these meetings? The women and men who come to
CTA annual conventions are usually those who are actively involved
throughout the year in a range of ministries. They include some clergy
and a number of women religious, but participants are principally lay
men and women—well-educated and informed, leaders in business
and the professions, parents of families, mostly people in middle age
but a growing number of young adults, mainly Euro-American but
striving to reach out to include both African Americans and Latino/a
Americans—for whom faith and commitment to service are the fore-
most interests of their lives. Perhaps the description given the movement by the *National Catholic Reporter*—"the principal engine driving
Catholic lay ministry in this country"—is somewhat inflated, but
there is no doubt that Call to Action has become a very important gathering place for those involved in ministry in the Church. As such, it
has the potential to be a highly effective and influential force in U.S.
Catholicism.

National Conventions

Its annual national convention has been the most visible activity of
Call to Action. At the 1996 convention—a twentieth-anniversary celebration of the original Call to Action assembly—more than 4000 attended. They included five bishops and a number of priests and
women religious, but by far the greatest proportion of attendees were
activist lay people. Talks and discussion groups and practical planning for action dealt, as they had in previous conventions, with topics
ranging from small Christian communities, to revitalizing liturgy, to
support for workers' rights, to fostering prayer in families, with a per-
vading emphasis on social justice. CTA serves a number of purposes
for the thousands who attend the annual convention: the convention
provides educational, organizational, personal, and liturgical resources.

Perhaps the most important service CTA provides is educational.
Although opportunities for deeper understanding of their Catholic
beliefs and lives have increased exponentially since Vatican II—
through periodicals, books, study groups, workshops, retreats, and
lectures organized on the parish level—the majority of American

Catholics are still relatively unaware of their religious heritage. Each year CTA assembles a roster of keynote speakers and workshop leaders that includes more than seventy prominent scholars and activists. Their range of experience and expertise provides a wide-angle lens on American Catholic practice and gives substantive information about developments in the Church and about controversial issues affecting Catholics worldwide. Often the keynote speakers draw attention to issues that are larger than Catholicism and invite participants to think globally. For example, at the 1996 convention, Hans Küng described the recent ecumenical formulation of a worldwide code of ethics, and Bishop Gaillot (bishop of Evreux in France until deposed by the Vatican in 1995) dealt with the religious imperative of overcoming worldwide poverty. Special sessions often explore sensitive topics like Christian attitudes toward homosexuality, ways to overcome racism in the Church, and improvements for boring liturgies in the parish.

Although the convention talks and workshops have been directed to practical action, to improving patterns and practices of life in the Church and in U.S. society, the general approach has been informative rather than hortatory. Understandably, some of the media reporting—in conservative periodicals like *The Wanderer*, or on television programs like CBS's *Sixty Minutes*—has highlighted controversial aspects of the gatherings. Actually, the atmosphere and tone of the meetings is notably non-confrontational. While the various talks and workshops acquaint convention attendees with a wide spectrum of information, a more valuable source of understanding is probably provided by the opportunity to spend three days with like-minded people. Individuals have the opportunity to exchange ideas, experiences, and enthusiasms with other interested Catholics from all parts of the country.

At the organizational level, the annual meeting facilitates a national network of activist Catholics. The collective energy of those interested in various ecclesiastical and political reforms facilitates large projects: lobbying Congress on social justice issues, developing youth leadership programs, and supporting small Christian communities—all efforts that link local groups in a national movement. One recent outcome of networking has been a sophisticated Internet linkage so that experiences and ideas can be exchanged worldwide. It is too early to assess the results of this continuing connection of people who first encountered one another at the yearly CTA meetings but it does suggest that new forms of Christian community, like CTA itself, are emerging in today's Church.

According to CTA members, the interconnection of like-minded people gives them a real hope for the future of the Church. As they meet thousands of women and men who believe in the implementation of Vatican II and are working to accomplish it, they find themselves energized in their local situation. Call to Action is not, of course, alone in this regard, but the movement provides many with the chance to meet large numbers of Catholics with the same interests and goals, and it provides also the realization that, despite difficulties and even some opposition, efforts at positive change in Church and society are producing results. Catholics who come to the annual convention are often isolated in their local parishes. At the meeting they say they are reinvigorated when they find thousands who share their enthusiasm and outlook.

On the personal level, CTA's annual convention has stimulated and supported the small Christian community movement in the American Church. For the past three years, a special day-long workshop immediately preceding the full convention has dealt with initiating and/or nurturing such small groups. These workshops have not resulted in CTA devising its own program for small communities, but rather have exposed people to "experts" like Bernard Lee, Art Baranowski, and Robert Pelton, who are already exercising leadership in small community development, and have facilitated linkage with national programs such as "BuenaVista."

Many of the participants in the annual convention mention opportunities for liturgy and prayer as one of the main reasons for their attendance. Carefully planned and celebrated, the principal Eucharistic liturgy of the annual convention has probably been the main object of national attention. Deliberate planning, inclusivity, creative use of the arts, and a joyous atmosphere of celebration have marked these liturgies. Liturgical dance is almost always part of the celebration, as is the presence of women at the altar in positions of prominence. Homilies are usually given by the non-ordained, the Eucharistic prayer is voiced by the entire assembly, and symbolism from African-American and Native-American cultures has been used. All these elements draw appreciative praise from participants and opprobrium from conservative Catholics. These strong differing judgments indicate the extent to which liturgical change is a neuralgic issue in progressive/conservative divisions in the U.S. Catholic Church.

In addition to a large celebratory Eucharist, a number of informally arranged prayer opportunities are scheduled throughout the convention. Quite diverse and reflecting a variety of approaches to personal or group prayer—from centering prayer as used by Benedictine monks, to daily prayer with an explicit feminist orientation, to biblically based daily reflection—these sessions have regularly drawn sizable participation despite the crowded schedule of the convention. This interest in non-official lay-organized prayer is one of the characteristic features of liberal Catholicism. Though participants in informal prayer sessions probably do not explicitly realize it, they are an expression of a widespread acceptance by lay people of Vatican II's teaching about the universal call to holiness.

Beyond Annual Meetings

While the annual convention continues to be a focus of Call to Action activity, the movement has gradually expanded its efforts. In addition to keeping in touch with its nationwide membership, now numbering close to 20,000, through its computer network and its three publications, the national office of CTA has been actively coordinating regional growth and fostering cooperation with other activist Catholic groups in North America, Europe, Asia, and Australia. Since just before the mid-1990s a spontaneous and growing development of regional branches of Call to Action has been taking place. Stimulated by their attendance at national conventions, lay men and women have formed local chapters—from San Diego to Maine and from Minnesota to Florida—in order to deal more directly and effectively with issues of Church renewal and structures of injustice in society. Whether it is this rapidly expanding regional growth or the insistence of its attention to vexing issues, Call to Action has drawn disapproval from some American bishops. The most well-publicized action was that of Bishop Bruskewitz in Lincoln, Nebraska, who condemned the local CTA chapter and threatened them with excommunication.

Reaching out beyond its own members, the national office of Call to Action has been actively engaged in Catholics Organized for Renewal (COR), a loose coalition of thirty-four Catholic organizations interested in working toward greater justice and equality in Church and society. Besides CTA, COR includes in its membership groups like the Association for the Rights of Catholics in the Church (ARCC), Dignity USA, the Fellowship of Christian Ministries (FCM), and Pax Christi, all part of the progressive wing of the U.S. Catholic Church. While individual member groups are active in various aspects of Church reform, COR itself functions as a clearinghouse for exchange of information and coordination of projects. The most recent expansion of CTA has been its interaction with the European group IMWAC ("We Are Church Movement"). So far, this connection has been informal, with attendance at one another's meetings, e-mail contact, and participation of IMWAC speakers at CTA's national conventions. One of the projects being envisaged by IMWAC is a convocation, early in the next century, of representatives from all the various Christian churches worldwide, to work toward full Christian reunion. Conversations are already underway with representatives of the World Council of Churches to consider the feasibility of such a gathering.[4]

Concluding Reflections

One indication of CTA's influence has been the attack mounted against it by more conservative elements in the American Catholic Church. When CTA met in Detroit in 1996, Mother Angelica, founding mother of the Eternal Word Television Network, organized a counter-meeting a few blocks away to denounce the "heresy" of CTA. Her meeting drew significantly fewer participants, but they were in a confrontational mood. When one of her followers showed up to picket at Cobo Hall, however, and was greeted congenially by CTA convention-goers, he gave up and left. That same year, in Lincoln, Nebraska, Bishop Bruskewitz declared CTA members in his diocese excommunicated. He has continued to attack CTA in his diocesan paper, referring to CTA members as "depraved" and "degenerate."[5] CTA remains a favorite target of right-wing papers like *The Wanderer*, and of arch-conservative groups like Human Life International.

There is no doubt that CTA has come to symbolize, perhaps more than any other Catholic group in the country, the desire of many progressive Catholics to share actively in the life of the Church and to help move it toward the ideals expressed by Vatican II. But beneath all the publicity, good and bad, what truly is Call to Action? What is it trying to accomplish? From its beginnings in Detroit in 1976 and particularly since its "resurrection" in the 1990s, the movement has had a double objective: Church reform and social justice. Essentially, its agenda is a continuation of the proposals adopted in Detroit in 1976 and tabled there by the American bishops.

Although Call to Action should not be seen as the paradigm of progressive Catholicism, it does embody many of the features that characterize progressive Catholic approaches to ministry. Its basic orientation is toward "ministries in the marketplace": CTA members generally work toward economic justice and social equality. At the same time the CTA approach to ministry is one that is involved in those issues of Church renewal that can both intensify internal Catholic life and better equip the Christian community for its ministry to the world. Its members take seriously the Vatican II teaching that they are the Church.

Despite some charges to the contrary, Call to Action is not anti-episcopal or anti-clerical. It is, admittedly, a strong group of lay people, but it does not set itself in any way in opposition to Church officialdom, even though it questions some Church policies. At the last few annual meetings, a handful of bishop-members have been warmly welcomed at national conventions and their attendance deeply and openly appreciated. At its home base in Chicago, CTA was quietly though not publicly supported by Cardinal Bernardin, a relationship cherished by the organization. Along with many other Catholics, members of CTA are concerned about the threat to regular Eucharistic celebration resulting from the diminishing number of the ordained. That concern is a factor in its espousal of both women's ordination and the ordination of married men, though another strong motive is its view that both issues involve injustice.

Many CTA members are chiefly interested in enlivening structures within the Church, especially in the exercise of ministries, while others, including the CTA national board, are working to direct the movement more to issues of injustice, nationally and internationally. Of its three regular publications, one is directed entirely to informing membership about issues of social and political concern. Although CTA members are concerned with issues like the minimum wage, reform of the welfare system, and closure of the School of the Americas, they are also very interested in justice issues within the Church. Such matters as the removal of Carmel McEnroy and Charles Curran from their teaching positions and the attempt to excommunicate CTA members in Nebraska are very much on the minds of CTA members. The organization was prominent in the international support for Tissa Balasurya that led to the Vatican lifting his excommunication, and members were delighted when Balasurya was a featured speaker at the 1997 convention.

With a national computer link, its own web page, and e-mail connections with similar groups throughout the world, Call to Action is very much involved in communications technology. What the future holds for Call to Action, no one can say. For the moment, however, CTA represents as much as any element in the Catholic Church in North America the outlook, objectives, and activity of progressive Catholics.

NOTES

1. *Origins* 6 (Nov. 4, 1976), p. 319.

2. See, for example, the cautionary remarks of Cincinnati archbishop Joseph Bernardin in *Origins* 6 (Nov. 4, 1976), p. 324, and 7 (June 2, 1977), pp. 29–32. By contrast, note Cardinal Dearden's report to the annual Bishops' Meeting a month later (*Origins* 6 [Nov. 4, 1976], p. 319).

3. Thomas C. Fox, "Made in Detroit," *Commonweal* 103, no. 24 (19 November 1976), pp. 746–748. Fox points to the tensions rising almost immediately because of the "radical" character of many of the Detroit proposals and the bishops' retreat from the process.

4. See "Attack on Crowley Part of a Bitter Harvest," *National Catholic Reporter* 34, no. 14 (6 February 1998), p. 24.

5. "Ask the Register," *Southern Nebraska Register*, Nov. 7, 1997.

8

WORSHIP IN THE SPIRIT
A Renewed Vision of Liturgy and Spirituality

ANNE E. PATRICK, BERNARD J. COOKE,
AND DIANA L. HAYES

Although the 1997–98 ABC television series *Nothing Sacred* routinely touched on issues of liturgy, spirituality, and ministry, one scene (aired on January 18, 1998) stands out for its clear portrayal of the clash between progressive and traditionalist ways of Catholic prayer and ministry. In the preceding episode, the (usually collarless) pastor, Father Ray, and his two associate pastors had all landed in jail on Christmas Eve because of a fracas surrounding the arrest of some illegal immigrants. Since social justice work abounds in this inner-city parish, neither refugees' seeking sanctuary nor priests' being put in jail for defending them is an astonishing event. But when Sister Maureen, a progressive pastoral associate, filled in for the absent clergymen by leading a Communion service at midnight Mass, she crossed a line. In the next episode—the one that embodies some of the divisive issues among American Catholics—the bishop has intervened by sending in conservative Father Martin to straighten out the situation. When the bishop's troubleshooter arrives on this scene, he immediately short-circuits the staff's usual collegial mode of operating by taking control of liturgy planning for the following Sunday, when he is to be officially welcomed to the parish.

The stage is thus set for a dramatic confrontation between Father Martin and the parishioners at Sunday worship. When he invites the congregation to join in reciting "the profession of our faith, that which makes us one true Catholic body of believers" and intones, "I believe in God, the Father . . . ," he is taken aback as the congregation adds, "and Mother." He is further dismayed by subsequent instances where credal language is changed for the sake of gender inclusivity, and finally interrupts the prayer to exclaim, "Brothers and sisters, this is the Profession of Faith!" They answer with, "Welcome to St. Thomas, Father!" and continue with their version of the creed, asserting that the mystery of the Incarnation is about the divine becoming "human" rather than "man."

It is probably safe to say that many American Catholics feel much more on the side of Father Ray and Sister "Mo" than on that of the bishop and Father Martin in this conflict. The fact that Father Martin was imposed on a parish less interested in maintaining rubrical precision than in dealing with the social and material needs of an inner-city neighborhood only sharpens the drama over the right way to pray. The regular staff members of St. Thomas (except for the agnostic Jew who handles the finances) are people of prayer, but are generally unconventional in their prayer forms. Many use gender-inclusive language, and Father Ray, when he retires to his room late at night, kneels so that he can look out into the city, and usually accompanies his meditation with a CD recording of a great jazz artist.

The fact that progressive Catholics generally endorsed this controversial television show while conservatives conducted a campaign to discourage advertisers from sponsoring it indicates that *Nothing Sacred* struck a nerve in the U.S. Catholic population. With this scene (Father Martin trying to pray against the tide of progressive parishioners) as background, we will analyze how assertive laity and independent-minded clergy and religious trace their roots to a theological vision that captured their imaginations during the Second Vatican Council. We will also explore progressive approaches to spirituality and ritual as they have expressed themselves in actual settings within this country.

Most Catholics in the United States experienced the decisions of Vatican II primarily in the worship life of their parishes. Before the council the Mass was typically classified among people's "religious devotions," something they attended. But by the mid-1960s, the Eucharistic liturgy had been reconceptualized as the heart and climax of Christian prayer, something requiring active involvement. In the first document promulgated by the council, "The Constitution on the Sacred Liturgy" (*Sacrosanctum Concilium*, 1963), the conciliar fathers observed that "the liturgy is the summit toward which the activity of the church is directed; at the same time it is the fountain from which all her power flows" (#10).[1] On this doctrinal basis they proceeded to mandate various reforms designed to promote the "full, conscious, and active participation" of all the faithful in liturgical celebrations (#14).

Characterizing their reforms as a "restoration" undertaken so that liturgical texts and rites would "express more clearly the holy things which they signify" (#21), the conciliar fathers allowed for the extension of the use of the vernacular in the Mass and sacraments. They also permitted variations in texts and actions that would reflect cultural diversity (##36–37). The changes were intended to bring the people into fuller and more active participation in the Eucharistic celebration, and thus to foster the realization among believers of a "closer union with God and with each other" (#48). The Eucharist was seen as the celebration of the entire community, and as expression and cause of the *communio* of the faithful, but the council fathers recognized that the salvific effectiveness of the celebration is conditioned by the extent to which the celebrating community is aware of what it is doing. Liturgy, in other words, had to be understandable to its participants.

Soon American Catholics were learning new hymns—often singing "Protestant" ones—and were actively participating in the Mass, now celebrated in English by a priest who faced them across an altar that had been moved from the back wall to the center of the sanctuary. Lay men and women were initially invited to read from the Scriptures, and later to help in distributing Communion, which now could include the cup as well as the Eucharistic bread. The Sunday obligation to assist at Mass could be fulfilled on Saturday afternoon or evening, the Eucharistic fast was reduced to one hour and largely forgotten, and many Catholics no longer felt they were offending God seriously if they missed participating for reasons other than illness.

In the years since the council, the changes designed to give central importance to the Eucharist and to enhance the active participation of the faithful have been broadly accepted. At the same time, practical implementation of the council's basic directives has varied widely, and responses to the revision of liturgical practice reflect one of the principal differences between progressive and conservative Catholics. On the liberal side of this line are those who tend to welcome the liturgical changes, along with new developments in spirituality and ministry, because they perceive them as leading to a deeper prayer life and a more involved sense of church than what they had known previously. Traditionalist Catholics, by contrast, tend to oppose change in this area because they believe it threatens, or even causes, the erosion of the sacred and supernatural elements of their prayer. Conservative Catholics, like those described in *Being Right*, accept the liturgical changes of Vatican II, but sometimes argue that contemporary changes are not authorized or that liberals have misinterpreted the council.

Changes in Catholic spiritual ideas and practices have been enormous since the 1960s. Not only are there dramatically different patterns of participation in central sacramental rituals like baptism and marriage, but older devotional practices such as novenas, First Friday observances, and wearing of medals and scapulars have diminished almost to the point of invisibility. Change is also evident in the increased emphasis on religiously motivated participation in various movements for peace, justice, and ecology.

The present chapter provides a map of liberal American Catholic views and practices about liturgy and spirituality in the post-conciliar period. We will discuss the patterns of change involved in these two dimensions of Catholic life, illustrate worship on the left by describing some examples of rituals conducted in progressive Catholic congregations in different regions of the United States, and conclude by noting the range of progressive approaches from moderate to radical.

Liturgy

The liturgical movement begun in Europe in the nineteenth century slowly generated an interest in revitalizing sacramental liturgies. By early in the twentieth century, it appeared to liturgical scholars that the Mass and the sacraments had become so routine that they were performed with very little congregational understanding in most Catholic parishes. The universal use of Latin was but one indication of how people's conscious and active participation was regarded as incidental. As liturgical scholars uncovered the history of early Christian practice, they began to suggest reforms that would ensure a greater sense of liturgical fidelity and revitalize Eucharistic celebration. The liturgical changes that most American Catholics now take for granted were considered strange and misguided during the first decades of this century. Nevertheless, a steady current of liturgical reform emerged in the United States under the leadership of Virgil Michel, a Benedictine priest based at St. John's Abbey in Collegeville, Minnesota. In 1926 he founded the progressive journal *Orate Fratres* (later renamed *Worship*), and he worked tirelessly to promote the kind of liturgical renewal that linked tradition, innovation, social consciousness, and a dynamic concept of the "Mystical Body of Christ."[2] As early as 1933 he called for use of the vernacular in the Mass and sacraments, evening masses, offertory processions, the priest's facing the congregation, and lay participation in the divine office.[3] As Michel insisted on a strong link between the liturgy and social justice, he also encouraged the leadership of lay women, including Dorothy Day, Catherine de Hueck Doherty, and Ellen Gates Starr.

Prior to the promulgation of Pope Pius XII's encyclical *Mediator Dei* (1947) there was little indication of official interest in or positive regard for a renewed liturgy. Indeed, the encyclical had little immediate impact on the conduct of Catholic liturgy save for some small but significant changes in the Holy Week rituals and the Eucharistic fast in the 1950s. Drastic change in liturgical practice had to wait for the Second Vatican Council, where liturgy was the subject of the council's first published document.

The "Constitution on the Sacred Liturgy" (1963) laid out a new vision of sacramental liturgies, especially the Eucharist. In addition, this document set the tone for the remainder of the council, especially by its emphasis on the laity and the model of church as *communio*, an image that laid stress on the "people of God" rather than on the hierarchical structure of the institution. In articulating far-reaching principles of liturgical worship, the constitution opened a whole new world of spiritual possibilities for Catholics and instituted a massive liturgical renewal. That renewal reflects and to a considerable extent has helped to cause a profound alteration in the religious attitudes of participants in worship. While most Catholics lack a clearly formulated understanding of soteriology (the theology of God's redemptive action), they do have a sense of God's action in the world through Jesus and can begin to describe the links between the obligations of the Gospel and their own personal salvation. What do we mean?

Until the last few decades it was almost universally understood that God called a few individuals to the priesthood. Upon ordination they received the power to transmit saving grace to others, whose task was to accept without question the teaching and grace-giving ministrations of the ordained, translate them into good moral actions, and remain faithful to a designated pattern of religious actions such as devotions, regular confession, and Sunday Mass. Today, many Catholic faithful still adhere to this worldview, but many others have come to understand salvation in a different light. Liberal Catholics see their religious lives as processes of personal maturation that involve not only their own judgments and responsibility but also their participation in a community of faith's endeavor to bring justice and peace ("the reign of God") to their world. God's role is understood as one of cooperating with this human ministry to the world by sharing the Holy Spirit. God is, thus, present to women and men on their spiritual journeys of transformation, journeys that have replaced old devotions with new practices and have reconceptualized "confession" as periodic discussion of one's spiritual growth with a "soul-mate," spouse, or spiritual director.

Depending upon which of these soteriological perspectives Catholics share, their understandings of what occurs in Eucharist are quite different from one another. The liberal or progressive view does not allow them to be content with assuming that something salvific automatically happens because they attend Mass. Nor does it permit a shift of personal responsibility to the shoulders of the ordained, or an unthinking acceptance of the authority claims of Church officials. Eucharistic liturgy is seen, at least in its ideal celebration, as a genuine sharing of faith by a community of baptized persons who join together to deepen their covenant relationship with one another and with God. In liturgy, they celebrate the saving presence of the risen Christ in their midst. Their lives are infused with the meaning of the liturgy that connects them to the whole people of God and generally propels them toward the world with ministries of care and healing.

The very centrality of this shift in theological understanding means that a wide gap has developed in American Catholicism. On the one hand are those who still function with the "automatic" viewpoint that understands official actions by themselves to be an effective means of grace. On the other are those who see the divine transforming power at work in proportion to the human effectiveness of the sacramental rituals. This second viewpoint is, in various forms and degrees, one of the determining characteristics of many liberal Catholics in the United States. An important element in this soteriological shift is the understanding that the Christian people function as the Body of Christ, making present in history the continuing influence of the risen Christ. This implies that the celebrant of Eucharistic liturgy is the risen Christ, who acts in and with the assembled community (including the ordained presider). In this view, it is the entire gathering that does the action, with various persons, including the presider, performing various roles. No one simply attends Mass. Instead, all celebrate it, much the way the entire family shares a meal on festive occasions, though there may be "consecrated" roles reserved for the elder members.

In many parishes that regard themselves as communities of faith, we find a new structuring of the liturgical action so that genuine participation can occur. In other contexts, small gatherings for prayer and reflection involve rituals of various kinds, including Eucharist. In some of these small communities, where ordained leadership is not available, or where the character of available ordained leadership is inappropriate (as it is experienced by some groups of women), sacramental rituals are celebrated without an ordained presider. Obviously this practice raises questions about such matters as the "validity" of the action and the "consecration" of the bread and wine. There is no unanimity on these questions, even among those on the left, and statistical information on the patterns of irregular Eucharistic practice is not available, although recent publications suggest a substantial trend in the direction of unofficial Eucharistic celebration. In *WomenEucharist* (1997), for example, Sheila Durkin Dierks observes that some women who feel alienated from typical Sunday liturgies have found a way to meet their spiritual needs by "gathering in informal groups, often in private homes, to celebrate Eucharist without inviting or including a priest to act as presider or celebrant." She continues:

> I have identified over 100 such gatherings in the United States. They reach out their arms from Seattle to Miami, from southern California to Vermont. They are six women, they are 30 joined in the name of

Jesus. They meet regularly (my definition: at least once a month).
Many are on a journey of discovery, some feel that they are finally
home.[4]

Such developments, as well as the authorized practice of having a lay-
person, sister, or brother lead a Communion service in the absence of
an ordained clergyman, are becoming more widespread. It is also the
case that the distinction between a Eucharist led by an ordained priest
and a Communion service conducted by a non-ordained Catholic is
lost on many Church members, who may refer to the latter as "sister's
Mass."

Today, we can find some formal theological reflection on the Eucharistic transformation of bread and wine along with a broad change
at the popular level in understandings of the Eucharist. From an almost exclusive focus on the moment of consecration of the elements as
the essence of the action there has been a movement toward regarding
the entire ceremony as an integrated unit, as a "word" that brings
about an intensification of Christ's presence to the community. Along
with this new sensibility has come—despite the bishops suggesting a
special Sunday Communion service when an ordained presider is not
available—less reception of Communion apart from the Eucharistic
action itself.

This is not to say that none of the older rubrical mentality remains.
Indeed, in many contexts both presider and congregation reject any
latitude in Eucharistic celebration beyond the explicit legislation of
Rome. Those who advocate adaptation, experimentation, and variety
tend to resist rigid adherence to official regulation of liturgical forms.
Most of the vital celebrations by caring communities—liturgies that
are often seen by conservatives as radically out of step with official
directives—vary only slightly in their externals from the official texts.
The difference between the older mentality and the newer one is,
rather, one of atmosphere: liberal Catholics are much more open to the
changes in language and understanding that are demanded by a variety of cultural settings.

Part of the atmospheric change one finds in contemporary Catholic liturgy is rooted in an important shift in language and understanding that resulted from Vatican II's encouragement of liturgical renewal.
What began as an emphasis on adaptation of the liturgy has turned
into an emphasis on inculturation. In other words, adaptation has
come to be seen by many Catholics as inadequate, as making superficial changes in the Roman rite without addressing the underlying
issues of cultural difference. By forcing different cultures to adjust to
predominantly Western European norms, the Church restricts some
essential "expressive" actions (clapping, for example, or spontaneous

verbal responses) and effectively undermines the spirit of liturgical renewal. Inculturation welcomes different liturgical expressions, finding that the "reincarnation of Christ in every culture" calls for an encounter of the Gospel with each culture to which it is brought, thereby resulting in a "new creation" that transforms both culture and faith. Theologian Peter Schineller describes inculturation thus:

> According to Pedro Arrupe, S.J., inculturation involves the incarnation of Christian life and of the Christian message in such a way that this experience not only finds expression through elements proper to the culture in question, but becomes a principle that animates, directs and unifies the culture, transforming and remaking it so as to bring about "a new creation."[5]

In fact, inculturation is not new for the Church, but rather has been an aspect of its missionary efforts throughout history (albeit more evident in situations where Christians were a minority group than in times when the Church was able to dominate cultures). It has re-emerged as an essential missionary strategy in this century and was underscored by the Vatican II document on the missions. Anscar Chapungco, who has written widely on the significance of the re-emergence, emphasizes this point:

> Through Christ, the non-repeatable historical event becomes actual, and Christ continues to be actively present in the world. The extent of the Church's incarnation in various roles and cultures will be the extent of Christ's universality. The incarnation is a historical event, but its universality lives on wherever the Church assumes the social and cultural conditions of the people among whom she dwells. . . . The Church must incarnate herself in every race, as Christ has incarnated himself in the Jewish race.[6]

Some results of inculturation in the American scene can be seen in liturgies such as the Gospel Mass of African Americans, which incorporate the values and traditions of cultures once seen as unfit to bear the weight of Christianity except in a style and form imported almost intact from Europe and alien to those who were celebrating.

Accompanying this new emphasis on inculturation are two other elements that reflect a different atmosphere among progressive Catholic communities. The first is a greater acceptance of the human aspects of liturgical action. Without losing a sense of mystery or reverence, people in more progressive or inculturated communities are more relaxed, more aware that people around them are not a distraction but part of the liturgical symbolism itself. One need only share in liturgies as distinctive as that of the Weston Priory in Vermont or St. Augustine's Church in Washington, D.C., to discover that this more human approach to Eucharist intensifies rather than diminishes the sense of divine presence. The second element, more pronounced among progressives though not completely reserved to them, is less emphasis on the moral obligation of attending Mass each Sunday. Regularity of participation in Eucharist is viewed as basically important, but not precisely because it is fulfillment of an ecclesiastical law whose non-observance constitutes a grave moral offense. Many progressive Catholics, especially if they belong to a vibrant parish community or an active small community, treasure the Eucharist. They understand the "obligation" of regular Eucharistic participation as an intrinsic need of their faith life and will search for liturgies that are carefully prepared and celebrated. They are distressed by the fact that the diminishing number of ordained presiders has reduced in many places the opportunity for regular Eucharistic celebration. On the other hand, some alienated progressives, especially women, do not attend Mass regularly and feel no obligation to do so.

The transformation of Catholic consciousness and practice where the Eucharist is concerned has been accompanied by developments affecting the faith life of progressives more generally. In the following section we shall consider these wider changes in what has come to be called "spirituality."

Spirituality

Developments occurring in Catholic devotional life since the 1960s can be summarized as a shift from supernaturalist understandings of piety and goodness to views that reflect more holistic interpretations of the ideals of Christian living and of the meaning of crucial religious doctrines (God, grace, sin, and salvation). So dramatic have been the post-conciliar changes in the theological discipline once called spiritual (or ascetical) theology that it has evolved into something of a new field, now called "spirituality."[7] Philip Sheldrake has noted three recent developments marking the maturation of this newly evolved discipline: the founding in 1991 of a journal, *Studies in Spirituality*, published in the Netherlands; the greatly increased number of courses and graduate programs in the field; and the establishment in 1992 of the Society for the Study of Christian Spirituality.[8]

Whereas ascetical theology was largely the province of those who trained seminarians and religious novices, spirituality has been increasingly important to lay Catholics, and indeed to many others in the wider culture. Sheldrake notes that "A paradoxical feature of contemporary western culture, particularly in the English-speaking world, is that alongside a decline in traditional religious practice there exists an ever-increasing hunger for spirituality." He accounts for the phenomenon by suggesting that in a postmodern era suspicious of dogma, there exists the presumption that "a coherent system of belief" is not required for "a valid spiritual quest."[9] In any event, however ordinary Catholics may regard dogma and doctrine, there is no doubt that spirituality has become an attractive subject for them, evident in the proliferation and popularity of publications, conferences, and study programs in this area. As theologian Joanne Wolski Conn has noted, "Religious publishers are selling more books about spirituality than any other kind."[10]

In contrast to the other theological disciplines, spirituality (and to some extent its predecessor, spiritual theology) has functioned to create a space where religious experience is free to interpret and express itself. Its tolerance for a limited form of pluralism is evident in the way Catholics have long distinguished, for example, Ignatian, Franciscan, and Benedictine forms of spirituality without ranking their acceptability. In the realm of doctrine and morals the magisterium has insisted on uniformity, but in matters of spirituality Catholics have enjoyed some liberty to search, experiment, and discern without pressure to be "correct" at every juncture.

This feature of spirituality is appealing to liberal Catholics who often have experienced religious authority as overly controlling in other aspects of life. Catholics disposed to assert their autonomy in spiritual matters have been influenced not only by the modern tendency to trust the "authority of experience" but also by the wave of historical consciousness about their tradition that accompanied the liturgical changes mandated by the hierarchy after the council. As these Catholics came to realize that even long-standing rituals and doctrines are products of human culture, their interest in social justice (long part of the tradition, but much more greatly stressed in the post-conciliar period) became central to their spiritual lives. Involvement in movements for peace and nuclear disarmament, racial and economic justice, equal rights for women, and care of the environment came to be seen as more important than weekly or monthly confession of sins in phrases borrowed from lists developed in another era.

Just as Ptolemaic astronomy eventually gave way to a more precise model of the universe, so also a paradigm for Christian living that stressed otherworldly, elitist, and individualistic forms of spirituality is currently yielding to a more integral vision of authentic discipleship. The eclipse of the old paradigm is not complete, but, as is clear from the literature of contemporary spirituality, very different interpretations of God and the Christian life are now widely accepted by many Catholics. Conn describes the shift in terms of a transition "from individualism, hierarchy, and male centeredness to a new paradigm of interdependence, mutuality, and inclusiveness."[11] She lists the following characteristics in contemporary work in spirituality: "sustained attention to feminist issues, concern for the link between prayer and social justice, reliance on classical sources for answers to current questions, recognition of the value of developmental psychology and its understanding of the 'self,' and agreement that experience is the most appropriate starting point."[12]

Spirituality is coming to be understood as involving not only prayer and pious practices, but the whole of the Christian religious life. Moreover, the latter is understood not merely as the vowed "state of perfection," lived by those in religious life, but as the graced reality of all the baptized. A central tenet of the Second Vatican Council was its stress on the "universal call to holiness." That millions are called to develop a spiritual life suggests the need to develop spiritualities that fit the life experiences and religious needs of an enormous variety of people. Spiritualities for lay women and men, for example, would not simply be adaptations of the rule of some religious order, but would instead grow out of and meet the exigencies of lay people's social locations and life experiences. Among other things, new spiritualities seek to remedy the historical lack of attention to spiritual dimensions of sex and family life. Moreover, Catholics influenced by the openness of the Second Vatican Council have come to appreciate the spiritualities of other religious traditions, as well as those of persons whose spirituality takes a non-religious form, for example, secular feminists or peace activists. In sum, the compass of what counts under the heading of spirituality has grown considerably in recent decades, and there has been greater affirmation of worldly values and appreciation for pluralism of experience and perspective.

Whereas pre-conciliar spirituality stressed the relationship between an individual's soul and God, the newer view emphasizes a God who is immanent in all relationships. Modern spirituality also expresses a much greater esteem for the earth and for human embodiment and sexuality.[13] According to this approach, God's valuing of our earthly existence fills history with intrinsic meaning. This divine concern for the world carries implications for Christian life quite different from those obtaining when earthly existence was regarded mainly as a testing period preliminary to "real" fulfillment in the afterlife. Whereas the spirituality of otherworldliness implicitly supplied a rationale for avoiding concern for justice and ecology, the newer approach considers these matters to be at the heart of discipleship. The new emphasis on justice and ecology is reflected in the various ways of describing this spirituality, including "creation-centered," "liberationist," "womanist," "mujerista," "feminist," and "ecofeminist." There are, of course, important differences among thinkers who claim these designations, but all share an appreciation for history and embodiment that contrasts markedly with the approach to spirituality dominant in the first half of this century.[14] This opening toward "the world" is consistent with the mandate of the council's Pastoral Constitution on the Church in the Modern World (*Gaudium et Spes*), which enjoined Catholics to be more responsible for culture and the major institutions of society and to be concerned with matters such as war and peace.

Liberal Catholics have welcomed this transformation of consciousness and the accompanying changes in the devotional life of parishes, religious congregations, and individuals. The once-thriving Holy Name Societies and Sodalities are less popular now, especially among younger Catholics. At the same time, Newman Centers, originally designed as campus ministry programs for university students, often function as parishes for progressive Catholic families and individuals who view these centers as islands of liturgical and ministerial excellence in a diocesan sea of mediocrity. Bible study groups abound, and in some instances "base communities" analogous to those in Latin American countries have emerged, either within traditional geographic parishes (as when programs such as Renew promote the growth of small "faith communities"), or apart from them. A national office for Hispanic ministry has promoted such communities among the burgeoning U.S. Latino population, which has also found nourishment in special retreats for lay men known as Cursillos, a Spanish name reflecting their purpose as short, intensive "courses" in Christianity.

Lay women and women religious have assumed leadership in providing spiritual retreats, which often include emphasis on the arts and the natural world as well as reflection on biblical themes. Whereas in the pre-conciliar period religious communities gathered monthly for common days of recollection and annually for a week of retreat preached by a priest, today it is quite common for religious sisters and brothers to seek out programs apart from their congregations or to have an individually directed or entirely independent retreat experience. The multiplicity of such options is evident in the long lists published in seasonal supplements by the *National Catholic Reporter*. In a particularly significant development, women have taken increasing responsibility for providing spiritual guidance in a range of settings. Spiritual direction has opened up many opportunities for Catholics who formerly relied only on the brief instructions of priests who often had to deal with long lines at church confessionals.

As the episode from *Nothing Sacred* discussed at the start of this chapter demonstrates, Catholic prayer and ritual life have been profoundly influenced by the feminist critique of language, not only concerning references to humanity, but also concerning images of God. In some instances presiders and readers take leadership in this matter, while in others individual Catholics simply pray against the tide of masculine images and linguistic forms on their own, omitting "men" from phrases like "who for us men and for our salvation," for example, or singing out "people" instead of "mankind." Progressive members of women's religious communities feel a particular alienation when male presiders insensitive to feminist concerns are assigned to lead their worship. It is not an exaggeration to say that many sisters have lost a Eucharistic center for community life as well as their traditional psalm-based daily prayer life.[15]

Meanwhile one finds marked diversity of spiritual expression among various ethnic groups of Catholics, as well as considerable exploration of meditative techniques and spiritual disciplines among progressive individuals. Centering prayer, Yoga, Tai Chi, and "New Age" practices, such as wearing crystals, are pursued by many who seek religious authenticity today, whereas in the pre-conciliar period these same Catholics might have attended novenas and Benediction of the Blessed Sacrament, worn St. Christopher or Miraculous medals, prayed the rosary daily, and given time to following Ignatian or Sulpician methods of mental prayer.

Although the current shift from what may be called an "otherworldly spirituality of Pilgrim's Progress" to a this-worldly spirituality of historical affirmation is neither complete nor proceeding without controversy, a consensus has developed among progressives in favor of the new model. Some of those alienated from official Catholicism are drawn to "survival spirituality," which addresses the experiences of darkness and aridity that are so prominent in today's Church. Others practice what is called "personally authentic spirituality," which carries positive associations of responsibility for others and openness to new movements of the Spirit. In either case, the spirituality of progressives has moved away from the dualisms of the earlier part of this century.

Spirituality is no longer relegated to the cloister, and matters of ecological, racial, gender, and economic justice are increasingly seen as central to Christian discipleship. The confident claiming of responsibility for one's religious and moral life is manifest in the burgeoning of organizations and networks such as Call to Action and Women-Church and in the growing popularity of holistic retreats as well as the practice of seeking spiritual direction from lay women and men. It may also be discerned in the spirit of communities distinguished by vibrant liturgies that draw on the gifts of lay Catholics as well as on those of ordained deacons and priests. In the final sections of this chapter, then, we describe instances where renewed understandings of Eucharist and Catholic spiritual life are expressed in rituals that nourish diverse communities of progressive Catholics.

St. Augustine's Church, Washington, D.C.

African-American Catholics have come to recognize that their silent and often passive presence in the Church is no longer viable, if, indeed, it ever was. They have in recent decades begun to affirm their presence in many ways more in keeping with their cultural heritage as a people whose traditions date back to Africa and the early Church.[16] No longer strangers and sojourners, they affirm the words of Pope Paul VI that they should see themselves as "missionaries to [them]-selves" and to all: "You must now give your gifts of Blackness to the whole Church."[17] Inculturation of the liturgy has been a critical aspect of the changes taking place in African-American Catholic churches. For example, some churches have installed crucifixes with images of a Black Jesus with African features, and have used cloth of African design to cover the altar and vest the presiders. The most critical shift, however, has been in the liturgical action itself. Without changing the basic Roman rite, African-American Catholics have managed to incorporate in their worship extemporaneous prayer, more fervent preaching styles, gospel songs and spirituals, and more active participation of the congregation, all of which reflect a renewed sense of Black history and tradition. In other words, they see Christ reincarnated as Black in their midst just as he has been European, Roman, and Jewish in other contexts and cultures. Black parishes in Washington, D.C., were among the first to install a baptismal pool in the church. They have led the way to a return to the full-immersion baptisms of early Christianity, and use them to baptize people during the liturgy in the presence of the entire congregation, a further symbol of the complete immersion of a person into their faith and community.

St. Augustine's Church in Washington, D.C., has been a forerunner among the many Black Catholic parishes that have developed liturgies reflective of the holistic spirituality of African peoples. Sparked by energetic and innovative priests who listened to and worked in solidarity with their congregants, St. Augustine's was one of the first parishes to institute a Gospel Mass, that is, a mass that celebrates being Black and Catholic. The parish accommodates the diversity in its predominantly Black membership by providing two different liturgies each Sunday. The 10:00 A.M. Mass, which has come to be known as the "traditional" Mass, is basically like that of white Catholic parishes, except for the addition of spirituals and occasionally a gospel hymn. The 12:30 Gospel Mass, however, is altogether different. The celebration is much more participatory, with congregants joining fully with the choir and celebrants in almost all aspects of the liturgy.

At the afternoon Mass, the large choir sets the tone and spirit of the celebration, exuberantly leading in singing spirituals and contemporary gospel songs, which are sung by the entire congregation. Leon Roberts, the former music director, has composed several Masses, including "The Mass of St. Augustine" and "The Mass of St. Martin de Porres," which helped to spread this style of worship to other parishes. Almost all parts of the liturgy are sung, from the processional to the recessional, in a gospel style that traces its roots to Africa.[18] The sign of peace is an opportunity for parishioners to move freely around the church welcoming strangers and old friends alike. One of the recurring comments of those attending St. Augustine's for the first time is about the "warm and welcoming" atmosphere. Time is seen as unimportant, and the service may flow for two hours in response to the presence and movement of the Holy Spirit in the community.

The welcoming atmosphere of the congregation, their energetic participation in the Eucharistic liturgy, and their continuing effort to make the Church an active participant in the lives of the people in the surrounding neighborhood—through senior citizen and low-income housing and support for the establishment of a federal credit union— all express the joyful, spirit-filled, holistic understanding of God and Church that are critical to the worldview of many African-American Catholics. This progressive, even radical, worldview is grounded in the present-day reality of ongoing racial and economic oppression in the Black community, which still persists in its expectation of a "new day coming" when all things will be changed. At St. Augustine's and other progressive Black parishes, the liturgy is seen as symbolic of the "Welcome Table" of the Lord, in which all are welcome to participate, regardless of race, class, gender, or sexual orientation.

Good Friday in San Antonio

One of the common features of progressive Catholic gatherings is the use of spontaneous prayers and rituals by lay women or men. San Antonio, Texas, provides an interesting example of the way in which such grassroots rituals occur side by side with more traditional practices. During Lent most of the local parishes hold the traditional Stations of the Cross. In addition, there is the distinctive practice in the Mexican-American community of having the Stations outdoors as people process through their neighborhood. On Good Friday, however, there is a full-scale public reenactment of the condemnation, way of the cross, and crucifixion of Jesus.

This drama begins at the Mercado, which ordinarily is a busy market that serves as the principal gathering place for the Latino community's numerous celebrations. There, on Good Friday, a stage is set, and amateur actors in the roles of Pilate, Herod, and Roman legionnaires enact the Gospel scene of Jesus' condemnation. Prior to the dramatization a number of local Latino dignitaries and politicians are invited to the stage and introduced to the crowd, which appears to comprise largely somewhat older Mexican Americans and their grandchildren. When the condemnation scene is ended, the procession toward the Cathedral of San Fernando begins, with the whole crowd joining in, walking along a major city street and stopping along the way for the Stations. No doubt because this ceremony has been celebrated for decades, the regular name of this street is "Dolorosa." An interesting feature of this "folk liturgy" is the involvement and support given it by many, both clergy and laity, who would be considered part of the progressive wing of the local Church.[19]

Much different is the social justice Stations of the Cross that generally takes place earlier in Holy Week. Organized by the San Antonio Peace and Justice Center, it occurs in the heart of the city amid banks and department stores and restaurants, with the obvious purpose of drawing attention to injustices and inequalities in the city and the world. As each station is reached, a particular group—students from one of the universities or members of Women-Church or representatives from Esperanza (a Latino peace and justice center), for example —prays for the suffering of those oppressed by a specific form of injustice. No one needs to make more explicit that this Via Dolorosa is symbolic of the ongoing passion of the Body of Christ. Neither supported nor opposed by the diocese, this annual street liturgy is an expression of the progressive members, most of them lay people, of the San Antonio Catholic Church. This ritual reflects the shift in soteriological understanding associated with progressive emphasis on social sin and this-worldly dimensions of salvation. It stands in marked contrast to the older emphasis on contemplating Stations of the Cross in church on Good Friday, with intense emphasis on the sufferings of the historical Jesus to atone for the personal sins of individuals.

Left and Further Left

The progressive approaches to spirituality and worship discussed in this chapter are by no means uniform in their expression. Although they all take inspiration from the teachings of the Second Vatican Council—particularly the documents on the liturgy, the Church, the laity, and the Church and modernity—there are other influences as well. As a result, today's progressives tend to line up along a spectrum ranging from those who have welcomed change more cautiously (and are now perhaps questioning certain developments) to those who continue to press exuberantly for still greater degrees of change in one or another direction.

Although they do not exactly define the range of this spectrum, two lay-edited publications help to frame a discussion of the differences among U.S. Catholic progressives at the close of the twentieth century: *Commonweal*, a biweekly magazine based in New York, and *The National Catholic Reporter (NCR)*, a weekly newspaper published in Kansas City, Missouri. A comparison of two October 1997 issues dealing with Catholic rituals makes these differences of degree quite clear.

"Celebrating Mass" is the title of a jointly authored report on the current state of Catholic liturgy that appeared in the *Commonweal* issue dated 30 January 1998. Fourteen contributors had all attended the liturgy for 19 October 1997 ("Mission Sunday," the "Twenty-ninth Sunday in Ordinary Time") and analyzed the experience for *Commonweal* readers. All these rituals were led by ordained priests, and nearly all were in churches, with the exception of two university chapels and one Catholic Worker house. In contrast to the mildly left approach of *Commonweal* was the front-page story "A Critical Mass," published in the *NCR* issue dated 17 October 1997. Written by Jane Redmont, who had danced in the event she describes, the piece is subtitled "Women break bread, break rules in experiment with liturgy." Redmont reports appreciatively on an outdoor ritual in Oakland, California (5 October 1997), in which a regular liturgy was begun and deliberately disrupted for the sake of expressing a feminist vision of what Eucharist should be. Organizers called the event "A Critical Mass: Women Celebrating Eucharist."

Commonweal's authors focused their analyses on various aspects of their worship experiences, but on the whole evinced enough satisfaction with post-conciliar changes currently under attack by conservatives—such as emphasis on Christ's presence in the assembly and the use of girl altar servers—that the designation "progressive" seems apt. Although Kathleen Hughes expressed a wish for "some nod to the existence of a Sacramentary" at the "decidedly low church" service she attended in a Minneapolis suburb, she clearly appreciated the youthful vitality and mutual affection of the worshippers. The equal balance of twenty men and women assisting the priest, and the care that "had been taken with inclusive language and in using a variety of metaphors for the name of God" impressed her.[20] The only contributor to describe a ceremony outside the U.S., Lynn C. Isabell, was highly critical of a London Mass led by a priest with his back to the congregation, which omitted the greeting of peace and required communicants to kneel at an altar rail. This "one-man show," she observed, "couldn't have been more off-putting," and Isabell was very happy to return to the "beautiful, communal Eucharist" of her home parish in San Francisco.[21]

Commonweal's editors summed up the reports by declaring that thirty years of post-conciliar reforms had not resulted in an excessively "horizontal" understanding of Eucharist at the expense of appreciation for the "vertical," or transcendent, dimension. In other words, the *communio* ecclesiology, with its emphasis on Christ's presence in the assembly, had not undermined faith in the "real presence" of Christ in the Eucharistic bread and wine, although Catholics may lack theological clarity on the precise "nature" of the Eucharist.[22] The editors, in fact, had entitled their lead editorial in the same issue "Liturgical Confusion," and used the space to attack Mother Angelica ("Rush Limbaugh in a wimple") for using her Eternal Word Television Network (EWTN) to accuse Cardinal Roger Mahony of Los Angeles of heresy because of his pastoral letter "Gather Faithfully Together: A Guide to Sunday Mass."[23] *Commonweal* insisted that "even cardinals" deserve courtesy and a presumption of good faith when they have not made heterodox statements, and defended Mahony's letter as quite orthodox and balanced in its effort to realize the conciliar ideal of "full participation of all Catholics in the liturgy." The editors confronted the position of two noted conservatives, Joseph Fessio, S.J., and Helen Hull Hitchcock, of the reactionary Adoremus movement, and exonerated Mahony of their charge that his emphasis on the assembly minimizes "the role or status of the ordained."[24] It may be the case that both sides of this debate are trying to claim the center, but in relation to Adoremus there is no doubt that *Commonweal* stands on the left.

When *Commonweal*'s discussion of liturgy is compared with the coverage in the *NCR*, however, its "leftness" appears quite moderate. The *NCR* coverage of "A Critical Mass: Women Celebrating Eucharist" includes a large photo depicting worshippers around an altar with chalice, book, and candles. Of those praying with arms raised, the two who are obviously wearing stoles are women. Jane Redmont's "commentary" emphasizes that "'A Critical Mass' had no identifiable 'presider(s)'—which was part of the point: not simply to have women as leaders in the celebration, but to transform the celebration itself."[25] A brief news article by John L. Allen Jr. notes that 300 women and men, mostly Catholics, attended the October 5 event. He observes:

> The liturgy opened with a priest in traditional vestments striding down an improvised aisle. As he intoned "In the name of the Father," a horn blew and dancers emerged, chasing the priest away and allowing those gathered to take over the service. The priest, who is married, reappeared several times, finally joining the celebration and expressing his solidarity with women.[26]

Whereas the liturgies discussed in *Commonweal* all used standard biblical readings from the official lectionary, the ritual reported in the *NCR* included selections by Teresa of Avila, Adrienne Rich, and Rosemary Radford Ruether. Allen quotes Karen Schwartz, one of the planners, on the significance of the Oakland ritual: "women's liturgies such as this are already being celebrated across the country and around the world in hundreds of feminist base communities. What makes this liturgy unique is our attempt to make it public, so that women and men in the pews of Roman Catholicism can know that liturgies such as this exist on the grassroots level."[27] NCR editors tended to agree with Schwartz's claim about the significance of the Oakland ritual. Their lead editorial declared, "One doesn't have to endorse the liturgy—and certainly there are liturgists and Catholic feminists who would take issue with the event in Oakland—to recognize the importance of taking it seriously." The tensions caused by women who speak up before everything is "all correct—liturgically, theologically, ecclesiastically tidied up"—the NCR editors suggest, are part of the ongoing historical process of the Church's development.[28]

Progressives toward the radical end of the left spectrum have always been more comfortable with such tensions than their more moderate counterparts, but the whole range of those who welcome change when it seems to bring the values of God's realm toward greater realization deserves the designation "left." What unites these progressive Catholics along a fairly wide spectrum is their faith that God's Spirit is present to these untidy historical processes, inviting all to courage and charity as they proceed.

NOTES

1. Conciliar statements quoted here are from Walter M. Abbott, S.J., ed., *The Documents of Vatican II* (New York: America Press, 1966).

2. For more on the significance of Virgil Michel, see R. W. Franklin and Robert L. Spaeth, *Virgil Michel: American Catholic, 1890–1938* (Collegeville, Minn.: Liturgical Press, 1988); Kenneth R. Himes, "Eucharist and Justice: Assessing the Significance of Virgil Michel," *Worship* 62 (May 1988), pp. 201–224; and Joseph P. Chinnici, *Living Stones: The History and Structure of Catholic Spiritual Life in the United States* (New York: Macmillan, 1989).

3. Franklin and Spaeth, pp. 83–84.

4. Sheila Durkin Dierks, *WomenEucharist* (Boulder, Colo.: Woven Word Press, 1997), p. 15. In some cases, participants in these groups are also active in Catholic parishes, as is Dierks herself, while in others the feminist groups are substitutes for parishes. For further information on these developments, see Miriam Therese Winter, Adair Lummis, and Allison Stokes, *Defecting in Place: Women Claiming Responsibility for Their Own Spiritual Lives* (New York: Crossroad, 1994), and Marjorie Procter-Smith and Janet R. Walton, eds., *Women at Worship: Interpretations of North American Diversity* (Louisville: Westminster/John Knox Press, 1993).

5. Pedro Arrupe, S.J., "Letter to the Whole Society [of Jesus] on

Inculturation," *Studies in the International Apostolate of Jesuits 7* (June 1978), p. 9; quoted in Peter Schineller, S.J., *A Handbook on Inculturation* (Mahwah, N.J.: Paulist Press, 1990), p. 6.

6. Anscar Chapungco, *Cultural Adaptation of the Liturgy* (NewYork: Paulist, 1982), p. 59; see also Diana L. Hayes, "Emerging Voices, Emerging Challenges: An American Contextual Theology," in David Schultenover, S.J., ed., *Theology for the Third Millennium* (Lewiston, N.Y.: Mellen Press, 1991), pp. 41–60.

7. This section on spirituality draws heavily on material from chapter 6 of Anne E. Patrick, *Liberating Conscience: Feminist Explorations in Catholic Moral Theology* (New York: Continuum, 1996). Other helpful sources are: Walter H. Principe, "Toward Defining Spirituality," *Studies in Religion/Sciences Religieuses* 12 (1983), pp. 127–141; Sandra M. Schneiders, "Spirituality in the Academy," *Theological Studies* 50 (1989), pp. 676–697; and Joan Wolski Conn, "Toward Spiritual Maturity," in Catherine LaCugna, ed., *Freeing Theology: The Essentials of Theology in Feminist Perspective* (San Francisco: HarperSanFrancisco, 1993), pp. 235–259. See also Michael Downey, ed., *The New Dictionary of Catholic Spirituality* (Collegeville, Minn.: Liturgical Press, 1993).

8. Philip Sheldrake, S.J., *Spirituality and History*, rev. ed. (1991; London: SPCK, 1995), p. 5.

9. Ibid., pp. 1–2.

10. Conn, "Toward Spiritual Maturity," p. 235.

11. Ibid., p. 253.

12. Conn, *Spirituality and Personal Maturity* (New York: Paulist, 1989), p. 31.

13. As womanist theologian Toinette Eugene has observed, "Spirituality is no longer identified simply with asceticism, mysticism, the practice of virtue, and methods of prayer. Spirituality, i.e., the human capacity to be self-transcending, relational, and freely committed, encompasses all of life, including our human sexuality." Quoted from "While Love Is Unfashionable: An Exploration of Black Spirituality and Sexuality," in Barbara Hilkert Andolsen et al., eds., *Women's Consciousness, Women's Conscience* (Minneapolis: Winston Press, 1985), p. 124.

14. In a chapter on spirituality in his volume *An Alternative Vision: An Interpretation of Liberation Theology* (New York: Paulist, 1985), theologian Roger Haight perceptively distinguishes this newer spirituality from "one-sided" forms that tend to affirm one half of a polar tension at the expense of the other, whereas liberationist spirituality affirms both poles of the tension at once. Thus pre-conciliar spirituality stressed the divine transcendence at the expense of God's immanence, affirmed the spiritual by denigrating the physical and material, favored contemplation over action, and emphasized the individual without due regard for social context. Liberationist spirituality, by contrast, seeks a balance of these factors (pp. 237–238). Other forms of spirituality on the left have also sought to restore this balance, sometimes in ways that can be considered "overcorrections."

15. One group that has addressed the inclusive language issue for the traditional prayer of the Divine Office is the Sisters of Our Lady of Mount Carmel, Indianapolis. Their *People's Companion to the Breviary* (2 vols.) features inclusive language and readings from a variety of contemporary sources. Their *Woman's Prayer Companion* is a sensitive modern translation of ancient Christian prayers into contemporary usage. For more information contact the Carmelite Monastery, 2500 Cold Spring Road, Indianapolis, IN 46222.

16. See Cyprian Davis, O.S.B., *The History of Black Catholics in the United States* (New York: Crossroad, 1991).

17. "To the Heart of Africa" (Address to the Bishops of the African Continent), *The Pope Speaks*, vol. 14 (1969), p. 219.

18. It should be acknowledged that Roberts was not the first to conjoin the ritual of the Mass with the musical traditions of African Americans. Father Clarence Rivers is the forerunner who, in the 1960s and 1970s, laid the foundations for Black Catholic liturgy.

19. The video *Soul of the City/Alma del Pueblo*, produced by the Mexican American Cultural Center (San Antonio, 1996), documents the Good Friday procession and shows the importance of the cathedral and its programs for San Antonio Catholics.

20. Kathleen Hughes, "Celebrating Mass: Minneapolis, Minnesota," *Commonweal* (30 January 1998), p. 18.

21. Lynn C. Isabell, "Celebrating Mass: London, England," *Commonweal* (30 January 1998), p. 14.

22. "Celebrating Mass," *Commonweal* (30 January 1998), p. 9.

23. Editorial, "Liturgical Confusion," *Commonweal* (30 January 1998), p. 5.

24. Ibid., p. 6.

25. Jane Redmont, "Women Stake Claim to Rites," *National Catholic Reporter* (17 October 1998), p. 4.

26. John L. Allen Jr., "Mass by Women Said in Public," *National Catholic Reporter* (17 October 1997), p. 4.

27. Ibid.

28. Editorial, "Mass in Oakland Too Critical to Shrug Off," *National Catholic Reporter* (17 October 1998), p. 32.

9

A MINISTRY OF JUSTICE

The 25-Year Pilgrimage of the
National Assembly of Religious Women

ANNE E. PATRICK

Within a decade of the Second Vatican Council, Catholic women had brought progressive ideas on spirituality and ministry to a level undreamed of by the bishops who endorsed the conciliar schemas. Over Thanksgiving weekend in 1975 they convened the historic Women's Ordination Conference in Detroit, Michigan, attracting some 1,200 persons to consider the topic "Women in Future Priesthood Now." The gathering was an expression of solidarity among lay women and women in religious vows (and some progressive men as well), but the majority of those who planned and attended the conference were nuns.[1]

The cooperation of many progressive individuals and groups contributed to the gathering's success, and one of these groups, the National Assembly of Women Religious (which in 1982 became the National Assembly of Religious Women to signify the full inclusion of lay members) is of particular interest to this volume because its members epitomized a particular post-conciliar vision of Catholic life. Since NAWR/NARW survived for only twenty-five years (1970–1995), its brief history provides a focused case study of the strengths and weaknesses of post-conciliar idealism.

Religious sisters in the United States have a history of significant achievement—and no little willingness to follow their own lights in the face of hierarchical incompetence when it was encountered— but their strategy before the council had been to minimize public expressions of conflict and to proceed with the "quiet grace" and "unshouted courage" of a subordinated class within a male-dominated religious institution.[2] Many sisters, moreover, had internalized the ideology of their own oppression and given the laity reason to think of them as "sweet," "pious," "unworldly," and generally incapable of assertive behavior or criticism of churchmen, much less organized opposition to a long-standing tradition such as the exclusively male priesthood.

In Detroit, however, hundreds of nuns spoke with the authority of their recently acquired graduate degrees in the sacred sciences and the power of their convictions. What accounted for this transformation, this willingness to object publicly to centuries-old practice and to assert their dissonant beliefs with such confidence? I will point to three factors that clearly contributed to the transformation of U.S. sisters after the council: educational, cultural, and religious.

In the first place, through farsighted planning in some communities and also the inter-congregational efforts of the Sister Formation Conference, women religious in this country had been highly educated. Moreover, because most sisters had earned college and graduate degrees while holding jobs in schools or hospitals, habits of continuing education were well established among them. Thus when opportunities to study the new theology became available, these women found ways to take advantage of them. In addition, many sisters with leadership experience in their own institutions were poised to bring this experience to bear on wider contexts of contemporary Church and world.

A second factor contributing to the transformation of American Catholic sisters involved the wider cultural context of the United States during the 1960s and early 1970s. Sisters were profoundly affected by the social movements for civil rights, peace, and women's liberation, and many who participated in these struggles applied what they were learning about injustice to their own situation in the Church.

Finally, and most importantly, nuns were explicitly religious in their reasons for doing what they did. Faith in God was quite deep, and their habits of prayer and spiritual reading led them to connect the above-mentioned cultural movements with the mandate experienced by biblical prophets to speak out in favor of changes that would bring justice to the oppressed. It was not a great leap to the position voiced by Nadine Foley at the Detroit conference in 1975: "The conflict between official Church pronouncements and the spirit of the Gospel with its message of freedom of persons through the redemptive activity of Jesus Christ is not merely theoretical."[3]

The 1975 Detroit conference took place when NAWR had been in existence five years. Organizationally strong, it had 103 diocesan organizations of sisters as "council" or "senate" members, with direct links to tens of thousands of nuns in these dioceses, and also some 3,500 dues-paying individual sisters as "grassroots" members, along with an unspecified number of clergy and lay associates. Within five years, however, membership had declined dramatically, to 23 sisters councils or senates and 1,400 individual members, and although some gains were made after lay women were admitted to full membership, the statistics of the early 1970s were never regained. By 1995 the decline in membership and turnover in the central office staff resulted in an insurmountable fiscal crisis, and NAWR disbanded.[4]

Why did this group flourish so briefly? What led to its demise? What does this case signify for American Catholicism, and especially for progressive members of the Church? I will suggest idealism as an important contributing factor. This organization's power was due in some measure to talented and dedicated women who were able to articulate a Gospel-based mission in terms of social justice. Once assembled, however, the idealists found it hard to choose among ways of focusing their efforts and structuring their membership. The conciliar spirit of openness and especially the value of inclusivity led them to invite increasingly diverse women into their ranks and governing board, and also led them to ponder their "Catholic identity." These changes may have caused the erosion of their original membership base. Although the ultimate explanation of NARW's demise was lack of funds, its collapse seems attributable, at least in part, to the increasing weight of its own idealism.

NAWR/NARW's history illustrates several liberal post-conciliar developments, notably an inclusive ecclesiology and a commitment to a feminist vision of social justice. Besides helping establish the Women's Ordination Conference in 1975, NAWR/NARW initiated the founding of the social justice lobby Network in 1971 and fostered other local and national efforts for justice in subsequent years.[5]

NAWR: Ministry, Social Justice, and Justice for Women

Although women's religious communities had worked in relative isolation from each other prior to the Second Vatican Council, the development of such groups as the National Catholic Education Association (1904), the Sister Formation Conference (1952), and the Conference of Major Superiors of Women (1956) (known after 1971 as the Leadership Conference of Women Religious, or LCWR), as well as diocesan organizations for religious educators and others, had provided some experiences of collaboration. Women religious built on these experiences with great energy in the years of renewal and adaptation immediately after the Second Vatican Council.[6] Nuns who had previously seen the apostolate primarily in terms of their duties in hospitals or schools staffed mainly by their religious communities came increasingly to use the term "ministry" for their activities and grew interested in diverse expressions of apostolic energy on an intercongregational basis as well as with lay colleagues. Sisters with experience in the civil rights movement or in local community-organizing activities were particularly influential in catalyzing the growth of new associations of women religious, first at local and regional levels, and eventually at the national level.[7]

From the first, NAWR's decision to have both corporate members (sisters councils and senates) and individual ("grassroots") members resulted in ongoing tension between those whose ties to diocesan structures led them to proceed somewhat more cautiously on controversial questions and many of the individual members, who were not accountable in the same way to women religious in their home dioceses. Indeed, a progressive group led by Margaret Ellen Traxler, S.S.N.D., had already decided in 1969 to found another organization, the National Coalition of American Nuns, precisely to establish the forum for speaking out independently and promptly on issues that NAWR's more cumbersome structures made difficult to achieve.[8]

Twin themes of "ministry" and "social justice" have marked the history of NAWR/NARW. A groundbreaking essay by Marjorie Tuite, O.P., distilled some of the material that she and community-relations trainer Sam Easley presented during numerous workshops on justice sponsored by NAWR and other organizations around the country during the 1970s. Tuite's insistence that women religious must "use power creatively—individually and corporately—to discover and empower the human agenda" found resonance among many NAWR members, who adapted community-organizing strategies to various Catholic contexts.[9] Books, booklets and resource packets dealing with such topics as "Lifestyle" (1975), "Models of Ministry" (1979), "Economics: Women's Cry for Change" (1987), "Sexism Is a Sin" (1990), and "Creating Inclusive Community" (1992) were published by NAWR/NARW and sent out to members. The emphasis on education for activism leading toward a more just society is a consistent theme of this literature, as of other NAWR/NARW activities, including the annual conventions and special workshops. The clientele for these meetings changed dramatically over the years, but the theme of "Empowerment, Justice, and Change," as a 1991 brochure describing several NARW skill-training workshops was entitled, remained constant.

Throughout the organization's history members regularly received *Probe*, which started out as a simple typewritten, photo-offset periodical and then adopted a tabloid newspaper format in 1981. Originally subtitled "What are sisters thinking?" *Probe* began as a sounding board for sisters' views on religious life, the contemporary Church, and new roles for women. It also provided summaries of convention resolutions and research reports on topics related to the organization's agenda, which had been expressed in terms of a "vision goal" adopted by the second House of Delegates assembly in Minneapolis in 1972, namely to exercise "a ministry of justice by the continuous use of our organized power to effect local and national policy for the liberation of all peoples from oppression."[10]

In 1973 NAWR established a committee on Women in Church and Society, which institutionalized the feminist spirit that had been growing within the group. NAWR also helped to form a national network of sisters who acted regionally to promote consciousness raising and feminist activism. A 1971 convention resolution had called for women's ordination to the diaconate, and the following year the delegate assembly had voiced support of women's "full participation in the priesthood." In June of 1974, Mary B. Lynch, the leader of the U.S. branch of the Association of Women Aspiring to the Presbyteral Ministry, approached me, in my capacity as the chair of NAWR's committee on women, about the feasibility of having a national meeting on ordination. We quickly drew up a plan for a small gathering to be facilitated by NAWR board member Nancy A. Lafferty, F.S.P.A., at the Catholic Theological Union in Chicago on 14 December 1974. It was this meeting of 31 representatives from seminaries, national Catholic organizations, and women's religious communities that led to the historic conference in Detroit the following November, "Women in Future Priesthood Now: A Call for Action," and the subsequent founding of the Women's Ordination Conference organization. Meanwhile some 650 NAWR members, assembled in St. Louis for the annual convention in August of 1974, went on record overwhelmingly in support of eleven Episcopal women ordained to the priesthood in a controversial July 29 ceremony in Philadelphia. In a telegram sent August 14, NAWR urged the Episcopal House of Bishops to "affirm and recognize" the ordinations because they are "a sign of hope authenticating the ministry of women in the church and a valid response to the Gospel values of human dignity, service, and justice."[11]

Membership and the Ideal of Inclusivity

NAWR reached its membership peak in the 1970s with approximately 100 sisters councils or senates and some 5,000 individual members. The ideal of inclusivity that led NAWR to extend full individual membership to lay women in 1978, however, did not increase overall membership. Indeed, the change in policy and resultant shift in identity were accompanied by a significant loss of the original membership base. In 1980 there were only 1,400 individual members and only 23 diocesan organizations of sisters. The name change to National Assembly of Religious Women (NARW) in 1982 signaled more clearly the organization's commitment to inclusivity, and the election of four lay women to the national board in 1984 brought this commitment to a new level of possibility. By 1985 NARW's board included six sisters and six lay women, and the board was co-chaired by two of the latter, Maureen Reiff and Pauline Turner, while Marjorie Tuite, O.P., served as national coordinator of the organization. Overall membership figures eventually improved, reaching by 1992 approximately 2,800 women who paid dues or contributed services. Although the membership had become one-third lay by 1983, the overall number of sisters had declined, and the statistics of the 1970s were never regained. By 1985 NARW reported 27 local groups of members in 20 states, but the links with diocesan groups of sisters had been relinquished. As a smaller, less-structured "movement organization," NARW continued to press the inclusivity ideal, and a 1990 report describes the "metamorphosis of NARW" as involving a "change from an organization of predominantly White women in religious congregations into a grassroots organization of women, more than half of whom are lay women and more than 15 percent of whom are African American, Latina, Asian, and Native American women."[12]

The ideal of inclusivity intensified with time, so that in 1981 the members who convened in Boston opened the possibility of non-Catholic women joining NARW by rephrasing the organization's "vision statement" in general terms: "We are religious feminist women committed to the prophetic tasks of giving witness, raising awareness, and engaging in public action for the achievement of justice."[13] The fact that Tuite, NAWR's national coordinator from 1981 until her death in 1986, was at the same time on the national staff of the largely Protestant group Church Women United provided new opportunities for ecumenical and interfaith collaboration.

By 1985 NARW's justice agenda, long voiced in opposition to racism, classism, sexism, militarism, and clericalism, began to extend also to the areas of heterosexism and environmental concern. Moreover, under the leadership of Judy Vaughan, C.S.J., national coordinator during 1987–1992, efforts to bring women of diverse economic and racial-ethnic backgrounds into NARW activities were greatly increased. When NARW celebrated its twentieth anniversary at a 1990 conference in Cleveland, more than 120 of the 300 who attended were Latina, African American, Asian, or Native American. The 1992 convention in Spokane, which was designed to counter celebrations of the Columbus quincentenary, was even more markedly multicultural, with particular emphasis on indigenous heritages. By then the inclusivity ideal had been extended also in the direction of youth, so that teenaged women constituted 10 percent of the 500 in attendance.[14] Meanwhile Spanish had been introduced into Probe in 1987, a reflection of the fact that NARW's vision statement was amended that year to emphasize working inclusively for justice.

Programs, Protests, and Collaboration

While the anti-racism imperative continued to dominate NARW's agenda, by the late 1980s attention to women's economic situation also led to a special focus on homeless women. Workshops on "Undoing Racism," "Creating Inclusive Community," and "Homeless Women: Creating Community, Creating Change" were prominent activities during NARW's final years. During 1989–1990 NARW sponsored skill-training sessions for homeless women in eleven cities, and in 1991 the organization was awarded a grant of $50,000 from United Way of Chicago for continuing this work under the program title "Empowerment, Justice, and Change."

In addition to programs, NARW's commitment to justice was expressed in many protest actions: boycotts in support of farm and factory labor movements, peace marches, vigils to end the violence in El Salvador, demonstrations against sexism in the churches, and protests against the Persian Gulf war were all part of NARW's public mission. Their 1981 vision statement—"We are religious feminist women committed to the prophetic tasks of giving witness, raising awareness, and engaging in public action for the achievement of justice"[15]—committed them to raise awareness and work for change.

Over the course of NAWR/NARW's history, its network of contacts and collaborators had extended in many directions, and increasingly they went beyond the borders of the United States. In 1975 I represented Sisters Uniting, an umbrella group of several national sisters' organizations at the International Women's Year Tribunal in Mexico City, and in 1979 NAWR sent Yolanda Tarango, C.C.V.I., and Mary O'Keefe, O.P., to participate in "Mujeres para el Diálogo" discussions held in connection with the Puebla meeting of the Latin American bishops' conference (C.E.L.A.M.).[16] In 1982 national coordinator Marjorie Tuite, O.P., participated in a peace march in Italy, and the following year she led a study tour to Nicaragua. Seven NARW members participated in Cuatro Encuentro Feminista de Latino America y el Caribe in 1987, and a year later NARW initiated a series of four retreat experiences in Ocotal, Nicaragua. In addition, NARW's national coordinator, Judy Vaughan, C.S.J., was among the official observers of the Nicaraguan elections in 1990.

Concluding Comments

Undoubtedly there were many factors that contributed to the fiscal crisis that caused NARW to dissolve in 1995. Finances may have been the bottom line, but I believe that six additional factors bear investigation. They are timing, erosion of the original membership base, a distrust of institutions in general, a very fast rate of change, the weighty burden of idealism, and the loss of a shared theological and liturgical tradition.

TIMING

Arguably the life and death of NAWR/NARW reflected a unique historical moment. Women religious in this country were poised to appreciate the progressive ideals of the Second Vatican Council and to implement them. NAWR also gained impetus from the 1971 Synod on Justice, and the organization's peak in terms of membership coincided with a general sense of optimism about the possibilities for continuing reform that lasted through the mid-1970s. The Vatican's explicit rejection of women's ordination in 1976, the distancing of American bishops from the more progressive results of their bicentennial hearings and the Detroit "Call to Action" conference that same year, followed by the ecclesiastical repression associated with the papacy of Pope John Paul II all contributed to the alienation of many progressive Catholic women from their own tradition, or if not from Catholicism altogether, from its hierarchical leadership.[17] NAWR/NARW's ambiguity about its relationship to Catholicism in the second half of its life reflects this alienation, which has been particularly strong among feminists.

This alienation deepened when the Vatican threatened twenty-four women religious with expulsion from their communities because they had signed a statement about the abortion issue, which was published in the New York Times in the heat of the U.S. presidential campaign of 1984. NARW's national coordinator, Marjorie Tuite, O.P., was among these signers, and this fact not only increased tensions on the board for many months, but also took a considerable toll on Tuite's health, as she gave much time and energy to dealing with the controversy. Tuite reported in May 1986 that her case had been closed, and a few weeks later she was hospitalized for surgery. A diagnosis of cancer was soon confirmed, and she died June 28, 1986. The entire episode, which also involved other prominent NARW members (including Judy Vaughan, C.S.J., who eventually succeeded Tuite as national coordinator), further distanced progressive Catholic women from the Vatican.

Another factor related to timing involves the less well-publicized personal situations of many of NAWR's original members. The organization's early days coincided with their decisions about changing from traditional works in schools and hospitals to a variety of new ministries, and as these women became educated to new professions such as law or theology they brought the organizational know-how obtained through NAWR to new settings, both professional groups and groups focused on Church reform.

EROSION OF ORIGINAL MEMBERSHIP BASE

The U.S. communities of women religious whose members first organized sisters councils or senates and then established national organizations like NAWR were at their peak of numerical strength immediately after the Second Vatican Council, with 1966 statistics showing 181,421 sisters in the United States. But the years of renewal and adaptation saw many departures from religious communities, and by the time NAWR was founded in 1970 the overall number of sisters had dropped by more than 20,000, to 160,931.[18] The steep decline continued, so that in 1978, when NAWR first welcomed lay women as full members, there were 129,391 sisters in this country. Four years later, in 1982, when the organization's name was changed to NARW, there were 121,370 sisters, nearly one-third fewer than immediately after the council. Indeed, the number of sisters continued to fall throughout the period of NAWR/NARW's history, with a count of 92,107 (a drop of nearly 50 percent since 1966) at the time the organization folded in 1995. Thus, one can read the difficulties of the group's later years to some extent as reflecting the decline of U.S. sisters more generally. Not only were the sisters fewer in number, but they were aging and increasingly burdened with financial worries about funding their retirement needs without a strong base of younger members. These congregations could no longer afford to subsidize ventures like NARW at the level needed when the staff were drawing even modest salaries at the national office. As funding became increasingly dependent on grants and donations, the organization could not sustain its programs.

DISTRUST OF INSTITUTIONS

An attitude discernible among many progressives is the impatience with which they sometimes regard structure and institutions. There is often more energy for critique and dismantling of structures than for rebuilding. Ironically, as the group sought to express the ideal of inclusivity more fully (and also to model a non-hierarchical team approach to leadership), it allowed its organization-maintenance (especially among the original base) to diminish, and the notion of regular replacement of national leadership was seemingly forgotten after 1981, when for reasons that warrant study, NARW allowed itself to become an organization increasingly identified with a single leader, Tuite, from 1981 to 1986, and Vaughan from 1987 to 1993.

THE RATE OF CHANGE

The many changes that NAWR/NARW implemented in its relatively brief existence led to gains, especially as women from more varied backgrounds learned of its ideals and activities, but also resulted in losses, particularly in continuity and stability of membership. Many women did not continue to pay dues after their initial interest had been sparked by a convention or other event .

THE WEIGHT OF IDEALS

Committed to a ministry of justice, NAWR/NARW felt the burden of injustice keenly, whether in the Church, in the wider society, or in its own ranks or those of its collaborators. With many justice issues constantly on the table, and various programs, protest activities, and strategies for change under discussion, tensions often ran high. The effort to institutionalize justice through bringing representatives of formerly excluded women onto the board naturally assembled an increasingly different set of interests and experiences. Perhaps more might have been done to deal directly with the tensions resulting when these differences were voiced. It may also be asked whether NAWR/NARW's prophetic stance (articulated explicitly as such in the 1981 assembly) aimed at such a perfection of justice that the journey itself became too difficult for most members to sustain over a long period of time. Also, the multi-issue approach that had always characterized NAWR/NARW led to a certain diffusion of energy, and it is likely that many women who initially benefited from the approach moved on in time to concentrate on specific local projects or became involved in national organizations with more limited but focused agendas.

LOSS OF SHARED THEOLOGICAL AND LITURGICAL TRADITION

NARW gained immensely from experiencing the variety of religious wisdom and women's ritual leadership available when it discontinued traditional Catholic celebrations of Eucharist at its gatherings. One may ask, however, if the loss of a worship tradition that included occasional attention to the Christian doctrine of sin and forgiveness as matters of daily life may have been associated with the organization's inability to hold members. Aspirations to prophecy and perfection can sometimes result in a moralism that brings discouragement and disunity. Psalms and Eucharistic prayers, which feminists may abandon because of their historic links with sexism, have served as reminders of divine transcendence and of human limitations.

CONCLUSION

Although these factors are reasonable speculations, we need a much more extensive history of the organization before we will be able to come to stronger conclusions. What is not a matter of speculation, but rather one of historical record, is the fact that thousands of women in this country were inspired by NAWR/NARW's vision of a ministry of justice. Through *Probe,* resource packets, books, conventions, workshops, and especially through personal contact with others who shared the ideals of liberation and empowerment, many women gained knowledge, experience, skills, and a wide network of associates who could be tapped for assistance with countless activities in behalf of justice and peace.

NOTES

1. See Anne Marie Gardiner, S.S.N.D., ed., *Women and Catholic Priesthood: An Expanded Vision: Proceedings of the Detroit Ordination Conference* (New York: Paulist, 1976).

2. These phrases are borrowed from Katie Geneva Cannon's groundbreaking study, *Black Womanist Ethics* (Atlanta: Scholars Press, 1988), and used analogously here. Jay P. Dolan writes in *The American Catholic Experience* (Garden City, N.Y.: Image, 1985) that sisters "were the Catholic serfs, having fewer rights and fewer options than priests, brothers, or lay people" (p. 289).

3. Nadine Foley, "Who Are These Women," in Gardiner, cited note 1, p. 4.

4. "The National Assembly of Women Religious (NAWR)—1968–1975" and *Probe* (Summer 1995). The 1975 flier includes a diagram showing the organization's complex structure as of 1975. The national executive board included representatives of fourteen geographic regions spanning the entire country, chairs of seven national committees, and three officers.

5. A comprehensive historical study of this significant organization has not yet been done. The group's archives are at the University of Notre Dame. Also important for research on NAWR/NARW are the papers of Marjorie Tuite, O.P., a key figure in NAWR from its inception until her death in 1986, which are stored in the Gannon Center at Loyola University in Chicago. Of particular help for this essay have been Judy Vaughan's article, "National Assembly of Religious Women (NARW)," in Sarah Slavin, ed., *U.S. Women's Interest Groups: Institutional Profiles* (Westport, Conn.: Greenwood Press, 1995), pp. 283–287, and the historical data given in the final issue of NAWR/NARW's periodical *Probe,* vol. 23, no. 2 (Summer 1995). I was a board member of NARW from 1972 to 1975 and consulted several people as I wrote this chapter. My thanks go to Ethne Kennedy, S.H., Rosemary Rader, O.S.B., Merle Nolde, O.S.B., Pauline Turner, and Judy Vaughan, C.S.J., for information provided in recent interviews.

6. Ethne Kennedy, S.H., reviews this early history in "The Changing World of Women: 1972," the foreword to her edited volume *Women in Ministry: A Sisters' View* (Chicago: NAWR Publications, 1972), pp. 9–18. Also valuable is the historical summary by Hildegarde Marie Mahoney, S.C., "Sisters Councils: Their Beginnings," *Probe* (September–October 1981), pp. 13–14, which gives an account of events leading to NAWR's establishment.

7. In addition to Marjorie Tuite, O.P., notable examples include Margaret Ellen Traxler, S.S.N.D., founder of the National Coalition of American Nuns (NCAN), and Carol Coston, O.P., the first executive director of Network, a Catholic social justice lobby. Traxler's and Coston's stories are found in a volume edited by another NCAN leader, Ann Patrick Ware, S.L., *Midwives of the Future: American Sisters Tell Their Story* (Kansas City, Mo.: Leaven Press, 1985), pp. 129–139 and 146–160.

8. A tenth-anniversary membership renewal form reflects NCAN's outspoken approach to justice advocacy: "During the 70s NCAN analyzed issues; took unpopular stands . . . published study guides on relevant issues; badgered, barraged, and buffeted the bishops." NCAN's newsletter had supported the Equal Rights Amendment, disarmament, civil rights for homosexuals, gender-inclusive language, and "'home rule' for nuns," along with other progressive causes of the 1970s. NCAN remains a small, efficient, and outspoken group today.

9. Marjorie Tuite, "Gospel Ministry," in Ethne Kennedy, ed., *Gospel Dimensions of Ministry* (Chicago: NAWR Publications, 1973), p. 7.

10. Quoted here from 1975 NAWR flier, "The National Assembly of Women Religious (NAWR)—1968–1975."

11. *St. Louis Globe-Democrat*, 16 August 1974, p. 8-A.

12. "NARW Annual Report: August 1989–July 1990," p. 2.

13. *Probe* 11 (September–October 1981), p. 1. Various opportunities for ecumenical collaboration led to some questioning of the "Catholic" identity of the group. A flyer from this period said that although a majority of members relate to the Catholic tradition, membership is open to women of all faiths. This interfaith focus complicated NARW's identity throughout the 1980s, though by 1990 the group had reclaimed "Catholic" in its self-description.

14. The ideal led next to the decision that "At least two young women will be invited to be part of the 1994 Conference Planning Committee," according to the NARW Annual Report (August 1992–July 1993), p. 4. This intended gathering on the theme "Celebrating Women's Sexuality: Healing Ourselves, Healing the Earth" never took place because of NARW's financial difficulties.

15. *Probe* (September–October 1981), p. 1.

16. For reports on the Puebla meetings, see *Probe* for April and May 1979.

17. For sociologically grounded accounts of this alienation, see Andrew M. Greeley and Mary G. Durkin, *Angry Catholic Women* (Chicago: Thomas More Press, 1984), and Miriam Therese Winter, Adair Lummis, and Allison Stokes, *Defecting in Place: Women Claiming Responsibility for Their Own Spiritual Lives* (New York: Crossroad, 1994).

18. The comparative value placed on priestly vocations and vocations of religious sisters and brothers by the hierarchy may be seen in the fact that worries about the loss of clergy were articulated much sooner and louder than notice was taken of what was happening to the non-ordained religious. It took fifteen years for the drop in the number of priests in this country to approach 1,000, from 59,193 in 1966 to 58,398 in 1981, which represented a decline of just over 1 percent (795). Meanwhile within the same period religious brothers had declined by more than 4,000 (by 1981 there were 4,489 fewer brothers, a drop of more than 36 percent from the 1966 figure of 12,255) and nuns had declined by nearly 60,000 to 122,653 in 1981 (58,768 departures and deaths within fifteen years caused a 32 percent drop from the 1966 peak of 181,421 sisters). All statistics are from P. J. Kennedy & Sons Official Catholic Directory.

Part 5

RACE AND ETHNICITY

10

CATHOLICISM IN THE UNITED STATES AND THE PROBLEM OF DIVERSITY

The View from History

JOHN T. MCGREEVY

It is one of the Christian community's oldest problems. The Pauline letters are saturated with discussion of how to define the boundaries of the early church community and what practices will count for authentic membership in the same. Catholics eager to further racial tolerance in the twentieth century frequently referred to Paul's admonition that all were "baptized into one body—Jews or Greeks, slaves or free —and we were all made to drink of one Spirit."[1]

It is also a peculiarly American dilemma. Historians of American Catholicism have long understood that their subject is at certain points almost coterminous with that of immigration history, but the point bears repeating. The United States became in the nineteenth century the most important destination for the largest voluntary mass migration in human history up until that time—the movement of Europeans across the Atlantic. The numbers are staggering: 33 million Europeans came to the United States between 1821 and 1924, and over two-thirds of these migrants remained in the United States for the rest of their lives. The percentage of these immigrants who were Catholic is unknown, but it is perhaps half that number, beginning with the waves of Irish and Germans in the 1840s and 1850s, and culminating with Italians, Poles, and Lithuanians before and during World War I.[2]

The still inadequate quality of the English language literature on these Catholic immigrants—especially from the vantage point of European religious archives—makes essays of this sort a hazardous endeavor.[3] What remains clear, though, is that this immigration determined the initial configuration of the modern Catholic "race" problem. Even though it sounds anachronistic to contemporary ears, most Catholics in the nineteenth century understood "race" conflicts as battles between Irish and Germans, or slightly later, Irish and Italians, or Lithuanians and Poles. The phrase "racial groups" when used by Catholics might refer to African Americans, but it more commonly suggested the various Euro-American populations. "It is true," explained Father Anton Walburg in 1889, "that the Irish vote and the German vote, still exist; but there is nothing more un-American in these than there is in the Labor vote, the Colored vote, the Saloon vote." Referring to battles between Irish and German priests, Father Walburg maintained that the Church should "not take part in the idiosyncrasies, in the antagonisms and war, of races."[4] When the Knights of Columbus sponsored a series of textbooks on "race" groups in order to promote tolerance in the 1920s, officials commissioned volumes on African Americans, Germans, Irish, and Italians.[5]

The internal Church "racial" question erupted with particular force in the late-nineteenth-century dispute termed Cahenslyism. On one side were an international group of Catholics, led in Europe by German Reichstag member Peter Paul Cahensly, Italian Bishop John Baptist Scalabrini, and a handful of French-Canadians. In the United States, Cahensly found support from virtually all German Catholic leaders and some of the more conservative Irish prelates. This diverse group became concerned that American bishops and pastors were hostile to unfamiliar worship and devotional traditions, as well as parochial schools using foreign languages. This hostility, according to Cahensly and Scalabrini, led to apostasy. On the other side, Archbishop John Ireland of St. Paul and his allies rallied Catholics worried that new immigrants would remain isolated on linguistic and cultural reservations, never contributing to the greater American whole.[6]

These struggles among German, Irish, and Italian Catholics extended from Rome across the United States and quickly became enmeshed with debates over the role of parochial schools and theological modernism. Vatican officials generally saw wisdom in Cahensly and Scalabrini's approach to the immigration question, and repeatedly asked American, Canadian, and Brazilian bishops to justify their treatment of Catholic immigrants. The same officials also tended to view national parishes for Italians, Germans, and Poles as a natural consequence of constant human traffic across the Atlantic.[7]

What remain intriguing for the purposes of this essay are the complicated alliances that were then already forming around the subject of what we might call Catholic multiculturalism. The tone of arguments made by those Catholics eager for the assimilation of co-religionists frequently edged into an intra-Catholic nativism. Archbishop Ireland consciously distorted the modest request of the 1891 Lucerne Memorial (signed by Cahensly and drafted by representatives of Bishop Scalabrini) for bishops of diverse ethnic origins into an "unpardonable" conspiracy to "meddle . . . in the Catholic affairs of America."[8] Ireland's friend, Minnesota Senator Cushman K. Davis, warned on the Senate floor of German Catholic attempts to "denationalize American institutions and plant as many nations as there are people of foreign tongue in our midst." By contrast, Ireland praised Irish immigrants for adopting "American ideas and manners" and the "national spirit."[9] Church historian John Gilmary Shea scolded German Catholics for forming "foreign camps" that would only heighten Protestant unease about Catholic intentions. The Reverend Edward McGlynn complained of "foreign born citizens [who] . . . make no concealment of their sense of superiority and of their contempt of Americans, and of American manners and traditions" and "an ecclesiastical power, secret and despotic in its methods."[10]

These same assimilationists or liberals, however, also tended to offer what limited support existed in Catholic circles for the integration of African Americans into either Church or society. It was Ireland, for example, who boldly attacked state laws prohibiting black and white intermarriage and urged the opening of all professions to African-American applicants. Significantly, Ireland also termed St. Paul's one African-American "national" parish a "temporary expedient," and was lionized by French-speaking Catholic Creoles in New Orleans then battling religious and public segregation.[11] And McGlynn was one of the few Catholic priests to offer support for Republican Party efforts to reconstruct the South.[12]

German-American Catholics and many of their allies took a more multiculturalist position, or as philosopher Charles Taylor puts it, they demanded "recognition" more than integration.[13] A memorial directed to the Vatican complained that German parishes needed "equality and independence because in many places they are denied to us." German pastors should not endure "dependence and subordination."[14] Bishop Scalabrini wrote that "Language is a mysterious means of keeping the faith. . . . experience teaches us that so long as a family living abroad preserves its native language, it does not lose its faith."[15]

Astonishingly bitter struggles among Polish Catholics, in particular, forced the issue of assimilation into sharper focus. In Chicago, Detroit, Omaha, and other cities, a group of younger, more nationalist Polish priests and parishioners accused older colleagues of exploiting faithful Poles by building large cathedrals even as Polish workers struggled for daily essentials. Such cathedrals were registered in the name of non-Polish bishops and archbishops—an especially neuralgic point—and these same bishops and archbishops could remove, or refuse to remove, pastors of Polish parishes. In Chicago, these complicated disputes produced a series of riots and confrontations, and in other cities the situation was barely more cordial. Chicago's archdiocesan chancellor explained to the apostolic delegate in 1895 that the archdiocese could not accede to the request of some unhappy Poles for a new pastor. "No city in the world [is] like [Chicago]," he insisted. "The same principle might if granted be applied by Germans and Bohemians."[16]

The vast majority of Poles remained firmly within the Roman Catholic communion, but frustration did lead to a series of unprecedented schisms. Most important, in Scranton in 1907, Father Francis Hodur formed the Polish Nationalist Catholic Church, which by 1925 counted 84,000 members and 71 parishes. Hodur repeatedly emphasized how Catholic denial of legitimate Polish aspirations had driven him to this step. As he wrote in the first church constitution, "The Polish nation is undertaking a terrible life-or-death struggle there in Europe . . . and here in America, where under the cloak of the community of the Roman religion Irish bishops try to exploit it, denationalize it, and harness it to their own political chariots."[17]

This fear of schism made the argument for national parishes and some concessions to ethnic interests more persuasive to Catholic leaders.[18] But it also may have quelled whatever impulse existed for Catholics to insist upon integration in either church or society. Advocates of more multicultural policies occasionally extended their interest beyond internal Church "racial" issues to matters outside church walls. German Catholic editor Arthur Preuss, for example, condemned lynchings of African Americans in the South even as he denied that Germans must assimilate to an as yet undefined American national culture.[19]

Still, those favoring the more multicultural position, unlike Ireland or McGlynn, generally attached themselves to the virulently racist Democratic party. Instead of praising the end of slavery and the Union effort in the Civil War, influential Catholic editors like James McMaster in New York City and Franco-American Jules Tardivel (writing from Quebec) regretted the abruptness of immediate emancipation, and opposed any expansion in federal government activities.[20]

Assimilationists such as Ireland triumphed on the specific Cahensly matter by persuading more conservative co-religionists that Roman bureaucrats and German nationalists were aspiring to direct American Catholic affairs. But the general portrait of American Catholicism in the early twentieth century was far less uniform than Ireland or his allies had hoped. In Detroit in 1933, Catholics could still hear the Gospel preached in twenty-two different languages. "How often," complained one priest in 1930, "is it said that this organization or that institution is 'Irish' or 'German'?" A 1920 Carnegie Foundation report described how "the great mass of [Catholic] immigrants belong to racial churches of their own."[21]

When African-American Catholics moved into the heavily Catholic urban North in the first decades of the twentieth century, then, they encountered a painfully achieved Catholic multiculturalism. African-American Catholics, like Poles, Italians, and other Euro-American groups, were expected to worship in their own parishes, receive the ministrations of religious order priests dedicated to work in their community, and learn from nuns devoted to working in their parochial schools. Some African-American Catholics used language similar to that used by German Catholics decades previously. As one Cleveland resident informed his bishop, "The Church in her wisdom, although looking ever toward the day when all nations shall be as one, nevertheless realizes that under earthly conditions religion and piety are best developed along ethnological lines and She therefore tolerates the division into racial groups."[22]

In practice, though, Catholic multiculturalism existed alongside a system of racial organization that emphasized the difference between "black" and "white." Students from various Euro-American backgrounds were accepted at all Catholic schools and institutions in the 1930s. Only African-American Catholics were denied admission. As African American Gustave Aldrich complained, "the second and third [immigrant] generations are absorbed into the general parish work; their separate churches become English speaking or disappear. Not so with the segregated churches for colored people."[23]

Two developments would alter this situation. First, Euro-American Catholics in the 1920s, 1930s, and 1940s came more vividly to think of themselves as both American and white. Spurs to this development included the forced end of mass European immigration in 1924 and the maturation of a Catholic community less aware of differences among Euro-Americans. Shared experiences in the Depression and World War II and, often, membership in the Democratic party and an industrial union also forged a new cohesiveness.[24] This more common Euro-American Catholic culture made it clear that barriers against African-American Catholics were a matter of racial prejudice, not cultural difference. Note the way in which one Brooklyn pastor discussed his neighborhood in 1938. "What was once an Irish German congregation," he wrote, "is composed at present of six thousand white people and four hundred Catholic Negroes." Irish and Germans, once ethnics, had become whites.[25]

The second development came from within the Catholic community, through the unlikely vehicle of a patrician Jesuit, Father John LaFarge. Deeply influenced by the emerging social doctrine of the Church, LaFarge decided that "the totally inadequate concept of race" could not be an acceptable Catholic category. Catholic institutions should open their doors to all qualified applicants, and African Americans in particular must be welcomed as members of Christ's Mystical Body. Unity must mark Catholicism in a divided and philosophically confused world. LaFarge even drafted part of a proposed Vatican encyclical that linked anti-Semitism and racial prejudice.[26]

This focus on integration made LaFarge and his associates uneasy with black Catholic advocacy groups, especially Thomas Turner's Federated Colored Catholics, which proposed to "perpetuate and increase the national solidarity" in much the same way as the Order of the Hibernians or the Polish Roman Catholic Union. By the early 1930s LaFarge and his allies had quietly but effectively edged aside the Federated Colored Catholics and formed their own Catholic Interracial Councils. These actions—taken by white clerics against African-American lay people—now seem less liberal than paternalist. And too, LaFarge's habitual caution—he once warned African Americans suffering from discrimination that "we may have to counsel patience and some degree of silence"—is less defensible in a post–civil rights age.[27]

Equally important, the view that "racial" organizations were not genuinely Catholic worked against much of recent Catholic history, which saw ethnicity and culture as natural organizing principles. Some Catholics opposed to discrimination disagreed with the very idea of "interracialism," arguing that cultural segregation of African Americans into Catholic associations and parochial schools was a useful way to strengthen African-American Catholic identity. Catholic schools especially, as opposed to integrationist activism, were seen as the key to African-American empowerment.[28]

Nonetheless, LaFarge's elegant prose and persistent activism provided a generation of Catholic bishops, intellectuals, and diocesan officials with a rationale for the integration of Catholic institutions. By 1959, LaFarge could confidently state that "the ideological controversy, the acknowledgment of the principle of interracial justice—has been won." The interracial argument formally triumphed in 1958 with a statement by the American bishops attacking discrimination. A more informal acknowledgment of victory was the growing reluctance of bishops to build national parishes for ethnic groups. One priest predicted that the "racial Church" [for African Americans] would disappear, "just as the national Church is gradually moving by itself away from its former isolation." When asked, "If Segregation is wrong now why wasn't it always wrong?" Catholic liberals were instructed to reply that "Precisely to help the Negro, as she did to help the Irish and the Germans and the Slavs . . . the Church did make special provision for them" but then to term these policies "temporary expedients."[29]

The power of this integrationist ideology was most evident in the response to Puerto Rican and Mexican immigrants in the 1940s and 1950s. Bishops confronted with Latino migrants in the early part of the century typically permitted the formation of national parishes, in accordance with practices established for German, Italian, and Polish immigrants. In the postwar period, however, at the exact moment when the Puerto Rican and Mexican migrations accelerated, bishops and Catholic intellectuals frowned upon this sort of "segregation." One 1955 clergy conference report for New York priests, for example, emphasized that new national parishes were "not advisable" because they halted the "process of integration."[30]

The moment of triumph for Catholic liberals convinced that integration could solve the race problem was brief. In retrospect, the focus by Catholic liberals on the universality of Catholic practice and the need to abandon distinctive ethnic rituals evokes the immediate postwar period, just as reassertions of the importance of ethnic identity instantly mark the late 1960s. David Hollinger terms this process the move from species- to ethnos-centered argument—first presuming that all humans are fundamentally alike, then beginning to stress the differences that mark particular cultural groups. Commonality becomes less interesting than diversity.[31]

The philosophical corollary to this broad process in American intellectual life was a conviction that universal claims conceal particularist agendas. "Man" means only men. Thornton Wilder's *Our Town* does not include Richard Wright's Chicago. The social movement most important for this intellectual transition was of course the civil rights movement, which by the late 1960s had evolved into Black Power and a focus on ethnic identity. African-American Catholics began this process within the Church, asking whether standard rituals, liturgical practices, and prayers were Catholic, or simply white. "The Church has tried to convert blacks to whiteness," charged one African-American Catholic nun. "Consequently, mental and physical harm has been caused to black people." Black Catholic organizations of lay people, priests, and nuns quickly formed in the late 1960s and early 1970s, a process that, as Gary Riebe-Estrella outlines in his essay for this volume, extended into the world of Catholic theology. Timothy Maitovina's essay in this volume points to a parallel process evident in the Latino community.

Even Catholic liberals fervently committed to integration in the first years of the decade began to have second thoughts. The director of the National Catholic Conference of Interracial Justice noted that when "Catholic Negro laymen recently organized a Council of Negro

Laymen in Cleveland many looked askance. The group replied that the Poles had their priests and their Church, the Irish had theirs, and the Italians theirs. . . . Not a very wide vision, perhaps; but who is to say that it is not a realistic one?" Cleveland's Commission on Catholic Community Action decided that "It is time now for the Church and the Commission to manifest and give evidence of the fact that the only way to help anyone is by having a special regard for that person's race and color."[32]

An equally powerful inspiration for new Catholic thinking about racial issues, however, did not stem from the American situation. Instead, the bishops at the Second Vatican Council, while reaffirming the long battle of interracialists against discrimination, altered the terms of discussion. No longer would the mark of the universal Church be its uniformity across time and culture. The most obvious change was the use of the vernacular in all liturgies, but conciliar documents also emphasized the link between evangelization, properly understood, and a sensitivity to local situations. According to *Gaudium et Spes*, the Church is "not bound exclusively and indissolubly to any race or nation, to any one particular way of life, or to any customary pattern of living."[33]

The emergence of liberation theology in the years immediately following the council cemented this transformation. The immediate impact on the North American Catholic milieu remains uncharted.[34] Catholics had been intimately involved on both sides of César Chávez's heroic effort to organize the United Farm Workers in California's Central Valley, but Chávez himself had received his theological education from the older papal encyclical tradition. Chávez's many liberal Catholic supporters tended to see the struggle simply as an analogue to Martin Luther King Jr.'s efforts in the South, and a natural outlet for Catholic energy following conciliar pleas to work for social justice. And, too, Chávez consistently stressed Gandhian nonviolence, while some advocates of liberation theology clearly drew upon Marxian analyses of class struggle.[35]

Still, the stress placed by Peruvian theologian Gustavo Gutiérrez and others on the need for theological reflection to grow out of specific social experiences resonated deeply with African-American and Latino Catholic intellectuals. Gutiérrez urged theologians to adopt the vantage point of the poor, but in the North American context poverty seemed inextricably intertwined with racial discrimination. (Indeed, Afro-Brazilians made much the same criticism of liberation theology.[36]) Mexican-American theologian Virgilio Elizondo recalled his excitement at first reading the 1971 Peruvian edition of Gutiérrez's *Teología de Liberacion*. "From the documents of Vatican II and our own experience of exclusion," he explained, "we pretty well sensed what had to be done but it was not yet clear. Reading Gustavo's work was like turning on the light switch." Gutiérrez, arguably the most important liberation theologian, spent a part of almost every summer in the 1970s and 1980s working with Mexican Americans in San Antonio.[37]

The current situation has its share of ironies. Beginning in the early 1970s a "liberal" position on identity matters within the Church has meant a willingness to tolerate division into ethnic groups, a fostering of a certain liturgical diversity, and an eagerness to promote devotional customs from varied cultures. Precisely the same attributes marked the "conservatives" of the late nineteenth century, making today's multiculturalists the figurative descendants of the German Catholic Central Verein and foreign-language Catholic groups. Catholic "liberals" of the mid-twentieth century stressed the importance of individuals from all cultures worshipping together in a uniform rite, a position rarely defended today, but certainly viewed as conservative.

The surge of Asian and Latin American immigration after the alteration of American immigration laws in 1965 has produced the most powerful echo of the Catholic past.[38] Vietnamese, Puerto Rican, Haitian, Cuban, and Mexican Catholic immigrants all claim the attention of Church and public authorities, making American Catholicism at once the home of a broadly affluent population of Euro-American Catholics and again an immigrant church. The very presence of these groups ensures the persistence of old debates about representation and integration.

Members of these immigrant groups are not uniformly "liberal" on Church and political matters, and some, especially Vietnamese and Cuban Catholics, are generally conservative.[39] Still, the intuitive sense that Catholics primarily concerned with racial matters and social justice are theologically liberal remains accurate. Catholic conservatives want a more just society as well, but it tends to be liberals who make the most vocal calls for the government to redistribute wealth, or who emphasize social service programs, not simply Catholic education, as a way to assist impoverished minority groups.

The situation of Mexican-American Catholics presents the sharpest break with American Catholic history. In one sense, Mexican-American Catholics might be understood as the late-twentieth-century equivalent of German Catholics, with Los Angeles as the new St. Louis and Phoenix as the new Milwaukee. And, too, in an echo of their German predecessors, Mexican Americans struggle to obtain Spanish-language Masses in multiethnic parishes, and repeatedly encounter clergy unfamiliar with Latino religious practices.[40]

But this analogy quickly collapses. Mexican-American Catholics are no longer a "minority" group—one million Latino Catholics (the vast majority of whom were Mexican) were added to membership rolls in the Los Angeles archdiocese during the 1980s, and Latinos are predominant not just in Los Angeles but in twelve American dioceses. Within roughly thirty years Latinos may total half of the American Catholic population, even as considerable numbers turn to evangelical Protestant churches.[41]

German Catholics, too, were once the majority in many American dioceses, but the combination of assimilation, waning immigration, and hostility to German culture during World War I effectively dismantled the once vast German Catholic network of institutions.[42] Predictions about a Mexican-American community with a substantial population solidly in the middle class, many of whom are more comfortable in English than Spanish, are equally perilous. But easy access to air travel, geographical proximity, the constant stream of legal and illegal immigrants, and even the ability to read Mexican newspapers on the Internet may produce a hybrid form of both American and American Catholic citizenship.

Mexican-American Catholics also emigrate from a Catholic culture far less shaped by the Tridentine and nineteenth-century Catholic revivals so important in Germany and Ireland.[43] In retrospect, German and Irish Catholics shared enthusiasm for parochial schools and ultramontane devotions, produced large numbers of religious vocations, and made Catholic institutions vital to immigrant communities.[44]

The situation for Mexican Catholicism has been closer to that of Italian Catholicism, with its anti-clerical heritage, a nationalism often juxtaposed against the Church, and a complex devotional life directed by women and existing in the home. Religious belief in both cultures has (at times) depended only indirectly on the efforts of the "institutional" Church.[45] The relatively small number of Mexican-American vocations to the religious life, until recently, has also ensured a paucity of Mexican-American voices in a clerical Church.[46]

Mexican and Mexican-American Catholicism, too, is changing, and any forecast should more honestly be termed a guess. What does seem evident, though, is that the Catholic integration problem of the twenty-first century will center around the contact between an overwhelmingly Euro-American Church structure and an increasingly Latino Catholic population. The result will be either the first American Church, combining the people and ideas of the northern and southern halves of the continent, or an impoverished vehicle.[47] John LaFarge once wrote of a Catholic "vision of the Kingdom" as one in which "all tribes and races . . . were united in love and . . . service." This optimism, and the example of the many Catholics still faithful after enduring discrimination, may serve as inspiration in the decades ahead.[48]

NOTES

Thanks to the editor of this volume for her enthusiasm, and to Peter D'Agostino for an especially insightful reading of an initial draft of this essay.

1. 1 Corinthians 12:13; Wayne A. Meeks, *The First Urban Christians: The Social World of the Apostle Paul* (New Haven: Yale University Press, 1983), pp. 74–110.

2. Frank Thistlewaite, "Postscript," in *A Century of European Migrations, 1830–1930*, ed. Rudolph J. Vecoli and Suzanne M. Sinke (Urbana: University of Illinois Press, 1991), p. 55; Walter Nugent, *Crossings: The Great Transatlantic Migrations, 1870–1914* (Bloomington: Indiana University Press, 1992), p. 14. Still useful on Catholics and immigration is Gerald Shaughnessy, *Has the Immigrant Kept the Faith? A Study of Immigration and Catholic Growth in the United States 1790–1920* (New York: Macmillan, 1925).

3. For example, Colman Barry's work on German Catholics is now almost fifty years old, but remains unsurpassed in its use of archival sources. Colman J. Barry, O.S.B., *The Catholic Church and German Americans* (Milwaukee: Bruce Publishing Company, 1953).

4. Rev. A. H. Walburg, *The Question of Nationality in Its Relations to the Catholic Church in the United States* (Cincinnati, 1889), pp. 14, 62.

5. Edward McSweeney to W.E.B. DuBois, May 10, 1922, frame 1199, reel 10, W.E.B. DuBois papers, microfilm copy.

6. The literature is large. Superb on the ecclesiastical dimension of the crisis is Gerald Fogarty, *The Vatican and the American Hierarchy from 1870–1965* (Stuttgart: Anton Hiersemann, 1982), pp. 35–194. Among the many relevant biographical accounts, Marvin O'Connell, *John Ireland and the American Catholic Church* (St. Paul: Minnesota Historical Society, 1988), is especially shrewd. Compelling on one of the conservatives is John Louis Ciani, S.J., "Across a Wide Ocean: Salvatore Maria Brandi, S.J., and the 'Civilta Cattolica' from Americanism to Modernism, 1891–1914" (Ph.D. dissertation, University of Virginia, 1992). Joseph Gerard Hubert, "'For the Upbuilding of the Church': The Reverend Herman Joseph Heuser, D.D., 1851–1933 (Volumes I–III)" (Ph.D. dissertation, Catholic University of America, 1992), is especially thorough.

7. Edward Claude Stibili, "The St. Raphael Society for the Protection of Italian Immigrants, 1887–1923" (Ph.D. dissertation, University of Notre Dame, 1977), pp. 11–187; John E. Zucchi, "The Catholic Church and the Italian Immigrant in Canada, 1880–1920: A Comparison between Ultramontane Montreal and Hibernian Toronto," in *Scalabrini Tra Vecchio E Nuovo Mondo: Atti del Convengno Storico Internazionale (Piacenza, 3–5 dicembre 1987)*, ed. Gianfuasto Rosoli (Rome: Centro Studi Emigrazione, 1989), p. 495.

8. O'Connell, *John Ireland*, p. 311. A copy of the Memorial is in Barry, *The Catholic Church and German Americans*, pp. 313–315.

9. Barry, *The Catholic Church and German Americans*, pp. 202–203, 296–97.

10. Barry, *The Catholic Church and German Americans*, p. 52; Rev. Edward McGlynn, "The New Know-Nothingism and the Old," *North American Review* 145 (August 1887), pp. 195–196, 202.

11. O'Connell, *John Ireland*, pp. 268–269; John Ireland, *The Church and Modern Society* (Chicago: D. H. McBride, 1896), p. 161; Douglas J. Slawson, "Segregated Catholicism: The Origins of Saint Katherine's Parish, New Orleans," *Vincentian Heritage* 17 (1996), p. 163.

12. Robert Emmett Curran, S.J., "Prelude to Americanism: The New York Academia and Clerical Radicalism in the Late Nineteenth Century," *Church History* 47 (March 1978), pp. 50–52.

13. Charles Taylor, *Multiculturalism: Examining the Politics of Recognition* (Princeton: Princeton University Press, 1994), pp. 25–74.

14. Barry, *The Catholic Church and German Americans*, pp. 53, 289–290.

15. Giovanni Battista Scalabrini, "Memorial of Bishop G. B. Scalabrini on the Congregation or Commission for Catholic Migrants (Pro Emigraits Catholicis)" [1905], reprinted in *Bishop Scalabrini's Plan for the Pastoral Care of Migrants of All Nationalities* (Staten Island: Center for Migration Studies, 1972), p. 24.

16. Robert Trisco, "The Holy See and the First 'Independent Catholic Church,'" in *Studies in Catholic History: In Honor of John Tracy Ellis*, ed. Nelson H Minnich, Robert B. Eno, S.S., and Robert F. Trisco (Wilmington, Del.: Michael Glazier, 1985), p. 200. For another view on events in Chicago, Joseph John Parot, *Polish Catholics in Chicago, 1850–1920* (DeKalb: Northern Illinois University Press, 1981), pp. 95–132. For disenchantment with the links between employers and Polish priests, Leo V. Krzywkowski, "Polish and Hungarian Reactions to Roman Catholicism in Nineteenth Century Northern Indiana," *PNCC Studies* 6 (1985), p. 96.

17. Hieronim Kubiak, *The Polish National Catholic Church in the United States of America from 1897 to 1980* (Warsaw: Nakl. Uniwersyteta Jagiellonskiego, 1982), p. 121; "Goals and Purposes of the Polish National Church of America" [1907], reprinted in *PNCC Studies* 9 (1988), p. 83.

18. Bishop Scalabrini made precisely this argument in "Memorial of Bishop G. B. Scalabrini," p. 29. Note also the routine appointment of specific priests (especially Polish priests) to serve as ethnic brokers within the Church. Parot, *Polish Catholics in Chicago*, pp. 158–160.

19. Rev. Rory T. Conley, "Arthur Preuss, Journalist and Voice of German and Conservative Catholics in America, 1871–1934" (Ph.D. dissertation, Catholic University of America, 1995), pp. 47, 105.

20. On the Democratic Party, Morton Keller, *Affairs of State: Public Life in Nineteenth Century America* (Cambridge: Harvard University Press, 1977), pp. 250–259. On German Catholics and the Democratic Party, Jon Gjerde, *The Minds of the West: Ethnocultural Evolution in the Rural Middle West 1830–1917* (Chapel Hill: University of North Carolina Press, 1997), pp. 312–317; Sr. Mary Augustine Kwitchen, O.S.F., *James Alphonsus McMaster: A Study in American Thought* (Washington: CUA, 1949), pp. 145–183; Pierre Savard, *Jules Paul Tardivel, La France et Les Etats-Unis, 1851–1905* (Quebec: Les presses de l'université Laval, 1967), pp. 32–35.

21. Leslie Woodcock Tentler, *Seasons of Grace: A History of the Catholic Archdiocese of Detroit* (Detroit: Wayne State University Press, 1990), p. 3; John O'Grady, *Catholic Charities in the United States: History and Problems* (Washington, D.C.: National Conference of Catholic Charities, 1930), p. 277; John Daniels, *America Via the Neighborhood* (New York: Harper and Brothers, 1920), pp. 242–246.

22. John T. McGreevy, *Parish Boundaries: The Catholic Encounter with Race in the Twentieth Century Urban North* (Chicago: University of Chicago Press, 1996), p. 32.

23. Ibid., p. 34.

24. On the Depression, Lizabeth Cohen, *Making a New Deal: Industrial Workers in Chicago, 1919–1939* (New York: Cambridge University Press, 1990), pp. 213–368. On American nationalism and World War II, Gary Gerstle, "The Working Class Goes to War," in *The War in American Culture: Society and Con-*

sciousness during World War II, ed. Lewis A. Erenburg and Susan Hirsch (Chicago: University of Chicago Press, 1996), pp. 105–127.

25. McGreevy, *Parish Boundaries*, p. 36.

26. McGreevy, *Parish Boundaries*, pp. 38–47; Georges Passelecq and Bernard Suchecky, *The Hidden Encyclical of Pius XI*, trans. Steven Rendell (New York: Harcourt, Brace, 1997).

27. The most important biography of LaFarge is David Southern, *John LaFarge and the Limits of Catholic Interracialism, 1911–1963* (Baton Rouge: Louisiana State University Press, 1996), esp. pp. 105–185. Also see Robert A. Hecht, *An Unordinary Man: A Life of Father John LaFarge, S.J.* (Lanham, Md.: Scarecrow Press, 1996).

28. McGreevy, *Parish Boundaries*, pp. 55–64.

29. McGreevy, *Parish Boundaries*, pp. 90, 140.

30. McGreevy, *Parish Boundaries*, p. 83; Jaime Vidal, "The Rejection of the Ethnic Parish Model," in *Puerto Rican and Cuban Catholics in the U.S., 1900–1965*, ed. Jay P. Dolan and Jaime R. Vidal (Notre Dame: University of Notre Dame Press, 1994), pp. 70–87.

31. David A. Hollinger, *Postethnic America: Beyond Multiculturalism* (New York: Basic Books, 1995), pp. 51–78.

32. McGreevy, *Parish Boundaries*, pp. 224, 226–227.

33. Walter M. Abbot, S.J., ed., *The Documents of Vatican II* (New York: Guild Press, 1966), p. 264.

34. A reliable history is Paul E. Sigmund, *Liberation Theology at the Crossroads: Democracy or Revolution?* (New York: Oxford University Press, 1990). Note that as early as 1970 an article by Gutiérrez was published in the leading Catholic theological review. Gustavo Gutiérrez, "Notes for a Theology of Liberation," *Theological Studies* 321 (June 1970), pp. 243–261. For an intriguing discussion of influence, Robert S. Goizueta, "The Preferential Option for the Poor: The CELAM Documents and the NCCB Pastoral Letter on U.S. Hispanics as Sources for U.S. Hispanic Theology," *Journal of Hispanic and Latino Theology* 3 (1995), pp. 65–72. Also see Archbishop Rembert Weakland, "How Medellín and Puebla Influenced North America," *Origins* 18 (13 April 1989), pp. 757–759.

35. A solid introduction to Chávez is Susan Ferriss and Ricardo Sandoval, *The Fight in the Fields: César Chávez and the Farmworker Movement* (New York: Harcourt, Brace, 1997). Also see Jon C. Hammerback and Richard J. Jenson, *The Rhetorical Career of César Chávez* (College Station: Texas A & M University Press, 1998), p. 30.

36. See various comments in the proceedings of the Theology in the Americas: 1975 conference held in Detroit. Sergio Torres and John Eagleson, eds., *Theology in the Americas* (Maryknoll: Orbis Books, 1975), pp. 175–252; Alan Doyle Myatt, "Religion and Racial Identity in the *Movimento Negro* of the Roman Catholic Church in Brazil" (Ph.D. dissertation, Iliff School of Theology, 1995), pp. 130–155.

37. Virgilio Elizondo, "*Mestizaje* as a Locus of Theological Reflection," in *The Future of Liberation Theology: Essays in Honor of Gustavo Gutiérrez*, ed. Marc H. Ellis and Otto Maduro (Maryknoll: Orbis Books, 1989), pp. 359–360.

38. A solid overview is Reed Ueda, *Post-war Immigrant America: A Social History* (Boston: St. Martin's Press, 1994).

39. On this matter generally, Allan Figueroa Deck, S.J., "'A Pox on Both Your Houses': A View of Catholic Conservative-Liberal Polarities from the Hispanic Margin," in *Being Right: Conservative Catholics in America*, ed. Mary Jo Weaver and R. Scott Appleby (Bloomington: Indiana University Press, 1995), pp. 88–104.

40. William Carroll Rickle, "Interethnic Relations in Hispanic Ministry Parishes in the Archdiocese of Philadelphia" (Ph.D. dissertation, Temple University, 1994). For a comparison of demands made by Hispanic Catholics in 1972 and those of German Catholics in the late nineteenth century, Ana María Díaz-Stevens and Anthony M. Stevens-Arroyo, *Recognizing the Latino Resurgence in U.S. Religion* (Boulder: Westview Press, 1998), pp. 184–189.

41. Deck, "'A Pox on Both Your Houses,'" p. 90; Mike Davis, *City of Quartz: Excavating the Future of Los Angeles* (New York: Vintage, 1992), p. 328. On religious affiliation see the contrasting views of Andrew Greeley, "Defection among Hispanics," *America* 159 (30 July 1988), pp. 60–63, and Thomas Quigley, "Overview: Myths about Latin America's Church," *Origins* 23 (28 October 1993), p. 366. See also Díaz-Stevens and Stevens-Arroyo, *Recognizing the Latino Resurgence*, p. 35.

42. The classic statement is Philip Gleason, *The Conservative Reformers: German-American Catholics and the Social Order* (Notre Dame: University of Notre Dame Press, 1968).

43. Orlando O. Espín, *The Faith of the People: Theological Reflections on Popular Catholicism* (Maryknoll: Orbis Books, 1997), pp. 68–71.

44. On the nineteenth-century revival, David Blackbourn, "The Catholic Church in Europe since the French Revolution," *Comparative Studies in Society and History* 33 (1991), pp. 778–790; Jonathan Sperber, *Popular Catholicism in Nineteenth-Century Germany* (Princeton: Princeton University Press, 1984); Patricia Byrne, C.S.J., "American Ultramontanism," *Theological Studies* 56 (June 1995), pp. 301–327; Jay P. Dolan, *Catholic Revivalism: The American Experience, 1830–1880* (Notre Dame: University of Notre Dame Press, 1978); Emmet Larkin, "The Devotional Revolution in Ireland, 1850–1875," *American Historical Review* 77 (1972), pp. 625–652.

45. Compare, for example, Robert A. Orsi, *The Madonna of 115th Street: Faith and Community in Italian Harlem, 1880–1950* (New Haven: Yale University Press, 1985), and Roberto R. Treviño, "La Fe: Catholicism and Mexican-Americans in Houston, 1911–1972" (Ph.D. dissertation, Stanford University, 1993).

46. One-third of seminarians in Texas and California are Mexican American according to Deck, "'A Pox on Both Your Houses,'" p. 90.

47. The recent Synod on the Americas in Rome is not a promising beginning. See Thomas J. Reese, S.J., "Synod for America," *America* 177 (13 December 1997), pp. 3–6; Michael A. Fahey, Jr., S.J., "The Synod of America: Reflections of a Nun-participant," *Theological Studies* 59 (September 1998), pp. 486–504.

48. John LaFarge, S.J., *Interracial Justice: A Study of the Catholic Doctrine of Race Relations* (New York: America Press, 1937), p. 194.

11
STRATEGIES ON THE LEFT
Catholics and Race

GARY RIEBE-ESTRELLA

Introduction

Racism is a recalcitrant issue in American society and no less so in American Catholicism. Any analysis of Catholic attitudes about race and ethnicity, therefore, is necessarily complex and not a little murky. Categories like "liberal" and "conservative" do not work to define the options, partly because there is no necessary connection between attitudes toward Church reform, on the one hand, and attitudes toward race on the other. It is possible, for example, for some Catholics to welcome liturgical change while maintaining racist attitudes in their neighborhoods. It is possible for religious leaders—like Cardinal Mahoney in his early days in Los Angeles—to be doctrinally conservative and socially liberal.

David Theo Goldberg explains such scenarios by way of "conceptual framing in terms of identity and difference."[1] In other words, uniformity of doctrine and discipline hold center stage *within the Church* because they are perceived as the basis for common ground: they define Catholic identity and guarantee unity. In the civic sphere, however, *outside the Church,* difference is allowable and even valued, since pluralism is a recognized characteristic of American society. But, even if we can say that most American Catholics today consider racism to be a moral evil, we must still notice that American Catholics in general do not put much support behind efforts specifically designed to help members of minority groups.[2] The commitment of Catholics to racial equality does not translate readily into social strategies. Although the old distinction between those who aim to change individual hearts and those who hope to change the world sometimes works to differentiate liberals and conservatives,[3] and although it is true that we can find these two attitudes in American Catholic life,[4] this distinction is not really helpful when it comes to race and ethnicity in the post-conciliar period.

Up to time of the civil rights movement, "whether in the North or South, every Catholic institution implicitly accepted segregation and secondary status as normative for blacks."[5] According to historian John McGreevy, in the reconstructionist South, the Catholic Church mirrored in its institutions and attitudes the segregationist position of the general society. Parishes, schools, church societies, seminaries, and even Catholic universities were usually segregated.[6] In the urban North during the first half of this century, the situation was not much different: racism was just more covert and harder to address. There was enormous urban tension between ethnic Catholics and poor Blacks who began to arrive in increasing numbers in the early 1940s. The hierarchy did not oppose segregation until the 1960s, and even then, threats of excommunication were necessary to pressure certain portions of the Catholic population to embrace episcopal moves toward integration.

If the bishops and the mass of working-class ethnic Catholics, the top and base of the Catholic pyramid, ignored racial justice until after the civil rights movement was well underway, dynamic segments of "middle management"—priests and women religious and lay pioneers—did not. These progressive Catholics built a history of attempts to deal more constructively with race relations. The interracial councils of John LaFarge, S.J., the Friendship Houses of Baroness Catherine de Hueck, the countless efforts of Black priests and sisters working in the Black community created a modest but influential precedent for subsequent Roman Catholic advocacy of racial equality.[7] Yet political terms, like conservative and liberal, do not quite fit the case. I will describe progressive Catholic attitudes in terms of two strategies (utopian and pragmatic) and two goals (integration and multiculturalism).

Utopian Strategies

Utopian strategies call for an entirely new social arrangement in American society and therefore usually begin by indicting society as a place where some people are marginalized. They seek to devalue the center and dissolve the margins. Two examples of this approach can show us that, however noble the intentions, utopian strategies have not worked. The Catholic Worker movement did not transform American Catholic consciousness, and polycentric ethnic societies like the Black Catholic Theological Symposium (BCTS) and the Academy of Catholic Hispanic Theologians of the United States (ACHTHUS) have not been able to transform the Catholic Theological Society of America (CTSA).

The Catholic Worker movement represents a radical utopian vision within American Catholicism. According to its founder, Dorothy Day, Catholic workers aim to make Christian love the foundation of social existence. Individuals begin this process by taking responsibility for themselves in personal conversion and then extend it by translating conversion to Christ into responsible social action. One must seek first to serve one's immediate neighbors and eventually work to transform society at large through the power of Christian love. Catholic Worker communities play out this strategy by living with fundamental mutual dependence, by establishing charitable programs out of Houses of Hospitality, and by engaging in social action, usually for the rights of workers or for the downtrodden. Historically, the locations of social engagement differed from group to group: some were intensely intellectual; others deeply involved in labor organizing, rent strikes, and similar forms of direct social action; still others focused on works of mercy and liturgical concerns. In each case, however, engagement in social transformation, seen as the road to personal transformation, was pivotal.[8]

The Catholic Worker directed its transformative energies toward society at large and toward the Church. As David O'Brien points out, Dorothy Day and Peter Maurin perceived the Church to be caught up "in bourgeois culture, too concerned with institutions, too filled with people, clergy, and laity, measuring success in the material terms of the larger society. Catholicism, for them, was too American, and not Christian enough."[9] What was needed, they thought, was a "communitarian revolution," which would act as an alternative to the structures of American society.[10] Race relations were not the first preoccupation of the founders of the Catholic Worker movement, not because they were blind to racism, but because racism was viewed as a part of bourgeois capitalist culture that is itself essentially un-Christian. One need not address racism specifically, therefore, since a communitarian revolution would end it.

Though its vision and strategies are clear, the Catholic Worker movement holds within itself an inherent polarity, which may account for some of the loss of appeal it has experienced in recent years. On the one hand, the movement is committed to living out the Gospel ideal with integrity. On the other, to effect social transformation it must witness that utopian vision to the larger society. According to historian Mel Piehl, "[e]fforts directed at maintaining the group's own hold on the ideal tend to turn it inward toward sectarian withdrawal, while attempts to present the ideal to others become entangled in social and moral complexity, thus eroding the purity of the original vision."[11] As appealing as the Catholic Worker movement might be, as a communitarian movement, therefore, it has not been an effective Catholic means to end racism.

A second utopian strategy, polycentrism, has appeared only recently. In some ways, it shares features with some of the more radical civil rights groups of the 1960s, such as the Brown Berets and the Black Panthers, albeit without the violent confrontations and penchant for separatism that characterized those groups. Like those groups, polycentrists see a need for "spaces" in American society for blacks, browns, and other racial and ethnic groups where their values and cultural traits can be maintained and lived. They do not, however, see these "spaces" as impermeable worlds of identity. Whereas the Black nationalism of the 60s sent a message of separatism,[12] a polycentric perspective "favors voluntary over involuntary affiliations, balances an appreciation for communities of descent with a determination to make room for new communities, and promotes solidarities of wide scope that incorporate people with different ethnic and racial backgrounds."[13] The attempt of polycentrists to balance communities of racial identity with a sense of community beyond race serves two purposes. First, it makes the white community one of many racial communities in American society, not *the center* of society, but one of the many centers created by racial and ethnic origin. Secondly, by promoting community beyond race, it refuses to acknowledge any of these centers as "autonomous, self-contained, and self-directed."[14] It, therefore, images a different social arrangement from that of a single center with margins because it proposes multiple centers or identities out of which people enter into voluntary affiliation around common goals or tasks to which they bring the richness of their communities of origin.

In the civic sphere, this image becomes the "e pluribus unum" of an American society that "is built and sustained by people who honor a common future more than a common past."[15] In the religious sphere, this image is seen by Black theologian Bryan Massingale as a kind of Pentecost, "as a biblical image of hope, sustaining ethical reflection and action which both critiques the present and strives to create a new social order: a society governed by the canons of neither 'integration,' nor 'assimilation,' nor 'separation,' but rather those of 'transformation,' the affirmation of difference, and the embrace of plural models of what is accepted as 'American'—or indeed 'human.'"[16]

Two liberal Catholic theological societies in their relationship to a third can be seen to demonstrate this polycentric strategy and its limitations. The Black Catholic Theological Symposium (BCTS) was founded in 1978 as just such a "center" among centers. The commitment of the Black theologians who make up the BCTS is to develop a Black theology that reflects their experience in *both* the Black and the Catholic communities.[17] Full membership in the BCTS is restricted to theologians who are both Black and Catholic. The Academy of

Catholic Hispanic Theologians of the United States (ACHTUS) was founded in Ruidoso, New Mexico, in 1988. Its goal is to promote research and theological reflection that is based on the experience of Hispanic Catholics in the United States in order to highlight this reflection as "a distinct theological enterprise whose depth and richness remain largely untapped by the Church."[18] Active membership is restricted to theologians who are both Hispanic and Catholic.

Each of these organizations has a dual identity, one based on race and the other on membership in the multiracial Catholic Church. Both the BCTS and the ACHTUS have regularly held their annual meetings close to the time of the annual convention of the Catholic Theological Society of America (CTSA), which is predominantly white in its membership. Many members of the Black and Hispanic theological societies are also members of the CTSA, and white members of CTSA have been participants at meetings of ACHTUS and the BCTS. Members of both groups sponsor workshops on Black and Hispanic theology that appear on the program of the CTSA. Yet neither group has an official organizational affiliation with the Catholic Theological Society.

Both ACHTUS and the BCTS propose themselves as theological "centers" based on racial identity but belonging to a larger communion and about a larger task. They both view the CTSA as another such center. Members move among centers, each of which has its own integrity and boundaries, and all are about a larger common task, the elaboration of theology reflective of the American scene. While the CTSA has been encouraging of both organizations and their members, it is more ambiguous in its understanding of the *equality of* the relationship. In its name it still claims to be the voice of American Catholic theology though it features white Catholic theology. Although it recognizes the value of the perspectives theologians of color bring, their theologies remain marginal to normative white theology. While the members of the BCTS and ACHTUS act on the basis of a new social arrangement, it is still unclear whether the members of the CTSA are yet willing to be part of a truly polycentrist approach. If they choose not to, it appears that there is little the other organizations can do about it.

Both the Catholic Worker and BCTS/ACHTUS have embraced a utopian strategy, hoping to transform society or an organization so that it no longer marginalizes certain of its members. Although each has surely raised consciousness about racism—within the Church and within the CTSA—neither has been able to be particularly effective, possibly because their goals were too lofty. The failure of the utopian strategy can serve as a background for more practical ways to address racism.

Pragmatic Approaches

Unlike utopian strategies that seek to transform a country or a society, pragmatic strategies aim to empower a particular group within a specific context. The model for this approach is the old Industrial Areas Foundation (IAF) founded by Saul Alinsky in Chicago in 1940. Although he was the son of Russian Jewish immigrants, Alinsky developed an early connection with the Catholic Church when his early organizing efforts took place in the heavily Catholic "Back of the Yards" area of Chicago's Southside. Those who have been inspired by his approach—men like Ed Chambers and Ernie Cortes, themselves Catholic—have elaborated an ever closer relationship with the Church as "an indispensable source of moral and spiritual authority, particularly among Mexican Americans," who form one of the largest constituencies, if not the largest, with which IAF works today.[19] In addition, especially under the direction of Ernie Cortes, IAF organizers use mostly Catholic theology in leadership training sessions and in Bible study classes for organization members.

IAF community organizers, though working chiefly among nonwhites, do not pursue racial or ethnic goals as such; they turn their energies toward practical matters. Unlike some utopian groups, IAF community organizers eschew class analysis in order first to deal with the "world as it is" rather than the "world as it ought to be." Put another way, Alinsky organizers aim their efforts at "getting a piece of the pie" for themselves and their organizations' members.[20]

The purpose of IAF community organizing is to teach people the skills to enter the political arena, not in supporting its partisan incarnation, but in making the political structures in American society responsive to goals the organizations' members have for themselves and their communities. People are taught that power is to be found in the group. As the organizers are fond of saying, "Power comes either from money or from organized people." And since the constituencies with which IAF works do not possess many monetary resources, the quest for power takes the road of organizing people. The organizing principle is "self-interest"; however, it is not naively understood. Leaders are taught to balance their needs and those of their immediate community with the needs of other leaders and groups in the organization. They are taught to move from self-interest to "enlightened self-interest."[21] And the kind of self-interest on which Alinsky organizing relies is founded on an organization's members having a stake in their local communities. These Alinsky organizers have always had the greatest success working with homeowners in stable working- and lower-middle-class neighborhoods with those who have already gained a foothold in the system and need added leverage to move further into the center. Seldom, if ever, have Alinsky organizers worked with the truly poor and destitute.[22]

The community organizing typified in IAF represents a kind of "empowerment" model for working with people of color who find themselves on the margins of U.S. society. Not content to remove barriers to participation in society, community organizing helps non-whites to understand the political system and teaches them the skills they need to use that system to secure their rights, to take their future into their own hands. While it does not normally call the system itself into question, it does empower the marginalized to access a greater number of opportunities within that system.

It is not clear to me that utopian or pragmatic strategies tend to appeal more strongly to liberal or conservative or middle-of-the-road Catholics. As I said earlier, I am not persuaded that those political distinctions help us understand the variety of approaches to racism within the Church. The differences between the two strategies I have outlined seem to be relatively simple: utopians are idealists who hope for the total transformation of society, whereas pragmatists do what they can in a particular situation. These strategies surely overlap in some instances—Catholic Workers can be pragmatic, community organizers can be idealistic—but they appeal to people differently. On the whole, the pragmatic strategy seems to be more effective even if it is less global in its aims. The aims, themselves, are also complicated. I find two general goals in this complex mixture of Catholic approaches to race and ethnicity: integration and multiculturalism, both of which can be approached via either strategy.

Integration

Perhaps the alternative to racism most widely embraced by Catholics has been that of integration. It can appeal to utopians, but generally, because it is predicated on a belief that the American system is essentially good, though in need of a rebalancing of its priorities, integrationists hope to bring into the center a greater number of those currently situated on the margins. A significant historical example of this approach, one that discloses one of its weaknesses, can be found in the National Catholic Council for Interracial Justice (NCCIJ), founded in 1958. At that time, some four hundred delegates from thirty-six Catholic Interracial Councils established this national organization to "fully implement the principles of Christian Social Justice and American Democracy in regard to race relations."[23] These Interracial Councils themselves had been born out of struggle, specifically, from the split within an earlier integrationist movement, the Federated Colored Catholics (FCC).

Founded by Thomas Wyatt Turner in 1924, the FCC was an organization for Black Catholics who sought to make their own determinations of their needs, and to advance their own ideas about how to address them.[24] Paradoxically, opposition to FCC came from a Catholic pioneer in race relations, John LaFarge, a white Jesuit priest. He believed that the integration movement needed to be an interracial organization, dedicated not only to fighting for Black Catholics' rights within the Church but also to educating white Catholics in the social justice doctrine of the Church as it applied to relations between the races. LaFarge's strategy to improve race relations was fundamentally one of education, since his analysis of racial tensions was that they were "not the result of prejudice so much as of ignorance."[25] Though the focus was different for each group, both Blacks and whites needed to be educated. For LaFarge, "Blacks needed education to equip them for a better social condition; whites needed education in the rudiments of justice based on Christian principles."[26] Whereas Turner espoused a more confrontational approach toward white racism, LaFarge thought that "racism could be combated by good manners and reasonableness."[27] The split between LaFarge and Turner resulted in LaFarge's founding the first Catholic Interracial Conference, a move that discloses a fundamental tension within integrationist movements: who gets to set the agenda. LaFarge, in effect, thought he knew more clearly what Black Catholics needed than Black Catholics themselves. Or perhaps he understood better what would appeal to American Catholics of the time. In any event, this heritage of the NCCIJ has marked the work of most of its local councils.[28]

Integrationism seeks to remove the barriers that keep people of color out of mainstream American society. Whether specific strategies of integration are confrontational or not usually depends on the posture of the racists being addressed. However, while they may often note the institutionalization of racism in the structures of American society, strategies for integration generally seek less to change the structures themselves than to open the structures to participation by non-whites.

At the same time, integration can hinder that move. There are integrationist movements—the white ethnic movement, for example —that effectively deny the significance of race in the construction of our society and effectively place the burden for inclusion on the marginalized themselves as they espouse the equality of all members of American society. Though few American sociologists are able to agree on the exact relationship of race and class in U.S. society, there is ample evidence that the two are interrelated. The comparative percentages of racial groups that are considered poor by the federal government in the 1990 census are symptomatic of this interrelationship: whites at 10.7 percent, Blacks at 31.9 percent, Hispanics at 28.1 percent. In 1989, only 9.9 percent of Hispanics and 11.8 percent of Blacks over 25 years of age had completed college, in contrast to the 21.8 percent of whites.[29] It is difficult to believe that it is purely by chance that persons of color are to be found in the bottom percentiles of all the indicators commonly used to measure well-being in American society.

Indeed, chance has little to do with the marginalization of racial minorities within North American society. Whether it be Blacks, Latinos, or Native Americans, each of these peoples entered the pages of American history as the conquered. Blacks entered as slaves; Latinos and Native Americans as victims of the expansionist policy of the United States. And though not new immigrants, none of these groups has been mainstreamed into American society.[30] In order to justify its actions, U.S. society has developed its own reading of its national history, one Latino theologian Justo González calls "an innocent history." That is, the American history that most of us learned in our elementary and high school education was an idealized history, one in which the losers were not present and the mixed motivations of the victors were not attended to:

> [T]he "fathers" [of our country] sued for independence, mostly in the name of freedom. That this was to a great degree the freedom to make money and to take lands from the Indians is again mentioned but is not allowed to play more than a secondary role in our understanding of the "revolutionary" war. . . . We seldom hear of the degree to which the leaders of the movement for independence lusted for Indian lands that the British would not allow them to possess. . . . The West was "won," we are told. But how, and who "lost" it, is not part of our national consciousness.[31]

According to González, this mythologizing of our national history is not an accident of fate.

> All this, and more we have not been told. But let us not deceive ourselves. We have not been told because we did not wish to be told. . . . If the Pilgrims, the patriots, and the pioneers were pure and just, they must have created a pure and just order, and it is our great fortune to have inherited it, and our task to defend it. Anything else is ingratitude and lack of patriotism.[32]

More pernicious than the justification of the actions of many of our national heroes is the concomitant need to portray the conquered as *deserving of their fate*. It is no wonder that Latinos, Native Americans, and African Americans are pictured in the American ethos as having a whole assortment of unsavory, un-Christian qualities, which are used to explain their failure to be integrated into mainstream society.

A critical approach to integration must ask how it is that white Catholics are able to move solidly to middle-class status within two or three generations.[33] This movement from poor immigrant to middle-class American is perhaps the most significant shift that has occurred in American Catholicism in this century.[34] It may also explain why we often find an enhanced patriotism among many white Catholics. I find it interesting that American Catholic churches are among the few that place the national flag in their sanctuaries. In their attempts to move beyond their "foreignness," some white Catholics have absorbed the version of American history written by the victors, one which depreci-ates non-whites as deserving of their own conquest.[35]

In addition to the time factor, we must examine critically the eco-nomic trajectory of white and immigrant groups and how it has con-vinced many white Catholics of the truthfulness of the American dream, that one can pull oneself up by one's own bootstraps. Many white ethnic Catholics who have "made it" do not understand why non-white groups remain poor nor why they should be asked to subsi-dize those groups with their tax monies.[36] Perhaps without meaning to do so, they blame the victims, believing that if non-whites experience marginalization in American society, the fault is ultimately theirs, as is its solution. Andrew Greeley, for example, appears to equate the situation of white ethnics with that of non-white ethnics by ignoring the role of race in the relationship of non-whites to mainstream U.S. society. Those who equate ethnicity with race and persist in believing that "ethnicity is a primordial, biological status"[37] fundamentally un-derestimate the symbolic nature of white ethnicity in comparison to the concrete constraints that people of color endure. As Mary Waters has observed:

> People who assert a symbolic ethnicity do not give much attention to the ease with which they are able to slip in and out of their ethnic roles. It is quite natural to them that in the greater part of their lives, their ethnicity does not matter. They also take for granted that when it does matter, it is largely a matter of personal choice and a source of pleasure.[38]

The integrationist aim, therefore, discloses some of the tensions as well as the possibilities between whites and non-whites. Those who es-pouse the white ethnic position envision a society open to persons of whatever race, but they believe that society is already at such a point and hold that whatever exclusion exists today is due, fundamentally, to characteristics and behavior in the excluded rather than to racial differences.

Multiculturalism

The goal of multiculturalism began to take center stage in the 1980s as it became clear to many in American society that the integrationist approach espoused so forcefully by the civil rights movement of the 1960s had achieved only limited success.[39] Multiculturalism did not emerge from the civil rights movement itself but rather from the counterculture of the 1960s,[40] a point of origin that played a decisive role in its development. At its heart, multiculturalism is committed to creating "spaces" in American society for non-white groups as alternatives to mainstream culture. However, its vision of the future seems to stop there. Unlike polycentrism, it does not engage in the promotion of a larger sense of community among the members of these separate spaces. As David Hollinger writes, *"Diversity* replaced *unity* in the slogans of those concerned to promote mutual respect and equality among the varieties of humankind found within the United States."[41] Perhaps without consciously intending to do so, multiculturalism creates either *permanent* spaces for racial minorities where they can feel at home but are not involved in the larger social project or *temporary* spaces where minorities wait until other factors such as economic advancement and suburbanization assimilate them into the mainstream of U.S. society. In either case, multiculturalism cedes the socially transformative project. The analysis of educator Peter McLaren is particularly astute in this regard: "Multiculturalism without a transformative political agenda can be just another form of accommodation to the larger social order."[42] In addition, by making race or ethnicity primordial categories of belonging it can effectively block the communication across racial lines that would be necessary to build linkages between groups around common goals or tasks.

> To put matters bluntly: the multiculturalist rhetoric has the rest of us on the run, unable to respond for fear of being branded unicultural, or racist. . . . In such a way does multiculturalism limit discussion; it makes people afraid to say what they think and feel; it presents dubious and cranky interpretations and analyses as self-evident, indisputable truths. It often operates, not through the usual means of civil discourse and persuasion, but via intimidation and intellectual decree.[43]

In the contemporary Church, the goal of multiculturalism has been to create a space for people not of the dominant culture to practice their faith according to the traditions and in the language of their country of origin. Though reminiscent of the national parish strategy of the first half of this century in its intent, it does not presuppose the existence of geographic enclaves. Rather, precisely the opposite. It is an approach generally used to deal with minorities who are intermixed with white Catholics by giving them space for their own practices but without systematically engaging them or white Catholics across racial lines.

For Latino Catholics, multiculturalism had its beginnings in the work of Archbishop Robert Lucey of San Antonio and thirteen other bishops who in 1945 established the Bishops' Committee for the Spanish Speaking. The goal of the Committee was to provide intensive programs for the social and spiritual welfare of Catholic Latinos. Though begun in the Southwest, the Catholic councils for the Spanish speaking, which were the local structures for the Committee, gradually spread. By the 1960s councils had been established in the Midwest, on the upper Pacific coast, and in the Northeast.[44] In 1964 the Office for the Spanish Speaking became national rather than regional in scope, and in 1970 it was moved by the bishops to Washington, D.C. Through the support of Pablo Sedillo, the director of the Office, the first of three National Encuentros was held in 1972. The First Encuentro had a confrontational tone, and delegates issued seventy-eight conclusions and demands they were making on the Church. The Second Encuentro resulted in forty-five conclusions. The Third National Encuentro, held in Washington in 1985, led to the elaboration of the *National Pastoral Plan for Hispanic Ministry*, a sixty-five-page bilingual document covering the areas of *pastoral de conjunto*, evangelization, the missionary option, and formation.[45] The whole Encuentro process was focused primarily on the demands by Latino Catholics that their needs as Catholics be met by the institutional Church and on the elaboration of strategies to implement that goal. The culmination of the Encuentro process, the *National Pastoral Plan*, was approved by the Bishops' Conference in 1987, but only on the condition that the funding figures for each strategy be eliminated.[46] The dollar amounts were replaced with a generic wording: "in keeping with the normal channels for plans and programs and budget procedures of the respective entities involved." Unfortunately, since most dioceses did not have an overall diocesan pastoral plan, there were, in fact, no "normal channels" into which the strategies of the *Plan* could be integrated. Those dioceses that did try to implement the *Plan*, therefore, turned the work over to their diocesan Office of Hispanic Ministry. That is, without an overall diocesan plan as the focus for integrating services for Latinos, those services became the building blocks for parallel structures within the same diocese, though usually not clearly articulated as such. Even in dioceses where the numerical majority of Catholics is Hispanic, there exist "special" programs and services for Hispanic youth, for instance, while the diocesan Youth Ministry Office provides the "normal" youth programming, which factually is aimed at non-Hispanics, without identifying its target audience by name but rather passing the programming off simply as "Catholic."

The "space" for language and culture envisioned by the Encuentro process and embraced by many multiculturalist Catholics, both Hispanic and non-Hispanic, becomes a concession by the majority in dealing with the needs of the minority. This is most clearly the case on the local level, where "multicultural parish" more often than not means that two racially different communities use the same parish facilities for the provision of parallel services, but only one of the two communities is the "owner" of the facilities.[47] As such, multiculturalism allows Catholics of color a space within the Church but does not engage them or white Catholics in building a new style of church with equality for all.

Concluding Reflections

The anti-racist strategies and goals adopted by American Catholics are not so clearly right or left on the political spectrum, but they tell us something about the ways in which people understand the kind of social transformation needed to produce equality. While it is possible to discuss various strategies and aims of those interested in race and ethnicity issues, that should not obscure the more basic reality with which this essay began: white Catholics interested in these issues are a minority in the Church in the United States. Though racism continues to tear American society apart, effectively creating two societies with an ever-widening gap between rich and poor, most American Catholics favor an individual "change of heart" as the best way to root out racism. Effectively, they do not favor action or policy change on behalf of non-whites. It may be that this preference for individual change is tied to white ethnic experience of American society, but whatever its source, it is a luxury that only a predominantly white Church can afford. When the effects of racism are perceived to be "outside" problems, having little or no relation to Church life, one can afford to be a passive observer . What will happen, however, as the effects of racism are experienced by a growing number of non-whites *within* the Church? Will their white co-religionists identify closely enough with them to be moved to a more aggressive stance against racism? Will the majority of white Catholics see their own experience of exclusion reflected in these "newcomers" and be galvanized into action? Or will the racism that divides U.S. society be allowed to divide the Church as well?

NOTES

1. David Theo Goldberg, "Introduction: Multicultural Conditions," in *Multiculturalism: A Critical Reader* (Cambridge: Blackwell Publishers, 1994), p. 12.

2. Jim Castelli and Joseph Gremillion, *The Emerging Parish: The Notre Dame Study of Catholic Life since Vatican II* (San Francisco: Harper and Row, 1987),

p. 186. Even though "American Catholics in general" may not support efforts to help members of minority groups, larger efforts in the Church, like the Campaign for Human Development, and the American bishops have been often in the forefront on their behalf.

3. Allan Figueroa Deck, *The Second Wave: Hispanic Ministry and Evangelization of Cultures* (New York: Paulist Press, 1989), pp. 93–94.

4. The Notre Dame Study of Catholic Parish Life, for example, shows that 62 percent of American Catholics involved in their parishes agree that social problems can be solved best by first focusing on changing the hearts (that is, attitudes, beliefs, consciences) of individuals, whereas only 38 percent agree that "social problems can be solved best by first focusing on transforming human institutions and environments in which people live." Castelli and Gremillion, *The Emerging Parish,* p. 183.

5. Dolores Liptak, *Immigrants and Their Church* (New York: Macmillan Publishing Company, 1989), p. 173.

6. John T. McGreevy, *Parish Boundaries: The Catholic Encounter with Race in the Twentieth-Century Urban North* (Chicago: University of Chicago Press, 1996), p. 8.

7. For an overview of the changing attitudes of Catholics to race approaching the time of the civil rights movement, see David J. O'Brien, *Public Catholicism,* 2d ed. (Maryknoll: Orbis Books, 1996), pp. 236–238.

8. Mel Piehl, *Breaking Bread: The Catholic Worker and the Origin of Catholic Radicalism in America* (Philadelphia: Temple University Press, 1982), p. 110.

9. O'Brien, *Public Catholicism,* p. 203.

10. James Hennesey, *American Catholics: A History of the Roman Catholic Community in the United States* (New York: Oxford University Press, 1981), p. 267.

11. Piehl, *Breaking Bread,* p. 95.

12. Ronald Takaki, *A Different Mirror: A History of Multicultural America* (Boston: Little, Brown and Company, 1993), p. 408.

13. David A. Hollinger, *Postethnic America: Beyond Multiculturalism* (New York: Basic Books, 1995), p. 3.

14. Peter McLaren, "White Terror and Oppositional Agency: Towards a Critical Multiculturalism," in *Multiculturalism: A Critical Reader,* ed. David Theo Goldberg (Cambridge: Blackwell Publishers, 1994), p. 33.

15. Hollinger, *Postethnic America,* p. 134.

16. Bryan Massingale, "The African American Experience and U.S. Roman Catholic Ethics: 'Strangers and Aliens No Longer?'" in *Black and Catholic: The Challenge and Gift of Black Folk,* ed. Jamie Phelps (Marquette: Marquette University Press, 1997), p. 93.

17. M. Shawn Copeland, "African American Catholics and Black Theology: An Interpretation," in *African-American Religious Studies: An Interdisciplinary Anthology,* ed. Gayraud Wilmore (Durham: Duke University Press, 1989), p. 241.

18. "Bylaws and Constitution of the Academy of Catholic Hispanic Theologians of the United States, Inc.," Article 1.

19. Peter Skerry, *Mexican Americans: The Ambivalent Minority* (New York: Free Press, 1993), p. 163.

20. Ibid., p. 160.

21. Ibid., p. 146.

22. Ibid., p. 145.

23. McGreevy, *Parish Boundaries,* p. 86.

24. Marilyn Wenzke Nickels, *Black Catholic Protest and the Federated Colored*

Catholics 1917–1933: Three Perspective on Racial Justice (New York: Garland Publishing, 1988), p. 43.

25. Liptak, *Immigrants and Their Church*, p. 181.

26. Davis, *The History of Black Catholics*, p. 226.

27. Ibid., p. 229.

28. The integrationist approach has been adopted by some Hispanic groups, like PADRES. See the essay in this volume by Tim Matovina for his analysis of the approach of PADRES to the integration of Mexican Americans into the mainstream of U.S. Catholicism.

29. National Council of La Raza, *State of Hispanic America 1991: An Overview* (Washington: National Council of La Raza, 1992), pp. 16, 9.

30. See my article, "Movement from Monocultural to Multicultural Congregations," *Review for Religious* 55, no. 5 (September–October 1996), pp. 507–510.

31. Justo L. González, *Mañana: Christian Theology from a Hispanic Perspective* (Nashville: Abingdon Press, 1990), p. 39.

32. Ibid.

33. McGreevy, *Parish Boundaries*, p. 80.

34. Joseph P. Fitzpatrick, "The Poor in a Middle-Class Church," in *Perspectivas: Hispanic Ministry*, ed. Allan Figueroa Deck, Yolanda Tarango, and Timothy M. Matovina (Kansas City: Sheet and Ward, 1995), pp. 7–8.

35. González, *Mañana*, pp. 38–41.

36. Andrew M. Greeley, *Why Can't They Be Like Us? America's White Ethnic Groups* (New York: E. P. Dutton, 1971), pp. 153–154.

37. Hollinger, *Postethnic America*, p. 40.

38. Mary C. Waters, *Ethnic Options: Choosing Identities in America* (Berkeley/Los Angeles: University of California Press, 1990), p. 158.

39. Nathan Glazer, *We Are All Multiculturalists Now* (Cambridge, Mass.: Harvard University Press, 1997), p. 97.

40. Richard Bernstein, *Dictatorship of Virtue: Multiculturalism and the Battle for America's Future* (New York: Alfred A. Knopf, 1994), p. 6.

41. Hollinger, *Postethnic America*, p. 64.

42. McLaren, "White Terror and Oppositional Agency," p. 53.

43. Bernstein, *Dictatorship of Virtue*, p. 8.

44. Moisés Sandoval, "The Organization of a Hispanic Church," in *Hispanic Catholic Culture in the U.S.: Issues and Concerns*, ed. Jay P. Dolan and Allan Figueroa Deck (Notre Dame: University of Notre Dame Press, 1994), p. 134.

45. National Conference of Catholic Bishops, *National Pastoral Plan for Hispanic Ministry* (Washington, D.C.: United States Catholic Conference, 1987).

46. Sandoval, "The Organization of a Hispanic Church," p. 145.

47. Allan Figueroa Deck, "Multiculturalism as an Ideology," in *Perspectivas*, pp. 31–33.

12

REPRESENTATION AND THE RECONSTRUCTION OF POWER

The Rise of PADRES and Las Hermanas

TIMOTHY M. MATOVINA

PADRES (Padres Asociados por los Derechos Religiosos, Educativos, y Sociales, or Priests Associated for Religious, Educational, and Social Rights) and Las Hermanas (literally "The Sisters") are post–Vatican II organizations that asserted the rights of Latinos in Church and society. Initially established as associations of Chicano priests and Chicana sisters, they evolved to include other Latinos/as as well. The foundation and subsequent activities of these two organizations illustrate Latino attempts to reform and transform the Roman Catholic Church in the wake of Vatican II.[1]

Context and Foundation

Las Hermanas and PADRES emerged as part of the wider movement for social and ecclesial change during the 1960s and early 1970s. While the Chicano movement was most visible to the general public in the efforts of César Chávez, Dolores Huerta, and the United Farm Workers (UFW), Chicano/a activism was also evident in organizations like El Movimiento Estudiantil Chicano de Aztlán (The Chicano Student Movement of Aztlán, or MEChA), the Brown Berets, the Mexican American Youth Organization (MAYO), La Raza Unida party, La Alianza Federal de Mercedes (the Federal Alliance of Land Grants), the Crusade for Justice, and Católicos Por La Raza. Early leaders in PADRES and Las Hermanas recognized their connection to the wider social currents of the day. In his public announcement that PADRES had been founded, for example, Father Henry Casso reportedly stated that "one of the main reasons for the founding of the group . . . was the example set by young Mexican Americans on college campuses and the barrios."[2]

Vatican II and the Latin American episcopal conference at Medellín in 1968 further motivated and shaped Chicano and Chicana religious leaders' analysis of their social and ecclesial situation, as did the emergence of Latin American liberation theology, which PADRES and Hermanas leaders affirmed as "significant in our struggle" in a 1975 statement at a Theology in the Americas symposium. When these priests and sisters examined critically the situation of their people in the Church, they concluded that Chicanos were relegated to a second-class ecclesiastic citizenry. Early Hermanas leaders pointed out that in 1970 approximately 27 percent of the U.S. Catholic population was Hispanic, while less than 1 percent served in the U.S. episcopacy. At the same time, 17 percent of the U.S. Catholic population was Irish American while 56 percent of the Catholic bishops were of Irish descent. PADRES members also protested the lack of Chicano representation in the hierarchy and even announced publicly the possibility of establishing a national Chicano church as a means to redress this situation of inequality.[3]

PADRES grew out of a Chicano priests' support group in San Antonio, Texas, initiated by Ralph Ruiz, priest-director of the Inner City Apostolate for the San Antonio archdiocese. Their conversations about their struggles in seminary formation and experiences in ministry led the group to convene a meeting of Chicano priests from other locales in Texas. To their surprise, on October 9, 1969, participants from as far away as New Mexico, Arizona, Colorado, and Illinois arrived at San Antonio, where they resolved to unite their efforts on behalf of their people. San Antonio priest Henry Casso announced publicly that the PADRES organization had been formed and that it had some fifty members from a seven-state area. The enthusiastic response to this announcement encouraged Ruiz, Casso, and others to call for a national meeting of Chicano priests, an aspiration they realized four months later when they convened the first national congress of PADRES in Tucson, Arizona.[4] In preparation for the Tucson congress, Ruiz and other PADRES met with members of the hierarchy, who agreed to form a liaison committee that would assist PADRES in presenting their resolutions to the National Conference of Catholic Bishops (NCCB). Members of the liaison committee included Bishop (soon-to-be Archbishop) Timothy Manning of Los Angeles and Archbishop Francis Furey of San Antonio.[5]

Participants from twelve states took part in the first national PADRES congress, which met from February 2 to 6, 1970, at the Pioneer Hotel in Tucson. Euro-American priests and sisters were among the more than one hundred participants; Chicano clergy made up less than one-fourth of the assembled body. Congress members endorsed the UFW's grape boycott and discussed a wide range of other issues, among them bilingual education, immigration, welfare reform, ministry with youth, funding for Catholic schools in low-income areas, a more equitable distribution of Church resources, the promotion of native Spanish-speaking pastors, and liturgical expressions that respect Hispanic cultures. They also called for the appointment of Chicano bishops and the promotion of a mobile team ministry to serve the numerous Spanish-speaking communities.[6]

The most controversial issue at the congress was the question of PADRES membership. Most of the Chicano priests perceived that "they first needed to solidify as a priests' group" before extending membership to lay collaborators. They contended that a clergy group would have more clout with the hierarchy, while a "diluted organization" would be more easily dismissed. Others disagreed, most notably a fairly large contingent from northern California who expressed the desire to be in solidarity with the laity rather than form an exclusively clerical association. Recognizing that they were outnumbered, the organizers of the congress, other Chicano priests, and a few Euro-American sympathizers walked out during the third day of the meeting and held separate sessions in a nearby parish. There they constituted the organization as a clergy group with full membership extended to Chicano priests and associate membership to non-Chicano priests, the latter enjoying voice and vote at all meetings except the plenary sessions of national conventions. They also elected a slate of Chicano priests as the organization's officers, among them Ralph Ruiz, who served as the first national chairman. PADRES leaders argued that their walkout was a "dramatic move" that was "necessary to insure the survival of PADRES as the voice of the Mexican American priests in this country."[7]

Not surprisingly, the controversy that resulted from these actions persisted after the congress. In April 1970 PADRES representatives went to San Francisco, where they joined delegates from four other organizations for a meeting with the aforementioned episcopal liaison committee. One of the other groups, the Confederación de la Raza Unida of San José, California, was a predominantly lay confederation that encompassed some fifty local organizations for the Spanish speaking. Like northern California participants at the PADRES congress in Tucson, Confederación members objected to PADRES's clerical exclusivity. Their leaders issued a press release in which they declared that PADRES "does not represent, nor does it have the authority to represent the Confederación de la Raza Unida in any manner, shape or form." According to a press report, a spokesperson later added that "the lay Spanish speaking must be represented by lay people." Subsequently PADRES leaders continued to defend the organization against accusations of practicing "reverse discrimination" and advocating a "separatist movement." Father Keith Kenny of Our Lady of Guadalupe parish in Sacramento, California, summarized the arguments against PADRES in a letter opining that the organization was "guilty of the same kind of paternalism and racism that they oppose in the Church."[8]

Despite ongoing disputes, PADRES's contention that Church officials would more readily listen to a priests' organization was somewhat vindicated when the Catholic bishops, at their 1970 meetings, gave PADRES grants for more than $50,000 and when, in 1971, the Campaign for Human Development (CHD) gave the organization an additional $100,000 grant. On May 5, 1970, PADRES member Patricio Flores became the first Mexican-American bishop. PADRES members perceived Flores's episcopal ordination, coming just three months after the PADRES congress had called for the appointment of Chicano bishops, as a further indication that their organizational strategy was an effective means to foster equality for Chicanos in the Church.[9]

Inspired in part by the vision and early success of PADRES, Chicana sisters established their own organization, Las Hermanas. Sister Gregoria Ortega, a Victoryknoll sister from El Paso and community activist, and Sister Gloria Graciela Gallardo, a Holy Ghost sister from San Antonio who had worked as a catechist and community organizer, founded the organization. On October 20, 1970, the two leaders sent a letter to Mexican-American women religious that, judging from the response it sparked, revealed that many sisters had a common experience and common frustrations in their religious vocation:

> We, as religious, exert much influence among our Spanish-speaking people because of their deep-seated religious principles. Many of us feel that we are not doing this to our fullest capacity. On the other hand, there are some of us who have tried to become more relevant to our people and because of this, find ourselves in "trouble" with either our own congregation or other members of the hierarchy. Then there are some of us who would like to be able to do more among our people but cannot, either because we are not yet quite sure of ourselves or because we are being constrained by the lack of understanding or communication in our congregation.[10]

The encouraging response led Ortega and Gallardo to convene a gathering of Chicana religious in Houston, Texas, from April 2 to 4, 1971, which was attended by some fifty Chicana sisters from eight states and twenty congregations. A few Euro-American sisters also attended, and (in a controversy reminiscent of PADRES's early history) some of them refused to support the newly constituted organization when participants decided that full membership would be open to native Spanish speakers only and associate membership to non-Hispanic women religious working among the Spanish speaking. Participants agreed on the organizational name Las Hermanas and the motto "Unidas en Acción y Oración" ("United in Action and Prayer"). They declared the purpose of the organization to be "to meet the needs of the Spanish-speaking people of God, using our unique resources as Spanish-speaking religious women," and endorsed four ways to achieve that goal. They agreed to put their efforts behind team ministry, the training of teams for religious congregations, a central religious formation center, and an information clearinghouse. The intention of these projects was to educate religious congregations about the needs of the Spanish speaking and the expectations of Chicana sisters who desired to work with them, as well as to coordinate ministerial initiatives with Spanish-speaking communities. Finally, participants selected Ortega and Gallardo as the organization's first president and vice president.[11]

While initially Las Hermanas comprised primarily Chicanas, other Latina religious, particularly those of Caribbean heritage, soon joined their Chicana sisters in forming the organization. At various times during their history Las Hermanas addressed the issue of extending full membership to non-Latina members, but the policy of full membership solely for Latinas has been retained due to concern for "the autonomy and self-determination of Hispanics" within the organization. The theme for the organization's fifth national conference (1975) was "La Mujer Laica" ("The Lay Woman"), symbolic of the extension of membership to Hispanic lay women; Las Hermanas became the first national organization of Hispanic Catholic women in the United States. Accepting lay members allowed those who left religious life to continue with the organization. However, it also led some sisters to withdraw from Las Hermanas because they felt the lay presence would dilute the organization's influence with religious superiors and other Church officials. Despite these resignations and some tensions between women religious and lay women who felt the sisters did not treat them as equals, the decision to accept lay members helped Las Hermanas expand its membership base and solidify as an organization.[12]

In addition to broadening the scope of membership by including lay women, at their second national conference (1972) Las Hermanas members opted for a team government concept in lieu of more traditional organizational structures, a contested decision followed by the withdrawal of Gloria Gallardo from the national coordinating team and the organization. Sister Carmelita Espinoza explained that the organization chose the team concept instead of electing a president, vice president, and other officers in order to "show the community in general, and the Hispanic community in particular, a new model within the structure, one that promotes creativity and co-responsibility in leadership." This commitment to co-responsibility in leadership included incorporating lay women on the national coordinating team; in 1976 Ramona Jean Corrales (who had been a woman religious) and then in 1978 Mrs. Sara G. Segovia began their respective terms as the first lay members in the organization's national leadership.[13]

The Struggle for Rights

While Las Hermanas and PADRES at times took prophetic stands on social issues, like farm workers' rights, their most consistent activism was within the Church itself. At their second national congress (1972), for example, Las Hermanas initiated the Proyecto México in response to the exploitation of Mexican nuns as cheap labor in U.S. Catholic institutions. In a subsequent 1973 report, national coordinators Carmelita Espinoza and María de Jesús Ybarra related that, out of economic necessity, at least fifteen Mexican congregations sent members to do domestic work in the United States; some received salaries as low as $50 per month. Espinoza and Ybarra denounced this injustice and asked rhetorically, "Is it necessary to profess vows to be a waitress or a house maid?" Further investigations revealed that about half of these Mexican sisters desired to have a catechetical apostolate among the Spanish speaking; many others feared losing their pay, which, though meager, was needed for the survival of their congregations in Mexico.[14]

PADRES joined the National Federation of Priests' Councils (NFPC) in 1974, and that year delegates Juan Esquivel and Juan Romero presented resolutions on training in cultural awareness for seminarians, national funding for Hispanic ministry, and the promotion of Hispanic bishops. Unfortunately, PADRES representatives were not aware that they had to submit their resolutions before a stated deadline, and NFPC delegates never considered their proposals. The following year PADRES withdrew from what their new executive director Manuel R. Martínez described as "a very lily-white priests' federation" that "should work to get that type of representation [Latinos and Blacks] through their local priests' councils, and not depend on a Hispanic organization such as PADRES to provide that [inclusive] image."[15]

During 1974 Las Hermanas's national coordinating team made an investigative visitation of some diocesan offices for the Spanish speaking, which resulted in an open letter to various bishops; they deplored the fact that the majority of diocesan directors for Hispanic ministry were not Hispanics, that many directors had little authority to implement their projects, that several were only part-time directors, and that most had little contact with the people. The following year Sister Clarita Trujillo represented Las Hermanas at the PADRES national convention. She proposed that PADRES support Las Hermanas's efforts to promote women's concerns, secure more diocesan posts for Hispanic women, and assist Hispanic women "who desire to prepare themselves for the priesthood." PADRES's response to these proposals included their collective affirmation that their organization "be open to the preparation of Hispanic women for the ministry of priestly orders."[16]

In February 1971, participants at a PADRES retreat and workshop in Santa Fe proposed to establish a cultural center with a strong pastoral orientation. Three months later PADRES held a three-week symposium in San Antonio that was facilitated by Latin American thinkers including anthropologist Alfonso Gortaire, theologian Edgard Beltran, and sociologist Manuel Velasquez. Then in September six members of PADRES and one from Las Hermanas participated in a program of pastoral training at the Instituto Pastoral Latino Americano (IPLA) in Quito, Ecuador; subsequently other representatives from PADRES and Las Hermanas participated in this program. Led by PADRES member Virgilio Elizondo, PADRES and Las Hermanas supported the 1972 founding of the Mexican American Cultural Center (MACC), a national training and research center modeled on IPLA that combined the lessons learned from Latin American liberation theology with analysis of the U.S. Latino experience and further advanced PADRES's and Las Hermanas's earlier advocacy for Hispanic ministry and rights. In the years that followed, Latin American Church leaders like Dom Helder Camara of Brazil and Gustavo Gutiérrez of Peru spoke at PADRES's and Las Hermanas's national conferences, continuing the process of adapting and applying liberation theology within the U.S. Latino context.[17]

Although both Hermanas and PADRES pressed Church authorities to create more Latino bishops, this struggle dominated PADRES, leading one of their presidents, Roberto Peña, to say that "the major thrust of PADRES should not be in trying to get more Hispanos appointed bishops but in political action on behalf of the poor." Nonetheless, beginning with the organization's first national congress, the promotion of Latino bishops consistently marked PADRES's official correspondence, newsletters, national and local meetings, and relations with U.S. bishops and the apostolic delegate. The newsletter of May 1974 proudly announced the forthcoming episcopal ordination of Gilberto Chávez as auxiliary bishop of San Diego. Two months later, PADRES member Roberto Sánchez became the archbishop of Santa Fe, the first Latino archbishop in the country. PADRES and Las Hermanas lobbied for both these appointments; they also agitated for Latino bishops in places with large Spanish-speaking populations, like Brownsville, Chicago, Denver, Phoenix, New York, Brooklyn, and the diocese of Orange in Southern California.[18]

In 1978, the Vatican formed a new diocese north of San Diego, the diocese of San Bernardino–Riverside, and named Philip Straling as its first ordinary. PADRES and Las Hermanas held their first joint meeting that August at Mesilla Park, New Mexico. Delegates sent a letter to apostolic delegate Jean Jadot protesting the appointment of bishop-elect Straling to the predominantly Latino see of San Bernardino–Riverside as "an insult to the Hispanic community of California and the nation." They also proposed demands echoing concerns about the lack of Hispanic bishops that PADRES board members had expressed to the apostolic delegate the previous August.[19]

Following the joint gathering of PADRES and Las Hermanas, the boards of the two organizations asked Archbishop Jadot for another meeting, and Las Hermanas and PADRES leaders set up a separate meeting with four California bishops. Meanwhile, PADRES's executive director, Brother Trinidad Sánchez, distributed a circular letter asking concerned parties to write California's two archbishops, John Quinn of San Francisco, the NCCB president, and Cardinal Timothy Manning of Los Angeles, the metropolitan overseeing San Bernardino–Riverside. Sánchez requested that his correspondents demand action on PADRES's proposals for episcopal appointments.[20]

The Decline of PADRES

After Trinidad Sánchez completed his tenure as executive director in 1981, PADRES continued to take activist positions on social issues like military spending, U.S. military aid to El Salvador, and the rights of farm workers, but the organization also adopted a more conciliatory position with regard to Church officials. A resolution from the 1981 national convention acknowledged "the contributions of [apostolic delegate] Archbishop Jean Jadot to minority groups in the Catholic Church of the United States and especially to the Hispanics" and proposed that PADRES engage in "an open and continuous dialogue" with him. Perhaps due in part to this more cooperative approach, during the mid-1980s the board of directors became less active and eventually ceased to meet. Meanwhile other organizations of Hispanic priests emerged in Florida and the northeast. Comprising predominantly foreign-born Hispanic priests, these two organizations merged with PADRES in 1989 to form a new group, Sacerdotes Hispanos (Hispanic Priests), which functions primarily as a fraternal support group for Spanish-speaking priests.[21]

The decision that PADRES remain a clerical group clearly influenced the organization's decline and eventual merger with other Hispanic priests' groups. Some members protested this decision from the very inception of the organization; as early as 1973 executive director Juan Romero warned in a report to PADRES members that "I do not think we can survive as a clerical organization too much longer. If we do not get lay and ecumenical involvement, not only on the national staff, but also on the Board and the membership soon, nothing is going to be left." During the late 1970s, two proposals to accept lay members both failed; after the 1979 national convention layman Armando Navarro concluded in frustration that "I guess leadership will just have to come from somewhere else." Even when the organization's vitality began to wane, delegates at the 1981 national congress voted down a proposal to offer the laity full membership, a controversial decision that led Luis Olivares to decline nomination for a second term as PADRES's national chairman.[22] While PADRES founding members achieved to a considerable degree the solidarity among Chicano priests that they had envisioned, the clerical eligibility requirements hindered the group's longevity by limiting the pool of potential members.

PADRES's founding as a predominantly Chicano clergy association also limited its membership, as did a lack of funding. Initially the U.S. bishops granted relatively significant financial support, as did some Protestant agencies and church boards. But as early as 1973 these funding sources refused PADRES's requests for additional grants, and the organization experienced a fiscal crunch. While PADRES received funding from ecclesial sources like the American Board of Catholic Missions into the 1980s, the organization's inability to broaden their base of monetary support eventually resulted in the loss of salaries and personnel, which clearly contributed to their demise and their 1989 amalgamation with other groups to form Sacerdotes Hispanos.[23]

Besides diminishing membership and funds, the decline of PADRES is also related to the rise of other spokespersons for Latinos in the Church. In this regard PADRES may have been victims of their own success. Today there are some twenty-five Hispanic bishops in the United States. Along with various Hispanic ecclesial organizations, they perform many of the leadership functions PADRES assumed at the time of the organization's founding. To the great disappointment of PADRES members, many of the spokespersons who replaced them (including some PADRES leaders themselves) did not take their same activist stance. In the words of PADRES member Vicente Lopez, "They beat us at our own game!" Historian Moisés Sandoval explains that "the assumption of PADRES and Las Hermanas had been that an Hispanic, by virtue of his ethnicity, would naturally take up the struggles of his people. It turned out to be an overly-optimistic estimate." While PADRES members applauded the episcopal leadership of bishops like Flores, Chávez, and Sánchez, they were frustrated with the "meek and mild" approach of many subsequent appointees. Ironically, PADRES struggled mightily for the appointment of Hispanic bishops who then overshadowed PADRES' leadership role and replaced their activist vision with a more patient and compromising approach.[24]

In his analysis of PADRES, Juan Romero offers a favorable interpretation of the organization's twenty-year existence. Pointing to developments like the empowerment of Chicano priests and the increased involvement of Church leaders in Latino ministry and social concerns, Romero argues that the rise and fall of PADRES is partly due to the fact that the organization "was a charism in the church, and that by nature is temporary. . . . Everything that PADRES originated has had positive influence in the church of today." PADRES founding member Edmundo Rodríguez echoes Romero's conclusion; he observes that as the organization declined, various key members continued the struggle begun in PADRES through efforts like community organizing and leading diocesan Hispanic ministry offices. A noted community organizer and advocate for Hispanic causes within the Church and society, Rodríguez attests that PADRES "will always be a part of who I am" and credits the organization with enhancing his formation and ministry as a Chicano priest. The lasting effect of PADRES in the Church and in the lives of PADRES members like Romero and Rodríguez is consistent with their claims that the organization served a vital purpose.[25]

The New Vision of Las Hermanas

Las Hermanas continues to exist in part because of their approach to the issue of membership. While the organization still restricts non-Latinas to associate membership, it has always accepted lay women as full members. At present there are approximately six hundred individuals associated with the organization, lay women being in the majority. Programs and activities are open to all Latinas. Las Hermanas's ongoing existence probably stems more from a gradual shift in identity and mission than from its membership composition, however. The organization was originally formed to empower Chicana women religious and advance Hispanic ministry and social concerns; its current constitution states that "the purpose of Las Hermanas is the development of leadership among Hispanic women, with a view to the needs of all members of the Hispanic community. The expressed priority of the organization is the promotion of the Hispanic woman."[26] This revised organizational vision has enabled Las Hermanas to endure even though, as with PADRES, Hispanic bishops and other ecclesial groups displaced the group's role as the sole spokespersons for Latinos in the Church.

While Las Hermanas's concern for women's issues was evident in early organizational efforts, a more focused commitment to Hispanic women emerged by their seventh national conference (1977), a meeting dedicated to developing a strategy for promoting women's concerns at the Second National Encuentro of Hispanic Catholics later that year. When participants discussed regional activities for the coming year, Teresita Basso moved that "the one specific project be the women's issue and each Hermana . . . involve herself in a Hispanic Woman's group that takes a liberation stance." This motion passed unanimously.[27]

At a joint meeting of Las Hermanas and PADRES the following year, a generally collaborative spirit was interrupted by the question of concelebration at the closing Eucharist. Hermanas insisted that the partnership and mutuality experienced during the conference would be symbolically nullified if those relationships were reconfigured within the Eucharistic assembly. In the end, a single presider led the Eucharist in order to avoid what one Las Hermanas member deemed the "obvious discrimination between them around the altar and the rest of us over here." At the joint board meeting following the general sessions Las Hermanas sought financial support from PADRES for Latinas in the Women's Ordination Conference (WOC). Although PADRES agreed to "support financially the participation of grass-roots Hispanic women" in WOC,[28] they refused to make a direct donation to that group.

By 1980 the shift of Las Hermanas to a national Hispanic Catholic women's group was clear: the theme for the tenth national conference that year was "Hispanic Women in the Church." Since then all national conferences have dealt with issues that Latinas face, such as sexuality, domestic violence, and leadership skills. Issues of *Informes* also reflect the shift. Not all Las Hermanas members agreed with the shift in the group's focus, however. Former national coordinator Verónica Méndez dropped out of the organization after a meeting in which some participants articulated their personal struggle with Church teaching on reproductive issues. Although Las Hermanas has never taken an official position on these issues, Méndez contended that this discussion contradicted Las Hermanas's purpose and role as a Catholic organization and that some opinions expressed in the conversation were out of touch with the concerns of grassroots Latinas.[29]

Despite such disagreements, the organization continued its vision of advocating for Latinas. At the Third National Encuentro of Hispanic Catholics in 1985, Hermanas members met daily to discuss strategies for promoting women's concerns. When Encuentro organizers re-jected a version of the "Línea Profética" (Prophetic Line) on women, Las Hermanas responded by organizing a protest demonstration of some five hundred delegates on the steps of the National Shrine of the Immaculate Conception, where sessions were held. Eventually the "Línea Profética" on women was restored to the agenda, although the wording was altered to remove an ambiguous passage that could imply a call for the ordination of women. Later a Las Hermanas repre-sentative criticized the National Pastoral Plan, which arose out of the Third Encuentro, for not giving due attention to Hispanic women, concluding that "we can no longer think that they [Church officials] are going to support us on projects for [Hispanic] women."[30]

Las Hermanas's focus on women's concerns is also reflected in the relationships they developed with coalitions of religious women and lay women. Unlike PADRES's, Las Hermanas's applications to Church funding sources like CHD were denied. Groups of religious women were a significant source of financial support: a 1976 report lists more than one hundred women's congregations that made donations to the organization in the previous year. Some religious communities have made substantial in-kind contributions, such as the Sisters of Charity of New York and the Sisters of Loretto, who funded their respective congregational members María Iglesias and Sylvia Sedillo while they served on the Las Hermanas national coordinating team. From 1988 to 1997 the Congregation of Divine Providence donated space for the Las Hermanas national office in the Center for Women at Our Lady of the Lake University in San Antonio, Texas.[31]

Participation in coalitions of women religious also increased Las Hermanas's recognition of sexism as a sin and aberration. Las Her-manas members have in turn voiced the concerns of Latinas within or-ganizations of women religious and other groups, especially the need for feminists to address the issue of racism in their own ranks. For example, in November 1978 María Iglesias, Ada María Isasi-Díaz, and other Las Hermanas members urged participants at a WOC confer-ence "that our Hispanic reality, cultural and economic, as well as the reality of other minority groups be recognized and affirmed as new models of ministry and priesthood are developed." At the 1987 na-tional meeting of the Leadership Conference of Women Religious (LCWR), Las Hermanas national coordinator Yolanda Tarango called on the membership not merely to incorporate Las Hermanas into their existing structures, but to accept Latinas as a transformative presence within the organization. Las Hermanas also withdrew official support for a Women-Church conference when Las Hermanas leaders per-ceived that the coalition was not responding to their challenge for a more inclusive approach. Las Hermanas leaders have consistently ar-

ticulated Hispanic women's concerns in WOC, LCWR, Sisters Uniting, the Women Church Coalition, and other organizations through
their insistence that Latinas shape the agenda of women's groups
rather than being presented with the predetermined agenda of the
dominant cultural group.[32]

The focus on Hispanic women's concerns enabled Las Hermanas
to play a leading role in developing theological reflection from the
perspective of U.S. Latinas. Besides participating in efforts like the
Theology in the Americas symposia and conducting numerous
courses, workshops, and conferences, Las Hermanas's leaders have
encouraged Latinas to articulate their own theological insights in
projects like "Entre Nosotras" ("Among Ourselves"), a small-group
weekend retreat that encompasses discussions of topics like sexuality,
decision making, support systems for Hispanic women, and other issues in participants' lives as Latinas. Las Hermanas's leaders have
also published significant theological works based on these discussions with grassroots women, further enhancing the organization's
mission of serving as a voice and advocate for Hispanic women.[33]

Las Hermanas, PADRES, and the Catholic Left

Like many of their progressive co-religionists, Las Hermanas and PA-
DRES promoted various reforms in Church and society and advocated
ideals like equality and inclusivity. Their social location as an oppressed group, however, differentiated them from most progressive
Catholic groups in the United States. Drawing on insights gained from
the Chicano movement and liberation theology, PADRES and Las
Hermanas developed an analysis that denounced the racism and ethnocentrism they perceived in other reform-minded groups like NFPC,
WOC, and the Women Church Coalition. As Juan Romero put it, PA-
DRES withdrew from NFPC because "they only wanted us as window
dressing to make them look inclusive."[34] Thus, while PADRES and Las
Hermanas can be considered participants in the Catholic left, clearly
their participation entailed a consistent critique of the Catholic left
itself.

PADRES defended themselves against charges of reverse discrimination and separatism by pointing out that they needed a Chicano/
Latino priests' association to build a power base that could effectively
gain access for them and their people within institutional Catholicism. They lamented the fact that "state and federal public institutions,
with their affirmative action programs, are more open to the idea of
equal employment opportunities and fighting discriminatory practices in hiring than the Catholic Church."[35] Drawing on the tactics and
insights of the Chicano movement, they embraced the progressive ideals proposed by their critics, but argued that combating inequality,

segregation, and discrimination necessitated strong organizations founded and led by Latinos themselves. Their contact with liberation theology enabled them to integrate their struggle for justice and institutional access with their vocation as Christians and Church leaders.

Like PADRES, Las Hermanas drew inspiration and strength from the Chicano movement and from Latin American theology's insistence that the struggle for liberation is a constitutive element of Christian faith. As women, however, Las Hermanas members had limited access to hierarchical power. While Hispanic bishops like Patricio Flores supported Las Hermanas's concerns, many members perceived the selection of Latino bishops as yet another example of their lack of representation in the episcopacy. If PADRES members experienced the difficult tension between critiquing the Church and serving as ordained leaders within it, Las Hermanas experienced the hopelessness of episcopal advancement and, at the same time, were relatively free from hierarchical recrimination. Thus it is not surprising that they more readily established networks and funding sources outside hierarchical control, especially through their association with women religious and other women's groups. Nor is it surprising that Las Hermanas were more flexible and adaptable than PADRES and eventually defined their mission as separate from the struggle for institutional access. Although both groups were actively engaged in grassroots struggles like those of farm workers and broad-based community organizations, PADRES more frequently demanded equal representation and institutional access as a strategy for improving the lot of their people. Las Hermanas, on the other hand, perceived power primarily as affecting changes in the lives of Latinas themselves and thus, in the words of one Las Hermanas member, "influencing change from the ground up."[36]

The history of PADRES and Las Hermanas illuminates strategies for people who lack access to leadership opportunities and other resources within a religious (or other) group. Their struggle for liberation and Church reform illustrates that, for oppressed peoples, movements for change can work inside and outside ecclesial and social institutions to confront discrimination, promote equality, bolster ethnic pride, foster group solidarity, and establish parallel networks and organizations to meet their own needs.

NOTES

1. Members of Las Hermanas and PADRES have not used one particular term to describe themselves, although in their early years they often em-

ployed the terms "Chicana" and "Chicano" (persons of Mexican heritage born in the United States) to name themselves and highlight their justice orientation. Early members also referred to themselves as "Mexican Americans" and "the Spanish speaking." As Puerto Ricans, Cubans, and other peoples from Spanish-speaking backgrounds joined the organizations, PADRES and Las Hermanas more frequently used the terms "Latino" and "Hispanic" to denote this wider scope of membership. Despite these general patterns, individual members' choice of terminology varied throughout the history of both organizations. In this essay I attempt to reflect the language used in primary sources, respecting both the diversity of terminology among individual members and the general shifts in usage (and consciousness) among Las Hermanas and PADRES as their organizations developed.

2. *San Antonio Light*, 10 October 1969, p. 7. For an overview of the Chicano movement, see Rodolfo Acuña, *Occupied America: A History of Chicanos*, 3rd ed. (New York: Harper and Row, 1988), esp. pp. 324–356; F. Arturo Rosales, *Chicano! The History of the Mexican American Civil Rights Movement* (Houston: University of Houston Press, 1996).

3. Hermana Mario Barrón and various PADRES, Statement at the Theology of the Americas symposium, August 1975, in *PADRES* (October 1975), p. 10 (quotation); Carmelita Espinoza and María de Jesús Ybarra, *La historia de Las Hermanas* (n.p.: privately printed, 1978), p. 6; PADRES's press release, 11 October 1971; Alberto Carillo, "Toward a National Hispano Church," presentation to the October 1971 PADRES national congress, as cited in Antonio M. Stevens Arroyo, *Prophets Denied Honor: An Anthology of the Hispanic Church in the United States* (Maryknoll: Orbis, 1980), pp. 154–157; PADRES national congress resolutions, October 1971; *Los Angeles Times*, 16 October 1971, part 1, p. 25; *National Catholic Reporter*, 29 October 1971, p. 4. *PADRES* was the organization's newsletter. The PADRES newsletter, press release, national congress resolutions, and other primary sources on the organization are from the private collection of Father Juan Romero, whom I gratefully acknowledge. Romero was an early member of PADRES and served as the organization's executive director from 1972 to 1976. Gilbert Cadena of California State Polytechnic University, Pomona, is preparing a more comprehensive archive of PADRES materials. *La Historia de Las Hermanas* and other primary documents about Las Hermanas are in the archival holdings at Our Lady of the Lake University in San Antonio, Texas.

4. "Origin and Development of PADRES," in PADRES national congress report, October 1971; *San Antonio Light*, 10 October 1969, p. 7; Juan Romero, "Charism and Power: An Essay on the History of PADRES," *U.S. Catholic Historian* 9 (Winter/Spring 1990), p. 150. An abbreviated and slightly revised version of Romero's article entitled "Mexican American Priests: History of PADRES, 1969–1989" is in *Hispanics in the Church: Up from the Cellar*, ed. Philip E. Lampe (San Francisco: Catholic Scholars Press, 1994), pp. 71–94. I am grateful to Father Romero for offering me his time and insightful commentaries in our conversations about PADRES, as well as for providing a helpful critique on an early draft of this essay. Thanks also to Trinidad Sánchez Jr., executive director of PADRES from 1978 to 1981, who also provided valuable comments on this essay.

5. "Origin and Development of PADRES"; *San Antonio Light*, 10 October 1969, p. 7; *Arizona Daily Star*, February 1970. The latter source is an undated photocopy from Father Romero's papers, but contextual evidence suggests that it is from the issue of 2 February 1970.

6. "Origin and Development of PADRES"; Romero, "Charism and Pow-

er," pp. 150–151; "PADRES Stand with Chicanos." The latter reference is a photocopy of a newspaper article from Father Romero's papers, but the date and name of the publication are not given.

7. Romero, "Charism and Power," pp. 151–152 (first two quotations); "Origin and Development of PADRES" (third and fourth quotations).

8. *Catholic Voice* (Oakland), 30 April 1970, p. 14 (first two quotations); Romero, "Charism and Power," p. 152 (third quotation); *PADRES* (December 1973), p. 1 (fourth quotation); letter of Keith B. Kenny, as cited in Moisés Sandoval, "The Church and *el Movimiento*," in *Fronteras: A History of the Latin American Church in the USA Since 1513*, ed. Moisés Sandoval (San Antonio: Mexican American Cultural Center Press, 1983), p. 399 (fifth quotation).

9. "Origin and Development of PADRES"; *National Catholic Reporter*, 10 September 1971, p. 23; Romero, "Charism and Power," pp. 152–153. See also *National Catholic Reporter*, 21 March 1975, p. 6; *PADRES* (December 1973), p. 3, (May 1974), p. 22, (October 1975), p. 3; *Entre Nosotros* 1, no. 1 (Fall 1978), p. 1; Special Issue (1979), p. 11. *Entre Nosotros* was a joint publication project of Las Hermanas and PADRES during the late 1970s. This publication and other cited documents that Las Hermanas and PADRES co-authored are in the archives of both organizations.

10. Gregoria Ortega and Gloria Graciela Gallardo to Mexican American Sisters, 20 October 1970. See also Gallardo to Mexican American Sisters, 11 November 1970. Many thanks to Sister Yolanda Tarango for all she has taught me about Las Hermanas and for her critical comments on an early draft of this essay. Sister Tarango is a long-standing Hermanas member and served on the national coordinating team from 1985 to 1991. I am also grateful to Lara Medina for her assessment of this essay and for sharing her current research on Las Hermanas. For an overview of Las Hermanas's history, see Yolanda Tarango and Timothy M. Matovina, "Las Hermanas," in Lampe, ed., *Hispanics in the Church*, pp. 95–120; Lara Medina, "Las Hermanas: Chicana/Latina Religious-Political Activism, 1971–1997" (Ph.D. dissertation, Claremont Graduate University, 1998).

11. Circular letter to Las Hermanas, 21 April 1971; *National Catholic Reporter*, 13 August 1971, pp. 1, 19; Espinoza and Ybarra, *La historia de Las Hermanas*, pp. 15–17; Interview, Sister Catalina Fresquez, 16 June 1997.

12. *Informes de Las Hermanas* (October 1975), p. 2; *Entre Nosotros* 1, no. 3 (Spring 1979), p. 15 (quotation); Minutes of the Tenth National Conference, 12–13 August 1980, p. 11; Ana María Díaz-Stevens, "Latinas and the Church," in *Hispanic Catholic Culture in the U.S.: Issues and Concerns*, ed. Jay P. Dolan and Allan Figueroa Deck (Notre Dame: University of Notre Dame Press, 1994), pp. 263–266; Medina, "Las Hermanas." *Informes* is Las Hermanas's periodic organizational newsletter. Although canonically religious sisters and brothers remain in the lay state, primary documentation from both Las Hermanas and PADRES reflected the widespread view that vowed religious are not members of the laity.

13. Carmelita Espinoza, Reporte sobre la organización Las Hermanas de '72/74 (quotation); Circular letter to Las Hermanas; Espinoza and Ybarra, *La historia de Las Hermanas*, pp. 16–21; *PADRES* (Fall 1976), pp. 3–4; *Entre Nosotros* 1, no. 2 (Winter 1978), p. 1; Medina, "Las Hermanas." Quotation cited is my translation of the text.

14. Carmelita Espinoza and María de Jesús Ybarra, Proyecto México report, as cited in Sandoval, "The Church and *el Movimiento*," pp. 407–408 (quotation); María de Jesús Ybarra and Mario Barrón to Las Hermanas, 25 August 1974; Clarita Trujillo, "Aporte de Las Hermanas," in PADRES national confer-

ence report, February 1975, p. 70; Espinoza and Ybarra, *La historia de Las Hermanas*, p. 24.

15. *PADRES* (March 1974), pp. 1, 3, (May 1974), pp. 11–12, (April 1975), p. 2, (Spring 1977), p. 19 (quotations); *National Catholic Reporter*, 2 April 1976, p. 2. See also *National Catholic Reporter*, 2 March 1979, p. 5.

16. Circular letter from Las Hermanas to select bishops, 27 May 1974; PADRES national conference report, February 1975, p. 70 (first quotation), p. 83 (second quotation), p. 88. Quotations cited are my translation of the texts.

17. "Origin and Development of PADRES"; Juan Romero, "The Chicano Culture and Pastoral Theology: A Summary of PADRES San Antonio Symposium," May–June 1971; Medina, "Las Hermanas"; *PADRES* (July 1973), p. 2, (Fall 1976), pp. 3–5, 17; Hermana Mario Barrón and various PADRES, Statement at the Theology of the Americas symposium, August 1975, in *PADRES* (October 1975), pp. 8–10.

18. *National Catholic Reporter*, 24 October 1975, p. 21 (quotation), 21 March 1975, p. 6, 13 May 1977, p. 5; *PADRES* (December 1973), p. 1, (May 1974), pp. 1, 7–8, 11–12, (August 1974), pp. 1–2, (November 1974), p. 16, (Summer 1976), p. 15; "Origin and Development of PADRES"; *Chicago Sun-Times*, 20 October 1974. See also PADRES to Archbishop Timothy Manning, 25 February 1971; PADRES of Region XI to select bishops (draft copy of letter), 16 September 1976; Minutes of PADRES–Las Hermanas joint board meeting, 18 August 1978.

19. *National Catholic Reporter*, 1 September 1978, p. 1; *Visitante Dominical*, 24 September 1978, p. 6 (quotation); Juan Romero, Report of meeting with Archbishop Jean Jadot, 5 September 1977. Quotation cited is my translation of the text.

20. Minutes of PADRES–Las Hermanas joint board meeting, 18 August 1978; Roberto Peña to Archbishop John Quinn, 9 October 1978; *Entre Nosotros* 1, no. 1 (Fall 1978), p. 1; Trinidad Sánchez, Circular letter, 20 October 1978.

21. PADRES national congress resolutions, 1981.

22. Romero, PADRES report, January 1973 (first quotation); *National Catholic Reporter*, 1 September 1978, p. 7; 2 March 1979, pp. 1, 5; 9 March 1979, p. 11 (second quotation); Romero, "Mexican American Priests," p. 86; Interview, Trinidad Sánchez Jr., 20 June 1997.

23. *PADRES* (May 1974), p. 22, (Winter 1977), pp. 10–11, (Summer 1982), p. 6; *Entre Nosotros* 1, no. 4 (Summer 1979), pp. 5, 11.

24. Romero, "Charism and Power," p. 158 (first and third quotations); Moisés Sandoval, *On the Move: A History of the Hispanic Church in the United States* (Maryknoll: Orbis, 1990), p. 78 (second quotation).

25. Romero, "Charism and Power," pp. 160–161 (quotations); Edmundo Rodríguez, "The Hispanic Community and Church Movements: Schools of Leadership," in *Hispanic Catholic Culture in the U.S.*, ed. Dolan and Figueroa Deck, pp. 225–226.

26. *Informes de Las Hermanas* (June 1989), p. 4. Quotation cited is my translation of the text.

27. Minutes of the seventh national conference, 14–17 August 1977 (quotation); *Informes de Las Hermanas* (September 1977), p. 3.

28. Interview, Sister Yolanda Tarango, 7 October 1997; Interview, Trinidad Sánchez Jr., 20 June 1997; *National Catholic Reporter*, 1 September 1978, p. 7 (first quotation); *Visitante Dominical*, 24 September 1978, p. 7; Minutes of PADRES–Las Hermanas joint board meeting, 18 August 1978 (second quotation).

29. Interview, Sister Verónica Méndez, 19 January 1997.

30. *Informes de Las Hermanas* (January 1986), p. 7, (December 1989), pp. 1–3; *Prophetic Voices: The Document on the Process of the III Encuentro Nacional*

Hispano de Pastoral (Washington, D.C.: United States Catholic Conference, 1986), p. 6, "Línea Profética" #9; Carmen Villegas, "Informes y análisis de la reunión de NAC," *Informes de Las Hermanas* (March 1987), p. 5 (quotation). Quotation cited is my translation of the text.

31. Espinoza and Ybarra, *La historia de Las Hermanas*, pp. 25–26; Ramona Jean Corrales, Teresita Basso, and María Iglesias, Circular letter to Las Hermanas, 8 October 1976; Minutes of the seventh national conference, 14–17 August 1977; Minutes of the executive board meeting, 20 October 1979. See also various issues of *Informes de Las Hermanas* and annual reports from Las Hermanas's leaders.

32. *Entre Nosotros* 1, no. 2 (Winter 1978), p. 9 (quotation); Interview, Sister Yolanda Tarango, 17 October 1997. See also various issues of *Informes de Las Hermanas*; Minutes of executive board meeting, 9 August 1981; Margarita Castañeda, Reporte de la coordinadora nacional a la asamblea nacional, 7–9 August 1981; Minutes of executive board meeting, 5–6 December 1981.

33. *Informes de Las Hermanas* (March 1987), p. 1, (July 1992), p. 2; Ada María Isasi-Díaz and Yolanda Tarango, *Hispanic Women: Prophetic Voice in the Church* (San Francisco: Harper and Row, 1988; reprint, Minneapolis: Fortress, 1992); Isasi-Díaz, *En la Lucha/In the Struggle: A Hispanic Women's Liberation Theology* (Minneapolis: Fortress, 1993); Tarango, "The Hispanic Woman and Her Role in the Church," *New Theology Review* 3 (November 1990), pp. 56–61.

34. Interview, Father Juan Romero, 18 March 1997.

35. Juan Hurtado to Archbishop Jean Jadot, 12 April 1976, as cited in *PADRES* (Summer 1976), p. 15.

36. Interview, Sister Yolanda Tarango, 6 November 1996.

13

THE BLACK CATHOLIC CONGRESS MOVEMENT

A Progressive Aspect of African-American Catholicism

DIANA L. HAYES

Despite their long presence in the Roman Catholic Church in the United States, Catholics of African descent have had to fight for their baptismal right to name themselves Catholic. Paradoxically, the effect of persistent bias has not been an exodus of Black Catholics from the Church. Indeed, the racism they encountered seems to have stiffened their resolve to remain in a church that has had African members since ancient times. Like their fellow Black Christians in Protestant churches, they affirm the legitimacy of their own faith while questioning that of their white co-religionists. Racism and its effects are not new to Black Catholics; they realize that the Church, in its relationships with people of color, is more a reflection of American society than a critique of it. Thus, they see their persistent presence as a challenge to the Church, a challenge exemplified by the Black Catholic Congress movement of the nineteenth and twentieth centuries: the institutional Church will not change until the "people of God" change their attitudes toward Black Catholics.

Are African-American Catholics progressive or conservative? On a fundamental level, they lead religious lives typical of other Catholics, following the rituals of the liturgical year, perhaps reading some Catholic newspaper, sending their children to Catholic schools when possible, and spending most of their energy on non-religious events. At the same time, they respond to issues within the Church not just as Catholics, but as Black Catholics, and their degree of comfort within the Church is relative to their acceptance of their Blackness and Black culture. Black Catholics often divide into liberal and conservative, as other Catholics do, over liturgical issues and over the appropriate speed of and means for change. Those from an earlier generation, however vocal they are in their demands for more Black priests, religious, and bishops, tend to prefer popular models of religiosity such as novenas, rosaries, and Benediction and thus can make common cause with some traditionalists. Conservative Black Catholics, like conservatives in general, resist some forms of change. As Gayraud Wilmore noted, "Radical and conservative Negroes agree as to the end in view [opposition to racism] but differ as to the most effective means of attaining it."[1]

I will describe progressive Black Catholics by way of the Black Catholic Congress movement. Like other Blacks, they work toward the eradication of white racism and ethnocentrism in the Church, but they are distinctive by way of their participation in or support for a Catholic movement of lay solidarity. The Black Catholic Congress movement in the twentieth century, related in spirit to its nineteenth-century forerunner, shows how Black Catholics have asserted the kind of self-determination that marks progressives in the Church. This is not to say that Black Catholics are generally liberal in their outlook. Black Catholics, like many other Black Christians, tend to lead the way on social justice issues while they are often behind on theologically progressive matters. For example, Black theology as a religious movement and intellectual phenomenon has not really had a significant impact in the pews. At the same time, progressive Black Catholics are very much involved in the kind of liturgical inculturation that leads to innovation, local authority, lay leadership, and advocacy of greater roles for persons of African descent—women and men—in all levels of Church life.

A Brief History

Cyprian Davis has shown that many persons of African descent were already Catholic when they first came to the shores of what is now the United States. Spanish-speaking and French-speaking Blacks helped to settle and colonize the Southwestern and Louisiana territories as early as the sixteenth century.[2] Other Africans were introduced to Catholic Christianity at the hands of their masters and given rudimentary religious instruction. After a brief catechesis and swift baptism, religious instruction stressed the responsibility of slaves to accept one's state as God's will and to be a good, honest, and obedient servant. As I have shown elsewhere, most Africans came from a culture with a worldview radically different from their captors'. Rather than an emphasis on sin and the "fallen nature" of humanity, they saw themselves as cared for by a loving Creator who participated in various ways in their lives. Their cosmic vision connected the living, the dead, and the unborn in a vast extended family.[3]

As slaves worked to reconstruct their religious lives in a harsh and unforgiving environment, many of them were attracted to Catholicism because of its sacramental richness, colorful vestments, emphasis on elaborate rituals, feasts and days of fasting, saints and sacramentals. Although Africans were drawn to Catholic ritual, they had difficulty adjusting to the solemnity and rigidity of the Roman Rite, which provided no space for spontaneity or the movement of the Spirit within their midst. Over time, however, usually in response to criticism by their fellow Catholics of other ethnic backgrounds, Black Catholics learned to reconcile themselves to the more subdued, less emotional, abstract style of worship that prevailed in the Church until the Second Vatican Council. They also found other outlets: syncretic Afro-Latino-Catholic religions such as Voudon, Santeria, and Candomble were important to many of them.[4] Others attended both Mass and then a more emotive service in a local Black Protestant community.

African Americans have been members of the Catholic Church in America for more than four hundred years. Through much of that time they have lived within a dialectical tension that Gayraud Wilmore describes as survival versus liberation. As he sees it, there is one Black expression of Christianity that overemphasizes a passive otherworldliness where social and political issues have no immediate role (survival), and another that, because of its emphasis on Black radicalism, has a more active, revolutionary spirit (liberation). "One of the continuing paradoxes of the black church," he says, "is that it is at once the most reactionary and the most radical of black institutions; the most imbued with the mythology and values of white America, and yet the most proud, the most independent and indigenous collectivity in the black community."[5]

Catholicism and Racism

After the Civil War, many Black Catholics left the Catholic Church, some because it had never filled their needs, others because of the negligent and hate-filled ways in which they were treated by the institution and its members. The treatment of African people by the Roman Catholic Church is a shameful page of Catholic history. Catholic countries like Spain and Portugal were heavily involved in the horrific Atlantic slave trade. Neither Scripture nor tradition was clear about the morality of human slavery, a system that had apparently been operative throughout human history. Slave masters quoted extensively from both Old and New Testament, especially the letters of St. Paul, to support their actions and were, in turn, supported by Rome's understanding of natural law. As less benign aspects of the slave trade became more widely known, often due to anguished letters by missionaries in the field, the Vatican slowly began to shift its emphasis from support to opposition. It was too little, too late. A legacy of racism that made persons of darker skin inferior human beings—if even seen as human at all—made it virtually impossible for freed slaves to be treated with fairness and civility by other Catholics, clergy, lay people, and the hierarchy.[6]

Efforts by the Vatican after the Civil War to encourage the establishment of a special vicariate to handle the particular needs of the freed slaves and to evangelize the fallen-away and those unchurched were strongly rejected by American bishops at the Second Plenary Council of Baltimore in 1866. They feared encroachment on their own diocesan territories and were, they thought, stretched thin in their efforts to serve what many believed were their true clientele, ethnic white Catholics and the increasing numbers of Catholic immigrants.[7] The bishops' failure to respond to Vatican appeals in this direction put Black Catholics in a cruel bind. Although these Catholics were often given encouragement from Rome, they found little support and often open hostility at the parish and diocesan level. Those who attempted to attend services in white parishes were rebuffed, often harshly. Those who attempted to enroll their children in Catholic schools were denied admission. This history of racist rejection ultimately led to the development of separate, segregated Black parishes—in both North and South—which were usually a bare step above a mission palmed off on a young, insecure priest or a broken-down old one with no idea of "what to do" with these strangely different people.

The stubborn refusal by Catholic bishops and rectors of seminaries to encourage priestly vocations among Black Catholics and a similar resistance by heads of religious orders had consequences that continue to impact the Black Catholic community today. Since Black candidates were not admitted to seminaries, Black Catholics had no way to foster indigenous clerical leadership. Religious orders with specific vocations to work within Black parishes eventually did the kind of work that led to the ordination of Black priests, though only after considerable time, and with a peculiar result. Black priests who were eventually ordained—usually in Rome where they were trained —found it impossible until this century to return to the United States for pastoral assignments, and were usually assigned to churches in Africa or the Caribbean.[8] In addition, it must be said that male religious orders founded for the benefit of Black Catholics were paternalistic in their leadership styles. Since they, like the Church as a whole, conceptualized Catholicism in segregated terms, this had the effect of isolating Black Catholic parishes even further from those of their co-religionists.[9] Nor did their efforts lead to significant numbers of Black priests. Leadership in Black Catholic churches, therefore, had to emerge from the ranks of the laity. The narrative of that struggle is the story of the Black Catholic Congress movement, a nineteenth-century phenomenon that emerged, was suppressed, and has re-emerged in the last twenty years.

The Black Catholic Congress Movement: Part One

The Negro Congress Movement of the late nineteenth century can be seen as a crucible for the dialectical tension between the otherworldliness promoted by the Church and the radical nature of Black faith. That tension led to the emergence of a fairly progressive, self-affirming lay movement, which held five national congresses between 1889 and 1894 in various northern urban centers. These convocations were the first lay-generated and lay-led conferences by Catholics of any race in the United States. What motivated them? It may have been the growing number of upwardly mobile, educated Negro Catholic lay men who felt that the time was ripe to claim their rights to active membership within the Church. Such was the case for Daniel Rudd, the man responsible for the calling of the first Congress. He was the founder of the first Black Catholic newspaper, the *American Catholic Tribune*, and saw the Catholic Church as the "single great hope for American Blacks" and as "the leaven which would raise up their people not only in the eye of God but before men."[10] Another factor could have been the growing frustration of Black Catholics as the Church continued to keep the doors of its seminaries, convents, monasteries, and chanceries closed to their brothers and sisters. Or it might have been the result of the hope kindled by the ordination of the first African-American diocesan priest, Father Augustus Tolton, for the Diocese of Joliet, Illinois, in 1886.[11]

Whatever its motivations, Rudd saw a three-fold significance for the congress:

> the importance of the general public seeing the large number of Black Catholics gathered together with the blessing of the Catholic Church . . . the large number of Black Protestants who regard Black Catholics as an anomaly to see [their] united strength . . . and finally the value of Black Catholics meeting one another and exchanging viewpoints.[12]

When the first congress met—January 1–4, 1889, at St. Augustine's church in Washington—Father Tolton celebrated the Mass. Participants and speakers included not only Black Catholic men but James Cardinal Gibbons, in whose archdiocese the meeting was held. William H. Elder, archbishop of Cincinnati, and priests working in the Black Catholic community also attended. The congress addressed issues within the Catholic community, such as education for Black children and greater participation in the creation of liturgy, as well as areas in the wider society, such as slum housing and union membership.

Although this and later congresses stressed the "deep devotion" of Black Catholics to the Church, the participants were not blind to its negative realities. They tended to place the blame for racism more on individual Catholics than on the institutional Church. Accordingly, they advocated the Church's increased participation on behalf of the civil and human rights of their Black faithful. As they continued to meet over the next few years, delegates at Black Catholic Congresses grew stronger in their demands, challenging the Church to bring its actions more in line with its teachings of a God-given equality among all human beings. The delegates also became more specific. As I have argued elsewhere, their line of questioning and dialogue can be said to be the first expression of a Black Catholic theological consciousness.[13]

At the second congress, held in Cincinnati in 1890, one of the speakers raised the school issue in sharp and clear terms:

> [T]he Church teaches that we must send our children to Catholic schools. We value our religion and Catholic training; we marvel that the Divines of the Church do not support their teaching by having Catholic colleges and schools open their doors to at least those of our Colored children who are well-behaved and able to pay.[14]

At the third congress (Philadelphia, 1892), delegates urged the foundation of a permanent national organization for the benefit of Black Catholics. In ensuing years, as little seemed to change, the challenges became more pointed. Delegates continued to press for equal access to Catholic education and to castigate the Church for its failure to live up to its own teachings. Racism was repeatedly condemned.

Why the congresses ended is not clear. Perhaps growing solidarity among Black Catholics along with increasingly strong demands for justice put the Church in a reactionary position. When Cyprian Davis questioned their demise, he wondered whether they ceased activity "because the Congresses had become more active and thereby perhaps more militant? Or was it because Rome itself became more wary of the activities of lay Catholic congresses in general?"[15] Whatever the reasons, this movement within the Black Catholic Church discloses the presence of an articulate, educated, active Black Catholic community that was unwilling to have others make all of the decisions for their role in the Church and their future as Catholic faithful. The assertive, self-determining, and challenging spirit that stirred the hearts and minds of those who had gathered over those five critical years was not quenched. Although the pendulum swung toward a more survival-oriented Black Catholic community, this phase of activism would return.

Black Catholics before Vatican II

In the early twentieth century, Black Catholics were able to consolidate their strength and to build schools and churches for themselves. They usually did so with little help from their bishops and with active resistance from other Catholics. Most Black Catholic parishes were designated as "mission churches," relegated to the margins of the Church and administered by religious orders with special vocations to "Negro and Indian Missions." Those who actively sought to bring the situation of Black Catholics to the forefront of the Church usually emerged from the ranks of the laity.

The great post-war migration from South to North meant that a rapidly growing Black population would inevitably intersect with vast numbers of first- and second-generation immigrant Catholics living in northern urban centers. This cultural clash led to growing fear, resentment, and disruption, a story that has been told by John McGreevy.[16] Yet, despite racial tensions, many Blacks who migrated north joined the Catholic Church. The reasons for the massive conversions are not entirely clear, but factors included a desire for social upward mobility (certainly a conservative movement) and the influence of Catholic religious in Catholic schools, to which many flocked for their emphasis on education and discipline. Initially the Church simply established Black parishes as they had fostered national parishes for the Irish, Italians, and other ethnic groups. Problems quickly arose, however, whenever and wherever Black Catholics moved into areas that had already established parishes. As McGreevy found, the greatest resistance to open housing and integration efforts for Black Americans came from white ethnic Catholics and their priests.

Although all too often local pastors aided and abetted the racist postures of their parishioners, other priests slowly began to move toward a reconciliation and advocacy for Black Catholics. Two results of efforts in this direction were the Federated Colored Catholics (FCC) and the National Catholic Council on Interracial Justice (NCCIJ). Thomas Wyatt Turner, the outspoken leader of the FCC, was adamant that leadership of the movement be both Black and lay. Turner and other Black leaders soon found, however, that hierarchical support for such ventures went to priests, not to lay men. And, to their dismay, they found that the Church was more willing to listen to white clerical analysis of and ideas for Black Catholicism than to Black lay men. John LaFarge, S.J., initially a supporter of the FCC, believed that Black Catholics ought to move away from emphasis on race—which he thought fostered separatism—to an emphasis on interracial justice. Despite assertions by Turner that LaFarge's suggestion was a move to "dethrone Negro leadership" and that interracial activity would dilute racial solidarity, his fellow Black Catholics eventually voted to dissolve the FCC and merge it into what later became the National Catholic Council on Interracial Justice, led by LaFarge. This conflict was one that was to be repeated in later years when Black Christians, both Protestant and Catholic, found themselves and their organizations co-opted by white liberals, religious and lay, who believed they had a better grasp of the situation of Blacks and their needs than did their Black brothers and sisters.[17]

In the second half of the twentieth century, a variety of social, political, and religious movements began to conspire to change the lives of Black Catholics in the United States. African-American Catholics became increasingly aware of the demand for Black liberation in the United States with the emergence of Dr. Martin Luther King Jr., but they were also aware of liberation movements in Africa, especially South Africa. Increasingly, South African Catholic bishops became more vocal and articulate in their attack on apartheid. Their assertion of papal doctrine over against the theology of separation, which supported the South African government, was enhanced by the fact that over 70 percent of the South African Church's members were of African descent. The Vatican began to compare the American Church and government unfavorably with those of South Africa, noting that "the church is completely and unalterably opposed to all forms of discrimination, in New Orleans as much as in South Africa."[18]

Despite the presence of nuns and priests in the civil rights movement, attitudes of most American Catholics toward their African-American co-religionists showed little change. In 1958, the American bishops issued their first major pastoral letter on racism, declaring that "the heart of the race question is moral and religious."[19] The statement received stiff opposition, especially from the bishops of southern dioceses concerned about membership loss, but it encouraged Black Catholics. Resistance increased on many levels as Black Catholics once again began to protest their treatment in the Church. Some became involved in the civil rights movement, where they underwent a significant conversion experience relative to their place and role in their own church. Some young Black Catholics—clergy and lay—although initially supportive of the interracial efforts of the NCCIJ, now began to raise questions about their own experience in the Church. They called for greater openness and change and emphasized the need for African-American Catholics to come together and work for that change as Black Catholics independent of well-meaning others. They were encouraged, therefore, when the Second Vatican Council described the Church as the "people of God" with a responsibility to work for Christ's extension throughout the world. The documents of Vatican II, particularly the pastoral constitution on the Church in the modern world and the one on the liturgy, gave Black Catholics an opening to explore and recover that part of their cultural heritage—their African and African-American roots—that had been put aside in an effort to become acceptably Catholic.

Vatican II set into motion a shift from an emphasis on unity and uniformity to an understanding of the diversity of the Catholic Church and the viability of cultures other than European for rendering the Gospel message. This shift was seen most clearly in the liturgical changes that were taking place: in Black parishes, images of saints and martyrs, Jesus and the Virgin Mary, and others in the early church were given what was believed to be their appropriate rendering in line with the fact that the Church was of Middle Eastern and African rather than Western European origins. At the same time, a liturgical retrieval of music and worship styles that had links not just with Black Protestantism but with the religion of the slaves began to stimulate the creation of Gospel liturgies rooted in the Black cultural heritage.[20] Encouraged by these movements, Black Catholics set out to reclaim their rightful place in the Church. As acceptance into seminaries had increased, albeit slowly, there was an increasingly vocal and educated group of Black Catholic clergy and religious women ready to act. With this critical mass, the stage was set for a renewed effort for self-determination in the Church, for a re-emergence of the Black Catholic Congress movement.

In April 1968, the first meeting of what would become the National Black Catholic Clergy Caucus (NBCCC) was held in Detroit. Attendees included sixty Black clergy; Harold Perry, the first Black Catholic bishop since Bishop James Healey in the nineteenth century; and one Black religious, Sister Martin de Porres Gray, R.S.M. After much discussion and four votes, a resolution was passed that stated unequivocally that "[t]he Catholic Church in the United States is a predominately white racist institution." A call was made for the establishment of a Black Catholic vicariate and the appointment of an episcopal vicar for all Black Catholics in the country, echoing the request made by the Vatican almost a hundred years earlier. Although this request may seem conservative relative to the assertion of racism, it signaled a move by Black Catholic leaders away from an emphasis on integration to an assertion that Black Catholics needed to look after their own needs in their own parishes.[21]

By the end of 1968, the NBCCC was joined by the National Black Sisters Conference, organized under the leadership of Sister Martin de Porres Gray, and in 1969, the National Black Lay Caucus was formed. A significant result of the development of these organizations was the growing emphasis on the recovery of their historical and cultural roots as both Black and Catholic. Black priests and religious, especially, recognized how much of that heritage had been sacrificed in their efforts to be accepted in religious orders and diocesan seminaries organized along European lines and values. Accompanying the development of an African-American Catholic identity were demands that Black Catholics have control of their own financial and institutional resources. They sought to make decisions for themselves, increasingly using the language of Black Power to couch their requests. They demanded to be involved in decisions about parish assignments and to be consulted about seminary and novitiate formation programs.

In order to promote cultural retrieval and freedom, Black Catholics sought funding from the Catholic bishops and others for an independent National Office of Black Catholics (NOBC), which would have as its mandate the specific needs and concerns of the still growing numbers of African-American Catholics. Although initially shocked and disoriented by these requests, the bishops offered a start-up grant of $16,000, much less than requested. Since subsequent requests received an even poorer response, Black Catholics began a fund-raising campaign of their own on the parish level. Once in place, the NOBC launched a series of programs designed to raise the consciousness of Black Catholics about their history in the Catholic Church. NOBC also embarked upon an inculturation program, which aimed to retrieve and reclaim Black history and culture in order to incorporate it into the liturgy.

The Black Catholic Congress Movement: Part Two

When I argue that the Black Catholic Congress movement is a progressive aspect of African-American Catholicism, I do so within a framework of Church life. Obviously, the Black Catholic community is not monolithic: their different cultural and religious traditions make the community inclusive and diverse. At the same time, the close-knit nature of the Black Catholic community means that they join to form a united front when threatened, especially from within. This sense of solidarity may explain, in part, the response of the majority of Black Catholics to the move by Black former priest George A. Stallings to create an independent Black Catholic Church. Although Black Catholics agreed with his charge of racism in the Church, they did not feel compelled to leave it. Whether the Catholic Church had been welcoming or not, it had been a home for most of them for generations. Most felt it more important to remain within the Catholic Church and to continue their struggle there.

One way to continue that struggle was by way of theological education and activism. In 1978, the first theological symposium held by Black Catholics took place. This gathering of predominately priests and religious discussed issues of Black Catholic identity, worship, and culture from a theological perspective.[22] An important institution that emerged as a result of this gathering was the Institute for Black Catholic Studies, established at Xavier University of New Orleans in 1980, under the leadership of Sister Thea Bowman, Father Joseph Nearon, Father Bede Abrams, and others. The Institute developed a program of study leading to a master of theology degree in pastoral studies, along with certificate programs in catechetics, youth ministry, and parish leadership. The goal of these programs was to enable anyone working with Black Catholics to understand Black Catholicism in its myriad manifestations.

By the 1980s, a Black Catholic identity was firmly established, acknowledged, and, to some extent, supported within the Church. Many bishops had created offices of ministry for Black Catholics at the diocesan level, some of which played key roles in the education of all Catholics about the cultural heritage of Black Catholicism. The battle against racism was not yet won, however, and Black Catholics continued to denounce the covert racism still all too prevalent in the Church. They also continued to seek greater participation at all levels of Church life. Much of this activity was led and sustained by Black clergy and religious, but the laity were about to re-emerge. When the NOBC virtually self-destructed because board members failed to agree on key issues and strategies, new organizations emerged. One of the most active of these new groups was the National Association of Black Catholic Administrators, representatives of the heads of Black Catholic Ministry Offices. Members of these organizations were instrumental in the revival of the Black Catholic Congresses in the last part of the twentieth century.

Although the modern Black Catholic Congresses depict themselves as the continuation of the five congresses held in the nineteenth century, there is no actual direct link between them. At the same time, both were the result of a growing desire by the Black Catholic laity to speak on their own behalf, to organize as a viable community, and to get to know each other and their history. In their modern incarnation, the congresses were designed so that Black Catholics at every level had an opportunity for input into the agenda and for the selection of the delegates. The first congress—or the sixth, if counted in continuity with the earlier movement, as is their accepted practice—took place in Washington in the summer of 1987. Despite the fact that this congress took place more than one hundred years after the first one, many of the issues were the same. Black Catholics called for evangelization of African Americans, greater leadership opportunities, recognition of and support for Black culture, opportunities for education, especially in light of the propensity for many dioceses to close inner-city schools, and attention to the particular needs of the Black family. As Albert Raboteau summarized it:

The papers presented at the 1987 National Black Catholic Congress remind the Church of how far it still has to go in the work of evangelization. Like the Black Congress of the last century, this one claims a primary role for Black Catholics in the process of converting Black people to Catholicism. These papers also reiterate that the goal of evangelization and the mission of social outreach are inextricably linked. . . . The Congress was in fact a reclamation of Black Catholic tradition and an assertion of present solidarity, pride, and activism among Black Catholics.[23]

This Congress took place in the context of a number of other significant events in the history of Black Catholics. The (then ten) Black bishops had issued their first pastoral letter in 1984, "What We Have Seen And Heard," proclaiming that "Black Catholics have now come of age."[24] After the congress, a historic visit took place between Black Catholic leaders, including lay leaders, and the pope on his visit to the United States. The pope urged them to keep their Black cultural heritage alive and active as a gift, which enriches the Church and gives credence to its universality. Sixteen hundred Black Catholics gathered in Washington in May of 1987. More than three thousand came to Baltimore in 1997 for the eighth congress.

Today, there are thirteen active Black bishops, four of whom head dioceses, and approximately two and a half million Black Catholics. Although Black Catholics make up just under 10 percent of the African-American population, they are the second largest African-American religious community in the United States. Although the numbers of priests and religious are still small and in many areas are decreasing and aging, an increasing number of Black Catholics are engaged in theological studies at the master's and doctoral level. Systematic theologians, catechists, liturgists, directors of religious education, and other professional ministers represent Black Catholics on their own terms. There is now a Secretariat for African American Catholics in the United States Catholic Conference as well as a Committee on African American Catholics in the National Conference of Catholic Bishops, with which it interacts. There is a permanent National Black Catholic Congress office, which organizes the congresses held every five years, and which also sponsors pastoral institutes to introduce Catholics to the Black cultural heritage as it is especially lived out in the Roman Catholic Church. Finally, Catholics who visit the Basilica of the National Shrine of the Immaculate Conception in Washington can see the "Mother of Africa" chapel recently dedicated there.

The spirit of assertive self-determination continues to move within the hearts and minds of Black Catholics in the United States, leading them to articulate "who and whose" they are, as a people of both African and American origins, a people Black and Catholic. Although they can be found along the entire spectrum from conservative to radical, in keeping with that dialectical tension between a passive other-worldliness and an active radicalism, it has been at the liberational pole that the most significant accomplishments for and by African-American Catholics have occurred, both in liturgical acculturation (see chapter 10) and in the congress movement. Many Black Catholic churches are now becoming home parishes for white Catholics as well who are disenchanted with the style of worship, the dull preaching, or the lack of community they find in their own churches. Many people of diverse ethnicities attend Gospel Masses in the United States today. Black Catholics persist in their refusal to be neatly boxed or categorized. Assertive of their particular self-understanding as truly Black and authentically Catholic, they also retain within themselves and their parishes a love for many of the "old ways" of that Church of which they have been a part for so long a time.

NOTES

1. Gayraud Wilmore, *Black Religion and Black Radicalism,* 2d ed. (Maryknoll: Orbis Books, 1983), p. xiii.

2. For a fuller presentation of Black Catholic history see Cyprian Davis, *The History of Black Catholics in the United States* (New York: Crossroad, 1990). Much of my historical information comes from that book.

3. See Diana L. Hayes, *And Still We Rise: An Introduction to Black Liberation Theology* (Mahwah, N.J.: Paulist Press, 1996), pp. 9–12, 32.

4. These religions, which flourish to this day, can be found especially in those countries in the Americas or areas in the United States where there was, and continues to be, a predominately Catholic population, such as Brazil, Haiti, Puerto Rico, and Louisiana. See two books by Joseph Murphy, *Santeria: African Spirits in America* (Boston: Beacon Press, 1993), and *Working the Spirit: Ceremonies of the African Diaspora* (Boston: Beacon Press, 1994).

5. Wilmore, *Black Religion and Black Radicalism,* pp. 220–242.

6. Forrest G. Wood, *The Arrogance of Faith: Christianity and Race in America from the Colonial Period to the Twentieth Century* (Boston: Northeastern University Press, 1990), pp. 353–365.

7. See Cyprian Davis, "The Holy See and American Black Catholics: A Forgotten Chapter in the History of the American Church," *U.S. Catholic Historian* 7 (1988), p. 157. Also Stephen J. Ochs, *Desegregating the Altar: The Josephites and the Struggle for Black Priests, 1871–1960* (Baton Rouge: Louisiana State University Press, 1990), pp. 1–48.

8. Ibid.

9. See Ochs, *Desegregating.* The two major religious orders were the Society of the Divine Word (SVDs) and the Society of Saint Joseph (Josephites). Their influence is still significant, as the majority of the Black Catholic bishops, of which there are 13 active today, have come from these two orders. There were two initial religious orders for Black women, both founded long before the men's orders: the Oblates of Divine Providence (1829) and the Holy Family Sisters (1842). They were and continue to be important figures in the evangelization and education of Black Catholics.

10. See Davis, "The Holy See and American Black Catholics," pp. 158–159.

11. Earlier Black priests never served in the United States except for the three Healey brothers, Patrick, James, and Sherwood. Although the children of a Black slave mother and a white plantation owner father who recognized them as his sons and sent them north for their education, the Healey brothers never fully identified with their Black ancestry. It was, however, known that they were of African descent. Patrick became president of Georgetown University, James the first bishop of Portland, Maine, and Sherwood, who died young, the rector of the cathedral in Boston, Massachusetts.

12. Davis, "The Holy See and American Black Catholics," pp. 159–160.

13. See my *And Still We Rise*, pp. 161–185.

14. Davis, *The History of Black Catholics*, p. 176.

15. Ibid., p. 193.

16. These observations are from John McGreevy, *Parish Boundaries: The Catholic Encounter with Race in the Twentieth-Century Urban North* (Chicago: University of Chicago Press, 1996), ch. 4 and p. 31.

17. Marilyn Nickels, "Thomas Wyatt Turner and the Federated Colored Catholics," *U.S. Catholic Historian* 7 (1988), pp. 215–232. In that same issue, also see Martin Zielinski, "Working for Interracial Justice: The Catholic Interracial Council of New York, 1934–1964," pp. 233–263.

18. As cited in McGreevy, *Parish Boundaries*, p. 88.

19. "Discrimination and the Christian Conscience" (Washington, D.C.: United States Catholic Conference, 1958), p. 91.

20. See two books by Clarence Rivers, *The Spirit in Worship* (Cincinnati: Stimuli, 1978) and *This Far by Faith: American Black Worship and Its African Roots* (Cincinnati: Stimuli, 1977).

21. James H. Cone and Gayraud Wilmore, eds., *Black Theology: A Documentary History, 1966–79*, vol. I (Maryknoll: Orbis Books, 1993), pp. 230–232.

22. The proceedings of the symposium, entitled *Theology: A Portrait in Black*, were published in 1980 by the National Black Catholic Clergy Caucus under the editorship of Fr. Thaddeus Posey, O.F.M.Cap. A second symposium was held in 1980. The symposium was reconstituted in 1991 and now meets annually.

23. Albert Raboteau, "Introductory Reflections," *U.S. Catholic Historian* 7 (1988), p. 300.

24. Cincinnati: St. Anthony Messenger Press, 1984.

Part 6

PUBLIC
CATHOLICISM

14

WHAT HAPPENED TO THE CATHOLIC LEFT?

DAVID J. O'BRIEN

What happened to the Catholic left? Veteran Catholic watchers understand that question, and know that it does not refer to people worried about birth control or women priests. Members of the Catholic left usually differ over such matters. Their common ground, instead, is a passion for social justice and world peace. They are people aroused by the moral scandals of nuclear weapons, third world poverty, domestic racism, and economic injustice—people like the late Dorothy Day, or the Berrigan brothers, or a Maryknoll nun or Jesuit priest just returned from Central America. The "what happened?" part of the question has to do with visibility: in the sixties and seventies Catholics of this sort seemed to be turning up all the time on the evening news, leading one sort of protest or another. Now we hear a lot about a Catholic right, but if the word "left" is heard at all, it refers to groups who are angry at the Church's clerical establishment, but who likely differ over political matters.

So what did happen to the Catholic left? The usual answer is that, in the Church as in American society, the left lost.

In this chapter we will reconsider the question. After defining our terms, we will examine the social and ecclesiastical context of contemporary Catholic life—the changes in society and in the Church that have had dramatic impact on Catholic participation in public life. Then we will suggest some interpretive categories for understanding the rhetoric of contemporary "public Catholicism." With that framework in place, we will argue that a Catholic left persists, and examine its constituent elements. Then, we will examine some reasons for its relative invisibility. Finally, we will suggest some ideas about where the left fits into the larger geography, the map, of Catholicism in the United States.

Getting the Subject Straight

The Catholic left is an aspect of what has come to be called "public Catholicism." At each historical moment the Catholic Church presents a public face—or, better, public faces—to other communities and to society at large. The Church in Latin America, for example, once cast its lot with the dominant political powers of the continent; today, more than a generation later, it has a radically different profile as a companion to the poor and defender of human rights. The example suggests that Catholicism, while it may entail everything from theology through Church politics to personal spirituality, is not a "private" faith; its mission to the world means that the Church inevitably plays a significant role in the public sphere. It cannot escape the political implications, whatever they may be, associated with this public role. For many Catholics, in the United States and elsewhere, whatever their political inclinations, this public role of the Church, or "public Catholicism," is what really matters. The Church's relationship to society—to "the world"—is at the heart of its mission to proclaim the good news of Jesus Christ.

Not all Catholics share this view, of course. In fact, perhaps the majority of Catholics think of the work of the Church as specifically "religious," by which they mean prayer, worship, catechetical instruction, efforts to win conversions, and charity toward the poor and suffering. These acts take precedence over the Church's efforts to transform society, important as those efforts may be. In this view, held especially by Catholics in societies where religious pluralism and religious freedom flourish, religion is entirely separate from the state. If not entirely isolated from politics, economics, and other realms of life, it conducts its affairs largely apart from those realms.

The advocates of public Catholicism, whether on the left or the right, reject this attitude, which they see as fostering the trivialization and marginalization of Catholicism. By contrast, they evaluate every work of the Church in terms of the Church's mission to transform society into the Kingdom of God. Whereas most Catholics believe that the Church's social mission is derivative or secondary, public Catholics believe that the phrase "social mission" is redundant: everything that constitutes the Church must be oriented toward societal transformation.

At issue between Catholics on the left and other public Catholics, however, is what is meant by societal transformation. Examining the attitudes and actions of the pope and Catholic bishops provides no clear answer. Pope John Paul II may tell some left-wing priests to stay out of politics, but he champions other priests who challenge governments, and still others who work closely with public officials. The pope and most bishops reject political partisanship as a matter of principle, but across the globe the Church exercises political responsibility by participating in civil society. Catholic educational and charitable institutions, newspapers, radio and television stations, social justice offices, community organizations—all are forms of civic participation and active public Catholicism.

In the United States there is an identifiable public Catholicism of the right, the center, and the left. Indeed the term is now quite popular among Catholic lay leaders who are strongly pro-life but more supportive of free markets and shrinking safety nets than are most bishops. From their perspective the bishops, acting through their national agencies on issues other than abortion, appear far too liberal. Most bishops, for their part, think of themselves as acting outside, perhaps above, such categories. But in practice, when dealing with economic and political matters they regard as morally open, they have clearly tried through consultation and compromise to stake out a center position. Most of all they have tried to encourage ongoing civic dialogue, within and beyond the Church, on the moral dimensions of public life.

The women and men of the Catholic left, by contrast, locate themselves, or are located by others, on the left side of the American political and cultural spectrum. Two corollaries of this definition bear consideration. First, Catholic social activism is not confined to the Catholic left. Many anti-abortion Catholics, for example, especially those who take a single-issue approach to the question, often associate closely with political groups normally identified with the right. To say that a person is a member of the Catholic left, second, does not indicate his or her position on matters internal to the Church. There is no direct correspondence, that is, between the political and ecclesial orientations of Catholics. For example, there are Catholics, including many associated with the Catholic Worker movement, whose politics in practice are "left" but whose theology and ecclesiastical opinions are often quite conservative. In the same way, political conservatives might be rather progressive in their views on the governance of the Church. And we know that Catholic leaders may adopt one position in principle, perhaps nonviolence, but sometimes end up in another position in practice, as on military service or economic sanctions, because the needs of the organized Church sometimes require moderation, even equivocation.

The Church's recent experience in many other countries, and indeed the leadership of Pope John Paul II, demonstrate the claim that there is no necessary correlation between advocacy of human rights, social justice, and world peace in the public arena and support for reform within the Church. In fact, the basic pattern of American Catholic episcopal leadership historically has been similar to that of the present pope: conservatism on internal ecclesiastical affairs but progressivism on matters of domestic social policy. United States bishops before the 1960s brooked no dissent on doctrine or discipline but gave strong support to labor unions and "bread and butter" social welfare policies. Since the sixties, the hierarchy has also been carefully critical of U.S. foreign and military policy, while regularly challenging elected officials on abortion, capital punishment, and welfare reform. Many within the Church regard the bishops as far too liberal on matters of public policy. At the same time, no one would accuse the vast majority of American bishops of excessive zeal in the cause of theological or ecclesiastical reform.

Similarly, Catholics on the political right often oppose "dissent" within the Church, especially when it is directed at matters of sexual morality, but they often are quite critical of episcopal leadership and urge greater attention to what they take to be lay experience in business, government, and the professions. As they see it, lay persons should submit without question to the Church's doctrinal and disciplinary teaching. But on worldly matters like money and power, Church authorities should speak only of general principles and leave their application to qualified lay persons.

While advocacy of progressive changes in Church and society are separable, there also are a significant number of Catholics who see their support for political causes considered to be "on the left"—government action to secure economic justice and human rights, for example—as being of one piece with their support of internal Church reforms aimed at shared responsibility and a greater role for women in the Church's ministries. Indeed, the Catholic left draws on papal and episcopal teaching to insist that the Church can be a credible advocate of social justice only if it eliminates racism, sexism, and class privilege from its internal affairs. As other essays in this volume make clear, many diverse groups advocating liberal or progressive reforms within the Church also champion causes of peace and justice. These groups probably provide the clues needed to answer the question of the decreasing visibility of the Catholic left.

In short, this exercise in mapping is complex, with the contours of the landscape determined by some combination of self-identification, others' perceptions and labeling, and the current meanings assigned to right and left in the Church and in society at large. And each of these factors changes constantly, along with the fluctuating currents in Church and society. For our present purposes we will attend to those who, whatever their views on controverted ecclesial issues, are united by their advocacy of social change in ways that identify them as on the political left. They range from Latino parishioners fighting for better schools to protesters sent to jail for acting against war and weapons on the basis of deep commitment to Christian nonviolence. Once that definition would have taken on flesh with names like César Chávez and Daniel Berrigan. If it seems less clear today, that may be a measure of the problem. What did happen to *that* Catholic left?

Contexts

At any point in its history, American Catholicism is formed by at least three distinct factors: (1) the social composition and location of the American Catholic people and their institutions; (2) the situation of the universal Church, and its relationship to the Church in the United States; and (3) economic, social, political, and cultural conditions in the United States. One way to understand the recent experience of American Catholicism is to examine the way these three factors have changed, simultaneously and at times with bewildering speed. The intersection of these three "streams of change," made especially intense by the events of "the sixties," gave to the immediate post-conciliar period in the United States that quality of accelerating change historian Philip Gleason characterizes as "disintegration."[1] The same combination of factors gave rise to the Catholic left.

THE SOCIAL COMPOSITION AND LOCATION OF CATHOLICS

Dramatic changes in the Catholic population took place well before the Vatican Council opened in 1962, so that even if there had not been a council, one might have anticipated significant strains in the American Church. The immigrant, working-class Catholic community was changing into a more multi-class, educated, assimilated population, as people left city neighborhoods, married across ethnic and later religious boundaries, and worshipped in "Catholic and American" rather than national parishes. Demographic change brought with it an easing of that minority self-consciousness that long marked Catholics, who more and more saw themselves, and were seen by others, as respected participants in America's "new pluralism." That "arrival" of Catholics reached a symbolic climax with the election of John F. Kennedy as president in 1960.[2]

Change in the social composition and location of Catholics continues. Numerous studies confirm the educational and economic advancement of Catholics and their attainment of leadership positions in all sectors of the society. There are also innumerable Catholics in the middle classes, wedded by economic reality to the dominant institutions but strained by the pressures of a changing economy and the accelerating polarization of wealth and income. At the same time, there are Catholic outsiders, many of them newer immigrants, arriving with little income and less wealth, some making dramatic economic progress, others less successful, but all conscious of their outsider status. Thoughtful commentators correctly refer to a "center and edge" or "mainstream and margin" image to describe the Catholic population, now composed of both the assimilated descendants of European immigrants and others excluded by race, class, or recent arrival.

These changes all influenced public Catholicism and perceptions of a Catholic left. Historically, at least on socio-economic issues, Catholics have always been an important segment of the American left. Immigrant, working-class outsiders found appropriate organizational forms in ethnic parishes and associations, in patronage politics of political machines, usually but not always with the Democratic Party, and in the practical "business unionism" that dominated organized labor. In each case, they articulated sharp criticisms of dominant institutions and ideas, placing them on the political left. Through such structures, Catholics became important participants in the New Deal coalition that dominated American politics for two generations.[3]

But that was not the whole story, for in retrospect it is clear that the very process of organizing, in churches, neighborhoods, or workplace, was an "Americanizing" experience that reflected aspirations for mobility and assimilation, not social transformation. These aspirations were often hidden by the separate Catholic symbols, and sometimes by the separatist rhetoric of ethnic group and social class. While Catholic workers often ended up in coalitions supportive of labor and the welfare state, they had little interest in socialism or basic changes in the organization of society. Nor did they coexist easily in the New Deal coalition with secular, Protestant, or Jewish liberals, who were allies on economic policy, but less close on civil liberties and civil rights, and outright opponents on what would later be called cultural issues, like birth control, censorship, or, most notably, abortion.[4]

Today, public Catholicism takes on a similar form and spirit among those working at the edge among the poor, immigrant outsiders. There a hard reading of daily realities argues for grassroots organization to gain a place at the economic and political table, while militantly defending traditional cultural values. The work of Texas community organizer Ernesto Cortes exemplifies this approach.[5] Community organizers want their Church to support their efforts at economic advancement and defend their cultural integrity, while they find in the Church resources for preserving their traditional faith and important cultural values, especially those associated with the family. For such Catholic outsiders, social attitudes and political positions arise from pressing self-interest. The Church's response—its defense of immigrants—is directly connected with its pastoral responsibilities, as was its defense of labor unions in the past.[6]

Catholic insiders, by contrast, no longer experience the world through the symbols and social reinforcements of ethnic groups, wage-earning industrial employment, or tightly knit parishes. Their religious life is marked by the same individualism, voluntarism, and diversity of opinion that distinguishes middle-class culture. They attend Mass less often, but they continue to identify as Catholic, whether or not they agree with the pope on one matter or another. They seek God and search for community, often finding both in vibrant parishes or spiritual renewal movements, sometimes in small groups connected to these. Neither ethnic solidarity nor class interest determines their politics. The majority are more liberal than non-Catholics, particularly on social justice questions, but there are more Catholic Republicans than a few years ago. Many more call themselves independents.[7]

Appeals for social responsibility addressed to insiders, in contrast to outsiders, rarely touch on group interest. Instead, public Catholics speak to ideals, to conscience, to a sense of civic responsibility. Such appeals reflect awareness of the most basic reality of middle-class American Catholicism: people will make up their own minds. They also reflect some less obvious, and less helpful, assumptions: that most demands for social justice, such as more taxes or more restrictions on business, probably run contrary to middle-class interests; that the first lesson of Christian social awareness is what we, the fortunate, should do more for them, the less fortunate; and that when dealing with serious matters, appeals to solidarity, the public interest, or the common good are incapable of overcoming middle-class self-interest. All this pushes the Church to avoid divisions by avoiding controversy: thus the illusory "stick to religion and get out of politics" argument. Or, as often, it forces a bland moderation featuring platitudes about social problems, frustrating to public Catholics of right and left alike.

This sense of the historical trajectory of U.S. Catholicism, from margin to mainstream, from opposition to responsibility, lends a peculiar artificiality to the rhetoric of much public Catholicism. Catholics of the right bemoan American materialism and individualism, often drawing on Pope John Paul II's denunciation of a "culture of death." Catholics of the left become equally passionate about their country's neglect of the poor and continuing love affair with weapons of mass destruction. In either case, it is not surprising that popular response is limited.

This rhetorical countercultural stance is common among public Catholics, but it obscures the fact that Catholics and their Church are now integral parts of that very culture; they help make it what it is. History has given weight to cartoonist Walt Kelly's famous quip, "We have met the enemy and he is us." What this means in practice is not that appeals for a countercultural challenge to American society run up against self-interested complicity, though that is part of it. It means that such appeals also run up against legitimate demands for responsibility. The Church may sound like an outsider challenging institutions dominated by others, but in fact Catholics are in the boardrooms and city halls, trying to figure out what to do. In that may lie one seed of an answer to the question "what happened to the Catholic left?"

Perhaps, that is, the left vanishes with success; those who have made it can no longer afford to be critical. Liberalism eased the way for some from margin to mainstream; at the end of the journey there may not be room for less pragmatic, more principled radicals. The left, it seems, must be left behind. But perhaps the story can be read another way. If liberation is, at least in part, a matter of winning economic sufficiency, educational advancement, and political participation, then for millions of Catholics recent history tells a liberation story. And the new question that arises, at the unfamiliar center, is liberation for what?

THE UNIVERSAL CHURCH

The Second Vatican Council initiated a process of change in the universal Church that, for better or for worse, has helped transform the Church in the United States. The fact that the meaning of conciliar renewal is disputed simply reinforces the disruption of the older, more liturgically and theologically unified and self-assured Catholic subculture. American Church leaders who have had to deal with changes in the social composition and location of Catholics, and with changes in American society, no longer operate from a base of confident understanding of the nature and purpose of the Church itself or the organizational unity and discipline that marked the pre-conciliar period.[8]

The council was an event that became a process, but it took place within an organization which remains extremely important in the life of American Catholics. The impact of papal decisions regarding bishops, theological orthodoxy, and moral teaching make that claim obvious. Pope John Paul II's stance has helped define the Church's response to numerous public issues, while his policies have reined in the emerging national episcopal conference, limiting the hierarchy's ability to influence public policy and public opinion. Conservative Catholics are in part defined by their professions of loyalty and obedience to the institutional authorities in the Church.[9] Catholics on the left are sometimes thought of as dissenters supporting a more independent American Church. Some are, of course, but many "left Catholics" are not dissenting Americanists but critics of American society and culture, like the pope, and concerned, like him, for the integrity of the Church as it lives in the sometimes suffocating embrace of modernity.

There is no necessary correlation between a "left" stance on public matters and support for or opposition to the ecclesiastical policies of Pope John Paul II. Recent conflicts, especially over questions of the role of women in the Church, have drawn many on the left to a preoccupation with internal Church matters, and made some feel marginal to Catholic life. Most important for the Church's public life is that those policies have driven a wedge between social activists working within church structures, parishes, Catholic charities offices, even parish-based community organizations, and others in more independent settings, in soup kitchens, sanctuary programs, and groups working on women's issues. To put the matter in its simplest terms, those employed by the Church are expected to keep their differences with controversial Church teachings to themselves. Those working independently are more free to express their views, and when those views are oppositional, the Catholic left with which we are concerned, advocates of justice and peace, become deeply divided and have reduced influence in internal Church politics.

On the other hand, the Catholic left has taken heart from the continuing development of Catholic social teaching, not just at the level of the Vatican but in sister churches in Asia, Africa, and especially Latin America, and in the United States bishops' pastoral letters of recent years. Pope John Paul's complex social thought at times provides powerful theological justification for public Catholicism generally and for such "left" ideals as the option for the poor, nonviolence, human rights, and the common good. Emphasis on social responsibility informs most other official Vatican documents, including the Catechism of the Catholic Church, which infuses demands for justice and peace throughout the text.[10]

The Catholic left in the United States has long drawn on official teachings to argue that struggle for justice and peace is integral to the Church's life and work. That teaching found its fullest expression in situations where the Church stood in opposition: in Poland, in those parts of Latin America where bishops adopted some of the tenets of liberation theology, even in the United States where the bishops placed themselves in opposition to racial discrimination, nuclear weapons, and abortion. To the degree the Church still stands in opposition to one or another "culture of death," the integral argument remains compelling. What is less clear is that it can sustain itself in a setting of insider responsibility, in post–Cold War Poland, in post–civil war Central America, or in the workplaces of post-immigrant American Catholics. If the historic American Catholic journey from margin to mainstream was a mistake, a pursuit of false gods, then the critical voice of Catholic social teaching should be heard as a call for renunciation, even conscientious objection. If that experience is viewed more posi-

tively, the question arises whether Catholic social teaching can provide now liberated Catholics with a positive understanding of their
civic responsibilities.

ECONOMIC, SOCIAL, POLITICAL, AND CULTURAL CONDITIONS
IN THE UNITED STATES

Between 1962 and 1972 Catholics dealt with social change and religious renewal at the same time that their country was undergoing a
series of wrenching events. The combination gave to the immediate
post-conciliar period that widely noted quality of explosive change.
Less noticed has been the impact of those events on thoughts and feeling about national symbols, including the thoughts and feelings of
those defined as on the right and on the left.

Religious groups on the left in the past often played a "muck-
raker" role, forcing attention to neglected dimensions of American life
and demonstrating that the nation's performance was less than its
promise of liberty and justice for all. From nineteenth-century aboli-
tionists through the civil rights movements to recent opponents of
nuclear weapons or Central American intervention, such consciousness raising has been a common technique of religiously oriented social action. It rested, always, on broadly shared understandings of social morality, sometimes articulated in Christian terms, but at least
as often in terms of the American experience. No one blended Christian and American symbols more powerfully that Martin Luther King
Jr., and a similar integration was evident among many Catholic radicals of the 1960s.[11]

In the mid-1970s Catholic activists eagerly joined the bishops in
exploring the demands of peace and social justice on the occasion of
the nation's bicentennial in the Call to Action program, whose theme
was "liberty and justice for all." Meeting in Detroit in October 1976,
the American Church's first authentic national assembly adopted a
series of recommendations that constituted an agenda for internal reform and vigorous social action, both aimed at national transformation. At that time modest pleas for reconsideration of matters like clerical celibacy and women's ordination seemed to arise from the same
ideals of liberty and equality that inspired Catholic social teaching.
But Rome and the hierarchy reacted negatively to the pleas for Church
reform while affirming the justice and peace agenda. Some, especially
those employed by the Church, felt that the price of participation in
the Church's social ministries might be silence on matters of pastoral
policy. Soon divisions appeared that fragmented what had become
known as the Catholic left.[12]

There was another, less noted problem: a dramatic challenge to
Catholic Americanism. At the moment of the Call to Action, Catholic
activists, perhaps inspired by Martin Luther King Jr., drew heavily on

American symbols to reinforce Christian arguments for human rights, social justice, racial equality, and world peace. Two decades later that language of prophetic civil religion is no longer common among Catholics of the left, who are more inclined to appeal to Christian Scripture and to argue for specifically Christian, as opposed to civic, responsibilities. Moderate and radical Catholics of the right are now more likely to appeal to patriotic emotions and national symbols, while liberal and radical Catholics of the left are more likely to appeal to Christian criteria to criticize national values and policies. In 1983 the bishops, discussing nuclear weapons, went so far as to compare contemporary American society to that of the Roman Empire of apostolic times. What they called for was active discipleship like that of the early church, prepared for the risks of persecution and martyrdom.[13] Similar language often envelops their opposition to abortion. To the degree it does so, public Catholicism becomes less public and more sectarian, less a matter of shared responsibility for public life, more a matter of witness to alternatives to prevailing practices.

In sum, not only has American society changed since the sixties, but Catholic perceptions of their country have changed even more dramatically, providing yet another clue to the question of the Catholic left. Until recently even the most radical Catholic protesters communicated a hope that America and its people would recommit themselves to their own deepest ideals. For Catholics, many here only a few generations, becoming American was a good thing, indeed an experience of liberation. Today voices from both ends of the spectrum, left and right, worry that the achievement of middle-class status came at the cost of Catholic identity, even Catholic integrity. Liberal appeals to share responsibility with other citizens for the common life once inspired many Catholics to work for social reform. Now such appeals seem less compelling, not because people disagree, but because the meaning structure provided by a sense of America's mission has all but disappeared.

If there is a powerful emotional appeal, it comes not from arguments for shared civic responsibility but from specifically religious appeals for resistance and countercultural witness against a society and culture deemed even by moderate voices to border on "neopaganism." That makes a tremendous difference in the public life and political and cultural possibilities of American Catholicism. The change is clearly registered in the languages of public Catholicism.

Styles of Public Catholicism

These changing conditions among Catholics, in the Church, and in the wider society set an important historical context for discussion of the Catholic left. The next step is to sort out public Catholicism of the left by examining the historical development of Catholic self-understandings. The plural is correct. As Catholics grappled over two centuries with the unique circumstances created by the disappearance of religious establishments, the guarantee of free exercise of conscience, and the rich pluralism of Christian voices and communities, three distinct, sometimes overlapping, forms, or styles, of public presence emerged. Each is present today, and assessment of them helps clarify the Catholic left. Let us be clear once again: each of these styles can give rise to a public stance of the left or right, one critical of prevailing social practice and one affirmative of that practice. Both the Catholic left, understood here in terms of advocacy of justice and peace, and the Catholic right make use of all three forms of public discourse.

The *republican* position arises from concern for the *res publica*, the public "thing." It represents a deliberate (though not necessarily ultimate) acceptance of religious pluralism, which, because it prevents the monopoly of culture by any particular religion, requires ongoing mediation between religious and civic obligations.[14]

The *immigrant* style also arises from the experience of pluralism, but here the focus is less on the public good, with its accommodation and negotiation, than the good of the group. Churches, like other institutions, have to organize to protect their interests; ethnic and working-class groups must do the same. The effectiveness of such organizations depends on their ability to claim the support of their members; thus self-interest rather than altruism or civic responsibility characterizes trade unions, ethnic associations, and community organizations.

The third style, an *evangelical* form of Catholicism, is a more recent phenomenon. Its adherents find the republican style too temporizing, the interest-group style too selfish. Instead, they would measure culture, society, and politics by Christian standards and act directly on the result, without the mediation of citizenship or group interests.

The republican style, once anathema in papal teaching, has dominated American Catholic social thought, and is seen best in the writings of people like John A. Ryan, John Courtney Murray, and J. Bryan Hehir and in the recent pastoral letters on public policy of the U.S. bishops.[15] The immigrant style dominates Catholic social action, from the organizing of ethnic associations, parishes, trade unions, and political machines through the community organizing efforts associated with the legacy of Saul Alinsky and his Catholic disciples and now institutionalized in the networks spawned by the Campaign for Human Development.[16] The evangelical style is best seen in movements of opposition to war, poverty, and violence, in the nonviolence promoted by Pax Christi and the Catholic Worker movement. Here the symbolic figures are Dorothy Day and Daniel Berrigan.[17]

These examples are drawn from what might be perceived as the

Catholic left, at various degrees of radicalism. But these styles arise from the structure of American culture, so they shape all forms of Catholic discourse. In the 1980s Catholic neo-conservatives made use of republican categories of Catholic social thought.[18] Right-to-life organizers, like opponents of birth control or immoral films in the past, used an immigrant approach of single-issue organizing to enter the contested arena of cultural politics. And the evangelical style of direct moves from faith commitments to public prescription occurs at least as often among those seen as conservative as among so-called radicals of the left.

Until the 1960s, most Catholic politics involved an interplay of the first two styles, with bishops upholding republican civic virtues in theory, occasionally winning respect and access by doing so, but adopting the interest-group approach in practice in order to defend Church interests or uphold Church teachings. Republican ideals aroused limited response among the laity. Instead, popular Catholic participation in political machines, trade unions, and community organizations represented clear expressions of the immigrant, interest-group style. Critics in and out of the Church correctly noted that both republican and interest-group approaches required modification, at least, of Gospel mandates and Catholic claims. Republicanism meant acceptance of civil and social equality with non-Catholics, thus assisting the assimilation of Catholic outsiders. It privileged the public interest, and regularly sought common ground. The immigrant style more or less excluded loving concern for those outside the group, and feared that common ground would require subordination to dominant others, but it was an appropriate means of securing institutional and group interests. In the United States, in so many ways, God seems to help those who help themselves. And despite frequent use of critical language to justify change, neither republican nor immigrant strategies provided powerful moral or emotional support for challenging, much less transforming, the common life. But a Church and a people on the move hardly noticed.

In recent history unavoidable moral issues like racism, imperialism, nuclear deterrence, and abortion drew from the margins of Catholic life a more explicitly religious stance. While few Catholics joined the Catholic Worker or the various resistance, peace, and social justice movements during and after the sixties, many did respond to a spirituality that called for fundamental commitment to the Gospel and witness of Jesus, and reflection on that commitment in light of all too obvious evils of contemporary history. The result was a new sense of distance from American culture and a renewed determination to salvage the credibility and integrity of Catholic Christianity. As the American bishops put it in their 1983 letter on nuclear weapons, Christian discipleship in "a society increasingly estranged from Christian values" requires an "adult" Christian community notable for its re-nunciation of prevailing values.[19]

Thus, while the three distinct approaches to the public presence of the Church persist, the most dynamic and influential is now the evangelical. Catholic faith and piety, like that of other American Christians, is increasingly centered on the Scriptures and the person of Jesus. As happened earlier among Protestants, social responsibility has come to be seen in personal terms. The question is less "what does the Church teach?" than "what would Jesus do?" In their 1983 pastoral on nuclear weapons the bishops came close to endorsing this position by emphasizing the dramatic demands of the Gospel, affirming nonviolence as an option for individuals and calling their people to a discipleship that might include several forms of conscientious objection. In their later pastoral letter on economics, they recommended a "fundamental," or "preferential," option for the poor, not only as a requirement of Christian discipleship but as a guideline for economic policy. And more recently, drawing on the statements of John Paul II, Catholic leaders have referred to the Church's responsibility to resist the "culture of death" believed to dominate modern societies. This image of a countercultural church strengthens radical voices on the left and the right and undermines the mediating discourse of liberals and neo-conservatives, who would continue to negotiate their way through a pluralistic society.

There are far softer forms of evangelicalism, where personal moral responsibility becomes an excuse for avoiding societal responsibilities. These are all too familiar in American Protestant history and are now an evident part of Catholic culture as well. Right-wing evangelicalism, in fact, provides a well-funded alternative to liberation theology, Catholic and Protestant, in Latin America and in some areas of the United States. But the hard edge of evangelical Christianity's challenge is also evident, and today constitutes an important component of the Catholic left. When Catholic activists for peace and social justice today look for allies in the other Christian churches, they are as likely to find them among evangelicals who read *Sojourners* as among mainline Protestants who read *Christian Century*.[20]

The preference for evangelical categories like "Gospel nonviolence" and the "option for the poor" over republican categories like "just war" and "distributive justice," even in texts whose overall direction is republican, like the pastoral letters of the bishops, helps explain the fate of the Catholic left. The strength of the evangelical approach is its appeal for integrity, calling the Church and its members to live out their faith and bear witness to the demands of Christianity. It exposes the impersonal character of the state and public life, condemns a spiritually empty pursuit of material self-interest, and expands the social imagination to embrace all human persons, including society's outcasts and unfortunates. It advocates fidelity to principle over pragmatic considerations. The evangelical style challenges the concern with effectiveness that marks republican and immigrant styles. "We believe that success, as the world determines it, is not the criterion by which a movement should be judged," the *Catholic Worker* maintains. "The important thing is that we adhere to these values which transcend time and for which we will be asked a personal accounting, not as to whether they succeeded . . . but as to whether we remained true to them even though the world go otherwise."[21]

The weakness of the evangelical approach is that by defining issues and responses in Christian terms, its proponents become marginalized in the larger public debate. Respected, even admired, they are not seen as offering an appropriate or reasonable way in which the American public as a whole can evaluate problems and formulate solutions. If social problems are at least in part problems of power, organization, and institutions, and if they almost always intersect with government policy, a pluralistic society simply cannot deal with those problems in explicitly Christian terms. Nor can the individual citizen effectively participate in the public debate, persuade non-Christians or indifferent Christians, or influence the larger culture by appealing to the authority of the Gospel. Thus, to the degree that the Catholic left, in spirit and discourse, has become more evangelical, it may also have risked becoming more sectarian, helping to explain both its persistence and its relative invisibility.

The Catholic Left: A Brief History

"The Catholic left" made attention-grabbing headlines in 1968 as the press picked up on the enormous public interest sparked by the surprising appearance of priests and nuns in dramatic protests against the Vietnam war. A few years earlier some prominent Catholics took to the streets with Martin Luther King Jr., first in Selma, later in Chicago. One of their number, Father James Groppi, entered the ranks of civil rights heroes as he marched for open housing with youthful Black activists in hostile ethnic Catholic neighborhoods of Milwaukee. He had counterparts in many American cities, where Catholics were shocked, and some angered, by priests who seemed to switch sides in disputes over open housing, education reform, and public employment.[22]

Race was the first wedge to shape what was really a "new" Catholic left; Vietnam was the next. A growing number of priests and religious joined longtime Catholic pacifists like Gordon Zahn and Dorothy Day in protesting nuclear weapons, the arms race, and, especially, the escalating American war in Indochina. What caught press attention in 1968 was a raid on a Catonsville, Maryland, draft board by a group of Catholics. They seized draft records, burned them in the parking lot with homemade napalm, then sang hymns and awaited arrest. The group's leaders, Josephite priest Philip Berrigan and his Jesuit brother Daniel, imprinted themselves on national consciousness as "the Berrigans," leaders of what seemed to be the most radical wing of the antiwar movement.[23]

From that moment on, the phrase "Catholic left" had a vivid meaning: a broad movement of Catholics who, on the basis of their faith, challenged national policy and sought to bring about substantial social change. At the radical edge were advocates of nonviolent direct action like the Berrigans. Dorothy Day and other members of the Catholic Worker movement practiced nonviolence and voluntary poverty and regularly joined protests, but they were modestly critical of the so-called ultraresistance, particularly when protest actions involved destruction of property.

These radicals were no longer alone. Backing them up were a growing number of priests and sisters in religious orders. Called to renewal by the Vatican Council, many orders thought deeply about their work in light of the Gospel and the needs of the Church and the world. The coincidence of this renewal movement and the conflicts of the sixties drew substantial numbers of religious priests, brothers, and sisters to support "peace and justice," either by enlisting directly in activist work or by supporting those causes in their existing ministries. While religious orders occupied the cutting edge of conflict, diocesan clergy were not far behind. The National Federation of Priests Councils, founded in 1967 to represent the new senates and associations of diocesan clergy, soon adopted a very progressive social agenda. While there were murmurs of conservative dissent among priests and religious, the momentum stirred by racial conflict, assassinations, and Vietnam created a powerful current to the left.

Advocacy of racial justice and opposition to the Vietnam war topped the peace and justice agenda, but there were other causes. Among them was the organizing movement of César Chávez and Mexican-American farm workers in California, which drew Church support locally and nationally and then, through a nationwide boycott of table grapes, enlisted the backing of thousands of lay people. At the same time, urban disorders, sometimes extremely violent, spawned a wide variety of reform efforts with churches at their core. While less inclined to nonviolent direct action than the Berrigans, the activists in these causes increasingly shared the radicals' pessimism about reform, suspicion of government, and alienation from mainstream American culture.

This process of radicalization received support from movements of liberation in Latin America and from the new liberation theology these movements spawned. Returning missionaries familiar with these currents confirmed suspicions that the deep poverty of the third world was systemic and that the United States government helped sustain authoritarian regimes determined to crush popular movements for social change, many led by priests, sisters, and lay catechists. This rapid transformation of attitudes toward American society was supported as well by the seemingly permanent national commitment to ever more dangerous weapons of mass destruction. In addition, in 1973, as American participation in the Vietnam war ended, the Supreme Court struck down state laws limiting abortion, opening yet another window on what appeared to a growing number of Catholic radicals as the deeply rooted violence and injustice of American society. Belief that reform had failed and that only systemic, structural change, even revolution, would open the way to social justice and world peace became a unifying conviction across the Catholic left.

In the 1960s Catholic social action across the country had the character of an authentic movement, aimed at working with other groups to bring about substantial change in the economic and social institutions of the country. The experience of the war on poverty, the failure of civil rights in northern urban areas, discovery of deeply rooted sources of poverty, particularly institutional racism, and the terrible violence that punctuated the decade, climaxing in the outbreaks that followed the assassination of Martin Luther King Jr. in 1968, all contributed to a radicalization of social discourse, secular and religious, Catholic and non-Catholic. The presence of a new left and a Catholic left shifted the center of society and Church, at least for a moment.

This social gospel spirit influenced many groups within the Church. The major Catholic provider of social services, the National Conference of Catholic Charities, representing diocesan social welfare agencies, engaged in a self-study which concluded that, while the Church should continue to offer direct social services, it should work to decentralize service delivery, strengthen its capacity to serve as advocates for the poor before public and private institutions, and rebuild parish capacity to deliver services and serve as catalysts for social change. This resulted a few years later in a major effort of Catholic charities to bring about parish-based community organizing aimed at challenging racism, systemic poverty, and structural injustice.[24]

Similar radical ideas shaped statements of commitment to social justice as a defining term for ministry emerging from the Major Conference of Superiors of Men, representing male religious orders, the Leadership Conference of Women Religious, representing women's orders, and the National Federation of Priests Councils, representing diocesan clergy. At the same time each of these constituencies generated new, more radical organizations aimed at social change, such as the Jesuit's Center of Concern, a think tank on global poverty and violence, the National Association of Women Religious, sisters organized to support local social action and nudge other sisters and the Church to the political left, and NETWORK, another organization, first of sisters, later for all women, formed to lobby Congress on specific issues.[25]

In 1974 the bishops themselves launched a national consultation on the theme of "liberty and justice for all" to mark the national bicentennial. That process climaxed with the Call to Action conference in Detroit in October 1976, when delegates from all the nation's dioceses and most of its Catholic organizations approved recommendations urging pastoral leaders to help the Church confront racism, economic inequality, global injustice, and the arms race. The delegates also urged the bishops to consider problems of injustice within the Church and to examine controversial teachings on women, marriage, and sexuality. When the bishops ignored appeals for Church reform and shared responsibility, the stage was set for a period of internal Church conflict that would divide moderates and activists and in the end all but destroy the Catholic left of the sixties.

But the Catholic left, while less visible, never disappeared. From the seventies through the nineties: (1) The radical edge of the peace movement persisted in actions against nuclear weapons installations by the Plowshares groups, linked together in a number of informal networks, many associated with Catholic Worker communities.[26] (2) Many priests, religious, and lay people worked openly to oppose the American war in Central America.[27] (3) Congregations across the country responded to the arrival of Central American refugees by declaring sanctuary for their churches. In the nineties, as anxiety about immigration gave rise to harsh legislation, a similar passion for justice among Catholics inspired a range of actions on behalf of immigrants, legal and illegal. (4) Throughout the period, almost every center of poverty and homelessness in the United States saw the creation of soup kitchens and shelters sponsored by parishes, independent groups of apostolic laity and religious, or movements like the Catholic Worker. Many were associated with advocacy of social reform. When the general assault against social welfare programs picked up steam in the 1980s, Catholic leaders, sometimes alone, spoke out strongly and consistently in opposition. Church leaders opposed many of the provisions of welfare reform that came in the 1990s; continued advocacy on behalf of the poor remains the accepted policy of the Church as a whole.[28] (5) The Catholic bishops, against opposition even from their own people, stood consistently opposed to capital punishment.

In sum, there has been no shortage of groups and actions that together constitute a Catholic left. If a Catholic left is defined by faith-based opposition to violence, racism, and social injustice, a structural as opposed to a reformist interpretation of these issues, and a determination to work actively to transform society, then the Catholic left, while more narrow as a movement than it was at the end of the sixties, is alive and well. What is missing in the nineties, as opposed to the sixties and early seventies, are the alliances with liberal Catholicism that give the Catholic left the character of a social movement.

The Strange Career of Liberal Catholicism

Use of the phrase "left," in any setting, raises the question: left of what? The Catholic left emerging from the sixties had a ready answer: left of liberal Catholicism. The reform bishops, clergy, and religious who dominated post-conciliar American Catholicism seemed to represent the moderate center of Catholic life, linking the radical demands of social and political activists to the pastoral life and organizational dynamics of mainstream Catholicism. This was the image of John Cardinal Dearden, an old-school bishop converted at Vatican II to an understanding of the faith that demanded shared responsibility and disciplined engagement with contemporary society. Presiding over the Call to Action conference, he served as an honest broker between Catholic activists of all sorts and clergy and lay Catholics worried about the Church's apparent shifts to the left. Later Joseph Cardinal Bernardin would embody a similar liberal center, most dramatically when he drew a powerful pastoral letter on nuclear weapons from a committee that included former military chaplain Cardinal John O'Connor on the right and nonviolence activist Thomas Gumbleton on the left.[29]

Such leaders, and there were many, were not ordinarily included in the ranks of the Catholic left, but in a real sense they made the Catholic left possible. And for support they could draw on a distinguished tradition of liberal Catholicism, long a minority stance in Catholic life but vindicated at Vatican II. The council finally approved church-state separation, renounced a specifically Catholic political agenda, and endorsed human rights, including religious liberty. Foundational theological changes, approval of ecumenical dialogue, and sharp criticism of the arms race and global economic injustices signaled a new stance for the Church, not countercultural but incarnational, within and not aloof from the struggles of the human family.

In the United States, liberal Catholicism, long known as Americanism, provided a body of ideas that sanctioned the assimilation of European immigrants by affirming the positive value of American democratic institutions and mainstream culture. In the years before the council, Catholic liberals advocated support for religious liberty, greater intellectual and cultural freedom in the Church, and a vigorous lay apostolate encouraging newly mobile Catholics to take up the cause of social reform. As renewal began after the council, it invariably intersected with the problems of the sixties, directing pastors and parishioners away from subcultural maintenance to a more active sense of mission, a process that reached its climax in the Call to Action.

The Catholic bishops by that time seemed to embody liberal Catholicism's public agenda. During and after the council they endorsed equal rights for African Americans, and many encouraged their clergy and religious to work for racial integration. When the cities exploded in riots, the hierarchy responded by launching its own war on poverty, the Campaign for Human Development. As the council ended with a document affirming conscientious objection and condemning the arms race and acts of total war, the United States government began massive bombing of North Vietnam and introduced large numbers of American troops into the south. Despite the wartime situation, the bishops for the first time endorsed the right of conscientious objection and even called for legal protection of selective conscientious objectors.

At Vatican II the U.S. bishops had lobbied against the more critical texts on war and peace, but as the Vietnam conflict escalated, a growing number of bishops cautiously challenged specific decisions, and gradually began to question the war itself. In 1971, in a remarkable move, the hierarchy concluded that by the standards of "just war" teaching, the war could no longer be justified. In subsequent years a growing number explored the Church's responsibility for peacemaking, some (more than one hundred) by joining Pax Christi, the international Catholic peace movement, others by regularly pushing the moral questions surrounding nuclear deterrence.[30]

After the Call to Action conference the bishops, while shelving its proposals for internal reform, continued to offer critical moral commentary on public policy, from abortion through economic justice to nuclear arms. They stood against American policy in Central America and challenged the drift of foreign and domestic policy during the Reagan administration. This was evident in two remarkable pastoral letters of the mid-1980s. In the "Challenge of Peace" (1993) the bishops set strict moral limits on deterrence while affirming in the strongest language the Church's responsibility for peacemaking. In "Economic Justice for All" (1986) they offered a stinging criticism of social policy based on a preferential option for the poor. In both texts they argued for reforms, specified concrete steps they thought should be taken, and urged their fellow Catholics to take up the cause of justice and peace.[31]

On the other hand, while their theological analysis and spiritual advice echoed the radical voice of the Catholic left—nonviolence and the option for the poor—their proposals were moderate: urging limits on the arms race, affirming job creation, supporting government programs in welfare, housing, and medical care. Similarly, while the bishops regularly endorsed specific reform legislation, they made little effort to mobilize popular support, in contrast to their activism on the abortion question. In theory they supported the idea that the pursuit of justice and peace was an integral element of the Christian life, but in practice their priorities seemed to lie elsewhere. Close followers of the episcopal conference knew the progressive stands the bishops took on controversial policies, but many more knew of their outspoken opposition to abortion, which seemed at times to align the Church with conservative politicians opposed to Catholic teaching on many other questions.

In one of the great ironies of American Catholic history, then, the leaders of the Church adopted a great deal of the liberal Catholic agenda, and when they had done so, they found that liberal Catholicism, as a coherent movement and compelling set of ideas, no longer enjoyed substantial public support. Instead liberal Catholicism came under attack, from the left because its Americanist reform solutions seemed religiously and politically inadequate, from the right because its social reform proposals seemed unnecessary and its religious stance seemed compromised by undue adaptation to secular culture. Perhaps most important, liberal Catholics among the hierarchy and clergy, and among Church employees generally, found it increasingly difficult to negotiate their way through an organization whose leaders required acceptance, or at least silence, on theological and ecclesiastical issues of growing importance and great moral force, particularly those dealing with women and with the use of power.

As Catholic piety became more evangelical, and as clerical and religious activists found themselves in conflict with Church authorities over a range of issues, with women at the center, liberal Catholicism seemed not wrong but irrelevant. Similarly, as national politics moved away from the New Deal legacy to policies anchored in the marketplace, liberal Catholicism learned how dependent it had been on (1) secular liberalism, with its agenda of social reform; (2) broad-based social movements, like those for peace and for civil rights; and (3) trade unions, the only sturdy defender of working people and the strongest bulwark of economic policies the bishops supported, like full employment and living wages. As each lost its hold on public opinion and popular politics, liberal Catholicism was left isolated, with limited backing within the Church and a sense of political homelessness in the wider society.

This meant a major shift for the more radical Catholic left, which had once defined itself in part by its differences with Catholic liberals: nonviolence as opposed to just war, structural analysis and systemic change as opposed to moral commentary and legislative reform, countercultural witness as opposed to dialogue, coalitions, and compromise. Still, the two groups needed each other more than they knew. Catholic radicals, by continually insisting on radical fidelity to the Gospel, helped keep liberals from too quick or close accommodation to power. Catholic liberals, in return, forced Catholic radicals to be responsible. They gave Catholic radicals dialogue partners within the Church, and provided them with access to the Catholic subculture, translating their radical message into language middle-class Catholics might understand. In a sense Catholics of the left, like those of the right, badly needed moderate, reformist partners if their countercultural strategies were to avoid sectarianism. When the links between liberals and radicals were severed, not only did the public Catholicism of the left lose leverage within the Church, but sectarian tendencies in its own ranks became more evident.

Community Organizing and the Catholic Left

In the 1960s Catholic social action had the qualities of a movement. Today, as many observers have noted, it is hard to locate a distinguishable Catholic left. There is no organization or network that shapes a Catholic social movement, while organizations of priests and religious are now preoccupied with problems caused by declining numbers and low morale. Some networks of activists are increasingly distanced from the institutional Church, and much of the Church's pastoral work is marked by conflicts arising over internal Church issues, particularly those dealing with women. While official teaching remains progressive, the organizing and educational work of the institutional Church is focused on parishes and diocesan offices.

Catholics on the left are always on the alert to distinguish between social service (the provision of food, clothing, shelter, and other forms of assistance to the poor) and social action (organized efforts to address the underlying causes of poverty). All Catholics acknowledge the obligation of charity, and dioceses, parishes, and a tremendous variety of independent groups and agencies manifest that Catholic commitment. Today, indeed, the phrase "option for the poor" enjoys official endorsement as a standard for Church practice and Catholic commentary on public policy.

Catholic social action is less clear. Parishes and schools are themselves forms of social action, of course, for they often provide important resources for communities struggling to overcome poverty and marginalization. But there are also many direct forms of Catholic social action, ranging from parish participation in community development projects through advocacy to legislative networks ready to lobby for specific programs. About half the nation's dioceses maintain social action offices, which represent the bishop in a variety of coalitions on public policy and seek to promote social justice education and action in parishes and schools. Each diocese has its Catholic charities office as well, shepherding a tremendous variety of Catholic welfare programs, usually stretching limited resources to add advocacy for the poor, especially to influence welfare reform, and social action to its heavy service commitments.

The most popular form of social action is community organizing, which provides the central work of the Campaign for Human Development and flourishes wherever the Church is active beyond service in situations of poverty. Catholic social action has drawn heavily on community organizing since World War II.[32] Today's work still relies on the legacy of Saul Alinsky but is adding many new features. As in the past, organizers emphasize the self-interest of participants, to better their lives and gain a place at tables where decisions are made, and they still use a combination of conflict and negotiation drawn from labor history. But today much of this work goes on in association with religious congregations in coalitions that are ecumenical or interfaith. They aim at justice, and power, for everyone in the community, regardless of faith, and they find justification less in pastoral considerations alone than in ideas of equity drawn from civic as well as religious sources.

Community organizing has always been hard to locate on the left-right spectrum. On the one hand mass popular organization to challenge elites and redistribute power is democratic. Organizing is an approach of the left because it takes the side of the poor and calls for more grassroots participation in deciding social-economic arrangements. But it has a local base and a practical orientation that allow for maximum flexibility. Most important, it seeks to integrate have-nots into the existing social and economic system, thus accepting that system and indeed seeking to strengthen it, at least at the local level. When the time comes to solve problems, community organizations seek active government help and partnerships with local institutions. They are the heart of Catholic social action everywhere, but do not fit the categories of a Catholic left.

Recently, national leaders close to this work have launched a new citizenship project to help local leaders develop the language and the skills required for citizenship. They see themselves building mediating structures to enable people to deal with remote bureaucracies and the domination of the marketplace, a process that requires civic space, which churches can provide, and an ethic and pedagogy for active citizenship. This sounds like a liberal agenda originating in radical consciousness of powerlessness, a renewed link perhaps between the radical and liberal wings of the left.

Is There a Catholic Left?

If there is a Catholic left today, its members probably read the *National Catholic Reporter*. That paper's editor, Tom Fox, believes that there is no Catholic left in the sense of a coherent movement, although there is plenty of radical nonviolent action in local pockets across the country. In the 1980s the sanctuary movement and the movement to oppose American policy in Central America both enjoyed remarkable Catholic participation and leadership, but each was a loose collection of local efforts linked by a variety of informal networks and publications. Similarly the peace movement now is centered on the Catholic Worker and small intentional communities that surface around Plowshares actions. In fact radical activists do enjoy considerable respect within the larger Church, but conflicts over sexual ethics, the role of women, and the exercise of authority limit cooperation and inhibit development of a movement.[33]

Papal actions and the work of the Catholic right, in Fox's view, have drawn many on the Catholic left, which is supposed to be about the pursuit of justice and peace, into internal Church conflicts. Thus in public perception, the Catholic left is defined increasingly by positions on women's ordination, clerical celibacy, homosexuality, and abortion, all linked to the larger question of papal teaching authority. While the activist left can seek Catholic legitimacy by quoting the pope and the bishops on questions of social justice and world peace, they are invariably portrayed as dissenters because of their unwillingness to accept Church rulings in other areas. This dilemma is rooted in nineteenth-century decisions that linked Catholic doctrine and discipline to private and family matters as the Church lost its influence over culture and politics.

Conclusion

All contemporary Catholics acknowledge the basic shift of Vatican II with respect to the Church's public presence. First, the council, by endorsing church-state separation, detached the Church from particular regimes and allowed the claim that the Church has no political agenda of its own. Second, the council reattached the Church to the political order around four mandates considered essential to its very existence as Church: the promotion of human dignity, the defense of human rights, the building up of the unity of the human family, and the search for meaning in human affairs. But in the United States, with the American Church's longer experience of detachment from regimes, it has long been clear that such a formulation is necessarily problematic: as an institution with concrete interests, the Church indeed has a political agenda of its own; as a community of moral discourse, it may at times also have a serious obligation to promote a specific moral position. Furthermore, human rights, human dignity, and human solidarity, however compelling as moral norms, can generate at best negative consensus: something is wrong and something must be done about it. What that something might be is ordinarily the political issue, and on that question the Church does not have, or claim to have, the answer. So, even if people take Church teaching seriously, divisions are natural and necessary. The problem is how the clarification of consensus and the debate about differences can be made constructive, both within the Church and in the civil community.

One suspects that, in the future, a public Catholicism of the left will have to avoid containment to any one of the three categories discussed in this essay. The force of evangelical Catholicism will undoubtedly grow as the realities of voluntarism assert themselves more fully among Catholics; thus the Catholic left will have to continue to make its case in evangelical terms, as in the specification of the demands and disciplines of discipleship. Republican ideals have always dominated episcopal political thought; whatever cost they may exact in terms of accommodation, they seem inseparable from the experience of pluralism. An effective Catholic left needs to include a Catholic liberalism grounded in lay experience of work and politics. The mutually beneficial dialogue of moderates and radicals, the tension between citizenship and discipleship that characterized the Catholic left at its most effective will have to be rebuilt. Finally, when the option for the poor takes place, the action required is organization; it always has been. Thus the immigrant style of interest-group organization of unions, neighborhood associations, and community organizations will persist as long as there are groups in need of power and as long as the Church feels insecure about the integrity of its witness to specific Catholic values or teachings. The alliance of Catholic radicals and moderates perhaps foundered in the past because each group lost touch with the Catholic people; ties to community organizing can help prevent repetition.

Evangelical Catholicism flourishes in movements, republican Catholicism lives most fully in the midst of society, immigrant Catholicism comes to life in the Church's own works of mercy and justice. The evangelical warns others of the dangers of accommodation and of self-interest; the institutional leader reminds others of the importance of organization and resources; the republican warns against sectarianism and self-isolation. A Catholicism of the left needs all three.

Catholics are remaking the map of their Church and, in the process, the map of their country. Whether the outcome of Catholic renewal is constructive, making a substantial contribution to the nation and the universal Church, or simply further fragments the American Church and weakens its witness and influence depends, in the end, on attitudes toward the faith, toward history, toward the human community, and, for purposes of distinguishing left and right, toward American society and culture. If Catholics and their Church can learn to understand and appreciate their history, if they can come to feel that this land, where they live, is their own, for which they are responsible, if they can come to see themselves as part of an American as well as a Christian people, then they may indeed help enliven public life and restore a sense of public responsibility in American institutions. That will best happen when there are vigorous and responsible voices of left, right, and center speaking to one another within the Church, acting on their faith in their daily lives, and offering their unique voices in public dialogues. The story of American Catholicism is not yet finished. The next chapter remains to be written.

NOTES

This essay results in part from the generous assistance of four consultants who joined the What's Left seminar when we dealt with public Catholicism: Anne Klejment, associate professor of history, University of St. Thomas; Elizabeth McKeown, associate professor of theology, Georgetown University; Frederick J. Perella, associate director, The Raskob Foundation; and Tom Fox, publisher and president of the National Catholic Reporter Publishing Company. The author and editor are enormously grateful for their help.

1. Philip Gleason, *Keeping the Faith: American Catholicism Past and Present* (Notre Dame, Ind.: University of Notre Dame Press), pp. 170–176.

2. Andrew Greeley, *The American Catholic: A Social Portrait* (New York: Basic Books, 1977).

3. David J. O'Brien, "Social Teaching, Social Action, Social Gospel," *U.S. Catholic Historian* 5 (Summer 1986), pp. 195–224; Gerald M. Costello, *Without Fear or Favor: George Higgins on the Record* (Mystic, Conn.: Twenty-Third Publications, 1984), pp. 14–28.

4. Thomas O'Dea, "The Catholic Immigrant and the American Scene," *Thought* 31 (Summer 1965), pp. 251–270. See also David J. O'Brien, *Public Catholicism* (New York: Macmillan, 1988).

5. On community organizing, see Charles Euchner, *Extraordinary Politics* (New York: Westview Press, 1996), and Leo J. Penta, "Organizing and Public Philosophy: The Industrial Areas Foundation," *Journal of Peace and Justice Studies* 6 (Summer 1992), pp. 17–32; on Cortes, see Mary Beth Rogers, *Cold Anger: A Story of Faith and Power Politics* (Denton: University of North Texas Press, 1990).

6. On the latter, see Neil Betten, *Catholic Activism and the Industrial Worker* (Gainesville, Fla.: University Presses of Florida, 1976).

7. George Gallup and James Castelli, *The American Catholic People: Their Beliefs, Practices and Values* (Garden City: Doubleday, 1987); James D. David-

son, Dean R. Hoge, and Ruth A. Wallace, *Laity: American and Catholic—Transforming the Church* (Kansas City, Mo.: Sheed and Ward, 1996).

8. R. Scott Appleby, "Crunch Time for American Catholicism," *Christian Century* 113 (3 April 1996), pp. 370–376.

9. For a characteristic statement, see Msgr. George A. Kelly, *The Battle for the American Church* (Garden City, N.Y.: Image Books, 1981), pp. 127–198.

10. *Catechism of the Catholic Church.*

11. David J. O'Brien, *The Renewal of American Catholicism* (N.Y.: Paulist Press, 1972), pp. 207–208.

12. O'Brien, *Public Catholicism,* p. 244.

13. U.S. Catholic Bishops, *The Challenge of Peace: God's Promise and Our Response* (Washington, D.C.: United States Catholic Conference, 1983).

14. O'Brien, *Public Catholicism,* pp. 230–252, delineates these three styles in greater detail. On republican Catholicism, see David Hollenback, S.J., and R. Bruce Douglass, eds., *Catholicism and Liberalism* (New York: Macmillan, 1994).

15. See, inter alia, John A. Ryan and Francis J. Boland, *Catholic Principles of Politics* (New York: Macmillan, 1948), p. 319; John Courtney Murray, S.J., "The Problem of Religious Freedom," *Theological Studies* 25 (1964), p. 569; J. Leon Hooper, S.J., "The Theological Sources of John Courtney Murray's Ethics," in J. Leon Hooper, S.J., and Todd David Whitmore, eds., *John Courtney Murray and the Growth of Tradition* (Kansas City: Sheed and Ward, 1997), pp. 106–125.

16. O'Brien, *Public Catholicism,* ch. 3; Jay Dolan, *The American Catholic Experience* (New York: Doubleday, 1985). On the Campaign for Human Development, see John D. McCarthy and Jim Castelli, *Working for Justice: The Campaign for Human Development and Poor Empowerment Groups* (Washington, D.C.: Life Cycle Institute, 1994).

17. Mel Piehl, *Breaking Bread: The Origins of Catholic Radicalism and the Catholic Worker Movement* (Philadelphia: Temple University Press, 1984). Murray Polner and Jim O'Grady, *Disarmed and Dangerous: The Radical Life and Times of Daniel and Philip Berrigan* (New York: Basic Books, 1997).

18. George Weigel, "The Neo-Conservative Difference: A Proposal for the Renewal of Church and Society," in Mary Jo Weaver and R. Scott Appleby, eds., *Being Right: Conservative Catholics in America* (Bloomington: Indiana University Press, 1995).

19. U.S. Catholic Bishops, *The Challenge of Peace,* par. 277.

20. For Protestant evangelical radicalism see Jim Wallis, *The Soul of Politics* (Maryknoll: Orbis Books, 1994).

21. "Catholic Worker Positions," *Catholic Worker* 52 (May 1985), p. 3.

22. John T. McGreevy, *Parish Boundaries: The Catholic Encounter with Race in the Urban North* (Chicago: University of Chicago Press, 1996), pp. 145–165.

23. Patricia McNeal, *Harder Than War: Catholic Peacemaking in Twentieth Century America* (Philadelphia: Temple University Press, 1992), ch. 6; David J. O'Brien, "American Catholics and the Vietnam War: A Preliminary Assessment," in Thomas Shannon, ed., *War or Peace: The Search for New Answers* (Maryknoll: Orbis Books, 1981), pp. 119–151.

24. R. Scott Appleby, "Present to the People of God: The Transformation of the Roman Catholic Parish Priesthood," in Jay P. Dolan, R. Scott Appleby, Patricia Byrne, and Debra Campbell, *Transforming Parish Ministry: The Changing Roles of Catholic Clergy, Laity, and Women Religious* (New York: Crossroad, 1989), pp. 1–107.

25. There is no history of this period, but a good sense of the leftward shift of these groups can be found in the published transcripts of the hearings held

across the country in preparation for the Call to Action conference. These book-length texts were published by the United States Catholic Conference in 1975 and 1976.

26. Like the production of these weapons, these actions, with lengthy jail sentences following, continue as the century nears its end. See the *Boston Globe*, February 13, 1997, on the March 1998 Philip Berrigan arrest.

27. Leaders of religious communities of men and women responded to the three symbolic moments that seemed to demand a prophetic response: the assassination of four American religious women in El Salvador, the assassination of San Salvador Archbishop Oscar Romero, and the murder of six Jesuit priests, their housekeeper, and her daughter at the University of Central America by an arm of the El Salvador military trained by the United States. On the Sanctuary movement, see Susan B. Coutin, *The Culture of Protest: Religious Activism and the U.S. Sanctuary Movement* (New York: Westview Press, 1993).

28. See, for example, the statement of the U.S. Bishops (on the tenth anniversary of their pastoral letter "Economic Justice for All"), published in the midst of the national debate over welfare reform, in *Origins* 25 (23 November 1995), pp. 389–393, and such pastoral exhortations as the statement "Everyday Christianity: To Hunger and Thirst for Justice," *Origins* 28 (26 November 1998), pp. 413–418.

29. For Bernardin and the construction of the pastoral letter, see James Castelli, *The Bishops and the Bomb: Waging Peace in the Nuclear Age* (Garden City: Doubleday, 1993).

30. On Pax Christi, see John A. Coleman and Thomas Leininger, "Discipleship as Non-Violence, Citizenship as Vigilance," in John A. Coleman, ed., *Religion, Discipleship and Citizenship* (forthcoming).

31. U.S. Catholic Bishops, *Economic Justice for All* (Washington, D.C.: United States Catholic Conference, 1986).

32. David Hollenbach, "Public Theology in America: Some Questions for Catholicism after John Courtney Murray," *Theological Studies* 37 (June 1976), pp. 290–303.

33. In his presentation to the What's Left seminar, Fox offered several reasons for the fragmentation of the Catholic left, including the importance of women religious in the past and their declining numbers and marginalization within the Church; the abandonment of the Catholic left by the hierarchy; the impact of the collapse of the socialist left around the world, leaving religious activists without a coherent alternative to dominant-market arguments; and the depth of divisions within the Church, most notably over the issue of women but also over moral teachings on sexuality and the use or abuse of teaching authority.

CONTRIBUTORS

John Boyle is Professor Emeritus in the School of Religion at the University of Iowa. He received his S.T.B. and S.T.L. degrees from the Gregorian University. He completed his Ph.D. at Fordham University with a dissertation on the ethics of Karl Rahner and Bernard Lonergan, directed by Gerald McCool, S.J. He is the author of *Church Teaching Authority: Historical and Theological Studies* (1995).

Gene Burns is an Associate Professor of Social Relations at Michigan State University. A sociologist interested in political culture, religion, and reproductive politics, he is the author of *The Frontiers of Catholicism: The Politics of Ideology in a Liberal World* (1992) and a forthcoming book tentatively titled *The Moral Veto: Stalemate and Change in American Debates over Contraception and Abortion.*

Bernard J. Cooke is a prominent Catholic theologian whose graduate studies were done at St. Louis University and the Institut catholique of Paris. He has taught in a number of U.S. and Canadian universities and is the author of more than twenty books and numerous articles. He presently teaches at the University of San Diego.

Diana L. Hayes (J.D., Ph.D., S.T.D.) is an Associate Professor of Systematic Theology at Georgetown University in Washington, D.C. She specializes in liberation theology in the United States with a particular emphasis on Black Womanist theologies. Her most recent work, co-edited with Cyprian Davis, OSB, is *Taking Down Our Harps: Black Catholics in the United States* (1998).

Mary Ann Hinsdale is Associate Professor and Chair of the Religious Department at the College of the Holy Cross, where she has been teaching since 1987. Her publications include *It Comes from the People: Community Development and Local Theology* (with Helen Lewis and Maxine Waller), and *Women and Theology* (co-edited with Phyllis Kaminski). She is a member of the Sisters, Servants of the Immaculate Heart of Mary, Monroe, Michigan.

Timothy M. Matovina is an assistant professor of theological studies at Loyola Marymount University in Los Angeles. He specializes in North American religion and the interplay between faith and culture, particularly with respect to Latino religion in the United States. He is the author of *Tejano Religion and Ethnicity, The Alamo Remembered,* and, with Virgilio P. Elizondo, *San Fernando Cathedral: Soul of the City.*

John T. McGreevy is Associate Professor of History at the University of Notre Dame. He received his doctoral degree from Stanford University, and he is the author of *Parish Boundaries: The Catholic Encounter with Race in the Twentieth Century Urban North* (1996).

David J. O'Brien is Loyola Professor of Roman Catholic Studies at the College of the Holy Cross. He is the author of six books on American Catholicism, most recently *From the Heart of the American Church: Catholic Higher Education and American Culture.* He is currently President of the American Catholic Historical Association.

Anne E. Patrick, S.N.J.M, is Professor of Religion at Carleton College in Northfield, Minnesota, and the author of *Liberating Conscience: Feminist Explorations in Catholic Moral Theology* (1996).

Gary Riebe-Estrella, S.V.D., holds an S.T.D. in Practical Theology from the Pontifical University of Salamanca, Spain. He is currently Vice President and Academic Dean at Catholic Theological Union in Chicago.

Susan A. Ross is Associate Professor of Theology at Loyola University, Chicago. She is the author of *Extravagant Affections: A Feminist Sacramental Theology,* and of numerous articles on contemporary constructive and feminist theology.

Rosemary Radford Ruether is the Georgia Harkness Professor of Applied Theology at Garrett Theological Seminary and Northwestern University in Evanston, Illinois. She is the author of 32 books and numerous articles on gender, religion, and social justice, the most recent being *Women and Redemption* (1996).

Mary Jo Weaver is Professor of Religious Studies at Indiana University. In addition to her early work on Roman Catholic modernism, she has published two editions of a textbook, *Introduction to Christianity,* and two books on feminism and American Catholicism, *New Catholic Women* and *Springs of Water in a Dry Land.* She is co-editor (with R. Scott Appleby) of a companion volume to this book, *Being Right: Conservative Catholics in America.*

INDEX

Abortion, 8–9, 27, 47, 67, 71–72, 84nn1,9, 114, 271; "culture of death" and, 78–79; pro-choice activism, 88–89, 90, 91, 93–97, 257, 267; pro-choice advertisement, 79, 86n36, 96–97, 106n16, 183. *See also* Reproductive rights; Women

Abrams, Father Bede, 248

Academic theology, 9–10, 96, 111, 126; historical consciousness, 111–113; religious diversity in, 120–121

Academy of Catholic Hispanic Theologians of the United States (ACHTHUS), 206, 208–209

ACHTHUS. *See* Academy of Catholic Hispanic Theologians of the United States

ACHTUS. *See* Association of Catholic Hispanic Theologians in the U.S.

Adoremus movement, 172

Affirmation, liberal goals for, 5

African-Americans, 151; Black Catholic Congress movement, 11, 238–250; churches, 193, 195, 240–242; Gospel Mass celebration, 161–163, 168, 175n18, 187n9; mission churches, 244–247; St. Augustine Church, 168–169; women, 20–21, 181. *See also* Racism

Ageism, 60

AGPIM. *See* Association of Graduate Programs in Ministry

AIDS, 72

Aldrich, Gustave, 195

Alinsky, Saul, 210–211, 266, 277

Allen, John L., 172

American Academy of Catholic Hispanic Theologians, 11

American Catholics: diversity among, 191–200, 218nn2,3, 257; opinion about John Paul II, 13–14; response to Vatican II, 2–3, 104nn3,5, 156–157,

159–160; rise to middle class, 213–214, 259; sexual morality, 68, 81–82, 84n9, 86n35, 95; social composition, 259–262; social conditions, 264–265. *See also* African-Americans; Bishops; Latino Catholics

Americanism. *See* Liberal Catholicism

The Analogical Imagination (Tracy), 117

Angelica, Mother, 153

Anselm, Father, 143–144

Apostolicam acutositatem, 137

Appleby, Scott, 6

The Approval of Catechisms and Catechetical Materials (CTSA), 123

ARCC. *See* Association for the Rights of Catholics in the Church

Ascetical theology, spirituality and, 163–164, 174n13

Ashley, Benedict, 112, 127n1

Association of Catholic Hispanic Theologians in the U.S. (ACHTUS), 129n25

Association of Graduate Programs in Ministry (AGPIM), 143

Association for the Rights of Catholics in the Church (ARCC), 32, 141, 152

Association of Women Aspiring to the Presbyteral Ministry, 180

Bailey, Derrick Sherwin, 106n17

Baranowski, Art, 151

Barrón, Hermana Mario, 234n3

Barry, Colman, 201n3

Basso, Teresita, 230

Baum, Gregory, 115, 127n7

BCTS. *See* Black Catholic Theological Symposium

Being Right (Appleby/Weaver), 6, 112, 157

Belief, 116, 127n4, 141, 144, 159, 215, 268

Beltran, Edgard, 226

Bernardin, Joseph Cardinal, 153, 154n2, 273, 282n29
Bernstein, Richard, 123
Berrigan, Daniel, 255, 259, 266, 270
Berrigan, Philip, 255, 270
Beyond God the Father (Daly), 20, 37, 118
Bible: feminist biblical criticism, 25–28, 46; interpretation of, 82–83; women's experience of, 24
Bible study groups, 166
Bilgrien, Marie Vianney, 90
Bishops: acceptance of academic theology, 9; African-American, 249; Episcopal, 47; Latin American, 115–116, 182, 215–216, 225–227; opposition to women's rights, 73, 74–76, 95–96; pastoral letters, 100–101, 138–139, 148, 263, 267–268, 274, 282n28; progressive and conservative policies, 29–30, 73, 98–101, 115, 121–122, 136, 137–138, 228–229, 258, 272, 274; relations with feminists, 48–49. *See also* American Catholics; Call to Action (CTA) movement; Jesuits; Priests
Black Catholic Congress movement, 11, 238–250
Black Catholic Theological Symposium (BCTS), 11, 206, 208–209
Black Panthers, 208
Black Sisters Conference, 59
Blessed Rage for Order (Tracy), 117
Body, critique of treatment of, 28–30. *See also* Embodiment; Sexuality
Boff, Leonardo, 35, 118, 128n19
Boston Women-Church, 51, 60
Bowman, Sister Thea, 248
Boyle, John, 9
Bread and wine, consecration of, 160–161
Briggs, Sheila, 12
Brooks, Delores, 49
Brown Berets, 208, 220
Bruskewitz, Bishop, 152, 153
Buchanan, Pat, 2
Burke, Ronald R., 79
Burns, Gene, 8
Buswell, Charles, 49
BVM Network, 51

Cahensly, Peter Paul, 192, 193
Cahenslyism, 192
Cahill, Lisa Sowle, 31, 94, 108n33
Call to Action (CTA) movement, 10, 32, 48, 51, 126, 141, 147–154, 167, 183, 264, 272, 274; liberal Catholic support for, 5; national conventions, 149–152
Callahan, Sydney, 102
Camara, Dom Helder, 226

Campaign for Human Development (CHD), 223, 231, 266, 274, 277
Canon Law Society of America (CLSA), 121, 123, 141
Capital punishment, 272
Carr, Anne, 48
Carroll, Beverly, 12
Casso, Father Henry, 220, 221
Casti Connubii, 75
Catholic Biblical Association (CBA), 141
Catholic Family Movement, 75
Catholic Hospital Ethics (CTSA), 122
Catholic immigrants: assimilation and acculturation, 191–200, 259–260, 273–274; sanctuary for, 272, 282n27. *See also* Latin America; *specific nationalities*
Catholic Left, 170–173, 255–280; community organizing, 276–278; components of, 96–97; ecclesiology and, 79–83; history, 269–273; identity, 21; Las Hermanas and PADRES, 232–233; sexuality issues, 67–83; strategies, 205–206. *See also* Liberal Catholicism
Catholic Perspectives on Baptism, Eucharist and Ministry (CTSA), 123
Catholic Theological Society of America (CTSA), 121, 122–124; doctoral women members, 19; politics, 6, 87n47, 206, 209
Catholic University of America, 121
Catholic Worker movement, 12, 206–209, 257, 266, 269, 270, 272, 278
Catholicism: public, 12–13, 256; racism and, 240–242. *See also* Conservative Catholicism; Liberal Catholicism
Catholicism (McBrien), 35, 119
Catholics for a Free Choice (CFFC), 8, 34, 47, 50, 55, 56, 60, 92, 93–97
Catholics Organized for Renewal, 152
CBA. *See* Catholic Biblical Association
CCL. *See* Conference of Catholic Lesbians
CDF. *See* Congregation for the Doctrine of Faith
Celibacy-optional policy, liberal goals for, 5, 28, 49
Center of Concern, 140, 272
CFFC. *See* Catholics for a Free Choice
Chambers, Ed, 210
Chapungco, Anscar, 162
Chávez, César, 198, 203n35, 220, 259, 270
Chávez, Gilberto, 226
CHD. *See* Campaign for Human Development
Chicago Catholic Women, 47, 50, 55, 56, 57, 60
China, women's conferences, 57

Chittister, Joan, 102
Christ: The Experience of Jesus as Lord
    (Schillebeeckx), 118
Christian Century (periodical), 268
Christian Feminists, 49
Christian Right, 72, 257. *See also*
    Conservative Catholicism
Christology, 36–37, 118
The Church (Boff), 119
The Church and the Homosexual (McNeil),
    78, 97
The Church and the Second Sex (Daly), 20
Civil disobedience, 12
Civil rights, 206, 269
Clark, Matthew, 102
Classism, 21, 25, 258
CLSA. *See* Canon Law Society of
    America
Code of Canon Law, 1
College Theology Society (CTS), 6, 38n2,
    124–125, 141
Commonweal, 124, 171–172
Community, Christian, 140–142, 145n16,
    151, 157, 191, 266, 268; relation to
    individual, 29, 129n20; Third World,
    120
Community of Anawin, 51, 55
Community organizing, 276–278, 280n5.
    See also Social justice
Comstock Law, 70
Concilium, 118
Confederación de la Raza Unida, 222
Conference of Catholic Lesbians (CCL),
    95, 102, 108n32, 127n8
Conference of Major Superiors of
    Women, 178
Congregation for the Doctrine of Faith
    (CDF), 101, 115, 124, 129nn23,24
Conn, Joanne Wolski, 10, 164
Conscience (publication), 56, 94
Conscience, personal, 79; role in
    morality, 33, 95
Conservative Catholic Influence in Europe
    (CFFC), 95
Conservative Catholicism: compared to
    Liberal Catholicism, 2–3, 15n2, 24,
    44n61, 205–206, 256–258; issues of, 95,
    157, 262–263. *See also* Catholicism;
    Liberal Catholicism
Consider Jesus (Johnson), 118
Contraception, 70–72, 90–91; issues
    about, 74–76, 80, 88, 90, 114, 267;
    rhythm method, 75. *See also*
    Abortion; Reproductive rights
Convergence (organization), 57, 58
Cooke, Bernard, 10, 11, 144n3
*Cooperation between Theologians and the
    Ecclesiastical Magisterium* (CTSA), 123
CORPUS (organization), 10, 142

Corrales, Ramona Jean, 225
Cortes, Ernesto, 210, 260
Coston, Carol, 186n7
Crisis (journal), 124
Critical theology, development of, 115–
    116, 128n9
Cross, significance of, 36, 37
Crossan, John Dominic, 118
Crowley, Patrick and Patty, 75
CTA. *See* Call to Action (CTA) move-
    ment
CTS. *See* College Theology Society
CTSA. *See* Catholic Theological Society
    of America
Cuatro Encuentro Feminista de Latino
    America y el Caribe, 182
"Culture of death," 78–79, 261, 263,
    268
Curran, Rev. Charles E., 77, 82, 86n40,
    87nn44,46, 90, 121, 154
Cursillos, 166

Daley, Dan and Sheila, 148
Daly, Mary, 20, 37, 57, 118
Davis, Cyprian, 239, 243, 250n7
Davis, Sen. Cushman K., 193
Day, Dorothy, 158, 207, 255, 266, 269, 270
Dearden, John Cardinal, 147, 273
"Dei Verbum," 105n11
Democratic Party, 194, 202n20, 260
Dennett, Mary Ware, 71
Derrida, Jacques, 123
Dialogue, embraced by liberal Catho-
    lics, 4, 14–15. *See also* Dissent
Dierks, Sheila Durkin, 160, 173n4
Dignitatis humanae, 113
Dignity (organization), 8–9, 92, 97–103,
    108n31, 152. *See also* Gay and lesbian
    rights
Dinges, Bill, 119
Directors of religious education (DREs),
    139
Dissent: as creative force, 3–4, 8–9, 82–
    83; cultural change and, 89–91; as
    marker of liberal Catholicism, 8, 94–
    95; sexual issues and, 91–93; Vatican
    opposition to, 77–78, 79–80, 89, 119,
    122, 258. *See also* Protest
Diversity, aspects of, 4. *See also* Catholic
    immigrants; Religious diversity
Doe v. Bolton, 72
Does God Exist? (Küng), 118
Doherty, Catherine de Hueck, 158, 206
Domestic violence, 23
Donovan, Mary Ann, 124
DREs. *See* Directors of religious
    education
Drucker, Peter, 135
Dualism, 28

Duddy, Mary Ann, 103, 108n34
Dulles, Avery, 124, 130n33

EATWOT. *See* Ecumenical Association
    of Third World Theologians
Ecclesiogenesis (Boff), 119
Ecclesiology: *communio*, 172; sexuality
    and, 79–83, 90
Ecumenical Association of Third World
    Theologians (EATWOT), 129n25
Education: by CTA, 149–152; by feminist
    groups, 55, 56; discrimination in,
    212–213
Egalitarianism: progressive goals for,
    32–33, 47, 52, 164; racial, 205–206. *See
    also* Social justice
Eight Day Center for Justice, 56
El Movimiento Estudiantil Chicano de
    Aztlán (MEChA), 220
Elder, William H., 242
Elizondo, Virgilio, 198, 226
Ellis, Monsignor John Tracy, 2
Embodiment: sexuality and, 33, 165;
    spirituality and, 28–31. *See also* Body;
    Sexuality
Environment, concern for, 34, 165
Episcopal Church, women's ordination,
    47. *See also* Protestant Church
Espinoza, Sister Carmelita, 224,
    235nn13,14
Esquivel, Juan, 225
Eternal World Television Network, 153
Ethics, social justice and, 31–35. *See also*
    Morality
Ethnicity, race and, 11–12
Eucharist: before and after Vatican II,
    156–157, 173n4; popular understand-
    ing of, 4, 171–172
Eugene, Toinette, 7, 174n13
*Everything You Always Wanted to Know
    about the Catholic Vote* (CFFC), 95
Excommunication, 73, 152, 153, 183
Experience: revelation within, 23, 92,
    113–115, 117, 127n2, 164; role in
    feminist theology, 21–22, 22–23, 113–
    115; theological method and, 22–25;
    universality and particularity of, 19,
    23, 24. *See also* Revelation
Experience-based theology: relation
    to dissent, 8–9; significance in
    Catholic life, 3. *See also* Liberal
    theology
An Experiment in Christology
    (Schillebeeckx), 118

Farley, Margaret, 8, 48, 89, 92, 102
FCC. *See* Federated Colored Catholics
FCM. *See* Fellowship for Christian
    Ministry

Federated Colored Catholics (FCC),
    211–212, 244
Fellowship for Christian Ministry
    (FCM), 142, 152
Feminism, moral theology and, 90–91,
    165. *See also* Women; Women's
    movement
Feminist Interest Group, 51
Feminist liturgy, principles, 30–31,
    43n46, 55. *See also* Liturgy; Women-
    Church
Feminist theology: alternative terms for,
    20–21, 31–35, 38–39, 40n10, 41n18,
    116; American Catholic acceptance
    of, 3, 6; origins, 20; universal and
    particular aspects, 23–25, 47;
    Women-Church movement and, 7–
    8. *See also* Mujerista movement;
    Spirituality; Womanist movement
Feminist Theology from the Third World
    (King), 129
Ferraro, Geraldine, 96
Fessio, Joseph, S.J., 172
Fiorenza, Elisabeth Schüssler. *See*
    Schüssler Fiorenza, Elisabeth
Fiorenza, Francis Schüssler. *See*
    Schüssler Fiorenza, Francis
Fleischer, Barbara, 10
Flores, Patricio, 233
Foley, Nadine, 177, 186n3
"Folk religion," 29. *See also* Religious
    diversity
Foucault, Michel, 123
Foundational Theology (Schüssler
    Fiorenza), 117
Fox, Tom, 13, 278, 282n33
Frankfurt School, 115
Freeing Theology (Hines), 119
Frei, Hans, 123
Friendship Houses, 206
Fuchs, Josef, 82
Fukuzawa, David, 12
Furey, Archbishop Francis, 221

Gaillot, Bishop, 150
Gallardo, Sister Gloria Graciela, 223,
    224, 235n10
Galvan, Ida, 59
Galvin, John, 117
Gaudium et Spes, 31, 113, 137, 166, 198
Gay and lesbian rights: attacks on, 60,
    72, 106n20, 114; Dignity, 97–103;
    liberal goals for, 6, 29–30, 78, 84n9,
    88–89, 91–93, 98–99, 106n17, 107n26.
    See also Dignity; Homosexuality;
    Sexuality
Gebara, Ivonne, 35, 42n67
German Catholics, 193, 200, 201nn3,9,10,
    202n14

Gibbons, James Cardinal, 242
Gilson, Etienne, 113
GLB Catholics, 100, 102–103
Gleason, Philip, 259
God, relationship with, 30, 35–36, 81–82, 92, 117–118, 159
God for Us (LaCugna), 118
Goldberg, David Theo, 205, 217n1
Goldman, Emma, 71
González, Justo, 213
Good Friday celebration, in San Antonio, 169–170
Gortaire, Alfonso, 226
Grail (organization), 47, 53–54, 55, 56, 63n14
Grammick, Jeannine, 98–99
Gray, Sister Martin de Porres, 246
Great Depression, 202n24
Greeley, Andrew, 214
Gregory XVI, Pope, 73
Groppi, Father James, 269
Guide for Prochoice Catholics (CFFC), 95
Gumbleton, Thomas, 101, 102
Gustafson, James, 123
Gutiérrez, Gustavo, 198–199, 226
Gyn/Ecology (Daly), 20

Habermas, Jürgen, 123
Haight, Roger, 118
Hamilton, Terry, 59
Häring, Bernard, 82
Hayes, Diana, 10, 11
Healy, Bishop James, 246, 251n11
Hearers of the Word (Rahner), 116
Hehir, J. Bryan, 266
Helms, Sen. Jesse, 72
Hermeneutics: feminist, 26–28; of suspicion, 111
Hick, John, 123
Hickey, Archbishop James A., 77
Hilkert, Mary Catherine, 118
Hines, Mary, 119
Hinsdale, Mary Ann, 9
The Historical Jesus (Crossan), 118
History: idealized, 213–214; reclaiming of, 21. *See also* Past
Hitchcock, Helen Hull, 172
Hodur, Father Francis, 194
Hollinger, David, 197, 215
Holy Name Societies, 166
Holy Spirit, experience of, 3
Homosexuality, 8–9. *See also* Gay and lesbian rights; Sexuality
"House churches," 46–47
Houses of Hospitality, 207
Huerta, Dolores, 220
Hughes, Kathleen, 171, 175n20
Human Life International, 153
Human Sexuality (CTSA), 123

Human Sexuality: A Catholic Perspective, 100
Humanae Vitae, 3, 6, 34, 75–76, 77, 79, 80, 83, 85nn21,22, 90, 114, 122, 127n5
Hunt, Mary, 7, 49, 106n16
Hunthausen, Archbishop Raymond, 77

IAF. *See* Industrial Areas Foundation
Idealism, 178, 185, 187n14, 207, 261, 267
Identity: African-American, 247, 248; Catholic, 53–54, 125–126; liberal, 2–5, 21, 273–276; "spaces" for, 208
Iglesias, María, 231
Immigrants. *See* Catholic immigrants; specific nationalities
IMWAC group, 152
Inculturation, 162
Industrial Areas Foundation (IAF), 210
In-Fire (publication), 56
Informes (periodical), 230, 235n12
INSeCT. *See* International Network of Societies of Catholic Theologians
Insight (Lonergan), 117
Institute for Women Today, 49, 50
Instituto Pastoral Latino Americano (IPLA), 226
International Network of Societies of Catholic Theologians (INSeCT), 129n25
International Women's Year Tribunal, 182
Internet, 150, 200
IPLA. *See* Instituto Pastoral Latino Americano
Ireland, Archbishop John, 193, 201nn8,11
Irish-Americans, 192–193
Isabell, Lynn C., 171
Isasi-Díaz, Ada María, 7, 48, 231
Italian Catholics, 200, 201n7

Jadot, Jean, 227
Jesuits, relations with feminists, 54. *See also* Bishops
Jesus: relation to women, 36–37; relationship with, 115, 171–172, 177, 207, 268
Jesus, Symbol of God (Haight), 118
John XXIII, Pope, 75
John Paul II, Pope, 13–14, 15n1, 77, 78, 115, 119, 124, 125, 146n21, 183, 256, 257, 261–263, 268
Johnson, Elizabeth, 45n84, 118
Johnson, Luke, 92
Josephites. *See* Society of Saint Joseph
Jüngel, Eberhard, 123

Kalven, Janet, 53, 61n14

Kauffman, Gordon, 123
Kelly, Walt, 261
Kennedy, Pres. John F., 259
Kenny, Father Keith, 223
King, Dr. Martin Luther Jr., 198, 245, 264, 269, 271
Kissling, Frances, 8, 47, 93, 94, 96, 106n16
Klejment, Anne, 13
Küng, Hans, 118, 148, 150
Kurtz, Lester R., 73–74, 85n12

La Raza Unida Party, 220
Laborem exercens, 115
LaCugna, Catherine Mowry, 118
LaFarge, Father John, S.J., 196, 200, 203n27, 204n48, 206, 212, 244–245
Laity: ministry and, 136–139, 160–161, 166–167; spirituality for, 165. See also Lay participation
Lamb, Matthew, 124, 128n15
Lamentabili sane exitu, 112
Language: androcentric/patriarchal, 120; inclusive, 35–38, 39, 174n15; oppressive, 91
Las Hermanas, 32, 49, 50, 59, 60, 63n19, 64n37; Catholic Left and, 232–233; context and foundation, 220–225, 233n1; new vision of, 229–232; struggle for rights, 225–227. See also Latino Catholics; PADRES
Latin America: Church politics, 256, 263, 272, 274, 278, 282n27; experience-based theology, 3, 120, 271; International Women's Year Tribunal, 182; "option for the poor," 115, 276; publications and outreach, 56–57
Latino Catholics: Encuentro process, 216–217, 230–231; Good Friday in San Antonio, 169–170; Hispanic ministry, 166, 226; immigration, 196–200; multiculturalism and, 215–216; theology, 198–199. See also Las Hermanas; Mexican-Americans; Mujerista movement; PADRES
Law, Cardinal Bernard, 124
Lay participation: Black, 244–247; liberal goals for, 5. See also Laity
Leadership Conference of Women Religious (LCWR), 49, 178, 231, 271
Lee, Bernard, 151
Leo XIII, Pope, 112, 116
Letter to the Bishops of the Catholic Church on the Pastoral Care of Homosexual Persons (Ratzinger), 99–101
Liberal Catholicism: compared to conservative Catholicism, 2–3, 24, 44n61, 205–206, 256–258; experience of Church leadership, 89; identity, 2–5,

21, 273–276; spirituality, 4–5, 114, 159, 164. See also Catholic Left; Catholicism; Conservative Catholicism; Progressive Catholicism
Liberal theology, academic theologians and, 9–10. See also Theology
Liberating Conscience (Patrick), 119
Liberation theology: components, 22–23; third-world, 3, 22, 271. See also Experience-based theology; Feminist theology
Lindbeck, George, 123
Liturgy: liberal approaches to, 10–11, 46–47, 139–140; visions for, 155–163, 243, 246. See also Feminist liturgy
To Live in Jesus Christ, 98
Lonergan, Bernard, 117
Lopez, Vicente, 228
Lorde, Audre, 20
Loretto Women's Network, 51, 53, 57, 58, 60, 64n39
Love, sexuality and, 80–81, 102
Lucerne Memorial, 193
Lucey, Archbishop Robert, 215–216
Lucker, Raymond, 49
Lumen Gentium, 114, 137
Luther, Martin, Reformation and, 43n40
Lynch, Mary B., 48, 180

MACC. See Mexican American Cultural Center
Mahoney, Cardinal Roger, 137, 145n7, 172, 205
Major Conference of Superiors of Men, 271
Manning, Cardinal Timothy, 221, 227
Maréchal, Joseph, 112
Maritain, Jacques, 112
Marriage, 157; contraception and, 80, 88. See also Ritual
Martínez, Manuel R., 225
Mass: before and after Vatican II, 156–157, 160, 175n20; laity participation in, 4
Massachusetts Women-Church, 54–55, 60
Massingale, Bryan, 208
Matovina, Tim, 11, 197
Maurin, Peter, 207
May, Archbishop John, 137, 138, 141, 145nn7,8
MAYO. See Mexican American Youth Organization
McBrien, Richard, 35, 119
McCool, Gerald, S.J., 112
McCormick, Richard, 90
McEnroy, Carmel, 154
McFague, Sallie, 123
McGlynn, Rev. Edward, 193

McGreevy, John T., 12, 206
McKeown, Elizabeth, 13
McLaren, Peter, 215
McMaster, James, 194
McNeil, John, 8, 78, 97
MEChA. *See* El Movimiento Estudiantil Chicano de Aztlán
Mediator Dei, 158
Memory of Her (Schüssler Fiorenza), 26
Method in Theology (Lonergan), 117
Metz, Johannes Baptist, 26, 117, 128n14
Mexican American Cultural Center (MACC), 226
Mexican American Youth Organization (MAYO), 220
Mexican-Americans: chicana/chicano, 233n1; Good Friday celebration, 169–170. *See also* Latino Catholics
Michel, Virgil, 158
Military policies, protest of, 57–58, 73, 181, 182, 227, 267–268, 269–270, 271, 272, 274, 278. *See also* Social justice
Ministry, Hispanic, 166, 226; liberal approaches to, 10–11; NAWR and, 178–180; at parish level, 139–140; progressive approaches to, 135–144; Vatican II and laity, 136–139
Ministry Renewal Network, 142, 146n19
Modernism, Vatican attack on, 72–74, 113–114
Moral theology, feminism and, 90–91
Morality, conceptions of, 32–33, 36, 83, 95. *See also* Ethics; Sexual morality
Mujerista movement, 23, 29, 31–33, 165; among Hispanic women, 21. *See also* Latino Catholics
Multiculturalism, racism and, 214–217
Murray, John Courtney, 266
Muschal-Reinhardt, Rosalie, 49, 51

National Abortion Federation, 93
National Assembly of Religious Women (NARW), 10, 32, 50, 57, 58–59, 63n19, 64nn32,38, 95, 176–186
National Assembly of Women Religious (NAWR), 49, 176, 272
National Association of Lay Catholics, 142
National Black Catholic Clergy Caucus (NBCCC), 246
National Black Lay Caucus, 246
National Black Sisters Conference, 49, 246
National Catholic Council for Interracial Justice (NCCIJ), 211, 244–245
National Catholic Education Association, 178
The National Catholic Reporter, 13, 142,

149, 166, 171, 278
National Center for Pastoral Leadership (NCPL), 142
National Coalition of American Nuns (NCAN), 49, 50, 57, 186n7, 187n8
National Conference of Catholic Bishops (NCCB), 121, 221
National Conference of Catholic Charities, 271
National Council of Catholic Women (NCCW), 96, 98
National Federation of Priests' Councils (NFPC), 225, 270, 271
National Office of Black Catholics (NOBC), 247, 248
National Sisters Vocation Conference, 49
Navarro, Armando, 228
NAWR. *See* National Assembly of Women Religious
NBCCC. *See* National Black Catholic Clergy Caucus
NCAN. *See* National Coalition of American Nuns
NCCB. *See* National Conference of Catholic Bishops
NCCIJ. *See* National Catholic Council for Interracial Justice
NCCW. *See* National Council of Catholic Women
NCPL. *See* National Center for Pastoral Leadership
Neal, Marie Augustus, 48
Nearon, Father Joseph, 248
Network (organization), 140, 272
"New Age" practices, 167, 265
New Deal, 260, 275
The New Republic, 101
A New Rite (CFFC), 95
New Ways Ministry, 98–99, 102
New York Times, 79, 86n36, 96–97, 106n16, 148, 183
Newman, John Henry, 114
Newman Centers, 166
Nidorf, Father Patrick, 100
NOBC. *See* National Office of Black Catholics
Nothing Sacred, 11, 155, 166
Nugent, Robert, 98–99

O'Brien, David, 12, 13, 207
O'Connell, Timothy E., 81, 82, 83, 86n41
O'Connor, Cardinal John, 72, 96, 273
O'Keefe, Mary, O.P., 182
Olivares, Luis, 228
On Being a Christian (Küng), 118
Oppression: internalization of, 176–177; multiple forms of, 21, 43n39, 95; as

sinful, 23, 37; Western European, 161–162
Orate Fratres (journal), 158
Ortega, Sister Gregoria, 223, 224, 235n10
Our Town (Wilder), 197

Padavano, Anthony, 10
PADRES (Padres Asociados por los Derechos Religiosos, Educativos, y Sociales), 11, 219n28; context and foundation, 220–225, 233n1, 234nn3,5,6, 235n9; decline, 227–229; struggle for rights, 225–227. *See also* Las Hermanas; Latino Catholics
Pascendi dominici gregis, 112
Past, remembrance of, 21, 26–27. *See also* History
Patriarchy: theology of, 21, 36; varied tools of, 20, 40n9, 120. *See also* Power relationships
Patrick, Anne, 10, 11, 119
Paul VI, Pope, 75, 77, 78, 124, 127n5, 168
Pax Christi, 126, 139, 152, 266, 274, 282n30
Pelton, Robert, 151
Peña, Roberto, 226
"People of God," American Catholic understanding of phrase, 3, 14, 37–38, 46–47, 79, 114, 137, 159, 245
Perella, Fred, 13
Perry, Harold, 246
Piehl, Mel, 207, 218n8
The Pilot (periodical), 124, 130n30
Pius IX, Pope, 112
Pius X, Pope, 74, 75, 112
Pius XI, Pope, 75
Pius XII, Pope, 75, 116, 158
Plowshares, 272, 278
Pluralism: among Catholic women, 20–21; Catholic, 88, 104n4, 111, 121, 126, 127n1, 256
Plurality and Ambiguity (Tracy), 117
Polish Catholics, 193–194, 202n17, 263
Political issues, social issues perceived as, 8–9
Polycentrism, racism and, 208–215
"Postmodern theology," described, 116
Power relationships: among feminists, 50–51, 58; critique of, 22, 35–38, 68–69, 282n33; political, 210–211. *See also* Patriarchy
Prayer, 156, 165, 167; novel and traditional forms, 4
Preuss, Arthur, 194, 202n19
Priests: African-American, 240–242, 251n11; shortages of, women's ordination and, 14, 86n37. *See also* Bishops
Priests for Equality, 49

Pro-choice advocacy. *See* Abortion
Probe (publication), 179–180, 181, 186, 187n13
The Problem of Second Marriages (CTSA), 122
Profession of Faith and Oath of Fidelity (CTSA), 123
Progressive Catholicism, structures and organizations, 140–142, 206. *See also* Liberal Catholicism
Protest: about Church conflicts, 56; about social and political issues, 57; by NARW, 182. *See also* Dissent
Protestant Church: liberalization of sexual morality, 74–76, 268; ordination of women, 61, 62n1, 180. *See also* Episcopal Church
Public Catholicism, 12–13, 256; evangelical, 13, 266, 268, 279; immigrant, 13, 266, 267, 279; republican, 13, 266–267, 279; styles, 265–269, 281n14. *See also* Catholicism
Publications: about spirituality, 163–164; progressive, 56–57, 142, 171, 179

Quinn, Donna, 47, 49, 51, 63n8
Quinn, John, 227
Quixote Center, 50

Raboteau, Albert, 248, 251n23
Race: Catholic, 192–195; effect on white consciousness, 22–23, 269; ethnicity and, 11–12. *See also* Ethnicity
Racism, 21, 25, 27, 182, 194, 258; against African-Americans, 194–197, 244–247; Catholicism and, 240–242, 267; introduction, 205–206, 250n9; multiculturalism, 214–217; polycentrism, 208, 215; pragmatic, 210–211; protesting, 58–60; strategies against integration, 211–214; utopian, 206–209. *See also* African-Americans; Latino Catholics
Radicalism, in feminist theology, 22
Ragan, Timothy, 142
Rahner, Karl, 116–117, 128n12
Ramsey Colloquium, 101
Ratzinger, Cardinal Joseph, 78, 98, 99–101
Ray, Father, 155
Redmont, Jane, 171, 172
Referenda: in American Church, 10, 15n9; international circulation of, 5
Reform, efforts at, 53
Reiff, Maureen, 181
Relationality, moral theology and, 36
Religious diversity: academic theology and, 120–121, 128n12; folk religion,

29; syncretic African religions, 240, 250n4. *See also* Diversity

Renewal of the Sacrament of Penance (CTSA), 122–123

Reproductive rights, 32–34, 38–39, 70–72, 93–97; Church opposition to, 49, 56, 67, 230. *See also* Contraception; Sexuality; Women

Retreats, 166, 167

Revelation: experience and, 23, 92, 113–115, 117, 164; feminist theology and, 28; liberation theology and, 23; theology and, 83. *See also* Experience

Rich, Adrienne, 172

Ricoeur, Paul, 123

Riebe-Estrella, Gary, 12, 197

Ritual, creative, 30, 173; patterns of participation in, 157–158

Rodríguez, Edmundo, 229

Roe v. Wade, 47, 72, 86n37, 93

Romero, Juan, 225, 228, 229, 232

Romero, Archbishop Oscar, 282n27

Rorty, Richard, 123

Ross, Susan, 7, 9, 89, 113, 116, 120

Rouselot, Pierre, 112

Rudd, Daniel, 242

Ruether, Rosemary Radford, 7, 27, 36, 48, 86n35, 95, 172–173

Ruiz, Father Ralph, 221, 222

Ryan, John A., 74, 266

Sabala, Joan, 48

Sacerdotes Hispanos, 227

Sacrosanctum Concilium, 156

St. Augustine Church, discussed, 168–169

St. Joan's Alliance, 49

St. Mary's community, 139

Saiving, Valerie, 23

San Antonio Women-Church, 51

Sánchez, Roberto, 226

Sánchez, Brother Trinidad, 227

Sandoval, Moisés, 228

Sanger, Margaret, 71

Sapientia Christiana, 129n23

Scalabrini, Bishop John Baptist, 192

"Scapegoat syndrome," 37

Schillebeeckx, Edward, 117, 118, 128nn16,17

Schineller, Peter, 162

Schreiter, Robert, 9

Schultenover, David, 88

Schüssler Fiorenza, Elisabeth, 25–28, 32, 39nn23,24, 48

Schüssler Fiorenza, Francis, 9, 117

Schwartz, Karen, 173

Second Vatican Council: changes occurring before and after, 1, 2, 46, 124, 136, 165, 178, 262; sexuality, 72–74, 91. *See also* Vatican

Sedillo, Pablo, 216

Sedillo, Sylvia, 231

Segovia, Mrs. Sara. G., 225

Sexism, 23, 27, 29, 32, 49, 181, 258

Sexism and God-Talk (Ruether), 36

Sexual morality: after Vatican II, 76–79, 114; dissent and, 91–93; liberal goals for, 5; personal determination of, 4, 89–90. *See also* Morality

Sexuality, 8–9, 30; abandoning suspicion of, 80–83; ecclesiology and, 79–83, 90; embodiment and, 33, 165; history of suspicion, 69; Left position on, 67–83; liberalization of, 70–72, 72–79; Vatican and popular views, 1–2, 68–69, 79, 89. *See also* Body

She Who Is (Johnson), 45n84, 118

Sheldrake, Philip, 163

SIGMA. *See* Sisters in Gay Ministry Associated

Sin, defined, 81, 83

Sister Formation Conference, 177, 178

Sisters in Gay Ministry Associated (SIGMA), 108n32

Sisters of Charity, 51, 57–58, 231

Sisters of Loretto, 50–51, 53, 57, 58, 60, 64n39, 231

Sisters Uniting, 182

Sixty Minutes (CBS), 150

Slavery, 194, 239–242. *See also* Racism

Social justice: efforts for, 57–59, 140, 158, 164, 177, 206, 257–260, 263, 268–269, 274, 276–278; ethics and, 31–35; NAWR and, 178–180, 182. *See also* Egalitarianism; Gay and lesbian rights; Military policies

Society of Catholic College Teachers of Sacred Doctrine, 124

Society of the Divine Word (SVDs), 250n9

Society of Saint Joseph (Josephites), 250n9

Society for the Study of Christian Spirituality, 163

Sodalites, 166

Sojourners (periodical), 268

Spirit in the World (Rahner), 116

Spirituality: embodiment and, 28–31; liberal approaches to, 4–5, 10–11, 96, 174n7; post-Christian (goddess), 54, 61–62; visions for, 155–158. *See also* Experience-based theology; Feminist theology

Starr, Ellen Gates, 158

Stecher, Reinhold, 14

Steinfels, Peter, 124

Stonewall incident, 72
Studies in Spirituality (Sheldrake), 163
Sullivan, Andrew, 101–102
SVDs. *See* Society of the Divine Word
Swidler, Arlene, 48
Syllabus of Errors, 73, 112
Systematic Theology (Schüssler Fioren-
    za), 117

Tarango, Yolanda, 182, 231, 237n36
Tardivel, Jules, 194
Taylor, Charles, 193, 202n13
Teología de Liberación (Gutiérrez), 198
Teresa of Avila, 172
Theological method, experience and,
    22–25
Theological organizations: Catholic
    Theological Society of America, 122–
    124; College Theology Society, 6,
    40n2, 124–125. *See also other specific*
    organizations
Theology: described, 9; revelation
    and, 83, 113–115; social locations for,
    119–122; traditional, women's ex-
    perience of, 24–25. *See also* Liberal
    theology; Liberation theology
Thomism, 112–113, 121, 127n1
Tilley, Terrence, 116, 128n11
Tolton, Father Augustus, 242
Torrance, Thomas, 123
Tracy, David, 117, 131n39
Tradition, reinterpretation of, 26–28
Traxler, Margaret Ellen, 47, 179, 186n7
Trujillo, Sister Clarita, 226
Tuite, Marjorie, O.P., 47, 179, 181, 182,
    183, 184, 186n7, 187n9
Turner, Pauline, 181
Turner, Thomas Wyatt, 212, 244

United Farm Workers (UFW), 198,
    203n35, 220

Vatican: anti-modernist crusade, 72–74;
    efforts at control, 14, 72–74, 76–79,
    79–80, 88–89, 104nn1,2, 118–119, 121,
    135, 205–206. *See also* Second Vatican
    Council
Vatican II, 20, 31, 46–47, 75–76, 113, 118,
    137, 140, 144n2, 148, 156; Black
    Catholics before, 244–247; sexual
    morality after, 76–79, 82
Vaughan, Judy, 181, 183, 184
Velasquez, Manuel, 226
Veritatis Splendor, 78
Vincent de Paul Society, 140
Virtually Normal (Sullivan), 101
"Voluntary motherhood" movement,
    70

Walburg, Father Anton, 192
Walker, Alice, 21
The Wanderer, 150, 153
WATER. *See* Women's Alliance for
    Theology, Ethics, and Ritual
Waters, Mary, 214
WCC. *See* Women of the Church
    Coalition
"We Are the Church" document, 5
Weakland, Archbishop Rembert, 34,
    145n12
Wilder, Thornton, 197
Wills, Gary, 2
Wilmore, Gayraud, 239
WOC. *See* Women's Ordination
    Conference
Womanist movement, 23, 29, 31–33, 165,
    167; among African-Americans, 21,
    186n2. *See also* Feminist theology
Women: Black, 250n9; Chicana, 229–232;
    in CTSA, 19, 123; in early Church,
    28–29; ordination, 14, 27, 32, 33, 47–
    48, 49–50, 51–53, 61, 62n1, 63n17,
    86n37, 114, 278; reproductive rights
    issues, 33–34, 38–39, 49, 56, 67, 70–72,
    93–97, 230. *See also* Body; Feminist
    theology; Mujerista movement;
    Women's issues
Women-Church movement, 6, 30, 46–62,
    64n38, 95–96, 141; feminist theology
    and, 7–8, 63n19; Las Hermanas and,
    230–232
Women Church Speaks, 50
Women-Church Speaks, 57
Women Eucharist (Dierks), 160
Women in Church and Society (CTSA),
    123
Women of the Church Coalition (WCC),
    49, 50–51
Women's Alliance for Theology, Ethics,
    and Ritual (WATER), 7, 50, 55, 56,
    57
Women's Auxiliary of the Knights of St.
    Peter Claver, 96
Women's equality, liberal goals for, 5
Women's issues: Church refusal to
    confront, 1–2, 31–32, 92–93; NAWR
    and, 178–180
Women's movement, Catholic accep-
    tance of, 3. *See also* Feminism
Women's Ordination Conference
    (WOC), 48, 50, 51–53, 57, 61, 63n9, 95,
    126, 176, 230
Women's Quick Action, 58
Worship (journal), 158
Wright, Richard, 197

Zahn, Gordon, 269